DRAMATIC GLOBAL POPULATION GROWTH EMBRACES THE GROWING OLDER POPULATION

"THE SILVER TSUNAMI"

EDWARD A MCKINNEY

authorHOUSE®

AuthorHouse™
1663 Liberty Drive
Bloomington, IN 47403
www.authorhouse.com
Phone: 1 (800) 839-8640

Published by AuthorHouse 11/15/2018

ISBN: 978-1-5462-6843-7 (sc)
ISBN: 978-1-5462-6842-0 (e)

Library of Congress Control Number: 2018913571

Print information available on the last page.

This book is printed on acid-free paper.

CONTENTS

CONTENTS

INTRODUCTION

Globally, continents, regions, and/or countries in the midst of the 21ˢᵗ Century are experiencing one of the most dramatic demographic trends, population growth in the history of humankind. What makes this phenomenon so much more dramatic is not just population growth in general or across all age groups, but an unprecedented growth in the older population 60 plus, the "Silver Tsunami." The phrase "Tsunami," according to Webster's 3ʳᵈ International Dictionary, "...is a destructive phenomenon caused by some seismic disturbance, and/or tidal wave, produced by a sub-marine earth movement or volcanic eruption." As the world knows a "tsunami" can be a very destructive force destroying physical infrastructures as well as human beings that get in its path. But, the "Silver Tsunami" takes on a totally different meaning. The world is now witnessing an unprecedented increasing number of older persons within the general population, the arrival of the "Silver Tsunami." The growing older population or the "Silver Tsunami" is touching down across all continents, countries and regions. Not like the well known destructive "Tsunami," the "Silver Tsunami" symbolizes an unprecedented global population growth of the ageing population, generally 60 plus. Sixty plus is considered the appropriate age for beginning the aging process in the more developed countries, but in the developing world and/or countries population ageing may begin between 48-55, depending on various social, economic, culture/customs/traditions and health factors. Also, in the more developed countries, such as the United States, Germany, France, United Kingdom, currently the fastest growing population age category from 60 plus is the age group 85 plus.

Unlike the "Tsunami" the "Silver Tsunami" as aforementioned is not some destructive force but symbolizes globally a growing number of older and active persons who bring, not destruction, but knowledge, skills, values, experiences, and a new "swagger" to the world; this population group also brings a new spirit of what growing old or ageing should really mean in the 21ˢᵗ Century. What this population group has plans for are destroying or doing away with all of the social injustices being experienced by persons across all age groups and especially the older population. The current and future generations of the older population, the "Silver Tsunami," refuses to be seen or viewed any longer as an old age problem and is demanding a seat at the decision-making tables with the goal of creating a society based on human rights and social justice for all irrespective of age. A major social action goal for the "Silver Tsunami" is to become proactive in the eradication of ageism in all of its hidden forms; also the assurances that this population group will have the opportunity to live in dignity and respect, not just income security but access to essential services for living, medical, health and social services including long-term care. Americans recall the "Grey Panther Movement of the 1960's, when the older population organized to challenge all forms of social injustices that were having a significant impact on their day to day lives. Well, the current growing older population, the "Silver Tsunami" is once again being called to action especially in the fight against all forms of ageism, stereotyping and most importantly obsolescence.

The United Nations in 1982 was proactive in organizing the First World Assembly on Aging. The primary focus for bringing together the international community was to become proactive in efforts to prepare the world for the unprecedented population growth in the aging population **(See Chapter III).** The world was finally beginning to recognize the impact this growth phenomenon was having and would continue to have on all societal systems. Most importantly, how does the world, continents/countries prepare to ensure that this population group would have income security such as social pensions in later life, also access to medical, health and social services including housing and transportation to live in dignity and respect. It is now three decades later since the First World Assembly on Aging and globally more than half of the older population does not have basic income security, a social pension. Furthermore, in Sub-Saharan Africa (forty-seven countries), eighty-two percent of the older population does not have a social pension or basic income security. Since the First World Assembly three decades ago there have been other World Assemblies on Aging as well as national and regional conferences resulting in Declarations and Policy statements that hopefully would enhance the quality of life for a growing older population. The subject of Chapter VII is "The Time is now for Action." Action will require a global commitment for enhancing the lives of the older population, especially related to income security, poverty and access to critical services as aforementioned. Considering little has happened in recent decades for ensuring a more quality of life for the growing older population (more than 50% globally without basic income security, and more than 80% in Sub-Saharan Africa) there is need for a human seismic force organizing and operating on principles such as human rights and social justice to become proactive. As aforementioned repeatedly the growing older population brings to the table years of experiences, knowledge and skills that will, if allowed to participate at the decision-making table contribute to developing a society for all ages with justice for all. This society will result in a new day for social and economic development across all continents.

Yes, there is an extraordinary difference between the seismic forces of "Tsunami" and that of the growing older population the "Silver Tsunami." Some examples of how destructive a "Tsunami" can be occurred off the shores of Kerala, India on December 26, 2004. Witness some of the reactions (their poems) of children of India who experienced this deadly and destructive force just fourteen years ago: Anjitha, Age 11, "Tsunami" was a terrific wave that wiped out thousands from the shore. We lost our houses, books and pencils…we lost our own dear playmates. "Tsunami" came to wipe out our joys. We are scared of those big waves; Anoopn, Age 11, "…I saw death before my eyes…I screamed in agony and ran for help. I did not see any faces before me. I was aghast by the fury of nature…" Amrita Kumar, Age 13, "Azheekkal was the land of fishermen…But their happiness was eclipsed one day…Mother sea, why did you destroy our happiness? Do you remember the children who collected shells from your lap? Why did you cheat them? Don't you see the tears in the eyes of parents who lost their children? Who can calm their burning hearts? Tell me mother, what was our sin? Why did you pour your fury upon us? (Nair, Murali D., Editor, "Tsunami" Victims: An Anthology of Writings of Children In Kerala, India," <u>School of Social work Publication,</u> Cleveland State University,

Cleveland, Ohio, pp. 11-15, August 2005). No one can expect the aforementioned comments from the "mouths of babies," to become part of reactions to the work or actions of the human seismic, the "Silver Tsunami."

Although population growth generally is extremely challenging for all of societal systems, equally or more challenging is the growth of the older population 50 or 60 plus, including the age group 85 plus, the fastest growing age group in the developed world. As aforementioned these demographic growth trends will have a tremendous impact on the family, as well as a country's social, medical/health occupational and economic systems. Globally, no continent, country, or region, despite its wealth, military and/or political power, will be immune to this population shock phenomenon, especially the arrival of the "Silver Tsunami." The low and middle-income and/or developing countries in Africa and globally will be confronted with the greatest challenges in responding to this population growth phenomenon, especially the "Silver Tsunami." Why? One response to the question is that the upper or higher income countries, or the OECD countries such as the United States, Switzerland, or France, have had many more years to prepare for this population growth shock, especially the older population than the developing countries globally. For example, in France it took over 100 years for the older population 60 plus to grow from ten to twenty percent. But, for the developing countries in Africa and other parts of the world it appears that the preparation will have to be completed overnight. **(See Appendix B: Definitions/Concepts and Special Notes when the question arises who are the OECD countries and their global mission?).**

As aforementioned the "Silver Tsunami" will include a new wave of activists who will be seeking opportunities within their countries, regions, communities, or villages, to become part of the decision-making, problem-solving process. A major goal of this group will be the elimination of ageism, or the eradication of aging stereotypes that have historically devalued the life experiences, knowledge and skills of older people. And, if given the platform and opportunity to share their years of knowledge, skills and life experiences, the "Silver Tsunami" would help to create a more humane society that respects the worth and dignity of everyone, regardless of age, gender, race/ethnicity, and creed, with justice for all. To meet this global challenge in the 21st Century, will require that all age groups have a seat at the decision-making table. Politicians and other "stakeholders" may not want to wait too long in providing a seat at the table for the growing older population, for this group the time is now. The initial campaign for the older population group will no doubt be the challenge of eliminating all of the ageing stereotypes and/or the matter of ageism especially obsolescence globally.

This particular era and/or time frame is especially critical if the goal, based on the United Nations Principles on social justice and human rights, is to create "A Society for All Ages." "A Society for All Ages" was the theme adopted by Help Age International, the global Non-Governmental Organization (NGO), during the organization's Regional Conference on Ageing in Nairobi, Kenya, year 1998-1999, in celebration of the International Year of Older People. The "Silver Tsunami" population can assist societies globally to rid themselves of all the ageing stereotypes, ageism and move forward towards a society for all. The results will be a society that allows ageing individuals an opportunity to live active (Ageing in Place – remaining in their homes as long as it is feasible to do so) lives to their maximum capacity regardless of age. Countries that invest towards this goal will benefit or will be rewarded from all of the knowledge and experiences that the active older population will contribute to decision-making as countries advance towards social and economic growth and transformation.

The book is about population growth in general but a major focus is on the growing older population globally, especially in Sub-Saharan Africa and. Sub-Saharan Africa is one of the developing regions of the world where approximately four/fifths of its old age population are without basic income security at the time of retirement. Globally, approximately fifty-one percent of older persons do not have a social pension at the time of retirement. A major question to consider is how prepared is Sub-Saharan Africa and the other developing regions of the world to respond to the social, health and medical needs of a growing older population, especially basic income in retirement? Specifically, as aforementioned approximately eighty-two percent of older persons in Sub-Saharan Africa are without a social pension, or basic income security in old age. The eighty-two percent represent the population of former workers that during their employment history were employed in the informal labor sectors in their respective countries. Unlike the formal labor sector, the workers did not have access to a traditional tripartite (worker, employee, public) collective bargaining system; the type of labor system that would have provided them with the opportunity to negotiate and bargain for their rights to workers' benefits related to social protection, especially in retirement. The workers representing the approximately 19 percent were part of a tripartite labor system, and for the most part, were employed in the public sectors, such as governmental agencies.

Most importantly as a causative factor to explain the 82%, is that this percentage of older persons without social pensions, represent the great/great grandchildren of the forced labor population in Africa during the era of colonization. This forced labor population contributed significantly to labor activities such as the extraction and processing of the natural resources from their native land, without permission, that were desperately needed for the development of the economic empires in Europe and the Western World. After all, in reality wasn't this the primary reason for the scramble for Africa? Because of global racism with all of the negative stereotypes about native Africans and their countries, there was more support, including that of the missionaries, for bringing Western style civilization to the Continent.

Once again, population growth, including the "Silver Tsunami," will have a tremendous impact on all societal systems, the family, medical, health, social/economical as well as political. Although all systems will be impacted the traditional family system in Africa will be critical in responding to a growing older population. As aforementioned a very critical question is how prepared is the family system for caring for an older population where less than twenty percent of the population in retirement does not have income, medical and health security? In the traditional extended African family systems the concept of reciprocity was a very important factor related to social protection and/or social security in the caring process, especially for the older population. The older members of the family took good care of the children and other vulnerable members of the family; the children, in turn, as they grew older felt somewhat obligated to care for the older members within the family, as they had been cared for during childhood. They realized that in old age the next generation would care for them. Social policies to ensure that the growing older population will live and carry on active lives in dignity and respect are an investment that can result in positive results for countries. Chapter V addresses the subject of the extended family in Africa, and the current challenges of urbanization and modernization in responding to the growing older population.

Despite all of the historical trials and tribulations from an array of injustices leveled against the native population during the era colonization, as well as post-Independence struggles, currently there is growing optimism in Sub-Saharan Africa **(See Chapters VII/VIII)**. The optimism is based on the fact that Sub-Saharan Africa currently has one of the fastest growing economies in the world. Also, there is a growing population the "youth bulge" generation (Africa's Demographic Dividend) and the recent "Rising Africa" Movement (Inauguration Day 2016) with the goal of witnessing an African Renaissance in the 21st Century. Finally, there is optimism that in the very near future the older population in Africa will have access to income security, and/or access to medical, health and social services that will allow them to live in dignity following retirement. Yes, the proactive growing older population as they take their places at the decision-making tables with knowledge, skills and years of experiences will play a major role in social and economic growth and development globally.

INTRODUCTION: OVERVIEW OF BOOK CHAPTERS:

Chapter I - The Chapter begins with a focus on how the world was witnessing an unprecedented demographic growth in population across all age groups, including a growing older population increasingly being referred to as the "Silver Tsunami." Globally, population growth reached the 1 billion mark around 1804 and the debate has continued as to the number of years it took globally to reach that one billion mark. The Chapter proceeds, based on modern scientific technology and/or techniques, to view population projections, not only including time frames from 1 billion to around 8 billion in 2011, also projections as far away as 2100. Most importantly, the Chapter addresses the historical timelines or phases whereas the global population finally reached the 1 billion mark around 1800 and is projected to reach approximately 11 billion by the year 2100. Although by some estimates it took thousands of years for the population to reach the one billion mark in 1800, the succeeding billion marks, 2 billion through 7 billion, most importantly and interesting, have taken significantly less time for each billion mark to be reached. The trends in population growth include all age groups including the "Silver Tsunami," "Baby Boomers" in the Western World and the "youth bulge" generation; the latter refers to the dramatic growth of the population age group 15-24 in Africa that is projected to provide Sub-Saharan Africa with a demographic dividend that will contribute significantly to economic growth and development in future years. Yes, the "Silver Tsunami" has also touched down in Africa.

Obviously the dramatic demographic growth did not happen without some significant causative factors. The Chapter addresses some of the most significant factors contributing not only to the growth trends, but the significant changes in the various timelines from 1 billion to the next billion and beyond. Some significant factors contributing to population growth especially after reaching the 1 Billion mark includes scientific inventions and innovations including medical, social, health, especially public health education and practices. The world cannot overlook the arrival and growth era of agricultural production and the mass distribution of food. Scientific knowledge related to food and nutrition played a major part in enhancing the quality of life across all age groups, especially the increase in life expectancy. Also, the coming of the industrial revolution that introduced and begin the development of electrical and transportation infrastructures including the construction of roads, highways, bridges, seaways and the arrival of the global automotive industry.

Most importantly to consider is that the dramatic rise in population growth is a global phenomenon affecting all continents, regions and countries regardless of political, financial, historical symbols or military power. There is no exemption for any continent or country to this dramatic trend in population growth. A major question for all is how prepared are the various countries, not just the developing countries also the higher income ones as well, in their preparation for responding to the needs of a growing population, including the "Silver Tsunami." Although the higher income countries, such as those that are part of the Organization for Economic Co-operation and Development (OECD-34 countries), have had more preparation time it does not mean that they don't have major challenges responding to the growing older population. Chapter I provide some examples of how OECD countries, such as the United States, Spain, Greece, UK, Norway, Germany and Japan, continue to search for innovative strategies in responding to the growth trends taking place, especially the growing older population. Globally, countries regardless of income, obviously some more so than others, have and will continue to experience major problems responding to this population growth phenomenon. A challenge may come for countries responding to the medical, health and social needs of the growing older population, 48 to 55 plus in the developing world, or 60 plus in the more developed world where the fastest growing age category is 85 plus. The 85 plus group will present major challenges not only to medical and health systems, but long-term care needs provided by families and institutional human services systems.

Chapter I introduced a most important subject area, not just the growing ageing trends globally, but the subject of ageism and the negative stereotypes confronted by the older population on a regular basis. The challenge for all continents will be to dispel all of the aging stereotypes passed down over generations. The continents now and in the future will be challenged to recognize that the aging population is not just a problem to be dealt with, but they bring years of knowledge, experiences and problem-solving skills that should be viewed from a strength perspective and become part of decision-making in social, economic growth and development. If given the opportunity political and civic leaders can use that knowledge, experiences and skills to bring about a society for all ages based on social justice and human rights. The eradication of ageism including all the social injustices implicated may require an organized human, not physical, seismic force globally, the "Silver Tsunami."

A very critical aspect of global population growth has been the arrival of the "Silver Tsunami," the growth in the older population 60 plus; as aforementioned a major challenge, especially for social (family caregiving, and professional home care), medical and health systems, as aforementioned will be the age category 85 plus, the fastest growth category of older persons. These demographic growth trends will have a significant impact, not only on all of the aforementioned systems, but these demographic trends will create demands for new and innovative systems as needs emerge. As aforementioned, the Chapter addresses how the global population growth trends will impact key societal systems, the family, medical, health, social, banking and/or commerce (including retirement and pension), and political. Although the aforementioned "youth bulge" generations is a very critical part of the discussions regarding demographic trends, the major focus will be the "Silver Tsunami," the growing older population. The narrative throughout all the chapters will highlight that more than eighty percent of the older population in Sub-Saharan Africa, fifty one percent globally will not have a social pension or basic income security following retirement. The Chapter makes the point that age inequalities related to social protection should be considered a major global crisis that violates all principles of human rights and social justice.

Chapter II - Considering that a major portion of the book addresses the dramatic growth of the growing older population or the "Silver Tsunami," Chapter II begins by asking a very important question, does Population Aging Matter? Research says yes it does and the Chapter addresses the major impact based on research findings of all the implications this demographic explosion will have on major or key societal systems beginning with the family. First of all, the Chapter addresses the very important family institution in regards to responsibilities for caring and/or socialization of family members from cradle to grave. A great deal of attention is given in the Chapter to the growing older family members, especially 60 plus or some less than 60 in the developing world. As a family member ages he/she becomes vulnerable to physiological, biological and/or psychological changes occurring which could affect limitations in mobility, auditory and visual. It is a strong desire of older family members during the aging process to reside at home and not in a nursing home or other institutional settings; in such instances, especially long-term care, homecare by professionals and/or family members becomes critical. According to research findings, family home care, for the most part by women, over a long period of time affects the caregivers' physically, medically and emotionally.

The Chapter also addresses other societal systems including retirement, pension systems, banking and other financial institutions, and most importantly medical, health and social welfare services. The concept of pensions and the current state of retirement will and continue to be impacted by increasing life expectancy. Because of increasing life expectancy the age of retirement has become a major discussion or debate globally. The Chapter addresses how some countries are currently considering, some have already made the decision of changing the retirement age of workers as part of their process related to pension reform. Another major discussion related to pension reform, especially on the part of workers is affordability of the pension, or does the pension provide an adequate income for workers and families following retirement? For workers and governments in Sub-Saharan Africa, the Chapter addresses the issue that more than eighty percent of retirees are without a social pension following retirement. Globally, the percentage of those without a pension at the time of retirement age is fifty-one percent. A major factor contributing to this problem is that most workers have been employed in the informal sector or self-employed during their work history; the Chapter addresses the dominant role that is played by the informal labor sector in employment. Also, the Chapter addresses the need for some partnership or collaboration between the two labor sectors, informal and formal that may reduce the number of retirees without a social pension following retirement.

Chapter II also addresses another system affected by increasing life expectancy or the growing older population, the Banking and Financial Industries. The Chapter addresses the need for a more age friendly banking environment. The older or aging population brings a different culture behavior to the banking industry that has to be seriously considered. The Banking Industry will need to recognize that a significant amount of financial assets will be under the control of an aging population especially females who continue to live longer than their male counterparts. The banking industry should expect changes in product and service demands of the growing older population. Accessibility to banking services and products will also become critical, including the use of modern technology in providing services to a growing older population. Also, addressed in the Chapter is the growing threat felt by the aging population regarding scam perpetrators and a challenge to the banking industry to find means to protect the financial interest of the older population. The Chapter provides examples of how some states such as Oregon and Texas have partnered with local law enforcement officials in protecting the financial interest of the growing older population.

Finally, extended life expectancy will probably have the greatest impact on the medical, health, and social welfare systems. A major focus in Chapter II is as the population ages there is an increasing risk for a variety of physical and mental disabilities resulting from an increase in chronic and/or long term illnesses. The transitioning from an era of communicable diseases to chronic illnesses will become a major challenge, especially for the developing and/or the low to middle-income countries. The developing countries, for example have not had the time to prepare for the growing older population with up to date medical, health and social welfare infrastructures as the more high-income countries. Increasing illnesses related to dementia and/ or Alzheimer's will require special medical, health and social needs, including long-term care in the home as well as institutional care. The Chapter highlights examples of the tremendous cost for institutional assisted living or home care services. The Chapter provides an example of the high cost of long-term care several years ago resulted in some countries such as the United Kingdom to close some of their institutional living facilities.

Chapter III – The Chapter addresses a time period when the world begins to become aware of the demographic growth explosion occurring across all age groups, but especially the dramatic increase within the growing older population. The international community in becoming more and more aware and alert to this demographic growth phenomenon began to consider ways to respond globally, national and regional; it was now time for a global call to action. Globally, the call to action dates back several decades, beginning with the First World Assembly on Aging in 1982. Not only was there a growing awareness of the demographic trends taking place the international community began a proactive movement that included organizing global assemblies, regional forums and conferences. The goal was to bring together delegates and representatives from member states for discussions and debates on how to respond. Also, a major focus of the Chapter is on the global or international community's recognition that the unprecedented growth in population, especially the "silver tsunami" will require not just a countries' response but there would be a need for a global collective response to this growth phenomenon. The global population growth shock considering the growth patterns/trends in recent decades awakened the world to the impact these demographic trends were having and would continue to have on all of societal systems such as the family, political, economical, social welfare, medical and health.

International organizations, including the United Nations, The International Labor

Organization, The World Bank, The International Social Security Association and Non-governmental organizations such as Help Age International, concluded that it was time to intervene and partner with not just member countries but all countries as they struggle to respond to this growth phenomenon. The Chapter highlights the role(s) of the international community in carrying out research on the subject and sharing the findings/results with the global community, especially the developing world; the sharing included research findings and technical assistance that helped to alert and prepare countries for responding to this unprecedented population growth phenomenon. A major focus of the international organizations, including non-governmental organizations, such as Help Age International, has been to ensure that the old age population would have social protection, such as income security, health and a safe environment to live in respect and dignity following retirement. The aforementioned necessary securities are equally applied to those with work histories in the informal sector and without a history of participation in the traditional tripartite collective bargaining labor system.

The Chapter provides an analysis of the various global assemblies, conventions and forums in addressing the needs of a growing older population and consequences, positively and negatively. In addition to the Declarations, Resolutions emerging from the assemblies, Chapter III addresses similar historical documents that had emerged from specific organizations, such as the International Labor Organization related to issues of human rights and social justice. Finally, the Chapter examines key planning and development documents related to population growth, such as the United Nations Minimum Development Goals 2015, and the Sustained Development Goals 2030 and their implications for improving the quality of life across all age groups.

Chapter IV- Globally, the unprecedented growth in populations across all age groups, especially the "Silver Tsunami" since 1800 has become a critical concern. The preparation and development of the necessary infrastructures, medical, health, and social for responding to this growth phenomenon will become quite challenging currently and in future years. Africa, Sub-Saharan Africa in particular, is an example of a continent not unlike a significant number of low to middle-income countries globally, that will be greatly challenged by an increasing growth in population; it is in such countries that the question of preparation for responding to the demographic growth trends becomes most critical. A major challenge for Sub-Saharan Africa will be ensuring that the growing older population has income security/social pension and access to medical, health and social welfare services.

Considering the major challenges being presented by the population growth "shock," especially the "Silver Tsunami," a major focus of Chapter IV is to take a look at how a continent, non-Western, historically has responded to vulnerable populations with very special needs. Sub-Saharan Africa is one continent that historically has been noted for its unique system of social welfare, the extended family network. Since the continent currently has more than eighty percent of its older population without basic income security or a social pension, its past history or responding to vulnerable populations will be a major focus or "case history" of Chapter VI. Historically, even prior to colonization, Africa had its own unique social, medical, and health infrastructures in place for meeting the needs of their populations across all age groups, tribes, clans and territories, especially the older population. The overall infrastructure in African societies was commonly referred to as the extended family system or network; the principles, duties and responsibilities of caring have been practiced for centuries, long before the Belgium

Conference of 1884-85, "Scramble for Africa," that resulted in three-quarters of a Century of colonization. A major question that emerged in the narrative of Chapter IV is does the past history of social protection and/or caring, especially for vulnerable members of society, become a problem-solving dividend in preparing for the trends in population growth, especially the growing older population in the 21st Century?

Chapter IV looks at how traditional African societies cared for members of the family kinship groups, especially the older population. Africa, not unlike other continents and/or countries, will be confronted with some major challenges in responding to these demographic growth trends such as the "Silver Tsunami." In regards to preparation for the "Silver Tsunami," the Chapter addresses several questions and/or issues related to the population growth phenomenon, and the African traditional systems of caregiving. First, what was the impact of historical events such as the era of colonization, including the land and natural resources take over, the separation of families, tribes, clans and forced labor, had on the extended family systems of caregiving, including the mutual aid societies? Secondly and most importantly, are their significant elements from the traditional extended family system that survived colonization that could be incorporated in the plans for responding to the growing older population? A very critical follow-up is can those critical elements that survived the era of colonization respond to the challenges presented during the current era of modernization, industrialization and urbanization taking place in African societies? For example, are their specific elements of the traditional African social welfare system that can be incorporated within the current conceptualization, preparation and planning for meeting the needs of the current and future growing older population?

Although it is recognized that the extended family system, historically played a key role in the caring of family members, it can be expected that in a more modern and urbanized society as life expectancy increases, the growing older population will require special needs and resources, including long-term care on the part of family as well as private and public institutions. Finally, the Chapter addresses the need for innovative policy initiatives as part of the preparation and response. This is why Chapter IV and other Chapters will continually focus on the need for new and innovative policies, including social pensions, access to health, social services and long-term care.

Chapter V- Chapter V is extremely important for the developing and or low to middle income countries such as Sub-Saharan Africa, Latin America and the Caribbean. Some of the countries within the aforementioned continents are transitioning from traditional to modern societies. Some of the countries are being challenged and confronted with problems and issues related to modernization, industrialization, urbanization as well as a growing cybernetic society. Progress towards a modern society will vary from country to country; in other words some countries, based on political, economic and social conditions are ahead of others. The population growth phenomenon including the growing older population, the "Silver Tsunami" is taking place in Sub-Saharan Africa at a time of modernization, industrialization and urbanization. Chapter V addresses the impact this transition towards a highly developed society, regardless of stage, will have on a continent's traditions, cultures and customs, especially the traditional or extended family network of caring for the older members, children and other vulnerable members of the extended family network. According to theories of modernization all societies over time move from a traditional, informal to a modern more formal society. Although a modern society is viewed by many as very positive in regards to a country's progress, such transition can result in some negative consequences as well; in other words, there can be some serious consequences or a weakening of traditional family kinship systems, especially in the caring for an older population, children/youth and other vulnerable family members. A key element of modernization is the dramatic increase in urbanization, especially of the younger population in search of education and job opportunities. Any significant movement of the younger age groups could leave members of the older population back in their home villages, especially caring for the younger children and other family responsibilities. The question is to what extent does urbanization and modernization threaten the significance of the extended family caring system? The pros and cons of such movement or transition are addressed in Chapter V.

The preparation of countries, such as those in Sub-Saharan Africa, becomes critical in responding to a growing older population in the 21st Century. It is even more critical considering the fact that more than 80% of retirees in Sub-Saharan Africa, 51% globally are without a social pension or sufficient income following retirement. Chapter V addresses some of the factors operating in a modern and urban society that make the task quite challenging. A modern and urbanized society may require new and innovative strategies for maintaining some of the strengths that were inherent in the traditional family kinship system as families continue the transition towards a complex urban and modernized society in the future.

The Chapter also addresses the critical relationship between the informal and formal labor sectors; historically the relationship between the two labor sectors has been non-existence. A major question, what are the possibilities of the two labor sectors working together or co-existing in the future that could potentially reduce significantly the number of individuals without income security? The Chapter examines the possibility of the two sectors working together or forming elements of a partnership, especially regarding a tripartite system of labor with the goal of increased social protection for workers and their families. The Chapter shares some current examples of the two sectors beginning to work together and progress to date. Globally, especially in Africa the informal sector continues to dominate the labor force. The Chapter addresses the fact that unless there is some form of a relationship between the two sectors the growing older population, not just in Africa will continue to live in retirement without basic income, medical, health and social services, including long-term care which becomes a necessity as the population ages.

Chapter VI – Chapter VI is probably the most important of the chapters considering the overall goal of providing the current state of social protection, social pensions for the growing older population in Sub-Saharan Africa. The continent is used as a case history to illustrate some of the success stories (not many) problems and issues of the older population residing on the continent. The statistical realities from current research are that the state of social protection/social pensions in Sub-Saharan Africa is not good in comparison with other countries including North Africa and globally. Chapter VI addresses the reality that despite several World Assemblies (First, UN: 1982), additional Conferences, Forums, and Conventions, over the past several decades, with few exceptions, Sub-Saharan African countries have made very little progress when it comes to social protection for the older retired population. It is interesting to note that although there has been little progress in recent years regarding social protection, Africa has become one of the fastest growing global economies. Despite the aforementioned reality, Africa with very few exceptions, have been unable to locate within their fiscal budget monetary resources needed for a social pension for those retirees who spent years working in the informal labor sectors or were self-employed.

The fact that less than 20% of older persons will have a social pension or basic income security in their retirement years illustrates little or limited progress. The workers and their families not only are currently denied the benefits of a social pension they have been denied benefits such as health care, including disability, maternal and child health care while working in the informal sector or self-employed. Chapter VI provides for the readers a profile of countries in Sub-Saharan Africa in response to questions such as: Does the country have a social pension, if yes what are the eligibility requirements or qualifying conditions and regulatory framework, pension scheme description, type of program coverage and/or benefits, sources of funds, exclusions (who are excluded from the scheme?) by countries' (example, self employed, agricultural workers). Most importantly, if a country does not have a social pension is it currently in the process of negotiating with the formal sector to become part of an existing tripartite system?

The major purpose of Chapter VI as aforementioned is to highlight the current status of social protection, specifically social pensions for each country in Sub-Saharan Africa. The data analysis does not just respond to whether a country has a social pension, but will also provide information regarding a country's progress, or the lack of progress, toward a social pension for the older population. The definition of a social pension is based on an international consensus and is used for the purpose of analysis. Each country has been assigned a grade by the Author, ranging from 1, highest to 5, lowest in accordance with the definition of a social pension. The grading process helps to determine the level of progress towards a social pension for each country.

In addition to factors related directly to a country's pension scheme, the Chapter also provide other social and economic data for each country, including total population, and the percentage of population 60 plus, dependency and family support ratios, life expectancy (male/female), statutory pension age, (male/female), GDP p/capita, human development index, corruption index and an index related to a country's governance such as day-to-day business and management practices. The purpose for the additional variables and/or information is to provide a broader view or profile of a country's capacity and readiness not only to introduce social programs also to sustain them over a period time. In summary, the data analysis from Chapter VI reinforced the statistical evidence, and conclusions that there is an urgent need for countries to enact social protection systems, especially social pensions in Sub-Saharan Africa as well as globally. It was obvious based on the grading or evaluative system used for analysis that some countries are significantly ahead of others.

Chapter VII - One of the major questions most frequently asked when the subject of countries not having a social pension is asked, is it affordable. Chapter VII shares research findings to illustrate that a social pension, not just in Sub-Saharan Africa but also in other low to middle income and/or developing countries is not only affordable, it is achievable and sustainable over a long period of time. The Chapter provides specific country examples, including low and middle-income countries reinforcing the aforementioned fact. The aforementioned countries include

Botswana, C. Verde, Kenya, Liberia, Swaziland, Namibia, South Africa and Lesotho. There are similar examples in Latin America and Caribbean countries as well. The aforementioned countries, including Liberia with a per/capita income of only $970.00 (has a social pension) compared to The Gambia with a per/capita income of approximately ten times that of Liberia does not have a social pension. Research has illustrated that low to middle income countries have been able to use a small percentage of their GDP to provide a social pension for retirees who were not part of a traditional tripartite collective bargaining system. The Chapter also shares research findings illustrating that the enactment of social pensions also has other very significant and important benefits, reductions in unemployment, poverty, children's growth and development, as well as contributions to economic growth and development.

Finally, the Chapter addresses the question if social pensions are affordable and achievable why is it that less than 20% of older persons in Sub-Saharan Africa do not have basic income security following retirement. What is more frightening and a reason to be alarmed is that unless there are immediate social polices in the very near future, the next cohort of older persons will face similar realities in their future years. Also, the same narrative will be true regarding the future lack of access to medical/health and social services, including long-term care. The Chapter concludes based on the evidence available reference affordability and the resulting benefits for countries, including economic growth, that "The Time Is Now" for the enactment of social pensions for the growing older population, the "Silver Tsunami." The case is made not just for countries in Sub-Saharan Africa but globally.

Chapter VIII – Yes, the growing consensus globally is that the "Time Is Now!!!" for global action for enacting a social or civic pension for all. Chapter VIII continues with the aforementioned question, if social pensions are affordable, and there are such great benefits, reduction in poverty, unemployment and contributions to social and economic growth, what are the countries waiting for? The question goes beyond what are the countries waiting for, what about the international community such as the United Nations, The World Bank? The international community including the United Nations recognized during the First World Assembly that problems such as a lack of social protection were a global issue requiring a global response.

The Chapter also addresses a "new spirit," and "Africa Rising," a social activist movement in Sub-Saharan Africa with a strong proactive commitment to getting things done on behalf of all citizens. The movement emerges from an increasing new generation of highly educated young social activists who are not willing to live in the past but moving forward. The changing attitudes and the optimism about getting things done are buoyed by several major factors: First of all, Africa is one of the fastest growing economies in the world. Secondly, there has been a significant improvement in overall governance and business management practices. Thirdly, expanded economic markets beyond the regional borders of Sub-Saharan Africa. Finally, the continent's current focus is on Foreign Direct Investments (FDI), not just Foreign Aid. In other words a major focus is on the development of appropriate infrastructures such as electricity and transportation systems that contribute to social and economic growth.

The Chapter calls attention to the naysayers who are fixated in the past focusing only on factors, such as corruption and yes to some extent still exist, but not see the citizens in South Africa, Zimbabwe demonstrating in the streets against all forms of illicit activities, including corruption. It does not make it right, but illicit activities are not just an African matter, but globally including the OECD countries! The Chapter concludes that here is a need for many of the naysayers to come to grips with the fact that Tarzan does not live in Africa anymore." Yes, there is a new spirit of getting things done or taking care of business, and economically "Africa Rising" is also a reality.

Although a number of success stories, especially economically in recent decades, Chapter VIII sends up some flags of caution for current and future planning. In addition to sharing selective factors contributing to economic growth during recent decades, the Chapter also identified a number of potential threats to economic growth and transformation that could have implications for the enactment of social programs and the continuation of economic growth. Those potential threats include: corruption or illicit practices, the continuing separation of the workforce into formal and informal sectors that does not allow for a tripartite collective bargaining system for all workers, and most importantly a failure on the part of countries to invest in the "youth bulge" generation, the demographic dividend with the potential of contributing to economic growth and development.

Finally, in response to a call for action in enacting social programs, especially social pensions, the Chapter has provided lessons from successful countries in Sub-Saharan Africa as well as those in Latin America/Caribbean. Furthermore, the Chapter addresses factors, based on findings from the successful countries, including globally, that should be considered as countries plan social protection programs such as Social pensions for the growing older population, the "Silver Tsunami."

OUTLINE OF BOOK CHAPTERS: I-VIII

CHAPTER I

The Global Population Growth Explosion: Challenges and Opportunities in the Twenty-First Century

CHAPTER II

Why Population Aging Matters in the 21st Century

I. **Introduction**

II. Family Systems

    A. Rural/Urban migration, modernization, industrialization and urbanization: Implications for a Growing Older Population
    B. The changing role of caretakers, especially older family members
    C. Changing dependency and family support ratios

III. Retirement and Pension Systems (Occupational)

    A. Early and extended retirement issues
    B. Inadequacy of pension programs for retires
    C. The lack of social protection for the informal and self-employed workforce

IV. Banking Systems: Changing the Banking Culture, Investing and Consumer Demands

    A. Major Challenges Confronting the Banking and Commerce Industries: Developing a Friendly Banking Environment for a Growing Older Population
    B. Enhancing Accessibility:
        1. Physical Structures Safety and Security
        2. Consumer and Staff Communications for Meeting the Special Needs of a Growing Older Population, including Preventive Measures for Protection Against "Scams" and Other Illicit Activities

V. Medical, Health and Social Systems:

    A. Financial and Physical Accessibility to Medical Facilities, esp. Long-Term Care
    B. Meeting the increasing needs of family and occupational caregivers
    C. Ensuring that resources are available that allow for Aging in Place/home for the Older population

Summary and Conclusion

CHAPTER III

The World Responds Belatedly to Unprecedented Population Growth, Including the "Silver Tsunami"

I. Introduction

II. Responding to the Global Demographic Explosion: Events and Actions Pre-Post First World Assembly on Ageing 1982

    A. The 26th Session of the International Labor Organization, Philadelphia, Pa., (USA), April-May, 1944

    B. The Founding of the United Nations – 1945

III. First World Assembly on Aging/Vienna Austria, 26 July to August 8, 1982

    A. Assembly's Preamble

    B. Principles Adopted by the First World Assembly on Aging: Human Rights and Social Justice for a Growing Older Population

IV. The United Nations General Assembly: Resolution 46/91 for Older Persons 1991: Social Justice and Human Rights

V. International Conference Population and Development (ICPD), Cairo, Egypt, 5 September to September 13, 1994

    A. Summary of ICPD Conference Principles

    B. A Program of Action and Member States' Commitment

VI. The Second World Assembly on Ageing/Madrid, Spain, 8 April to 12 April 2002

VII. The United Nations Economic Community for Europe Ministerial Conference: Ensuring A Society for All Ages, 18-20 2012, Vienna, Austria

VIII. Ageing in the Twenty-First Century: A Celebration and a Challenge – 2012

CHAPTER IV

Social Welfare Protection Practices in Traditional African Societies: Implications for the "Silver Tsunami"

I. Introduction

II. Africa's Traditional Social Welfare System: The Extended Family Network providing for The Overall welfare of Family Members When Needed, food, shelter and clothing

The Matriarchs' of Mthatha Village/South Africa

III. The Traditional Medical System of Caring for Families

    A. Medicine and Practitioners
    B. Maternal and Child Health
    C. Herbal Medicine

IV. Utilizing The Strengths of Traditional and Modern Medicine

V. The African Extended Family Kinship Network: The Chances of Survival in a Modern, Urbanized, Industrialized and Cybernetic Society

Summary/Conclusion

CHAPTER V

Pre-Post Independence Sub-Saharan Africa: The Challenges of Modernization, Industrialization and Urbanization

I. Introduction

II. Pre-Independence Era of Colonization: Impact on Culture, Traditions and Social Protection

"The Forced Labor Era"

III. European Views Pre-Post Colonialism of Africa and Africans: Implications for Future Partnerships Related to Economic Growth and Development

IV. The Europeans Zero contributions to Social Welfare and Economic Development in Africa: Pre-Post Independence

    A. Social Security/Social Protection in the Colonies: For Expatriates Only
    B. Plans for Economic Growth and Development: On Behalf of Europeans Only

V. Theories of Social and Economic Development: Modernization, Dependency and Social Development Schools of Thought

    A. Modernization School
    B. Dependency School
    C. Development School

VI. Economical and Developmental Perspectives of African Leaders: Post Independence

"Selective Views on Modernization:"
Dr. Chigozie Obioma
Dr. Bruce Gilley

CHAPTER VI

The Current and Future Status of Social Pensions: Sub Saharan Africa

X. Future Projections: Coverage of The Next Generation of Older Persons in Sub-Saharan Africa

XI. The United Nations Developmental Goals (MDGs): The Inclusion/Exclusion of Social Statutory Social Pensions

    A. The 2015 Millennium Developmental Goals
    B. The 2020 Sustainable Developmental Goals

Summary/Conclusion

CHAPTER VII

Social Pensions for the Growing Older Population in Sub-Saharan Africa: Affordable, Achievable and Sustainable

CHAPTER VIII

Economic Growth, the "Youth Bulge" Generation and the "African Rising Spirit:" Implications for Social Policies, Programs and Enhanced Quality of Life for All

I. Introduction

II. Africa's Economic Renaissance: Current and Future Projections

    A. Past, Current and Future Economic Projections
    B. "Africa Economic Rising"

III. Selective Factors Contributing to Economic Growth/Development in Sub-Saharan Africa

    A. Improved Inter-Intra continent/country economic partnerships
    B. Improved infrastructure developments, including energy, and railroads development
    C. A New spirit and Growing Optimism in Africa
    D. The "Youth Bulge" Generations
    E. Africa and China: A Growing Partnership

IV. Potential Internal Threats to Economic Growth and Transformation

    A. Poor/Inadequate Business and Management Practices/Regulatory Reforms
    B. The "Elephant in the Room:" Corruption
    C. The Continuing Separation of the Labor Sectors: Informal and Formal
    D. Political and/or Governmental Failures to Take Advantage of the "Youth Bulge" Generation, the Demographic Economic Dividend

V. The Non-Contributory Social Pensions Movement: Valuable Lessons From Other Countries Including Developing and Low to Middle Income

VI. The Ultimate Goal is Social Pensions For All: Factors to Consider in Conceptualization, Planning and Implementation.

A. Affordability and Fiscal Space in Countries' Budgets, Including Sustainability

B. A Country's Diversity: Political, Social/Economical and Cultural Traditions

C. Non-Contributory Cash Transfers: Lessons from Other Countries, especially from Africa (Botswana, Namibia, South Africa, Liberia, Swaziland, C. Verde)

D. Administrative Use of "Means" or "Pension" Tests in Determining Program Eligibility

E. The Need for Collaboration with all Stakeholders Across Policy Lines

F. A Thorough Review of Management and Business Practices

G. Conceptualization and Implementation of an Environmental Scan related to Factors contributing to the aging process (medical/health/social issues) and resulting implications for the "Silver Tsunami"

Summary and Conclusion

THE GLOBAL POPULATION GROWTH EXPLOSION: CHALLENGES AND OPPORTUNITIES IN THE 21ST CENTURY

INTRODUCTION

Globally, according to demographic scholars, United Nations and other international organizations, continents and countries have been and will continue to experience an unprecedented demographic growth process of transition resulting in an increasing number of individuals across all age groups; most importantly has been the significant increase of those in the 60 plus age group. Currently, the fastest growing age group in the Western World or the more economically developed countries in the category 60 plus, is the age group 85 and over. In the developing and/or low to middle income countries age 60 plus may be inappropriate to be considered as the beginning of the aging process; in considering the beginning of the aging process in the developing world factors such as cultural, customs, social, medical and health factors should be part of the formula. Globally there are significant differences when it comes to life expectancy across various continents and/or countries. An important question for future considerations, when discussing the beginning of the aging process is wouldn't it be more appropriate, considering the aforementioned factors, if each continent and/or country had the opportunity for determining when its aging process begins? (**For further discussion reference the aging process See Growing Older/Aging: Defining the Concept from A Global Perspective, Chapter I, pages 18-27).**

As aforementioned every continent and it varies from continent to continent, is currently experiencing a demographic phenomenon of growth in population including an increasing percentage of the proportion of older persons within its total population. Global population growth including the "Silver Tsunami," the growing older population, is being discussed as one of the most significant occurrences in social transformation of the 21st Century. The 21st Century that began on January 1, 2001 and projected to end on December 31, 2100, represents the First Century of the Third Millennium.

Why does this unprecedented population phenomenon or demographic shock wave matter? It matters primarily, as research has already pointed out, because of the significant impact it is having and will continue to have on all of the critical societal systems such as the family, labor and/or occupational, political, financial, housing, transportation, social services, health and medical institutions including long-term care. Most importantly for the growing older population globally there will be an increasing demand and need not only for social protection such as social pensions and/or income security, but more specialized medical, social and health infrastructures including specialized personnel as well. A major challenge for all countries, developed and/or developing, will be searching for new and/or innovative ways for developing, maintaining and strengthening institutional physical and human infrastructures, including family intergenerational ties in a modern, urbanized, industrialized and cybernetic society (UN: World Population Ageing 2015 Report, Division Economic Social Affairs (DESA) Population Division, New York, 2015).

The fact that this demographic growth phenomenon will have such an impact on all societal systems should help to alert and inform the world, including continents, countries, regions and international organizations to begin, if not already in process to conceptualize and develop appropriate strategies of action for responding. The response should include populations across all age groups, especially the growing older population, the "Silver Tsunami." The international organizations and their members and non-member countries, governmental and non-governmental entities, political leaders and social advocates can expect to be confronted with some of the greatest challenges in the history of humankind. The challenges will be even greater in responding to the "Silver Tsunami," the growing older population whose age group within the next couple of decades will outnumber the age group 15 and under; the growing older population is becoming the new majority. Just imagine how such a change in age structure will begin to impact critical factors such as age dependency and/or family support ratios in future years.

But, prior to a more explicit narrative(s) or discussions of all the implications of the current and continuous demographic explosion across all age groups the primary goal of Chapter I is to put into a historical perspective some of the significant factors contributing to the current era of global population growth beginning from around the year 1800. It was the year 1800 when the world, after thousands of years of population growth reached the 1 Billion mark in population. A significant part of the narrative in Chapter I will also include some of the dynamics, especially factors contributing to changing timelines surrounding the population growth process. As aforementioned it was the year 1800 when global population growth reached the 1 Billion mark. Some demographers have used the year 1800 and others based on their research have used the year 1804; for this latter group 1804 seems to be the most valid date when the global population reached the 1 Billion mark. In considering the fact that it took thousands of years for the world to reach the 1 Billion mark in population growth, it should not be of too much significance whether it occurred in 1801 or 1804 or somewhere in between. In other words four (4) years should not make too much of a significant difference for analytical purposes.

GLOBAL POPULATION GROWTH: HISTORICAL PERSPECTIVE: 8000 BC TO 2100

For all of the Homo sapiens around at the time to witness the grand occasion, reaching the 1 Billion mark in 1800/1804 also represented the beginning of the 19th Century. At this time in history it has been estimated that the global population was growing at the rate of approximately 0.5 % annually (UN: Population Division, World Population Prospects: The 2000 Revision, Volume III, Analytical Report, 2001, p 155). (**See Appendix A: Tables/Charts, Chapter 1, Table I).**

For the population to double from 1 Billion in 1800/1804 to 2 Billion around 1927 required only about one Century or approximately 127 years. During the year 1927 when the population reached the 2 Billion mark the population growth at the time was occurring at the rate of about 1% per/year (UN: Population Division, The 2000 Revision, ibid. 2001). When the 21st Century began around January 1, 2001 the global population had reached the 6 Billion mark requiring only about 200 years for this remarkable achievement in population growth to occur in such a short period of time. It is remarkable considering that it took thousands of years to reach the 1 Billion Mark.

It was around the beginning of the 1950's, approximately 145 years following the achievement of the 1 Billion mark, when globally the mortality rates begin a very significant decline, especially in the developing countries such as Sub-Saharan Africa. This was an important time in history with the introduction and use of vaccines, antibiotics and insecticides that had become available globally. These medical advances, including the decline in mortality begin to result in a significant increase in the rate of population growth. Globally, between the years of 1965-1970 the annual growth rate was around 2%. The world witnessed a decline in the growth rate after 1970; between 2000-2005 the growth rate stood around 1.2%. The projections are that when the world reaches the halfway mark of the 21st Century global population growth annually will be around 0.5%. Further projections are that the annual rate for the years 2045-2050 will range between 0.05 and 1% (UN: Population Division, The 2000 Revision, ibid, 2001, p 155). **(See Appendix A: Tables/Charts, Chapter I, Tables 2-5).**

How Many Years to Reach the One Billion Mark?

Historically one major question that has been asked repeatedly is if it took only 127 years to go from 1 Billion in 1800 to 2 Billion in 1927, and only197 years, around 2001 to go from 1 Billion to 6 Billion, how long did it take for the global population to reach the 1 Billion mark in 1800/1804? Globally, countries entered the 21st Century, 2001, experiencing what some demographers have been describing as a demographic explosion or a demographic "time bomb." As aforementioned the world had reached the 1 Billion mark around 1800/1804 around 200 years prior to the beginning of the 21st Century. Some demographers using the concept referred to as "Guesstimate" have speculated that it may have taken, based on research available to them at a particular time in history, approximately 50,000 years for the world to reach the 1 Billion mark in population. But, as researchers, including the paleontologist, anthropologist and demographers, working with new technology and techniques continued their research the date(s) begin to change over time. Following a period of time there were other scientific experts, utilizing new technology available in the their field of study, who speculated and/or reported that the number of years to reach the 1 Billion mark was more like 200,000 or 195,000 years. The main question when considering a time frame was when did human beings or Homo sapiens first make an appearance on earth? Based on available research at a given time some experts begin to use the timeframe 195,000 or 200,000 years for the approximate time it took to reach the 1 Billion mark in population. Some historical records have illustrated that Homo sapiens may have actually emerged around 200,000 B.C. or more specifically 195,000 years earlier on the African continent. In other words, the population based on historical documentation, Homo sapiens first made an appearance in Africa around 195,000 or 200,000 years ago; they were described as anatomically modern or human like in features. But, in reference to life style of the population that appeared in Africa around the year 200,000 there was little change over a very long period of time from their contemporaries, Homo erectus and Neanderthals. Historically referred to as "Neanderthal man" this extinct species of humans possessed somewhat of a receding forehead and pronounced brow ridges that resided in Africa approximately 30,000 to 200,000 years ago; these extinct humans referred to as Homo erectus were discovered in Africa around 1.9 million years ago. So, the debate continues with the introduction of new research and technology (Haub, C., Senior Scholar Population Reference Bureau (PRB), "How Many People Have Ever Lived on Earth," PRB, Washington, DC, 2016). (Merriam Webster Dictionary and Wikipedia).

Once again based on advanced research findings and technology the time frame would continue to change overtime. Other experts have proposed, based on more recent scientific discoveries, including the famous Lucy remains in Ethiopia, Homo sapiens may have made an appearance approximately 400,000 years ago on the Continent of Africa. "Around 400,000 years ago, Homo sapiens appeared and had evolved into what would be recognize as modern humans. Perhaps the most well-known sites associated with Homo sapiens again are from the opposite ends of the continent, Omo Valley in Ethiopia and Border Cave in South Africa, dating from 100,000 years ago" (Kasule, Samuel, The History Atlas of Africa: From the First Humans to the Emergence of a New South Africa, New York: A Simon & Schuster Macmillan Company, 1998, p. 14).

A new challenge or more recent research reported in 2017 challenges the conclusion that it was 200,000 years ago when Homo sapiens first appeared on the African continent. According to the Archaeologists informing the world, the "…Oldest Homo sapiens bones ever found shake foundations of the human story…idea that modern humans evolved in East Africa 200,000 years ago challenged by extraordinary discover of 300,000 year old remains in Moroccan mine. Fossils recovered from an old mine on a desolate mountain in Morocco have rocked one of the most enduring foundations of human history: that Homo sapiens arose in a cradle of humankind in East Africa 200,000 years ago" (Sample, Ian, Science Editor, the Guardian, England, Wednesday 7/June/2017). The Archaeologists during the evacuation that lasted for years discovered the remains or bones of five people. When date test were completed the discovery from a tooth and stone tools were approximately 300,000 years (Sample, I., Ibid, 2017).

It is obvious, even among experts in the field, of the difficulty based on available data and technology to make a precise determination about when the human race first appeared or came into existence. For some scholars "Various ancestors of Homo sapiens seem to have appeared at least as early as 700,000 B.C. Hominids walked the earth as early as several million years ago…Modern Homo sapiens may have appeared about 50,000 B.C. The long period of 50,000 years holds the key to the question of how many people have ever been born" (Haub, C., ibid, 2016, p. 1). It has been suggested by some experts that the counting should really begin around 50,000 years BC. The reason given, according to these experts, is that this was really the time when modern Homo sapiens first appeared on earth; the time line should not begin at 700,000 years ago or before when the ancestors of Homo sapiens appeared several million years ago during the time hominids were present (Haub, C., ibid, 2016).

Most importantly, not that the previous historical estimates are unimportant, whether it took 700,000, 400,000, 200,000 or 50,000 years to reach the global 1 Billion mark but what follows centuries later. What is remarkable, based on advanced technology and techniques is that it took approximately 200 years for the population to advance from 1 Billion in 1800/1804 to 6 Billion in 2001. What the world has witnessed, especially since around 1800/1804 and the achievement of the 1 B mark in global population, has been not only a significant astronomical growth in population across all age groupings, including the 60 plus group, but what is more remarkable has been the extremely short time periods in advancing from 1 B to 2B, to 3B, to 4B and from the 6 B mark to the 11 B mark in just a few years in comparison to 200,000; the global population reached the growth mark of 7 B around the year 2012 requiring only 12 years after reaching the 6 B (Haub, C., ibid, 2016) Population Reference Bureau). During the post 1 Billion mark demographers and other experts have had at their disposal more scientific tools/ techniques for measuring population growth than were available during the growth period leading up to the 1 Billion mark; in other words, the concept "guesstimate" had become past history.

Globally a great deal of attention, preparation and actions are desperately needed in responding to the current demographic explosion, especially the impact it is having on all societal systems, political, social, health and economic. The response to this demographic explosion by global or international organizations, such as the United Nations and member countries being affected will be addressed in **Chapter III.** The primary focus of Chapter I was to put the subject matter of population growth into a global historical perspective, especially population growth trends, timelines and significant factors contributing to the growth phenomenon.

As aforementioned the world population reached the 1 billion mark around 1800/1804 at a time referred to as the beginning of the First Industrial Revolution (time frame - roughly 1760-1840). In the year 2015, approximately two centuries and a decade later, the global population had reached the mark of 7.3 billion people; to reach the global population mark of 7.3 billion from the 1 Billion mark required only about 215 years, significantly less time than the 50,000 years speculated to reach the 1 B mark. This was a remarkable accomplishment considering that some demographers and/or historians have estimated (or used the concept Guesstimate) that it may have taken approximately 50,000 years or longer to reach the 1 billion mark around 1800/1804. In regards to subjects or topics related to the beginning of the human race, demographers do caution that attempts to conclude the exact time when the human race appeared on earth can be highly problematic; the conclusions reached in response can be quite questionable (Haub, Carl, "How Many People Have Ever Lived on Earth," Population Reference Bureau (PRB), Washington, D.C., 2016).

It is interesting to note that it was about 50,000 years ago that history began to recognize significant discoveries of artifacts on the continent of Africa; it was on the African continent that artwork, including bone artifacts appeared. This period, especially around the time 50,000 to 45,000 was when the use of tools and/or tool technology began to spread to Europe and other parts of the world. It was also during this period, 50,000 years ago that emerged for the first time organized settlements of people; in the midst of these early settlements were what would be considered campsites, that included storage areas, cave paintings, carvings and engravings. Also with advances in agricultural knowledge and technology, what followed were advanced tools, and improved and more reliable food supplies. It has been suggested, based on the available evidence that it was during this time-span that group identities and/or the concept of ethnicity emerged. Sociologists, such as Tonnies, may view this era as the beginning of what modern society refers to as Gemeinschaft or the beginning of traditional societies. Another very interesting note regarding the time period 50,000 - 30,000, is that migratory records indicate that significant numbers of humans begin spreading out across the globe, into Australia, Europe, Japan, and Siberia above the Arctic. By the end of the Upper Paleolithic period the migratory history indicates that human populations had crossed the Bering land and within a very short period of time had settled throughout North and South America (Haub, C. ibid, 2016).

Although somewhat difficult to scientifically verify global population size historically, there is some consensus that the population around 8000 B.C. was approximately 5 million people; estimates are that the population by the year 1 AD had grown to 300 million. Also, it has been estimated that the average rate of growth during that particular time period was approximately 0.0512 per/year; obviously this trend in growth rate during modern times would be considered as an extremely slow growth rate (Haub, C., Population Reference Bureau (PRB), ibid, 2016).

In somewhat of a different perspective than Table 1, Chart 1 below provides data in reference to population growth with certain timeframes, births per/1000 population and the number of births between the various timeframes. Chart 1 represents a summary of population growth following the time period 8000 B.C. to around 2011.

Chart 1
Global Population Growth1800/1804 - 2011

Year	Population	Births per/1000	Births Between Birth Periods
8000 B.C.	5,000,000	80	1,137,789,769
1 AD	300,000,000	80	46,025,332,354
1200	450,000,000	60	26,591,343,000
1650	500,000,000	60	12,782,002,453
1750	795,000,000	50	3,171,931,513

(1800/1804)		**THE HISTORIC 1 BILLION MARK**	
1850	1,265,000,000	40	4,046,240,009
1900	1,656,000,000	40	2,900,237,856
1950	2,516,000,000	31-38	3,390,198,215
1995	5,760,000,000	31	5,427,305,000
2011	6,987,000,000	23	2,130,327,622

Globally, The Percentage of Persons Ever Born Living Today

Another continuing and a very interesting question or inquiry for some scholars and/or amateur demographers is how many people have ever lived on the earth? One conclusion that has been put forward in response to the question is approximately 106 Billion people have lived on earth. A second question frequently asked is the percent of individuals who have been born are actually living today? The global population in mid-2011 was around 6,987,000,0000, and it was concluded that the percent of all those ever born, those living in 2011, approximately 5 years ago, was around 6.5% of the population (Haub, Carl, "How Many People Have Ever Lived on Earth?" Population Reference Bureau, Washington, DC: 2016; World-o-meters Information, Latest News extracted from the U.S. Census Bureau, 2017).

For the Population Reference Bureau an article first published in 1995 and updated in 2002 created much scholarly conversation and debate. The article was in reference to a previous article that had been written in the mid-1970's that concluded that 75% of people ever born was alive in 1970. The response to such a bold conclusion was that such statistical fact of 75% was highly unlikely. According to PRB scholars in order for such a conclusion to occur the birth rates during the 20th Century would have had been significantly higher than those in past centuries; furthermore the evidence would have to demonstrate "…an extraordinary number of extremely old people living in the 1970's" (Haub, PRB, ibid, 2016).

It is of interest to note that during the early existence of human history, life expectancy averaged approximately 10 years. During the Iron Age in France, life expectancy ranged between 10-12 years. Just imagine that during the early years of history, the birth had to have been approximately 80 per 1000 people in order for the human species just to survive. Compare with some of the more modern countries in Africa where the birth rate is 45 to 50 per/1000 (Haub, ibid, PRB, 2016).

From An Era of Hunters and Gatherers to an Agricultural Economy and Most Importantly, the Emerging Concept of Community

On the one hand population growth is critical and it is important to consider during the process the interactions of people, or how communities emerged. Therefore, one major question beginning with the hunters and gatherers era is what did people do to occupy their time during this era of history. Long before the introduction or dawn of the agricultural economy human beings making up the populations were known as hunters and gatherers. One can assume by estimation or guesstimate that from a family perspective the population during the hunters and gatherers era or time span was comprised of small families; the population estimates at a peak time were approximately 10 million people. The population of hunters and gatherers during this era eventually discovered a new way of life, agriculture. Agriculture or farming probably subsistence farming for the most part became known as the agricultural era. What probably happened next was the introduction of an agriculture economy requiring more people, larger families, with added roles and responsibilities (UN: Population Reference Bureau, DESA, World Population Revision, July, 2015; Population Reference Bureau, "Human Population: World Population Growth," Washington, DC, 2015).

It was during the transition from an era of hunters and gatherers to an agricultural era when the concept community began to evolve. Now, with a combination of an agricultural economy and communities emerging, families began to increase in size and roles in response to the demands expected from an agricultural economy. Now, with subsistence farming or an agricultural economy evolving, more children and adults could now share various divisions of labor required for carrying out family and community tasks and responsibilities. Also, with family composition increasing, including the clarification of roles and responsibilities, members of the family could be cared for as well, especially children, the older population, as well as other vulnerable family members and society at large. One could conclude that during this era of history, dominated by hunters and gatherers, and eventually the transition to an agriculture era, the world was beginning to observe the beginning of a society as described by the German Sociologist, Ferdinand Tonnies (1855-1936). Tonnies viewed society as allowing for an evolutionary process beginning with the concept Gemeinschaft. The concept symbolized a traditional society over a period of time that would eventually evolve into a modern society to be referred to as Gesellschaft. The time frame or period for each society would vary based the level or progress related to social, economic, cultural and political circumstances (See Chapter IV for a more explicit discussion of the two concepts). Tonnies, from a sociological/anthropological perspective would suggest that the hunters and gatherers were not unlike other human species, but social beings that eventually would create communities as well as structured societies. Human beings, including the hunters and gatherers from past centuries, possessed a need for interdependence, and the sharing of occupational, physical, mental, and spiritual elements. In other words, all human beings have a strong or tremendous need to be in contact with other human beings even though this need may result in warfare or other conflicts. Anyway, it is not difficult to understand why communities began to emerge during this era (Tonnies, Ferdinard, Community and Society (Gemeinschaft and Gesellschaft), Translated and Edited by Charles P. Loomis, Dover Publications, Inc., New York, 2002; Tonnies, Ferdinard, Community and Civil Society (Gemeinschaft and Gesellschaft): Cambridge Texts in the History of Political Thought, Editor, Jose Harris, Cambridge University Press, 2001).

By the year 1 AD, or the year the baby Jesus was born (Christian perspective), globally there were approximately 300 million people and the population was growing at what was considered at the time to be at a very moderate rate of growth. At this point in history the world begins the transition from a dominant agriculture society to an era that would be one commonly described as the Industrial Revolution beginning around the 18th Century. As communities evolved during the agricultural era the world now with the coming of the industrial era, including the introduction scientific, medical and technological inventions, began to witness overall improvements in the quality of life and/or living standards of people. Also, this was an era that witnessed a significant decline in epidemics and famines; these global changes contributed significantly to population growth.

But, because of regional diversity, especially economically, the degree or levels of improvements would differ or vary by region or country. It was during this era that population growth began what is referred to as a take off period. By 1750 the population had increased to approximately 760 – 795 million, and by 1800/1804 it had reached the 1 billion mark. Not only had the world reached the 1 billion mark the diverse populations and/or diversity were highlighted. Eighty-five percent of the population of 1 billion people in 1800/1804 lived or resided in Europe and Asia, but 65% of the 85%, resided in Asia. In comparison with all recognized regions in 1804, 10.9% of the people lived in Africa, 0.7% in North America, 0.2% in Oceania, 20.8% in Europe, and 2.5 % in Latin America and the Caribbean (UN: World Population Prospects, Revision 2015, ESA/P/WP. 241, 2015). (**See Appendix A: Tables/ Charts, Chapter I, Table 1.**

After reaching the 1 billion mark in 1800/1804, it is interesting to note, as aforementioned, that globally it took only 127 years, 1927, to reach a population of 2 billion people. In reaching the 3 billion mark it took only about 33 years, 1927 to 1960; the 4 billion mark was reached in 1974, 1960 to 1974 taking approximately 14 years; the 5 billion mark was reached in 1987 in about 13 years; the 6-7 billion mark was reached around 2001 and it took approximately14 years, and the global population count of 7.3 billion was reached in 2015 requiring approximately 14-15 years for this accomplishment. The projections are that the 8 billion mark will be reached around 2024, taking approximately 12 years; the 9 billion count will be reached around 2039, and the projections are that the global population will reach 10.6 billion by the year 2100. The Twentieth Century may best be described, globally, as the era of an astronomical rise in population growth (United Nations: Population Division, DESA, 2000, 2008, 2012 Population Revisions). The 2015 Revisions by DESA updated or revised some of the projections that had been published in the aforementioned 2012 Revision by the DESA. The 8.5 billion mark will be reached around 2030; the 9.7 billion mark around 2050; and the 11.2 billion mark in 2100 (United Nations: Populations Division, DESA, 2015 Revisions).

The most recent update from the United Nations indicates that the population 60 plus will reach the 1Billion mark by the year 2018 and the 2 Billion mark by 2050. Children age 15 and under by 2050 will represent one-quarter of the global population; the global median age will be 30. It is projected that by the year 2050 more than half of the global population will be residing in Sub-Saharan Africa; the global population will reach 8 Billion in 2023, and by the year 2050 9.8 Billion. Approximately half of the population growth will take place in nine countries: India, Nigeria, Democratic Republic Congo, Pakistan, Ethiopia, Tanzania, United States, Uganda and Indonesia. By the year 2050 seven of the most populous nations globally will be Africans. Finally, another very significant projection from the United Nations latest survey was that by the current year, 2018 there will be more men than women globally, 102 men for every 100 women. Nine Eastern European countries will be negatively affected, 15% decline, by the latest population growth trends: Bulgaria, Croatia, Latvia, Lithuania, Poland, Republic of Moldova, Romania, Serbia and Ukraine (United Nations: World Population Prospects 2017 Revisions, DESA, Working Paper ESA/P/WP/248, New York, 2017); (Guardian Staff, Wednesday 21/June/2017, 14:12 EDT).

Estimates are that when the 1 billion mark was reached during the years when estimates could be made prior to 1800/1804, the annual population growth rate had been approximately 0.5% or less. Also, Indicators are that following the milestone reached of 1 billion people the average annual population growth continued at a rate of less than 0.1%; this moderate rate continued well into the 19th Century. Between 1950 and 1955 the average annual rate of population change was 1.77% globally; however, during the next five years, 1955 to 1960 the rate increased to 1.80 %. But, during the years from 1960 to 1965 there was an increase to 1.92 %, and reached a peak between the years 1965 to 1970 up to 2.6%. But, the annual rate began to decrease between the years 1970 to 1975 to 1.96; and between 2010 and 2015 the rate had decreased to about 1.18% (UN: Population Division, DESA, ibid, 2015 Revision; UN: DESA, ibid, World Population Prospects, The 2000 Revisions).

The World Bank projections are that by the year 2025 the world population will reach approximately eight billion people; if the previous projections are somewhat accurate this means that the population should reach 8 billion in about 12 years; the population is projected to reach 9.6 billion people in 2050, and approximately 10.9 billion people by the year 2021. The population of 7.3 billion is an increase from 6.1 billion in 2000, and increase of approximately 1.1 % in just twelve years. Globally, the population grew dramatically in the twentieth century. In 1900 there were approximately 1.6 billion people, and by the year 2000 the rate was 6.1 billion, and by the year 2010 had reached 6.9 billion. As indicated it was not until the early 1800's for the world to reach 1 billion people, now "… the world now seems to gain approximately 1billion people every 12-14 years" (The World Bank, 2013). (**See Appendix A: Tables/Charts, Chapter I, Tables 3 and 4).**

The World Bank projections in 2013 differ slightly from the more current projections from the United Nations, DESA/Population Division in the Revisions 2015 and 2017. For example, as aforementioned the World Bank projected that that the population would reach 8 billion by the year 2025; the United Nations projects that the 8.5 billion mark will be reached in 2030. Considering the difference in a half billion individuals, the projections among the two are extremely close. By the year 2021 the World Bank is projecting 10.9 billion people but for the same year the UN Revisions are projecting that number to be 11.2.

The differences in populations by the various global organizations may be explained by more recent methodology shared by the Population Division of the United Nations in its 2015 Revision. According to the Population Division, the "World Population Prospects is the twenty-fourth round of official United Nations population estimates and projections that have been prepared by the population division…The population provision builds on its earlier revision "… by incorporating additional results from the 2010 round of national population censuses as well as findings from recent demographic and health surveys that have been carried out around the world. The 2015 Revision provides the demographic data and indicators to assess population trends at the global, regional and national levels and to calculate many other key indicators commonly used by the United Nations" (UN, Revision 2015, ibid, p 1). The aforementioned approach by the United Nations Population Division, may account for slight differences in projections.

SIGNIFICANT FACTORS CONTRIBUTING TO GLOBAL POPULATION GROWTH AND WELLBEING

A key question historically has been what was and continues to be the various societal factors, including technological changes, contributing to this unprecedented demographic phenomenon? The following factors have been considered significant in response to the question:

Medical Innovations/Discoveries/ Advances in Public Health Education and Practice

Global population growth has been attributed to a number of factors, such as the triumph of modern medicine, including inventions, health education prevention practices and/or technological advances and industrialization. Demographic experts view the astronomical growth in human population as a major scientific victory of historical medical achievements, as well as social and economic development. The Medical and public health advancements probably begin with Louis Pasteur and his discovery of the anthrax vaccine that became a major deterrent to rabies; the vaccine proved useful in saving the lives of children and animals. Almost a half century later, penicillin was introduced to the world. Penicillin as an antibiotic made a significant contribution in preventing the spread of bacteria. It was a decade later when a biochemist discovered a method for processing penicillin that made it available globally. Also, there was the introduction of Asepsis that contributed to the early decline in child mortality rates; it was discovered that fever in children could be prevented if medical personnel, especially doctors would just wash their hands following medical procedures. The discovery of antibiotics, including the vaccination for tuberculosis (TB) represented major historical moments of medical achievements. A major factor is not just the Scientific Medical advancements alone, but the introduction and implementation of preventive and curative methods as part of the process and accomplishments (Teeple, John B. Timelines of World History, London: DK Publishing, 2002; Time Tables of History, 2nd Edition, New York: Random House, 1996).

By the year 1927, as aforementioned, the global population had reached 2 Billion people in approximately 127 years from the 1 Billion mark in 1800/1804; annual population growth at this time was about 1% per/year. In the 1950's the use of preventive measures such as vaccines, antibiotics and insecticides were now part of common everyday practices. Population growth seemed to have reached a peak around 1965 to 1970 when the annual rate reached 2% (UN: Population Division, World Population Prospects, 2000 Revisions, Vol. III, Analytical Report p. 155).

Advances in Agricultural Production and Distribution

Although medicine and public health played a major role in population growth, major technological advances during the transition from an agricultural to an industrial economy, contributed significantly as well. From an agricultural perspective not only did selected breeding improve crop production but increased the amount of food available to the growing number of families. Although medical advances and inventions played a significant role in increasing life expectancy and mortality reductions, the contributions of the agricultural era cannot be ignored. Some scholars have pointed out that the significant increase in life expectancy had begun in the mid-1800s after the 1 Billion mark in population had occurred. "In fact, the major impact of improvements in medicine and sanitation did not occur until the late 19th Century. Prior innovations in industrial and agricultural production and distribution, which improved nutrition for large numbers of people, were powerful forces in mortality reductions" (Kinsella, Kevin and Phillips, David R., Population Bulletin, Global Aging: The Challenge of Success, Vol. 60, No. 1, Publication of the Population Reference Bureau, page 12, March 2005).

During the latter part of the agricultural era and the coming of the industrial revolution, countries globally with some exceptions, begin an era of stable and increased incomes, improved social standards resulting from public health education and practices especially related to prevention. With the industrial revolution came sustained economic growth and development resulting in an overall improvement in the quality of life for most people globally; new agricultural techniques contributed significantly to improved standard of living. The improvements in agriculture brought about efficiency, not only crop production, but an increase in the volume of nutritious food for people to consume. Another contributing factor was the period of reproductive health, especially contraceptive methods and education. Related to the aforementioned was the women empowerment movement resulting in enhanced public health education, and decision making by women, as well as access to healthcare (Teeple, ibid, 2002).

The Era of Industrialization: Infrastructure Development, Including Roads, Bridges, Housing, Electricity, Transportation and Jobs

Technological inventions and developments, including the spinning wheel, the rotary and steam engines, the revolution in communications (electric telegraph), and the mechanization of the textile economy gave strong notice that era to become known as the Industrial Revolution was now underway. The transition from the agricultural era and its unique economy had begun to give way to a new global industrial economy. Now, with the availability of trains and ships, there was an on-going migration of people from the agricultural villages into the cities in search of jobs and new opportunities. The increasing availability of raw materials, especially mineral resources such as iron ore and coal would also contribute greatly to these developments during the industrial era (Teeple, J. B., ibid, 2002). Also, the scramble and colonization of the African countries, especially the exportation of the continent's natural resources and/or raw materials to Europe, and the era of forced labor contributed significantly to the building of economic empires in Europe.

Significant Changes in Fertility, Mortality and Life Expectancy

Although all of the aforementioned factors played a major role in population growth, there is a global consensus that population growth and the coming of the "Silver Tsunami" is very much related to significant declines in mortality and fertility (UN: World Population Ageing, 2013). The foundation for declining or decreasing mortality and fertility had a great deal to do with medical and public health advances. The world had been witnessing for a number of decades a decline in the number of children in the population and an increasing percentage of older persons, including those 60 plus; the fastest growing group of older persons 60 plus are those in the 85 plus category, now being referred to as the oldest old.

In some of the Western countries, especially the United States, when discussing population growth and its impact on all societal systems, the conversations at some point include the "Baby Boomers. Although the astronomical rise in population growth began long before the era of the "Baby Boomers," many view the era as relevant when discussing population growth. The phrase, "Baby Boomers" is used not only to describe a specific birth age group, most importantly the changing role of the family, and other social/health, economical, and political systems with implications related to overall population growth, including the "Silver Tsunami." This is the age group born between the years 1946, shortly following World War II, and 1964. From the first wave, some seventy-seven million Americans turned 62 around 2008. Some of the implications for this large cohort of age 62 are, they are now eligible for the first level of social security; secondly, just three years later eligible for Medicare/Medicaid; thirdly, the entire cohort by the year 2030 will have reached the age of 65 plus. By that time in history the "Boomers" will represent approximately 20% of the total population; in comparison with 2015, the 65 plus group represents only about 12.5 %, or a little less than half of what the representation will be fifteen years from now.

One very significant factor contributing to overall population growth is a process referred to as the 'demographic transition' whereas mortality and fertility decrease from high to low levels. As a result of the process, decreasing fertility rates accompanied by increasing life expectancy have significantly changed or "...reshaped the age structure of the population in most regions of the planet by shifting relative weight from younger to older groups. The role of international migration in changing age distributions has been far less important than that of fertility and mortality" (UN: DESA, Population Division, World Population Ageing, 1950-2050, New York: United Nations, 2002, p. 5). Other factors to consider regarding population growth are: fertility at this point in history is significantly in what are considered the more developed countries globally, dropping from around 2.8 children in the mid-1950's to a level of about 1.5 by the year 2005; the decline in fertility in what are considered less developed countries globally begin later than the developed world, but are now moving at a much faster pace. During the past five decades the fertility rates in the less developed countries have declined by approximately 60%, from about 6 children per/woman to 3 (UN: DESA, ibid, p. 5).

Population growth is "...determined by the relative size of the younger and older cohorts in the population at different moments in time. The initial size of each cohort depends on the population in childbearing ages at a given point in time, and the prevalent fertility rates. The mortality is determined by the number of people of each cohort that survives to old age. Now, it is expected that "The average age will increase as fertility slows and people live longer" (Badiee, S., The World Bank Atlas of Global Development 2013, 4th Edition, UK: Harper Collins, 2013).

Fertility is a major contributing factor related to global population growth, as well as the "Silver Tsunami." Therefore, any discussions around overall population growth, especially the growing older population, fertility has to be a significant part of the process. Total fertility has been defined as "...the average number of children a woman would bear if fertility rates remained unchanged during her lifetime—is 2.53 children per woman in 2005-2010 at the world level…This average masks the heterogeneity of fertility levels among countries and regions (UN: DESA/Population Division, "World Population Prospects" The 2012 Revision, page 11). As indicated the 2.53 rate is global and does not give a picture of the various regions of the world. In the more developed regions of the world the rate 1.66, in the less developed regions of the world it is 2.69, the least developed countries 4.53, and what is labeled less developed countries, the rate is 2.40. From a regional perspective, Africa's rate is 4.88, Asia 2.25, Europe 1.54, Latin America and the Caribbean, Northern America 2.02, and Oceania 2.47 (UN: DESA, ibid, 2012, page 12).

Projections are that between 2045-2050, the countries that were below replacement level during the period of 2005-2010 will double. So, "…by mid-century 7.1 billion people or 75.2 percent of the world population will be living in these countries." "Under this medium fertility variant, it is assumed that 184 countries will reach below-replacement fertility by 2095-2100, and more than 81 percent of the world population will be living in a country where the average number of children per woman will be below 2.1" (UN: DESA, ibid, page 11). Since the 1970's fertility has declined by approximately 20 percent in about 155 developing countries but by more than 50 percent in 40 of those countries At one point in the 1970's there were only 24 countries with a fertility rate of 2.1, and they were all classified as rich (UN: DESA, ibid).

It has been reported that the drop in the fertility rate to the 2.1 replacement level may be responsible for several global uprisings or demonstrations in recent years. Several examples are, Students' engaged in demonstrations "…against their clerical rulers in Iran…in rural Malaysia in emptier villages surrounded by mechanized farms" …It almost certainly contributed to the rising numbers of middle class voters who backed the incumbent governments in Indonesia and India" ("Go Forth and Multiply Lot Less," The Economist (Digital), Oct. 29th, 2009). The declining fertility rate obviously has brought about significant changes in traditional families customs. But, the trend allows for more opportunities for women to participate in the workforce, as well as more opportunities for children to be educated in preparation for life in a changing technological world (The Economist, ibid, 2009). (**See Appendix A: Tables/Charts, Chapter 1, Tables 3 and 4).**

Fertility will play a major role in population growth between 2015 and 2050. Africa is a high fertility country and will continue to be a major contributor to population growth in the future. Considering the astronomical growth in population globally, half of the world's population growth will be concentrated in only nine countries during the time span 2015-2050. The nine countries are India, Nigeria, Pakistan, and Democratic Republic of the Congo, Ethiopia, United Republic of Tanzania, United States of America, Indonesia, and Uganda. Five of the countries are located in Africa; one of the African countries Nigeria is also one of the world's largest countries and projections are that it will surpass the United States of America by the year 2050 becoming the third largest country in the world. In addition to Nigeria in Africa, five of the largest countries in the world are located in Asia (Bangladesh, China, India, Indonesia, and Pakistan); two countries are in Latin America (Brazil and Mexico), one in North America (United States), and one in Europe (Russian Federation) (UN: DESA/Population Division, Revision 2015, ibid).

Despite the discussions regarding fertility decline there are countries, specifically

Sub-Saharan Africa where the population is young. Africa is a good example of having a young population; in 2015 children under the age of 15 represented 41% of the population, and those in the category 15 to 24 accounted for 19%. So, young people between the ages of 1 to 24 in 2015 represented more than half of the population, or 60%. Countries such as Latin America the Caribbean, and Asia who have experienced a greater decrease in fertility rates than Africa, in 2015 had "…smaller percentages of young people, (26 and 24 percent, respectively) and similar percentages of youth (17 and 16 percent, respectively)…these three regions are home to 1,7 billion children and 1.1 billion young persons in 2015 (United Nations, DESA/Population Division, World Population Prospects 2015 Revision, p 7, UN: New York, 2015. The aforementioned countries "…have the possibility of benefitting from a 'demographic dividend,' provided that appropriate labor market and other policies allow for productive absorption of the growing working-age population and for increased investments in the human capital of children and youth" (United Nations, DESA/Population Division, ibid).

The projections are that even if Africa experiences a significant reduction of fertility, the anticipated population growth or increase will occur. "The medium variant projection assumes that fertility will fall from 4.7 children per women in 2010-2015 to 3.1 in 2045-2050, reaching 2.2 by 2095-2100" (United Nations: DESA, ibid). Following the year 2050, it is interesting to note that only Africa, globally, will continue to experience significant population growth. Not only will Africa continue to experience substantial population growth but the region's share of the population globally will also increase. It will grow from 25% in 2050 to 39% by the year 2100 in comparison, while Asia's share of the global population will decline to 54% and to 44% by the year 2100.

Once again there are some slight differences of reported projections in population growth between the 2012 and 2015 Revisions. Examples are, "The 2012 Revision projected a median population in 2100 of 10.9 billion, 359 million lower than that projected by the 2015 Revision. This difference is made up of discrepancies between the two Revisions in the starting population and the numbers of births and deaths projected. The 2010 population, which was the starting point for the 2012 Revision, is higher in the 2015 Revision by nearly 14 million. Between 2010 and 2100, the number of births projected in the 2015 Revision surpasses that projected in the 2012 Revision by 194 million and the number of deaths is lower by 152 million. That is, the 'median path' (also called the 'median variant') "…of the 2015 Revision projects higher fertility and lower mortality than the 2012 Revision" (Zlotnik, Hania (Former Director, UN Population Division), "Future World Population: The Latest United Nations Projections," Population Connection, Washington, DC, October 2015, p. 12).

The above differences in fertility between the time period of 2015 and 2012 are highest during the years of 2010 to 2030. These differences were (…influenced by the upward revision of total fertility in 2005-2010, when the total fertility of the least developed countries in particular underwent a substantial revision, increasing by a tenth of a child" (Zlotnik, ibid, 2015, pages 12-13). Some significant or key findings based on the 2015 Revision is a world population of 8.5 billion by the year 2030 and by the year 2050 the global population is projected to reach 9.7 billion. Note the differences between the 2012 Revision and the 2015 Revision. In order to achieve the 'median variant' of the 2015 Revision, the global population will have to (… increase by 2.4 billion between 2015 and 2050, 1.3 billion of which will be added to Africa and

0.9 to Asia" (Zlotnik, ibid, 2015, p. 13). During the aforementioned time frame the developed countries will experience very little population growth, and this result will be due for the most part to migration patterns. But, in regards to the developing countries whereas there will be no significant population growth, there will be somewhat of an exception in Europe who will experience a decrease in population growth. Another very significant factor from the 2015 Revision is that Africa's share of the World population will go from 16% in 2015 to 20% in 2030, 25% in 2050, and 39% in 2050 (Zlotnik, ibid, 2015).

Globally, not only in recent decades have there been a decline in fertility rates, but also a significant decline in mortality rates. "In 1950-1955, life expectancy at the world level was 47 years and it had reached 69 years by 2005-2010. Over the next 40 years, life expectancy at birth at the global level is expected to reach 76 years 76 years in 2045-2050 and 82 years in 2095-2100" (UN: DESA, ibid, page 15).

But, the mortality rates will vary depending on region and/or countries. Examples, life expectancy at birth for the World was 68.7, 2005-2010, and projected at 75.9, 2045-2050, and 81.8 by 2095-2100. For the Continent of Africa in 2005-2010 life expectancy was 55.6, projected to be 68.9 in 2045-2050, and 77.1 in 2095-2100, the lowest of all the regions. Among the least developed countries of the world, almost half (20) have been "…highly affected by HIV/AIDS… and experiencing higher mortality than other development groups. Their life expectancy at birth was 58.4 years in 2005-2010, and expected to remain relatively low, reaching 70.4 years in 2045-2050…During 2050-2100, provided a continued decline in mortality rates from HIV/AIDS as well as from other major causes of death, it is conceivable that life expectancy at birth will further climb to reach 77.6 years in 2095-2100" (UN: DESA, page 15).

With declining mortality and fertility and an increasing life expectancy, the world will now witness some of the most challenging demographic trends in modern history. Historically, it has been a common assumption strongly supported by empirical evidence from the beginning of recorded history that children would always out number their parents/grandparents/elders. The world and/or countries or regions, will now have to confront the reality that within the next decade the projections are that the population category of persons 65 plus will outnumber children under the age of 5 years. The projections are that the number of persons in the 65 plus category will increase from approximately 524 million in 2010 to 1.5 billion by the year 2050. The developing countries and/or regions will be confronted with the greatest challenges in subsequent decades considering that the most significant increase will occur in the developing world (Department of HHS/WHO/NIH: Global Health and Aging, Publication #11-7737, October 2011).

As a result of these demographic trends, declining mortality, and increasing life expectancy taking place globally, there will be significant or remarkable changes related to morbidity and mortality, especially for the growing older population. For example, historically, infectious and parasitic diseases presented the greatest threat in the survival of infants and children especially during their first year of life. But, due to advances in medicine, including research and technology, public health prevention/education, and the global family planning movement, there have been great accomplishments, especially declining infant and maternal mortality rates. Now, the trend from infectious and communicable diseases, are shifting to chronic and/or long-term illnesses that affect and present the greatest challenges for a growing older population (Global Health and Aging, Publication #11-7737, ibid, 2017).

As population growth continues, the projections are that life expectancy will increase significantly globally. The world has seen a significant increase in life expectancy at birth in recent years. But, there are still some significant variations in life expectancy when viewed from birth. For example, women continue to live longer than men globally, and there continues to be a correlation between high and low-income countries when analyzing life expectancy at birth. "Globally, life expectancy at birth rose by 3 years between 2000-2005 and 2010-2015, that is from 67 to 70 years. All major areas shared in the life expectancy gains over this period, but the greatest increase was in Africa, where life expectancy rose by 6 years in the 2000s after rising only by 2 years in the previous decade. Life expectancy in Africa in 2010-2015 stood at 60 years, compared to 72 years in Asia, 75 years in Latin America and the Caribbean, 77 years in Europe and in Oceania and 79 years in Northern America (UN: DESA/Population Division, Revision 2015, pp. 5-6).

There is great news in recent reports in reference to life expectancy among the least developed economically, and/or the poorest countries in the world. In what is considered the poorest countries in the world, there was a six-year gain in life expectancy, "...from 56 years in 2000-2005 to 62 years in 2010-2015...roughly double the increase recorded in the rest of the world. While significant differences in life expectancy across major areas and income groups are projected to continue, they are expected to diminish significantly by 2045-2050" (UN: DESA/Population Division, ibid, p 10). (**See Appendix A: Tables/Charts, Chapter I, Tables 5 – 13**).

GROWING OLDER/AGEING: DEFINING THE CONCEPT FROM A GLOBAL PERSPECTIVE

Population growth across all ages is occurring globally. Most importantly is the growth of the proportion of those 60 plus, especially in the Western world, within the general population. Yes, the "Silver Tsunami" or the growing older population has arrived; as aforementioned the ageing of the population is occurring on all continents and will present major challenges for all societal systems and groups. First of all, before proceeding with the discussion/narrative of global ageing, and all of societal implications for this group, the question what is the meaning of the concept ageing should be addressed. Most importantly, what are the factors used by persons and institutions to determine that someone has reached concepts described as old age, elderly, oldest-old, or a senior member of the community, village or society? In other words how are these labels determined?

Biological Perspective of Aging

Let's began with a biological perspective of the concept ageing. First, in reference to the concept of ageing biological experts note that the various factors influencing the ageing process are complex. "At a biological level, ageing is associated with the gradual accumulation of a wide variety of molecular and cellular damage. Over time, this damage leads to a gradual decrease in physiological reserves, an increased risk of any diseases, and a general decline in the capacity of the individual…But these changes are neither linear nor consistent, and they are only loosely associated with age in years. Thus, while some 70-year-olds may enjoy good physical and mental functioning, others may be frail or require significant support to meet their basic needs. In part, this is because many of the mechanisms of ageing are random. But it is also because these changes are strongly influenced by the environment and behaviors of the individual" (WHO: World Report on Ageing and Health, WHO 2015, Geneva, Switzerland, 2015, p 25).

Other scholars have a very similar perspective on aging, "…aging is a gradual biological process that differs among individuals; people do not suddenly become old age at 65…A chronological based level is convenient for defining population groups, but is a poor descriptor of biological function… Although 65 is a chronological definition of the onset of old age, there is no scientific marker of old age…definitions of the elderly based on chronological age are artificial" (Technology of Aging in America – Washington, D.C: U.S. Congress, Office of Technology Assessment, OTA-BA-264, p 35-36, 1985). According to scholars there are some distinct differences between those classified as 65 plus and those 65 and under. The older population, 65 plus, in the U.S. is more heterogeneous in areas of social, political, economical, health and other characteristics than the population group 65 and under (Technology of Aging, ibid, 1985). It should be noted that although 65 is used mostly in the developed or OECD countries it does not necessarily apply especially in the developing word; in other words, there is no global consensus on a chronological age for use in determining a person's age.

Sociological/Anthropological Perspectives

Beyond the biological perspective of ageing is the sociological and/or anthropological perspectives that have to be considered or part of the discussion. It has been suggested that there are those who "…define seniors as those who have used up their fair measure of our communal resources. They're the ones who had their chance and now are, at best, superfluous. Some academics call this the 'fair innings' argument, one that suggests that we all have our chance at bat, and by definition, all seniors have had their chance" (Koch, Tom, Age Speaks for Itself: Silent Voices of the Elderly, CT, Praeger Publishers, 2000, p. 4). The aforementioned perspective on the aging population created quite a controversy and debate several decades ago at the suggestion/recommendation by some politicians and ethicists, that due to rising health care costs a country should consider rationing as a possible solution. In other words, seniors have had their turn at bat, or have had their opportunities and life's chances. By continuing to utilize modern medical advances and/or interventions in caring for seniors it would only extend their life expectancy as rising health care costs would continue (Koch, Ibid, 2000).

The debate arose as the United States, not unlike other countries globally, begin to recognize, and take seriously, the coming of the "Silver Tsunami" or the growing older population. Globally, countries, such as the United States were beginning to feel the impact, especially on medical and health systems. From an intergenerational policy perspective one question that emerged was "who shall live, and who shall die?" In other words, why spend millions of dollars prolonging the lives of seniors when the younger population of children and young adults, have not had their chance at the plate? **(See Appendix A: Tables/Charts, Chapter 1, Tables 5-10).**

Global Factors In Determining the Concepts "Old," and/or "Aging"

The major questions at this time are what are the factors determining when a person is considered old; does the concept aging clearly define the growing older population globally? During a perusal of books, journals, governmental documents, newspapers, one could identify a half-dozen or more labels or tags that are used to identify a person, or group that society refers to or assign one of the following to the older population: Ageing, Aged, Elderly, Seniors, Old-age, Old, Oldest-old, Older Persons, and Older adults, for categorizing the person or group of persons. Institutions or others utilizing one of the aforementioned tags include researchers, scholars, political leaders, family members, and occupational workers in human services. As aforementioned there are several questions that need to be addressed as the dialogue continues. When does someone begin the aging process, or what factors determine a person is now old, a senior, or elderly? Is there a global consensus in response to the aforementioned? Although a variety of terms are used to describe a person and/or group, globally, there seems to be a lack of global consensus. Despite a lack of global consensus on the subject, it has been pointed out by some global scholars that, "…there is an increasing awareness that the terms used should acknowledge the tremendous diversity inherent in a group of people whose ages can span a range of 40 or more years (Kinsella, Kevin and Phillips, David, "Global Aging: The Challenge of Success," Population Reference Bureau, Population Bulletin, Vol. 60, #1, March 2005, p 6).

It has been suggested by some gerontologists that some commonly used terms, such as "elderly," or "senior citizen," are such generalizations that the phrases actually leave negative stereotypes of persons as being frail, socially isolated, as well as being physical and/or financial dependent (Kinsella and Phillips, ibid, 2005). Beyond the negative stereotypes, one scholar has strongly suggested that, "We do not like our seniors, nor do we understand them. They are wrinkled, shrunken in stature, and speak too often in dry, querulous voices. Our assumptions of physical beauty and social responsibility are violated by the elderly, who rarely work and are free of the obligations that plague us younger adults" (Koch, ibid, 2000, p 1). The aforementioned observations are some of the reasoning behind the current movement focusing on social justice and human rights for a growing older population. A primary goal of the movement is to combat all of the negative stereotypes associated with the concept aging.

From a sociological and/or anthropological perspective the current or more modern view of aging has changed tremendously during what one may consider an era of modernization, urbanization, a cybernetic and technological society. **Chapter IV** discusses the past and current role(s) of the older persons within the extended family in Africa, the process of reciprocity that existed among the old and the young family members and their obligations in caring for each other. In the Western and/or the postindustrial world, the process of aging has been reduced to that of obsolescence, weakness and decline" (Koch, ibid, 2000, p 3).

Chronological age is commonly used globally to determine a person's eligibility for social programs, such as a social pension. It appears from a search of the literature that often a chronological age, for example 65, for program eligibility has been determined arbitrarily. Botswana, for example uses age 65 for social pension eligibility, but life expectancy in the country is only approximately 49. Recently, April 2018, Kenya instituted a universal statutory pension plan; the age eligibility requirement for a pension in Kenya is 70. The life expectancy in Kenya for males is approximately 49 and 51 for females. Although chronological age is commonly used there is an increasing awareness that it has some significant shortcomings. For example, "...chronological age may differ from functional age; some people can work productively until age 70 or 80, whereas others become unproductive much earlier. A 45 - year old female might be considered old in Zambia, where life expectancy (at age 15) is 59, but still young in Japan where life expectancy (at age 15) is 83 (World Bank Policy Research Report, Averting the Old Age Crisis, NY Oxford University Press, 1994, p 28).

Currently countries globally are discussing a need to increase the pension age as one way to manage the growing pension crisis as the population growth continues. Therefore, it appears that a major challenge in the future will focus on determining an appropriate retirement age for each country based on factors relevant to the country. The United Nations and other international organizations have expressed through research and scholarship that global population ageing, is an unprecedented phenomenon. Such an astronomical growth in the older population is unknown or not recorded in the annals of human history. The global consensus is that the population is considered ageing when there are significant increases in the proportion of older person who are age 60 plus, when there are reductions in the proportion of children under the age of 15" (UN: DESA, "World Population Ageing, Executive Summary, 1950-2050). One question becomes, what factors are used to describe an individual who is now considered to be old? Is chronological age such as 60 sufficient for making such a determination? Is there a global consensus that ageing commences when an individual reaches 60, or are there factors related to culture, customs and traditions more relevant in making such determination?

In the US, the ageing process has been divided into three categories: the first category is old, referring to those age 60 to 64, the second category is old-old, referring to those 65 to 84, and the third category is oldest-old, those individuals 85 plus. Each of the categories can have different implications, especially medical and or health issues. Research tells us that for the age group 85 plus, there can be an increase in disabilities, especially related to Alzheimer's, resulting in the need for additional medical attention, especially long-term care as well as the cost of providing care. Although there have been significant demographic trends in the population group sixty to sixty-four, sixty-five to eighty-four, there have also been dramatic trends in the age population group eighty-five and above. The significant increase in the eighty plus, especially 85 plus population has major implications for psycho/social, including caregiving responsibilities, health/medical issues and concerns (Population Bulletin, Vol. 60, No.1, ibid, 2005). The aforementioned categories may be appropriate for the United States but can or should they apply globally?

There does not seem to be a consensus on how we identify a person who is considered ageing. As aforementioned a number of tags or concepts have been identified, even globally, for describing such individuals or groups. Because of global diversity or variations in cultures, customs and traditions it seems unrealistic for the researchers, academics, as well as policy makers, to engage in the task of agreeing on a particular global label or concept for describing a person or group. It is probably more realistic for countries to define their own concepts, definitions for aging, based on culture and customs, as long as they are operationally defined for the purpose of sharing globally.

Globally one has to consider or cannot ignore how some citizens, including professionals, and scholars are beginning to ask the question of what is and/or what are the factors that determine any of the aforementioned concepts relating to the aging process. It is common knowledge that in many countries, developed and developing, the labels imply a chronological age for determining eligibility requirements for a particular program or service. The Profession of social work for example uses the concept holistic when referring to people. In other words an individual who has lived to reach the chronological age of 65 is more than just the number. Therefore, in describing a human being or someone the reference is the whole person, physically, biologically, culturally, socially, and not just a part, such as the age. For the world to benefit from the wealth of knowledge, experiences, skills that the "Silver Tsunami" brings to the table of sharing, one has to view people from a holistic perspective

In response to the question what is aging, a focus group of participants from Nairobi, Kenya in a workshop sponsored by the National Institute of Health responded in a variety of ways. For some of the participants the use of chronological age was not at the top of their list. For some participants "…chronological age…may be a poorer indicator of being elderly than social standing." Furthermore, some participants indicated that chronological age differed significantly from functional age, "…which can be the most important dimension of aging in a rural subsistence agricultural context." It appears that for some cultures if the question is what factor(s) should determine one's status, the conclusion would be a person's level of day-to-day functioning, and/or their social status in a community. Participants concluded "…that old people can be identified in a variety of ways: by their physical attributes or appearance (e.g., gray hair, wrinkles, obvious frailty), by their life experiences (e.g., their reproductive history), or by the roles that they sometimes play in their community" (Cohen, B., Menken J., (Editors), "Ageing in Sub-Saharan Africa – Recommendations for Furthering Research," Washington, D.C.: National Academia Press (US), 2006, p 3). NOTE: Research Panel/Advisors for the Report: Alex Ezeh, Edwell Kaseke, Barthelemy Kuate-Defo, David Lam, Alberto Palloni, Stephen Tollmans and Robert Willis.

The concept of old age or who is old seemingly varies according to social/cultural traditions and practices. This is especially the case in Africa, more specifically Su-Saharan Africa. Also, in reality a major factor that determines who is old is influenced by social welfare policy, especially in determining eligibility for social pensions, as well as other entitlement programs; there does not seem to be a global consensual definition for old age. The United Nations, The International Labor Organization, or any of the major international organizations do not have a specific definition for old age. "However the United Nations identifies exclusively for the purpose of demographic comparisons populations which have reached the age of 60 years as "older persons." This classification was also used at the 2002 World Assembly in Madrid Spain. The International Labor Organization defines older workers "… all workers who are liable to encounter difficulties in employment and occupation because of an advancement in age" (The ILO Older Workers Recommendation, 1980 (No. 162). Although in its numerous publications The ILO uses 15-64 in reference to population at working age. But the organization makes the point that this is primarily for comparison purposes.

Therefore, in definitional discussions related to social security/social protection, policy makers, and professionals, although recognizing the needs for program eligibility requirements, should also consider the aforementioned concepts within a cross-cultural context. Fox example, when discussing the more formal levels of social protection/social security schemes, one should not ignore altogether the diversity of socialization. Therefore, on the one hand chronological age maybe used for the purpose of an operational definition to determine program or service eligibility, other factors as previously noted cannot be ignored in describing or speaking of all human beings.

There is little or no evidence of a "life span" formula, biologically based, that can operationally separate or divide '…maturity from seniority. It is always a relative phenomenon, a cultural definition that shifts with the success of medical science and the determinations of society's leaders" (Koch, ibid, 2000, p 8). Now, if one returns to the previous question of "who shall live and who shall die," a response to consider follows: (If the question is cost, wouldn't the healthy and active senior be more valuable than the infant with a congenital heart malfunction whose continuance will require a risky heart transplant and lifelong medical attention (Koch, ibid, 2000, pages 8-9)?

In regards to the stereotyping of the older population let's not forget that "ageism" can have a similar or very negative impact on individuals and groups as "racism," and "sexism." A negative view of a senior person, or an older person, maybe that he or she has reached a dependent stage in her/his life and now only needs to be taken care of. All of the research and observations of women working into their 70's and 80's, in the agricultural economy, caring for grandchildren and other vulnerable members of the their families in villages and communities globally, but sometimes stereotypes are very difficult to "cut loose." The "Silver Tsunami" population if allowed, as aforementioned, will bring a new level of activism, social justice and a new spirit to global decision-making.

Age 65, for the most part in developed countries, has been used primarily as a point of reference in determining eligibility for a social security pension. In reviewing the ISSA country profiles it seems as though developing countries are using an arbitrary chronological age, i.e., 60 for the same aforementioned purpose. As aforementioned Botswana, one of nine countries in Sub-Saharan Africa with a statutory social pension for the older population, has a life expectancy of 49 years; the statutory pension age in the country is 65. As indicated there is no global acceptable chronological definition of old age. Chronological age is primarily used to determine pension and/or an entitlement grant, and as a research tool for comparative purposes. There are examples other than chronological age used within certain cultures to determine or define old age. Some consider a change in social role activities, becoming a grandparent, to be more important than a chronological age designation; others define old age in terms of a significant decline in functional, mental, and physical activities. The latter grouping, functional, mental, and physical decline were seen by an older age focus group/interview as more important than chronological age (Help Age International, UNFPA, Ageing in the 21st Century, 2012).

Globally, a future challenge for determining or defining age has to consider changes in life expectancy. "Around 1900, the average life expectancy was between 45-50 years in the developed world countries at that time. Now life expectancy in developed countries reaches 80" (Help Age International, 2012, ibid, p.19). Life expectancy has also increased among countries in the developing world as well. Therefore, there needs to be some discussions regarding a more realistic chronological age for developing countries as well.

Prior to the Madrid World Assembly in 2002 a MDS Workshop on Ageing under the auspices of international groups, WHO, Help Age International, and the National Institute of Health, accepted (during a meeting in Harare, 2000) the use of the chronological age of 60 in defining old age. The group was influenced by the acceptance at the time of the UN's decision to use 60 as the defining age for old. The age of 60 had been adopted as part of a United Nations Resolution 35/129. But, the MDS Project Group on further discussions/deliberations at its follow up Workshop in Tanzania 2001 brought the subject up again for deliberations. The final conclusion of the work group was the chronological age of 60 did not represent reality for the developing countries, especially for countries in Sub-Saharan Africa. So, during the 2001 Workshop, the group changed the age from 60 to 50. Although the feelings of the group were that the chronological age of 50 was similarly arbitrary, it was a better representation of the realities that existed in Africa.

The reference to chronological age, according to this focus group, may not be recognizable in Sub-Saharan Africa. The group expressed that chronological age would be a less useful indicator of being an old person in the community than social standing. Within the group it seems that functional age may be much more important indicator of old age, especially geographically rural or farming areas. There are countries in Sub-Saharan Africa where people work into their 60's, 70's; it is very sad to say but in many instances it is due to the fact that they do not have a pension, or an adequate income to rely following retirement (Cohen and Menken, ibid, 2006). In terms of chronological age, for some scholars it has little or no significance for those living in the developing world. In the developing world old age seems to begin when the person can no longer make a significant to his/her culturally designed or defined roles. Also, for the purpose of this manuscript classifications such as 60 or 65 plus will be used primarily for comparison purposes only.

Finally, the world is so diverse, inter-intra country with numerous different cultures, customs and traditions, based on some of the aforementioned comments coming out of workshops; it raises once again the very important question, how realistic is it to consider having a consensus concept, especially chronological age. There are significant differences, based on biological, socio/economic and cultural factors, related to life expectancy, pension age or retirement age that may it becomes a very challenging task for a global consensus on the subject. Some countries are currently debating the subject of changes in retirement age, and some have already made changes in retirement age based on social, and especially economic factors occurring in their respective countries.

A statistical definition of old age, such as 60 or 65 is now commonly used as the official retirement age, especially in administering social benefits such as social pension. In regards to country differences retirement age in Africa can range from 55 to 65. According to some African scholars such a specific chronological age is not compatible with life experiences in Africa. One major factor to consider in the use of a specific age is that a very small percentage of Africans will have social, economic, and health benefits following retirement (Apt, Nana, Ageing in Africa, Aging and Health Programs, Geneva: World Health Organization, 1997).

A NEW VISION FOR A GROWING OLDER POPULATION: THE FOUR FREEDOMS OF AGING

Beyond all of the discussions/debates focused on the concept aging and/or an appropriate definition of aging, especially for operational purposes (example, determining eligibility for entitlement programs), there is a global movement calling for action to eliminate all of the negative stereotypes related to the older population. Organizations, such as the Association of Retired Persons (AARP), United States, is promoting a bold new approach as they respond to the "Silver Tsunami," calling for a new vision for the growing older population. At an AARP National Convention in 2014, the CEO, AARP, focused her presentation around "A new vision for living and doing in America" (Jenkins, Jo Ann, AARP's Ideas at 50+ National Member Event, California: San Diego, September, 2014, AARP International, The Journal, Washington, DC, Spring, 2016).

A highlight of the aforementioned Conference centered on a new phrase, Disrupt Aging, the basic theme of a forthcoming book by the CEO of ASRP Jo Ann Jenkins. The phrase "Disrupt Aging" is all about introducing and implementing new pathways and challenges for the older population to become active in living their lives to the fullest regardless of age. According to the Author the response to the challenge has been overwhelming; it has been the kind of challenge, it seemed, that the growing older population has been waiting for. The impression is that the growing older population has been searching for new models as they advance chronologically, biologically, socially and psychologically in age. In other words, the current growing older population appears to be demanding new choices, including solutions that should enhance their overall level of independence. According to the Author, it is not just a matter that people are living longer and more healthy, but the time-span referred to as middle-age has been significantly extended, resulting in the introduction of a new world offering of challenges and opportunities (Jenkins, ibid, 2016).

Although some progress, although very little, has been made in eliminating stereotypes of aging, "…most conversations around aging still view it as a problem to be solved…the conversation can't be about how to take advantage of the opportunities we have so we individually and as a nation can thrive…we need to get rid of the outdated beliefs and stereotypes about our aging and spur new solutions so many of us can choose how we want to age" (Jenkins, ibid, 2016 p. 1). The major challenge becomes the elimination of the historical and/or traditional models that no longer work for enhancing the quality of life for older people, and creating new ones that will allow for older persons to live as independently as possible in dignity (Jenkins, ibid). The aforementioned symbolizes what the phrase "Disrupting Ageing is all about" (Jenkins, ibid, 2016).

The process of "Disrupting Ageing" include the Four Freedoms of Ageing: (1) The Freedom to choose; as one ages she/he should have the primary say of how one wants to live her/his life, including where. If a person has the capacity to live at home and in her/his community, it's the person's choice. (2) The Freedom to earn; institutional barriers, such as chronological age for retirement, should be eliminated. Chronological age should not be the only criteria for leaving work. (3) The Freedom to learn; as persons continue to age with the desire to remain engaged, especially in community affairs, including social development, they should have the opportunities as provided to other age groups, to continue the learning process. (4) The Freedom to pursue happiness; the growing older population should have the opportunities, "…to pursue happiness by discovering and fulfilling our purpose…longer lives gives us an extraordinary opportunity to become the people we have always wanted to be" (Jenkins, ibid, 2016).

The Global Challenge: The Eradication of Ageism Now!!!

A major and/or important step in doing away with or eliminating all of the negative stereotypes related to ageing is to "…recognize that quality of life is no less important than longevity, and that the ageing should therefore, as for as possible, be enabled to enjoy their own families and communities a life of fulfillment, health, security and contentment, appreciated as an integral part of society" (International Plan of Action, Preamble, Item 2, First World Assembly on Ageing, Vienna, Austria, 1982). Secondly, one global goal that all age groups, political and civil leaders, should become proactive in is "Ensuring a Society for All Ages" (UN: Economic Commission for European Ministerial Conference, Vienna, Austria, 2012). Thirdly, in order to achieve and sustain successfully social and economic development, it is critical that no age group is left out of the policy, program and implementation process, especially the older population. The goal should be, "The recognition of the importance of inter-generational, inter-dependency, solidarity and reciprocity for social development" (Second World Assembly, Madrid, Spain, 2012). The principles that have been put forward by AARP and those from the First World Assembly on Aging are critical as the world continue to prepare for the "Silver Tsunami." Secondly, those principles should establish the foundation for creating a society for all ages and most importantly the elimination of global ageism.

The Growing Older Population, the "Silver Tsunami:" The Need for Autonomy in Decision Making Affecting Their Lives

The above title is the major focus of a publication from <u>Help Age International</u> that shares dialogue representing various "…themes and issues raised by 450 older people from 24 countries in a consultation on their rights to autonomy, independence, long-term care and palliative care" (Help Age International, <u>Freedom to Decide for Ourselves</u>, London WC1A 9GB, UK, 2018). The primary purpose for the gathering of this very critical input by Help Age International from many older persons globally, was to prepare for the upcoming 9th session of the Working Group (OEWG) on Aging at the United Nations in July 2018. As aforementioned the Age Demand Campaign has been petitioning the United Nations to convene a special session on the needs of the growing older population. According to key findings from Help Age International global research older persons are demanding to have the freedom "…to lead autonomous and independent lives. Autonomy and independence are highly valued" (Help Age 2018). The results from listening to the older population that a significant number strongly expressed not being able to make their own decisions, especially in regards to "…their finances, employment, management and disposal of their property, who to vote for, where and with whom to live, access to health services, family life and participation in community, voluntary or social activities" (Help Age, "Autonomy and independence," 2018).

The second and most critical area of concern that was expressed by the older respondents related to long-term care and support services. This is a very critical area considering the increase in life expectancy with the social, medical and health implications. Globally, research has pointed out that older persons' preference is to live active and independent lives. The Report indicates that "Many older people have no access to, or choices and control over, the care and support services they may need to live independent lives…Family members are the only care and support providers available to most older people…There is no explicit standard on the right to care and support for independent living in older age in international human rights law" (Help Age, "Long-term care and support services," 2018).

Another very critical area for concern related to long-term care is palliative care. First of all as aforementioned above, "There is no explicit standard on the right to palliative care in international human rights law… Many older people have no access to palliative care to help them die free from pain and unnecessary suffering…The concept of palliative care is completely new to many older people…Palliative care services are limited or non-existent in all countries included in the consultation" (Help Age, "Palliative care," 2018).

A surprising finding in reading the report was that international organizations have not been proactive in ensuring that critical global issues and concerns such as long-term care, palliative care, autonomy and independence are part of international human rights law.

GLOBAL AGEING: SOCIAL, CULTURAL AND PUBLIC POLICY IMPLICATIONS

The astronomical rise in global populations, especially the "Silver Tsunami" has and will continue to have significant implications for those who are considered old or 60 plus, or in some instances, especially in developing countries less than 60. As illustrated in the previous section, the chronological age of 60 for determining the beginning of the aging process is not applicable globally. The impact or implications of aging will not only affect the person/family, but key systems, medical/health, retirement/pensions, and banking and financial institutions as well. Globally, the number of persons 60+ will triple by the year 2100, increasing from 841 million in 2013 to approximately 2 billion in 2050 and 3 billion by the year 2100. Currently, 66% of the world's older population lives in the less developed regions of the world, and it is projected that by 2050, 79% will do so, and reach 85% by the year 2100 (United Nations: World Population Aging, 2013). (**See Appendix: A, Tables/Charts, Chapter 1 Table 3**).

The Growing Older Population: Implications for Low to Middle Income Countries

In regards to the tremendous challenges facing the developing world in reference to population ageing, the more industrialized countries had a much longer time period to prepare for their growing older population. Because of factors such as the "…diffusion of medical technology, and declining fertility, developing countries are ageing faster than the industrialized countries did" (World Bank: 1994, Ibid, p.1). Belgium, France and United States are very good examples of the difference between industrialized countries (OECD) and those in the developing world in reference to population ageing. In Belgian, "…it took more than 100 years for the share of the population over 60 to double from 9% to 18 %… In China the same transition will take only 34 years and in Venezuela 22 years" (World Bank: 1994, Ibid, p.1). In France it took approximately 115 years to double its aging population (Kowal, 1996); in the United States the time frame for tripling (from 4% to 12%) the population 65 plus was approximately 96 years, from 1900 to 1996 (Torres-Gil, 1995). What about Sweden? It took Sweden 85 years, and the United States 69 years for their populations 60 plus to go from 7% to 14%, whereas it will take a country such as Brazil only 21 years, and Colombia 21 years (UN: World Population Ageing 2013, Population Division, DESA, NY 2013). It does appear that countries in the developing world, including Sub-Saharan Africa, the doubling of the population will take place overnight in comparison with the more developed world. These latter regions of the world will have to respond very quickly, especially policy wise, in preparing for an older growing population. These countries will not have the same time frame for preparation as countries such as Belgian, France, Sweden, and the United States.

Once again population ageing, or the increasing number of older persons in the population will have a profound impact on all countries regardless of classification, developed or developing. The impact of population ageing on the social, economical, and political processes of each country or region will be most challenging. There are two major questions that countries, developed and/or developing will have to address. First, how prepared is the country to respond to this "Silver Tsunami?" Secondly, how committed is the country to ensuring that social justice will be a top priority in responding to the basic human needs of all age groups? Basic human needs, especially for the older population should include, an adequate income, decent housing, access to health and social care, including long-term, adequate sanitation conditions, and safety.

Globally, there was estimated to be approximately 205 million people 60 plus in the year 1950. Approximately a half century or six decades later the number of older people 60 plus had reached approximately 810 million; by the year 2050, the 60 plus group was expected to double in size to approximately 2 billion (UN: Population Fund/Help Age International: Ageing in the 21st Century, "Global Population Ageing," New York, 2012). To be more specifically in reference to the 60 plus group, the age category "…80 or over is growing faster than any younger age group within the older population. The population of Centenarians, those aged 100 years or over is growing the fastest" (UN and Help Age International, Ibid, p. 19). During the year 2013 the percentage of the age population 80 plus globally was 13% but approximately thirty years ahead, 2050, this particular age group (oldest old) will climb to 19%, averaging approximately 2% every 10 years. The projections are that by the year 2050 there will be almost 400, more specifically 392 million persons 80 plus; this age group, globally, will have tripled in approximately 30 years (UN: Department of Economic and Social Affairs (DESA), Population Division, World Population Ageing 2013, ST/ESA/SER.A/348, United Nations, New York, 2013).

From a country or regional perspective, population growth of the older population, with some variations by country and/or region, will affect all regardless of income group. In 2012 there were approximately 15 countries with a 60 plus population of at least 10 million, and

7 of the 15 were classified as developing countries. Approximately four decades later, "…33 countries are expected to have 10 million aged 60 or over, including 5 countries with more than 50 million older people. Of these 33 countries, 22 are currently classified as developing countries" (UN and Help Age International, ibid, p.19).

The astronomical rise in the number of older persons globally, especially beginning in the middle of the Twentieth Century, is also along side overall population growth a global phenomenon. The average life expectancy at birth has increased by some twenty years since 1950, and projections are it will increase another ten years by the year 2050. The United Nations is projecting that the proportion of persons we define as old will increase globally from ten (10%) percent in 1998 to fifteen (15%) percent by the year 2025 (International Plan of Action, 2002). (**See Appendix A: Tables/Charts, Chapter 1, Tables 5-6**).

Although the increasing number of older person is a global phenomenon, there will be variations among countries depending, especially on factors such as their social and economical status. Globally, despite deplorable, health, and social and economic conditions, people representing all continents, countries, regions, are living longer. Why is this major phenomenon happening? As aforementioned a number of factors are responsible, especially medical, health practices and the overall enhancement in the socio/economic conditions of people globally.

The "Silver Tsunami" and its potential impact on countries, especially social and economic policies, were initially noted by international organizations, several decades ago (See Chapter III). The evidence of their concerns and recognition of the need for global leadership in responding to this phenomenon initially resulted in several major World Forums and/ Conferences, including the International Conference on Population, 1994 in Egypt, the First World Assembly on Aging, Vienna in 1982, and the Second World Assembly in Madrid, Spain in 2002. Population scholars, social/public policy analysts, and the leadership of these International organizations, began to alert the world that the "Silver Tsunami" would have significant social/economic implications.

Another significant finding from the 2015 Revision is the continuing of the "Silver Tsunami." The current percentage of the global population for the age group 60 plus will increase from 12% to 22% by the year 2050. "Africa will remain the region with the youngest population, with the share of those aged 60 plus rising from 5% to 9% in 2050. However, to achieve such slow population aging, Africa will have to maintain a rapid rate of population growth, averaging well above 2 % per year until 2040" (Zlotnik, Hania, "World Population Prospects, 2015 Revision, DESA, Population Division, New York: United Nations, 2015, p. 13). It is interesting to note that the aforementioned growth "…will mainly be distributed among the population aged 15-59 (1.6 billion) and 60 or over (1.99 billion), as the number of children under age 15 in developing countries will hardly increase. Growth is expected to be particularly dramatic in the least developed countries…which are projected to double in size from 898 million inhabitants in 2013 to 1.8 billion in 2050 and to 2.9 billion in 2100 (UN: World Population Prospects, 2012 Revisions, Executive Summary, p xvi).

In regards to the focus of the manuscript on Sub-Saharan Africa, a very significant volume of population growth between 2013 and 2050 will be occurring in what are considered high fertility countries, especially Africa, including countries such as India (UN: World Population Prospects, Ibid, 2012) The current and future population size as occurring in developing countries will present some major challenges regarding the growing older population, now being referred to as the "Silver Tsunami."

What about beyond 2100? Data published under the auspices of the United Nations long-range projections are that the global population will peak or reach 9.22 by 2075. The United Nations, based on its revised methodology, is sharing from its database some new long-range projections reference global population growth. The United Nations and its DESA Division, has been providing estimates and/or projections for the world, including regional and national population size, s well as their demographic indicators. The DESA long-range projection or horizon has been the year 2050. But in its recent projections, the long-range horizon has been extended to the year 2300. The explanation given is that the extension to the year 2300 will allow for the stabilization of populations. Now, the projections will be based on all countries in the World, rather than the major areas and/or selected larger counties (United Nations DESA, Population Division, "World Population to 2300," ST/ESA/SER_/236, 2004).

The projections by DESA are that the global population will reach or peak at 9.22 billion by the year 2075. "Populations therefore grow slightly beyond the level of 8.92 billion projected for 2050 in the 2002 revisions on which these projections are based. However, after reaching its maximum, world population declines slightly and then resumes increasing, slowly, to reach a level of 8.97 billion by 2300, not much different from the projected 2050 figures" (UN: DESA, Ibid, World Population 2300). Based on the revised database and projections Europe and Africa will move in different directions. For example, Europe will reach its low point in growth by 2050, whereas Africa will not reach its peak until some 80 years later. So, Africa will reach its peak after all of the major areas have done so (UN: DSEA, Ibid).

But, the projections are that between 2000 to 2100 Europe's share of the global population will be halved, 12.0 to 5.9 percent, whereas for Africa the population will double, 13.1 percent to 24 percent. It is interesting to note that smaller regions within continents will see different patterns of growth. For example, several African regions, East Africa, Middle Africa, and Western Africa, will grow "...unusually fast in comparison with every other region through 2100, even though total fertility will be close to replacement by 2050...Southern Africa is seeing a decline in life expectancy to a lower level than anywhere else, but life expectancy will rebound, rise quite rapidly, and overtake other African regions." (UN: DESA)

Once again, the question is how prepared are the developing countries, especially a region such as Sub-Saharan Africa to respond to the needs of a growing older population. It is interesting to note considering the population age distribution is that of the 9.6 billion projected in the developing countries, approximately 1.6 will be young people 15 to 19; and approximately 1.9 will be those in the age range of 60 plus. These two age groups combined will constitute approximately 3.5 million of the total population (UN: World Population Prospects 2012 Revision). In comparison with what is considered the least developed countries the challenges will be the greatest. The population in the least developed countries has been projected "...to double in size from 898 million in 2013 to 1.8 billion in 2050, and 2.9 billion in 2100" (World Prospects, 2012 Revision, page vii, Explanatory Notes Ref. Developing and least Developed). There is a very significant difference when considering the population growth in the more developed areas of the world. The change in population will not be as dramatic as indicated for the least developed regions; the projection for the former is 1.25 in 2013, to just 1.28 in 2100.

The most important trend related to population increase in the more developed countries will be the migration of individuals from the developing countries to the developed world or countries. This particular migratory trend is "…projected to average about 2.4 million persons annually from 2013 to 2050 and 1 million from 2050 to 2100 (World Prospects).

In comparison with the more developed regions, the population in the less developed countries is considered very young. The children, 15 or less currently account for approximately 28% of the population; the population age group15-24 accounts for about 18 percent. There is a major difference between the less developed and least developed countries regarding the population of children; in the least developed countries, children under the age of 15 account for 40 percent of the population, and those 15-24, 20 percent. In comparison with the more developed countries, children under 15 accounts for 16 percent, and those 15-24 accounts for 12 percent (World Population Prospects, 2012 Revision).

There are some changes in reference to the age group 15-24 reported in the 2015 than previously reported in the 2012 Revision. The 2015 Revision projects significant changes globally in the size of the age group 15-24; (…children under 15 and young people aged 15-24 will increase from 1.9 billion and 1.2 billion, respectively, to 2.1 billion and 1.3 billion in 2050. Africa which accounts for 25% of the world's children and 19% of the world's young people today, will account for 39% and 34%, respectively, in 2050 and will be the only region with an increasing population of children and youth at mid-century" (Zlotnik, ibid, 2015, p. 13). Yes, not only will Africa has the tremendous challenge of preparing the children and youth for the more advanced cybernetic society, but meeting the needs of a growing older population as well.

Beyond the concept "population aging" there are other related factors/indicators that are crucial in preparing for and responding to the needs of a growing older population: These factors/concepts include age index, or the number of people who have reached the age 65 plus per 100 children under the age of 15; another second indicator is the median age of a country's population. An example, the median age in most developed countries, is approximately 32, and approximately 25 in most developing countries (Population Bulletin, Vol. 60, ibid).

Some 30 countries in the year 2013 reported a median age higher than 40 years; almost all of the countries were classified as developed countries. Some examples were Japan was listed as having a median age of 45.9, Germany 45.5, and Italy 44.3. By comparison countries listed as developing, such as Niger, Uganda, and Chad, listed median age in the below 16 category. But, by 2050 there will be significant changes in the median age; it is projected that approximately 100 countries will have a median age of 40, and more than half will be countries in the developing world. In 2100 some 158 countries will have a median age of 40, and two/thirds will be in the developing world (UN: World Population Prospects, 2012 Revision, 2013).

Beyond the concept "population aging" there are other related factors/indicators that are crucial in preparing for and responding to the needs of a growing older population. These factors/concepts include age index, or the number of people who have reached the age 65 plus per 100 children under the age of 15; another second indicator is the median age of a country's population. An example, the median age in most developed countries, is approximately 32, and approximately 25 in most developing countries (Population Bulletin, Vol. 60, ibid).

Age Dependency: Older Persons' Support Ratios

Another indicator is referred to as the elderly support or dependency ratio. The elderly support ratio is defined as the number of persons 65 plus per 100 persons within the age range 20 to 64 within a given population. For the purpose of planning, especially for social welfare purposes, these are crucial factors related to the population ageing processes. The elderly support ratio is a crucial policy and planning indicator. It is projected that support ratios will rise in the developed countries with low or declining fertility rates and increasing longevity. But, in countries where the fertility rates show only a modest change, support ratios were expected to change very little between 2000 and 2030. **(See Appendix A: Tables/Charts, Chapter I, Tables 15-16).**

Age dependency ratio is another crucial factor in population aging that has to be considered, especially in preparing for and responding to the needs of a growing older population. The age dependency ratio refers to the ratio of older dependents, individuals who are older than 64 years of age, to what is described as the working group in the population, 15 to 64 years of age. The World Bank Group and it interpretation of what is referred to as "Inverse of Dependency Ratio, how many independent workers have to provide for one dependent person (The World Bank Group, Working for a World Free of Poverty, 2003 World Development Indicators, The World Bank: Washington, DC, 2003)?

A very significant factor, especially in the industrialized countries of the world is that the number of people reaching the age of retirement is and will continually to increase whereas the number of the younger working age population will continue to decline. More importantly, the number of older persons 85 plus has become the fastest growing category of any age group. The implications create serious social policy issues because there is a declining number of the working age younger population contributing to social protection, such as social pensions/social security for the for those in retirement. An indication of such change is there were twelve working age individuals in 1950 to support each person age 65; more than a half century later, in 2010 there were only nine for each person 65 plus (Patterson, Lindsay, "Carl Haub on the Graying Global Population," Human World, Earth Sky Communications, January 19, 2011).

Countries with a high dependency ratio normally will devote a significant portion of their budgets or expenditures toward health/human services, housing, food/nutrition, and social security. The aforementioned categories are directed towards the needs of the youngest (15 and under) and oldest (64 plus) members in the population. In other words, the less number of individuals in the population in a position to support their school systems, pension plans, as well as other entitlement programs, for what are considered to be the most vulnerable members, the youngest, 14 and below, and the oldest 64 plus. The relationship between dependency ratio and fertility is crucial. With a continuing decline in fertility rates, the dependency ratio will continue to increase. As the proportion of the older age groups within the general population continues to increase and/or grows older, there will be significant pressures on retirement and pension systems such as social security, medical and health systems, including long-term care (World Bank Group, ibid, 2003).

The National Institute of Health has put forward a number of factors that call attention to some of the major challenges confronting families, economic, political, as well as health/

human service institutions as the world continues to prepare for the "Silver Tsunami." Most importantly, within the next couple of decades the age group 65 plus will outnumber the youngest age group five years and under. This particular trend will have a significant impact regarding the age dependency ratio. As life expectancy continues to rise and fertility drops, there will be growing concerns and/or questions regarding the care and support for the older population (Department of Health and Human Services, National Institutes of Health/ National Institute of Aging: Why Population Aging Matters, A Global Perspective, Publication No. 07-6134, March 2007).

The dependency ratio becomes extremely important as economic growth continues resulting in rising incomes. As income rises there is a tendency for families to have fewer children, and this happens as people are living longer. "Over the next several decades the inverse of the dependency ratio is expected to plummet in much of Latin America, Central Asia, Eastern Europe, and China. By the year 2050 only Africa will still be young" (World Bank Policy Research Report: Adverting the Old Age Crisis, Oxford University Press, 1994, p. 303). Presently Kenya a country considered young in comparison with other countries globally remains young until around the year 2030. The year 2030 is approximately the time that the current population of young girls in Kenya begins to bear children. This is roughly the time when Kenya's demographic transition has been projected to begin; this is much later than most other countries. This could mean that the African countries may not only have time to prepare for the old age population, but can learn from the experiences of the countries reaching the peak of demographic transition earlier. The demographic transition referred to has already been taking place in the OECD countries (World Bank Policy Research Paper, ibid, 1994).

Additional research from the Pew Research Center extends the dependency/ratio projections into the year 2050. One conclusion is that the total dependency ratio as the year 2050 approaches will significantly increase in most countries. The countries mostly affected will be Germany, Italy, Spain, Japan and South Korea. By the year 2050 the dependency ratio in the aforementioned countries is projected to range from 83 in Germany to 96 in Japan. The conclusion is that German and Japan can expect to have as many dependents by the year 2050 as the working age population. Countries including Egypt, Pakistan, India, Nigeria, Kenya and South Africa are projected to have a more positive demographic change. The working age population in the aforementioned countries will increase in size in comparison to the youth and older person/ senior population combined by the year 2050. The Pew Research Center suggest that this results will could make available more or additional resources for economic development in the aforementioned countries. Several countries, Pakistan, Kenya and Nigeria, are projected to witness the most significant declines in dependency ratio; these three countries currently have very high levels of dependency ratios as a result of such large populations of children. In reference to the concept demographic dividend relatively to African countries, projections are that those children will grow up and make their way into the labor markets in very large numbers (Pew Research Center, "Aging in the United States and Other Countries 2010-2050, Washington, D.C., 1/30/2014). See **Appendix A: Tables/Charts, Chapter II, Table 1).**

According to Pew Research the global population by the year 2050 is projected to increase by approximately 38% from the 6.9% mark in the year 2010 to approximately 9.6%. Most importantly, children under the age of 15 are expected to increase only by 10% as a result of declining birth rates. The population on the African Continent is projected to have the highest increase and make up a much greater share of the global population by 2050. Also of note India is expected to replace China approximately 400 million by the year 2050. A population of 1.6 Billion in India is projected to equal the combined total of the United States and China. The most significant population losses by 2050 will be the countries of Japan, Russia and Germany; the decreases are expected to reach 10% or more by 2025 (Kochhar, Rakesh, "Ten Projections for the Global Population 2050," Pew Research Center, Washington, D.C., February 3, 2014).

As aforementioned beyond the concept "population aging" there are other related factors/indicators that are crucial as countries prepare for the needs of a growing older population. These factors/concepts include age index, or the number of people who have reached the age 65 plus per 100 children under the age of 15; another second indicator is the median age of a country's population. An example, the median age in most developed countries, is approximately 32, and approximately 25 in most developing countries (Population Bulletin, Vol. 60, ibid).

One major theme question throughout the book chapter is are the countries prepared for the "Silver Tsunami"? But, in regards to children, are the countries, especially those in the less and least developed one, prepared for the socialization of children to reach their highest potential? The largest percentage of the population growth will be taking place in the developing world, especially the less and least developed, primarily in Africa. The number of children is at an all time high, and the challenges are if the aforementioned regions have the resources, education, health to ensure their overall growth and development. The United Nations recent Report on Investment in Children, 2014, presents a very critical discussion on how youth, especially in Africa, represents a demographic dividend in future economic development. More discussion on this particular topic is presented in Chapter VIII. (**See Appendix A: Tables/Charts, Chapter I, Tables 14-15**).

The Global Non-Changing Ratio: Males/Females

Despite all of the demographic changes over the past couple of centuries the one factor that has remained constant is the ratio between males and females. Women continue to live longer than men, or globally, the common fact is that women continue to have a higher life expectancy rate than men. Although there are variations by country and regions, the fact remains that women have a tendency to have a longer life expectancy than men. Although the gender gap has somewhat widened in recent decades, projections are that the gap will not significantly change over the next several decades. Also, the projections are that in "…less developed regions…the gains in female life expectancy are to be larger than the gains for men, and this will lead to a widening of the gender gap in mortality…In contrast gender gap in life expectancy in the more developed regions is expected to narrow from a 6.8 years in 2010-2015 to 5.8 in 2045-2050" (UN: World Population Ageing, DESA, Population Division, 2013, p.8).

Gender Inequalities: A Continuing Barrier for Women Globally

Although women continue to live longer than men, or life expectancy is longer, there continues to issues related to social justice or inequalities that prevent them from experiencing a quality of life equal to that of men. Globally, the consensus is that women have made significant progress when it comes to matters related to education health, and improved access to the labor market. But, there is also a consensus that gender inequality continues to be a major issue. Research seems to point out that gender gaps in regards to primary school education have been eliminated or closed. The estimations are that, in "One/Third of developing countries female students outnumber male students in secondary and tertiary education" (UN: DESA, ibid, 2013, pp.46-50). But, it has to be pointed out that in 2010, of the 800 million illiterate adults, from age 15, approximately 64% were women; there has not been a very significant change since the year 2010 (UN: DESA, ibid, 2013, p.49).

In regards to labor force participation, it is estimated that women now represent some 40% of the global labor force, and approximately of the world's farming workforce. Although there is significant improvement in workforce participation, it is the types of employment, and the levels of earnings that continue to raise questions related to gender inequality. There continue to be a significant difference in earning power between women and men. The income gap is very much related to types of employment/jobs that are open to women. Societal and cultural norms, and it varies by country and/or region, continue to have a significant influence on employment choices (UN: DESA, ibid, 2013).

Women continue to gravitate towards the jobs that are considered vulnerable occupations or less secure areas in the labor market. These are the jobs and occupations that also social security/social protection and/or safety net for worker and her/his family, and usually are informal sector jobs. In these jobs women, "…earn only 10 to 80% of what men earn (UN: DESA, 2013 ibid, p. 50).

Although globally there have been improved access for women in education, especially higher education, there are occupational careers where women are limited. In a review of women graduates on a global level, it is interesting to note that some 70% to 90% of women university graduates are in the more traditional areas such as education and health careers. By contrast when one looks at career lines such as law, engineering, manufacturing, only 10% to 30% women (The World Bank: Women, Business and the Law 2016: Getting to Equal, The World Bank, Washington, D.C., 2016, pp. 1-23). The United Nations Human Development Report, 2013, focuses on some of the major sources of inequality confronted by women globally. The 2013 Report states clearly that women and girls have and continue to be discriminated against in all of the labor markets such as health, education and labor (United Nations Human Development Report, 2013).

Banking and financing are two very important areas where women are still struggling to become key players. These are crucial areas when considering the fact that women are living longer than men and their contributions in the areas should be considered crucial. But, historically women have had limited or less access "…to productive assets and services, land capital, financial services, and information communication technology" (The World Bank: ATLAS of Global Development, ibid, pp. 49-50).

Despite all of the gender inequalities that women confront on a daily basis, globally "women play a major role as providers of family support and care for all generational groups, especially children and older people" (UN: World Population Aging, 2013, p. 1).

Although women continue to be the primary care givers, especially in the caring of older members of the family, children, and other vulnerable members, this major historical responsibility is no substitute for social justice for women in the work place. Social justice in the work place and the eradiation of all forms of discrimination for women is a major area to be addressed by all countries. "As fertility has fallen, women's labor force participation has been globally on the rise, although women still engage less than men in paid work" (UN World Population Ageing, ibid, 2013). A major challenge for all countries will be social justice in the work place for women. **(See Appendix A: Tables/Charts, Chapter VI, Tables 5, 7, 8, 9).**

POPULATION GROWTH: SOCIAL, ECONOMIC AND CULTURAL IMPLICATIONS FOR SUB-SAHARAN AFRICA

Population Growth Trends

Although the overall focus of the manuscript is on global population growth Sub-Saharan Africa (SSA) is selected as a case history to highlight how one continent that has experienced years of colonization, including all forms of social injustices has been and will continue to be impacted by various demographic, social and economic shocks. Also, SSA is a continent that has historically been noted for its social welfare system of caring, especially for the older population, children and other vulnerable members of society. As aforementioned the continent will be significantly impacted by the growth explosion and presented not only with challenges but opportunities as it responds to the "Silver Tsunami" in Africa.

Projections indicate that Africa, especially Sub-Saharan Africa, will become the fastest growing region of the world. Yes, the "Silver Tsunami" has reached the Continent of Africa. It has been projected that over the next thirty-five years, between 2015 and 2050 "…more than half of global population growth among major areas, growing at a pace of 2.55 percent annually in 2010-2015…" will take place in Africa. Consequently, of the additional 2.4 billion people projected to be added to the global population between 2015 and 2050, 1.3 billion will be added in Africa (United Nations: DESA Population Division, World Population Prospectus 2015 Revisions, New York: United Nations, 2015, p 3). The projections are that Asia will become the second major region next to Africa in population growth, 0.9 billion people during the aforementioned time-span. Africa and Asia will be "…followed by Northern America, Latin America and the Caribbean and Oceania, which are projected to have much smaller increments. In the medium variant, Europe is projected to have a smaller population in 2050 than in 2015 (United Nations: DESA, ibid). **(See Appendix A: Tables/Charts, Chapter I, Tables 14 - 17).**

The "Silver Tsunami" as aforementioned has and will continue to land on every continent, country, region prepared to engage and contribute overall social and economic growth and development. The goal is to ensure social justice and/or human rights for all. A significant factor related to global population growth is that more than ninety (90%) percent of the aforementioned growth will occur within the developing countries; more than half of that growth will take place in Sub-Saharan Africa. A major challenge awaiting the "Silver Tsunami" are projections that approximately ninety (90%) percent of the growth will occur in urban areas. Countries in Sub-Saharan Africa are projected to have the largest proportional increase, from 12% of today's world population to approximately 21% by the year 2050. Another major challenge is that the majority of the newcomers globally will reside in urban areas. The projections are that globally one-third of families/individuals will be living in urban areas; in Sub-Saharan Africa approximately 60% of the population will be urban slum dwellers. Historically, slum areas have been noted to not have the basic services and/or resources, such as clean water and sanitation, access to health care, as well as decent housing (The World Bank, 2013). Another question what strengths that were such a significant part of the traditional family kinship system for caring, especially for the older populations in rural African villages, transfer to urban homesteading in a modern, industrialized and urban society?

Globally, population growth presents major challenges and countries cannot overlook this reality as they engage in developing their social and economic, five or ten year plans for the future. A major challenge will be preparing for the growing older population that will present unique medical, social, and health problems and issues that will require innovative thinking and additional resources. But, the challenges will vary because of country and/or regional political, economic and social diversity. The population ageing demographics we see happening in Africa are quite different in comparison to what took place in the more developed world, including the countries that colonized the African continent. As repeatedly mentioned in the previous narratives, it took countries such as France and Belgium more than 100 years and France 140 years to double their ageing population (Kowal, 1996). What about the US? It took approximately 90 years, 1900 to 1986, for the percentage of Americans age 65 and older to go from 4% of the country's population to the current 12%, or triple in size (Torres-Gil, 1995). But, African countries will not have that much time to prepare for its growing older population. It sees like the growing older population in Africa may just double or triple overnight.

As aforementioned the largest increase, proportional of the growing older population globally, will take place in Sub-Saharan Africa. The population is expected to grow from approximately 12 percent of the world's population in 2013 to around 21 percent in 2050; in comparison, East Asia and the Pacific, currently at 29 percent is projected to decrease to around 23 percent by 2050. Practically all population growth will take place in urban areas, and for the most part in developing countries (The World Bank: Atlas of Global Development, Fourth Edition, 2013).

Some Major Challenges

Modernization, Industrialization and Urbanization, - Population growth in Africa, especially in Sub-Saharan Africa, will present major challenges for families, as well as political, social and civic organizations. In 1804 the global population for the first time reached 1 billion. A little more than two centuries later, the year 2009, Africa as a continent reached the 1B mark. Almost 400 million or about 40% at the time were living in urban areas. It took the continent some

27 years to double from 500 million to the 1 billion mark. It is projected that to reach the next half-billion mark will take approximately 17 years. It has been projected that the demographic growth in Africa will begin to slow down. It will now take Africa approximately 24 years to reach the 2 billion mark, the year 2050. Approximately 60 percent of continent's population at the time will be residing in the urban areas. The urban population around 2050 is projected to be approximately 1.23 billion (World Bank: Atlas).

According to the Vice-President, African Region World Bank, the Sub-Saharan Region of Africa, from a demographic perspective, displays two very unique characteristics. According to Diop, Africa, including sub-Saharan Africa, is unique in that it is the only region globally still at a very early stage of the demographic transition. A strong positive for being in this position is that countries in Sub-Saharan Africa will have an opportunity of gaining knowledge from the experiences those going through the process, especially those who have reached advanced stages (Diop, Makhtar, Africa's Demographic Transition: Dividend or Disaster (Editors: Canning, David, Raja, Sangeeta, and Yazbeck, Abdo S.), Africa Development Forum Series, World Bank Group, 2015, Foreword 2015).

The lesson to be learned is that the path through the transition can be extremely difficult requiring a variety of strategies, tactics along the way. There is no "cookie cutter model" to serve as a guide because of countries' intra-inter diversity. Diop describes the second uniqueness of the region as its heterogeneity. "While a small number of countries are far along the transition, with fertility rates that are below replacement levels, many are exhibiting surprising delays in the transition in the last ten years. Some countries are showing very little movement along the national transition and are stuck at very high fertility rates...these large differences that target different sectors and processes (Diop, ibid).

The most significant increase of persons considered old are projected to be residing in developing countries, especially Sub-Saharan Africa and Asia. It is projected that there will be approximately 100 million older people in Africa by the year 2025 of which 75 million will be living in Sub-Saharan Africa (Brundtland, 2002). In 2000 Africa had approximately 42 million older people representing about 5% percent of the world's population. Eight (8%) of the 42 million were over 80 years old. It is projected that by the year 2050, the population of older Africans will reach 205 million (Ageing in Africa, 2004). Sub-Saharan Africa is expected to "...remain relatively young..." from the mid-nineties to the year 2050, there will be significant changes in the dependency ratios. The projections are that the "...young dependency ratio will be reduced by 57%, its old age dependency burden will increase by 93% within the same period" (Kalasa, UNFPA, Ethiopia).

Although the females to male ratios may vary, not unlike other countries globally, there are more elderly females than males in Africa. The aforementioned includes the age groups 60 plus, but also an older age category, for example, 75 and over (in the U.S. the older old is 80 plus). From the time period "... between 1980 and 2025, the 75 years and over age group will increase by 434% in East Africa, 385% in Central Africa, 427% in Northern Africa and 526% in Western Africa (Editorial, East African Medical Journal...). Now, with an increasing life expectancy globally, females will continue to live longer than their male cohorts. The factor will have major policy implications considering all of the social injustices women have faced, especially related to issues such as social protection, social pensions or basic income security.

Poverty - The increasing ageing population will face one of the most deadly forces known to humankind, extreme poverty. Forty-seven (47) million people aged 60 and over are chronically poor. This can have a major impact on family households, especially where children are being housed and cared for by their grandparents. It is understandable why the Millennium Development Goals for 2015, is the eradication of extreme poverty. Also, it should be noted that in addition to being chronically poor, more than 80% of the current older population does not have a social pension or basic income security following retirement.

The Continuing Struggle with the Impact of the HIV/AIDS Epidemic: An Expanded Role for Grandparents - Although increasing life expectancy on one hand symbolizes progress and an enhanced quality of life, the ageing population in Africa will bring about some negative consequences as well. Not only will an increasing older population not have sufficient financial supports (pension/retirement funds), but will be called on to accept more family responsibility such as the rearing and/or socialization of their grandchildren. A growing number of children are being made homeless as a result of the HIV/AIDs epidemic. It has been estimated that globally approximately 6000 children are losing one or both parents to AIDS daily. Approximately ninety (90%) of these children are residing in Africa. In the year 2002, there were some thirty-four (34) million orphans in Sub-Saharan Africa; one-third of these children became orphans due to HIV/AIDS. It was projected that the number would reach forty-two (42) million by the year 2010 (Help Age International, Ageing in Africa, 2003).

Globally, it has been estimated that 30 million people, over several decades have died as a result of the AIDS epidemic. The epidemic has had a major impact on children; approximately16 million children have been orphaned during the same time frame. A vast majority of these children are living with grandparents. In 2010 it was estimated to be approximately 33 million people now living with HIV, but approximately half or less may not be aware that they have the infection. In 2010 there were approximately 1.8 million AIDS related deaths compared with2.2 million in 2005. Even though the decline from 2.2 to 1.8 between 2005 and 2010 is a positive sign, it is estimated that some 7,000 new cases happen each day. Although Sub-Saharan Africa has about one-tenth of the world's population, but approximately two-thirds, the majority of women, of those globally living with HIV/AIDS (World Bank: Atlas of Global Development, 2013).

The HIV/AIDS epidemic has had a devastating impact in Africa, including decreasing life expectancy, morbidity, and mortality. In some countries affected by the epidemic, the adult HIV prevalence rate reached a peak during the last decade. In the Southern region of Africa known to have the highest prevalence level, life expectancy decreased "…from 62 years in 1990-1995 to 52 years in 2005-2010. Life expectancy in the Southern Region is not projected to recover back to the 1990s level possibly until around the year 2030 (World Population Prospects, 2012).

Although HIV/AIDS has had a tremendous impact regarding children, malaria continues to be a major threat for children. There were some 216 million cases of malaria, resulting in 655,000 deaths in 2010. The majority of these deaths occur in Africa "… where a child dies every minute from malaria (World Bank Atlas, 2013, p. 12). Globally, the positive news is that tuberculosis cases peaked around 2004, but in Sub-Saharan Africa the prevalence is still high. Although some regions, such as the Southern Asian countries have returned to the prevalence levels of the 1990s, that has not been the case for Africa. A very important factor is that developing countries will have a much shorter time period to prepare than what was experienced in the more developed world.

In regards to HIV/AIDS globally of the 49 countries listed by the United Nations as least developed, 20 of those countries have been significantly affected. The life expectancy in those countries at birth was around 58.4 years between 2005 and 2010; life expectancy for those countries will remain somewhat low slowly reaching 70 years around or between 2045 and 2050. The projections are that due to a decline in mortality rates from HIV/AIDS between the years 2050-2100, as well as from other major causes of death, life expectancy is expected to reach approximately 77 years between the years 2095 and 2100 (UN: DESA/Population Division, World Population Prospects: The 2012 Revision.

A major concern for all countries as population growth continues is the financial wellbeing of the older population. But, practically all developed or OECD countries have developed over the years some formal or tripartite labor system with a collective bargaining process. The goal has been to provide basic income supports (social security/social protection), including, including health and social services. On the other hand, countries in Sub-Saharan Africa for the most part, a significant majority of those who have reached retirement age do not have a social pension, or some basic income at the time of retirement. In Sub-Saharan Africa only 16.9% of older persons currently have a social pension following retirement from the workplace. (**See Appendix A: Tables/Charts, Chapters VI, Tables 2-3; Who Represent OECD Countries? Their Mission, See Appendix B: Concepts/Definitions and Special Notes**).

SUMMARY/CONCLUSION

Chapter I has several major goals, the first one is to highlight the unprecedented global population explosion or phenomenon occurring now for decades, and most importantly the growing older population or the "silver tsunami." In regards to the latter, the goal is to highlight a beginning global awareness and/or recognition by international organizations, political and governmental entities and civic groups, of the importance of a growing older population or the "silver tsunami." The intent was not just for the global community to gain an awareness of an unprecedented growth in population, including the "silver tsunami," but recognize a need for a call to action in responding to these important demographic trends that will have a tremendous impact on all societal systems. Also, the Chapter highlighted the fact that this unprecedented demographic phenomenon will have a significant impact on societal systems across all continents, regions or countries regardless of political, military, social and economic capital. Finally, the Chapter considered it critical in discussing demographic changes to evaluate the changes occurring within a historical perspective beginning prior to 1800.

Chapter I introduced the concept "Silver Tsunami" in order to bring a new meaning or significance to a growing older population, especially their social activism and the contributions they will make in creating a global society all across all age groups. The concept "Silver Tsunami" unlike the well known traditional cosmic tsunami, represents and increasing number of older persons that bring not destructive forces for destroying physical and human infrastructures, but knowledge, experiences, human and social justice commitments and values to the decision-making table for shaping a new world; a world for all people, across all age groups, gender, racial/ethnic, religious and sexual orientations. Most importantly, the Chapter addresses how negative perspectives regarding the older population represent a form of ageism or prejudices toward this population. Ageism, especially the use of chronological age rather than a holistic perspective presents barriers that do not allow this population to live and perform to their full potential. The growing older population represents the new majority and when it comes to social injustices they will come out of the "trenches." Americans should remember dating back a few years ago the social justice and human rights movement for the older population spearheaded by the "The Grey Panthers' Party.

A major factor in highlighting the growing older population is to call attention to the fact that globally half of the older population does not have basic income security or a social pension at the time of retirement; this is especially the situation for those with no history of participation in formal occupational and/or collective bargaining systems. In Sub-Saharan Africa 82.5 % of the current retired population does not have basic income security. In other words approximately four/fifths of the older population in Sub-Saharan Africa is without basic income security or a social pension. Furthermore, there is little research to demonstrate that this ageing population has adequate access to critical medical, health and social physical and human infrastructures, including long-term medical care. The Chapter highlights the impact this reality has on the growing older population, especially those who have an increasing responsibility in the socialization of grandchildren.

Chapter I also responds to the question of what are the causative factors responsible for this growth phenomenon? The growth in population across all age groups and countries has been attributed to a number of factors, medical and health practices, especially preventive measures and education and economical improvements related to overall quality of life. Medical advances have been remarkable as far back as the introduction of vaccines, and other medical discoveries; one cannot overlook great improvements in sanitation and sanitary conditions. Most importantly, Chapter I addressed the impact the "silver tsunami" will have on societal systems, including the countries in Sub-Saharan Africa.

Yes, the chapter also raises questions and challenges in regards to the continuing global practices of ageism and/or all of the applied concepts with negative connotations affecting the older population. Not only should the "Silver Tsunami" has income security, access to health and social services, but the right to social participation involving all societal matters, especially affecting the growing older population. In other words, in responding to the current and future needs of the older population, the older population is no longer expecting others to just work on their behalf, but will be demanding to sit at the decision-making and problem solving tables providing input. The chapter takes a look at the various concepts that are used by countries in describing, depending on the different cultures, the criteria used in referring to persons as old, old-age, senior or older person; some of the concepts have similar negative consequences as racism and sexism.

As stated, the world is witnessing a dramatic demographic growth trend, including the "silver tsunami," or a growing older population. The growth is taking place across all regions, countries and continents. The question of the hour is how well prepared are countries, developed, less or least developed prepared to respond to this unprecedented growth shock? A key factor is that population growth, including the growing older population will impact every essential societal system, political, economical, medical, health, social welfare and family. For developing and/or low-income countries timing for preparation becomes extremely critical. In regards to medical and health issues, as an example, low-income countries will begin to struggle in finding ways to respond to chronic illnesses such as heart, cancer, dementia and Alzheimer that normally accompanies increasing life expectancy. Unlike the developed countries, the developing countries will need time and resources for developing the necessary infrastructures, physical and human for responding to a growing older population.

In its conclusion the chapter addresses some of the issues and challenges that are unique to a continent such as Sub-Saharan Africa. Sub-Saharan Africa comprising some forty-seven countries has some major challenges in preparing for the growing older population of the "silver tsunami;" eighty-two percent of the current older population does not have a social pension, or basic income security. Furthermore, a large percentage of the older population is living in poverty. The growing older population as a result of public health issues, urbanization, political and military conflicts, is being asked to take on additional family responsibilities, especially the socialization of grandchildren. For the most part theses are grandparents without basic income security.

CHAPTER II

WHY POPULATION AGING MATTERS IN THE 21ST CENTURY

INTRODUCTION

The demographic growth phenomenon being addressed is happening across all age groups, but the major focus within the manuscript will be on the unprecedented growth of the growing older population, the "Silver Tsunami." The growing older population has and will continue to have a significant impact on all societal systems; historically the ageing population has been put aside, ignored or labeled obsolesce. In other words, "ageism is alive and active globally. Furthermore, special attention will be focused on the growing older population in the developing or low to middle income countries where social protection is in desperate need; an example is the continent of Sub-Saharan Africa where 82.5% of the retirees from their perspective workplaces do not have basic income security or a social pension.

Globally, the growing older population or "Silver Tsunami" matters now and will continue to do so as the world transition through the 21st Century. Why is this global demographic phenomenon the growing older population receiving such worldwide attention? As aforementioned it matters because of the significant impact this demographic aging phenomenon will have on all of the critical societal systems including the family, medical, health, social welfare, culture, economical, political, banking/commerce and occupational. Furthermore, beyond the demographics of aging there is a growing movement globally that is challenging how the concept aging has been and continuously being viewed historically. In other words, what does it mean to be defined by such terms or phrases as old, old age, elderly or senior? There is a global movement, the Age Demand Campaign that is demanding that the ways in which society has historically viewed and labeled those 60 plus, less than 60 in some countries such as in Sub-Saharan Africa, be reconsidered. The concept aging, or as some say old age, can no longer be defined strictly by chronological age. A person's value or holistic makeup in society, including participation and contributions should no longer depend only on a person's chronological age alone. There is a growing recognition from a biological, physiological, sociological, anthropological and psychological perspective that there are individual differences during the aging process beyond chronological age that should be seriously considered when relating to the growing older population, the "Silver Tsunami."

Currently and in the ensuing years, continents, regions and/or countries are expected to develop the capacity, and be prepared with the appropriate societal systems in place, for responding to the growing older population. The primary goal globally is to create a "Society for all Ages," including the 60 plus. Also of great importance, it is now the time that society began viewing the aging population as an asset and not just a state of dependency defined by some arbitrary chronological age; some countries based on a variety of social, cultural traditions, or economic factors will begin viewing the aging process at a time line less than 60. The world needs to begin recognizing that the growing older population brings forth years of decision-making experiences, knowledge, skills, including personal and group survival skills that can be useful for countries in the mist of social, economic development and transformation. The life experiences of the aging population represent a major strength or an asset; if allowed the opportunity, and not pushed aside because of some historical stereotypes related to chronological age, the aging population could make a significant contribution globally towards the creation of a "Society for all Ages." There is no doubt that this unprecedented demographic shock or explosion, the growing older population, will present major challenges but also opportunities for countries and all of their current and future operational and/or helping systems. The traditional decision makers can no longer overlook the assets that the aging population brings to the table; it is time that the aging population becomes a major part of the solution and not just viewed as a societal problem.

The growing older population or the "Silver Tsunami" as aforementioned will have a significant impact on all societal systems regardless of a country's wealth, military power, political strength and/or power or other historical cultural symbols. Countries will differ according to their political, economic, social and cultural systems, including past success or lack of success in responding to problems and/or challenges; in other words some countries based on a variety of reasons such as economic growth, cultural traditions, are more prepared than others. Although the developing countries can learn from the more developed ones based on years of experiences, but because of countries' diversity, there is no "cookie cutter" model for all to follow. Developing countries, such as those geographically located in Sub-Saharan Africa, symbolize in comparison with the OECD countries, the current "HIP-HOP" musical rendition by the artist/vocalist known as Drake; the artist now famous song begins with the words, "Starting from the Bottom Up." The second part of Drake's verse is, "Now I am here." The words of this HIP-HOP tune symbolize some countries such as in Sub-Saharan Africa who will be to some extent, "Starting from the Bottom UP" in developing the necessary infrastructures, physical and human, in responding to the growing older population. It will probably take a longer time period beginning from the bottom, for low and middle-Income countries globally to get there or to the level of developed ones. Many of the more advanced industrialized and richer countries, such as France, Germany, and the United States have had many years, some a century, preparing for a growing older population. Sub-Saharan Africa, not unlike other developing countries, does not have this luxury of time in responding to the "Silver Tsunami;" the time is now! Sub-Saharan Africa and other developing countries has a major strength when it comes to caring for the growing older population, children and other vulnerable members of society; the strength is in their past commitment and success historically of operating and/or managing its extended family network system of caring. Sub-Saharan Africa as well as other low and middle-income countries globally will be challenged to respond it seems over night, not having years to prepare as the Western countries, to this demographic shock wave with all of the accompanying implications. There are countries, some more so than others, with the necessary systems in place at least for a beginning response to the "Silver Tsunami," but there is global recognition that a great deal of preparation will be needed and urgently for most countries including the more developed ones.

The lack of preparation is not just a matter of concern for low to middle-income countries but research in recent years has illustrated that some problems in responding to the growing older population currently and will continue to exist among the highly developed and/or OECD countries as well **(OECD Countries and Mission, See Appendix B: Definitions, Concepts and Special Notes)**. A major problem that is challenging the developed countries, such as those listed in the OECD category currently, is long-term caring as a result of the transition from communicable to chronic diseases, not only for the medical/health systems, but family care giving in the home as well. Another matter or challenge to consider is that although some countries have various levels of systems currently in place, additional and/or expanded systems may have to be added in response to more specialized service needs and demands in an era of increasing chronic illnesses. Societal systems directly related to the growing older population that will be impacted by this growth phenomenon as aforementioned include the family network system, retirement and pension, as well as the banking and financial institutions. Most importantly will be the Medical, Health, and Social Welfare Systems, including Long-term care (Institutional and Family Care in the Home).

The growing older population, the "Silver Tsunami" and its potential impact on a country's, medical, health, social and economic system, including social and public policies, were initially noted by international organizations such as the United Nations, and the International Labor Organization (ILO) several decades ago. The evidence of their concerns and recognition of the need for global leadership in responding to this phenomenon initially resulted in several major World Assemblies and Conferences, including the International Conference on Population 1994 in Egypt, the First World Assembly on Aging Vienna in 1982, and the Second World Assembly in Madrid, Spain in 2002. Population scholars, social/public policy analysts, and the leadership of these International organizations, began to alert the world that the "Silver Tsunami" were having significant impact: political, social, economic, health and medical implications. For example, from a medical health perspective, research illustrates that as persons increase in age their health begins and continue to deteriorate; as a result of the aging process, their needs and demands on the medical/health systems increases, especially for long-term care. The medical and health needs of older persons not only become a challenge for the medical, social and health systems, but family caregivers as well (UN: "World Population Prospects 2002," ESA/P/WP 180, DESA, UN: New York, 26/February/2003).

FAMILY SYSTEMS: WHY POPULATION AGING MATTERS

Rural/Urban Migration, Modernization, Industrialization, and Urbanization: Implication for a Growing Older Population

The family network system globally, historically known for it commitment to caregiving, especially in the socialization of children, and caring for the older population is an appropriate place to begin in response to the question why does population aging really matter? The family system considering the demographic, political, social and economic changes occurring globally, will be greatly affected. The current changes that are occurring include an unprecedented population growth across all age groups, increasing life expectancy, changes in dependency and support ratios, grandparents taking on additional family responsibilities, and most importantly the transition from a rural to a modernized, urbanized and cybernetic society. As previously stated the family and/or kinship systems historically in Africa have been the primary support systems for family members, especially the older population, children, youth as well as other vulnerable members of the extended family network. But, the family's kinship/network system of reciprocity between the young and old is changing rapidly in response to and era of modernization, industrialization and urbanization. As predicted by sociologists and social theorists, all countries eventually transitions from a traditional informal, to a modern formal type society. The process, although depending on the country, varies over time and is irreversible **(See Chapter V Modernization).** The major and most challenging question globally is how prepared are countries, especially in the developing world to respond to the "Silver Tsunami," and all of the accompanying challenges?

The Changing Role(s) of the Traditional Extended Family System

Historically, especially in African societies, within the family and/or kinship network the expectations have been one of "reciprocity," where parents and older members took care of the young and vulnerable members of the family, and likewise the children and/or younger population would eventually take care of the older members of the family. In other words, African societies based on customs and traditions possessed their own form of a social welfare system; the system extended beyond immediate family members reaching out to tribal and clans within certain geographical regions. Now, with industrialization, urbanization, modernization and a growing movement of the young from rural to urban areas in search of educational and job opportunities, the traditional family system will be challenged to find innovative ways for keeping some of the key elements of the helping process afloat or operative, especially in responding to the growing older population.

Economic development and transformation, which includes meeting the basic needs of family members is one major goal for all countries; achieving and maintaining such a goal in a modernized urban society will present major challenges but also opportunities. The challenges to the family system can be critical as populations, especially the growing youth population, considered to be a demographic dividend, especially in Sub-Saharan Africa, make the transition from a rural to an urbanized society. In the modern and urbanized societies, "...opportunities for market employment open up for the young. The value of time contributed by old people diminishes. And people live longer, so the proportion of old people in the population increases" (World Bank: Averting the Old Age Crisis: Policies to Protect the Old and Promote Growth, New York: Oxford University Press, 1994, p 5). Industrialization, modernization, urbanization, and now a more cybernetic society, families become smaller in size and not as geographically close to each other as in a traditional society. Families, when reasonable will continue to provide for family, including geographically external families, but composition of family and distance will present a major challenge. A major question for those preparing for the "Silver Tsunami," is what historical strengths, especially from the extended family network system from the past, are feasible or applicable in responding to a growing older population in a modern society?

Also, a major challenge to the family system is that the growing older population regardless of geographical location in the 21st Century, is being called on for carrying out additional responsibilities within the family extended kinship system. Because of social, health and political circumstances, such as HIV/AIDS, Ebola, military, political conflicts and unemployment among the youth, older persons are being asked to take on more child caring responsibilities. Many of these grandparents in Sub-Saharan Africa do not have a social pension, or basic income support to assist in these expanded or additional roles (World Bank, ibid, 1994). The fact that a significant number of older persons in Sub-Saharan Africa do not have a social pension or basic income security at the time of retirement for this reason a significant number continue to work, especially in the agriculture sectors beyond retirement age. Although most countries are now making an effort to provide income support for families, including grandparents caring for the orphan children, only a few countries, including Botswana, Cape Verde, Kenya, Mozambique, Mauritius, Namibia, Lesotho, Liberia, Seychelles, Swaziland and South Africa, have a statutory provision for this purpose (See Chapter VI).

The reality of having to continue working duties/responsibilities is much more pronounced in the least and/or less developed regions, globally. For example, during the year 2010, persons 65 plus represented 31% of the labor force in the less developed regions, but only 8% in the more developed regions globally. The need for income support for older persons, especially in the less developed regions is crucial. This need is not just for the economical survival for the older person(s) but the added expenses of caring for vulnerable family members, especially the socialization of children. The aforementioned observations reinforce the need for public support and/or public transfers for the growing older population not just in Sub-Saharan Africa, globally as well. If public transfers or social pensions are a significant part of old age assistance or support in the developing countries, one can only imagine the need in the least or less developed regions of the world (UN: DESA, World Population Ageing, ibid, 2013).

The HIV/AIDs epidemic that continues, but less severe than previous decades, to present social, health, and medical challenges for almost four decades is an excellent example of how a family, especially the older members, can be impacted in so many ways. Several major studies going back to the late 1990's and in early 2000's highlighted a new role and additional family kinship duties for older persons, especially in Africa and Asia, resulting from a health epidemic known as HIV. The growing older population, now becoming part of the "Silver Tsunami," instead of looking forward to an extended life, was now being asked to take on additional responsibilities, beyond the traditional ones, caring for their children and grandchildren, affected by the HIV or Ebola epidemics.

Research results or estimates reported in early 2000 indicated that approximately 19 million people had expired as a result of the HIV disease. One can conclude that with so many reported young deaths, many young children were left behind in the world to be cared for by their grandparents, more specifically grandmothers. In addition to the 19 million deaths it was estimated that approximately 37 million young people at the time were living with the disease HIV. What becomes so much more alarming was the fact that 95% of new infections at the time had been identified, specifically in what was classified as less developed countries. It was also estimated at the time that of the 14 million children below the age of 15 living without a mother or both parents, were residing in Sub-Saharan Africa. The question is who will care for the children? The most logical response would be the grandparents (Lamptey, Peter et al., "Facing the HIV/AIDS Pandemic," Population Bulletin 57, no. 3, 2001).

Studies in Zimbabwe and Uganda during the aforementioned era concluded that the older population had become the primary caregivers for their terminally ill children affected by the HIV epidemic, or the grandparents for their grandchildren. One of the major issues reported from the research was the loss of financial support from their children who had been affected/stricken or died due to HIV. It was also noted that there were issues beyond providing food and shelter, but there were school fees to be paid, including books and uniforms where required. Also, the day-to-day caring on the part of grandparents had a major impact on their physical and emotional wellbeing, or health (World Health Organization, Impact of AIDS on Older People in Africa: Zimbabwe Case Study Geneva; WHO, 2002; Williams, Alun and Tumwekwase, Grace, "Multiple Impacts of the HIV/AIDS Epidemic on the Aged in Rural Uganda," Journal of Cross Gerontology, 16, no. 3, 2001, pages 221-36, Direct Quotes in Population Bulletin, Vol. 60, No 1, March 2005).

Although research points to the fact that the problem (s) related to HIV/AIDS have decreased significantly in recent decades, research also indicates that continents such as Sub-Saharan Africa continue to feel the impact. More current research related to HIV/AIDS and caregiving by grandparents indicates that '...more than 60% of orphaned children in Namibia and Zimbabwe, for example, are looked after by their grandmothers. This care function is also important in everyday settings of poverty or labor-related parental absence—In the urban slums of Nairobi, Kenya...more than 30% of older women and 20% of older men (aged 60 years or older) care for one or more non-biological children' (Aboderin, Isabella A G, Beard, John R, "Older People's Health in Sub-Saharan Africa," The Lancet, Vol. 385, No. 9968, 14 February 2015.

The World Population Prospects in its 2012 Revision, states that following some three decades of the HIV/AIDS epidemic "...its effects on the populations of the highly-affected countries is still evident. In the 2012 Revision, the demographic impact of HIV/AIDS is explicitly modeled or estimated in 39 countries, down from 48 in the 2010 Revision. In most of these countries, HIV prevalence reached 2 per cent or higher in the period from 1980 to 2011 among the population aged 15-49 years. Among the highly affected countries, 32 are in Africa, one in Asia, and six in Latin America and the Caribbean...The 2012 Revision confirms yet again the devastating toll HIV/AIDS has in terms of increased morbidity, mortality and population loss (UN: DESA, Population Division, World Population Prospects, the 2012 Revision, NY, 2013, page 18). It is unrealistic to think that all of the elements of the traditional family kinship system will remain in place in the process of continuing to transition from a traditional to a modern technological, informational and cybernetic society. The family system regardless of all the external factors, political and military conflicts, diseases such as HIV/AIDS, urbanization, and Direct Foreign Investments, will continue to play some role in maintaining in some form the family kinship system. The aforementioned include caregiving for the growing older population and children.

There is consensus that the family is an important system globally to consider when preparing for the "Silver Tsunami," especially in preparation for meeting basic needs, including income and access to medical and health services, including long-term care. Globally, how is a family household defined or what comprises a household can be critical in determining eligibility for social programs such as a social pension or other social protection programs? Household is a concept that needs some clarification when discussing family composition in countries in Sub-Saharan Africa in comparison to the Western world. Historically, the extended family, including its older members, has been the primary support system, especially in caring for the elderly, the children, and other vulnerable family members. Although socially threatened by modernization (See Chapter V), the extended family with its key principle of reciprocity remains a key kinship support system. In regards to extended families in African societies one has to keep in mind that "…households are more likely to be larger, multigenerational, and less nuclear than in Western societies (Cohen and Menken, ibid p. 3). Rural to urban migration in an era of modernization can be very challenging when it comes to maintaining family unity. The possibility of households being separated across geographical lines or to maintain both rural and urban dwellings or households for the purpose of allocating their labor resources becomes a reality in an era of modernization. A major reason for such a choice by families is to protect, maintain and/or maximize family income and unity (Agesa, R., Review of Economics of the Household, "One Family, Two Households: Rural to Urban Migration in Kenya," Vol. 2, Issue 2, pp. 161-178). But, when it comes to the use of a means or pension test for determining program eligibility for entitlement programs, such as a social pension, the concept household can become a key variable.

The Changing Dependency and Family Support Ratios

Changes in the dependency and support ratios can have a major impact on the family system as well. With a growing older population and a declining category of young people the expectations or projections are some significant changes in dependency ratios. For example, will population-ageing matter when it comes to the Potential Support Ratio (PSR)? The PSR is globally "…defined as the number of people aged 20 to 64 divided by the number of people aged 65 and over. In 2015, African countries have approximately 13 individuals aged 20 to 64 for each person 65 plus. In comparisons, Asian countries have a PSR of 8.0, Latin America and the Caribbean 7.6 and Oceania has a PSR of 4.8. Europe and North America's PSR is 4; Japan is at 2.1 and has the lowest PSR globally. There are seven Asian countries, twenty-four European countries, and four countries in Latin America and the Caribbean that are being projected to drop below PSR 2 by the year 2050. The drop in SPR's for these countries below 2 highlights some of the major challenges for social protection systems, especially in caring for a growing older population" (UN: DESA/Population Division Revision 2015, ibid, p. 7). (**See Appendix A: Tables/Charts, Chapter II, Table 1**).

In reference to the pension support ratio and/or dependency ratio Sub-Saharan Africa is projected to experience during the next several decades (2050) what is referred to as a demographic dividend considering the growth of the younger population. For example, countries such as Kenya and Nigeria are currently considered to have a very young population in comparison to most other countries globally. The population is projected to remain quite young until around when a significant birth rate begins. The young children will grow up and are expected to enter the labor market; the working population will increase in size and significant declines in dependency ratios will follow (Chapter I, page 31).

A major factor currently and in the future affecting the family is how to respond to a growing older population with special needs such as long-term care at home or institutionalized. Globally, population aging is occurring and developing countries could very well learn from the countries that have experienced and continue to experience the problems and issues related to a growing older population. Sub-Saharan African countries are already experiencing some of the problems and issues of the transition from a traditional to modern urbanized society. The traditional family system was ideal for caring for the needs of the older population, but faces more complex and different demands in a modernized urban society. If history is on course, the future, if not already began, will see the need not only for nursing facilities (homes), but what is known in more developed countries as assisted living facilities; these facilities are designed for those not quite ready for a nursing home. The biggest growth industry in the Western world presently is home care for the older population not in need of a nursing home, or an assisted living facility, but with adequate home care support can continue to remain in one's home. The home caretakers are either family members, or professional home care assistants. As indicated the primary medical issue as persons grow older is referred to as Dementia and/or Alzheimer's illness, which can require around the clock care by family members, or by professional caretakers.

RETIREMENT AND PENSION SYSTEMS: WHY POPULATION AGING MATTERS

Retirement and Pensions: Major Issues and Concerns

Current aging demographics, especially related to retirement and pension systems are critical in decision making for ensuring that persons 60 plus or younger at retirement have an opportunity to live in dignity and respect at the end of their working years. For the growing older population a social pension or basic income security, access to medical care is most important; yes, aging really matters when considering social protection programs for a growing older population. There are a number of very important factors/issues that have to be seriously considered regarding retirement and pension, especially when it comes to issues of occupational reforms. First, the obvious challenge for countries globally, is the growing 60 plus population and/or increasing life expectancy. Another issue that enters the discussion is an increasing high unemployment rate of youth, and a significant decline in recent years in the practice of open-end labor contracts/agreements. One of the most important issues in recent years being addressed globally are discussions, debates, regarding the appropriate retirement age. In other words, globally what is an appropriate retirement age? Also, what factors should ne considered in the determination of retirement age? Related to retirement age is the debate focused on the adequacy or inadequacy or pension incomes. Another very important factor has been, and seemingly will continue, is the increasing number of temporary jobs, including the informal and/or self-employment sectors, especially in countries such as Sub-Saharan Africa. The self-employed and/or the informal sectors still dominate in low-income as well as some low to middle income countries; these are the countries that represent the extremely high numbers of retirees without a social pension or other social protections in retirement, such as access to health care and social services. There is an obvious need for actions on the part of public and private sectors to ensure that the informal sector workers and/or self-employed, will be included in some form of a social pension scheme during their working years. Also, there are workers, especially women and younger workers, for whatever the reason(s) are separated from the work place for short or long periods of time; these time gaps in the work place will affect their pension at the time of retirement resulting in lower benefits and/or incomes to rely on following retirement. The growing consensus globally is that unless countries begin to take the appropriate actions, such as making pension systems more affordable, including the strengthening of safety nets, future pension systems will not be sufficient for meeting basic needs, especially income security (OECD Library "Pensions at a Glance 2015," OECD and G20 Indicators, OECD Publishing). **(See Appendix B: Definitions, Concepts and Special Notes Reference Mission of OECD Countries).**

Pension benefits following retirement will vary globally, including the OECD countries. On average, the percentage of average earnings during one's work history, social security benefits in the OECD countries is about 22%; the variations by country is very significant, Korea 6% and 40% in New Zealand (OECD Library, ibid). It is projected that the average worker retiring in the UK will have a pension averaging approximately 38% of salary after the state and private pensions have been combined. This is in comparison with 90% in the Netherlands and Austria, and 80% in countries, such as Spain, Italy, and 105% in Turkey. The State pension age in the UK is expected to change in not to distant future from 65 to 68; the current issues in the UK related to pensions seem to be urgent enough that changes in the current systems are imminent and the country are planning to commence with some actions soon. Countries, globally, with the earliest retirement ages are the French and Belgium, 59.4 and 59.8 respectively (Collinson, Patrick, "British workers will have worst pension of any major economy and the oldest," Guardian and Observer, 12/1/2015).

Population growth and ageing and the impact on the age of retirement are becoming a major area of concern globally. The age of retirement is projected to increase, including the OECD countries from age 64 to about 65.5. Globally, retirement age has increased significantly in recent years. What has been considered the model age of retirement, 65, has become questionable and legislative momentum in some countries are considering a change to age 67. Countries such as The Czech Republic, Denmark, Ireland, and Italy are considering a change in their pension system as high as 70, not 67. It should be noted considered the global discussions focused on increasing the retirement age that in 2014 the average age of persons leaving the labor market was for women, 63.1 and for men, 64.6 (OECD Library, 2015 ibid).

A short or long-term absence from the labor market or workplace, including a delay in entry, and especially short careers will have a significant impact on an individual's pension. An example is a woman who over an average time period of five years choose to stay at home to care for the children, could lose approximately four percent in pension income on retirement (OECD Library, ibid, 2015). Research indicates that with population ageing the demands made on family caretakers will increase, especially the needs of the older persons with chronic illnesses such as Alzheimer's. The primary caregivers, or the great majority who remain at home caring for older family members are women. Caregiving responsibilities have been and will continue to have a major impact on the overall health and wellbeing of family members, primarily women. Any significant time taken in carrying out this responsibility can have an impact on one's pension at the time of retirement. Yes, aging does matter!

The Global Pension Reform Movement

A major concern in discussions regarding pension reform, not just in the developing world but the developed world as well, has to do with the population of older persons who will not meet eligibility requirements for the traditional tripartite pension system. Pension reform measures will need to ensure that those individuals on retirement will have sufficient income as well as provisions for social and health care, including long-term care. The average payment for older persons not meeting the eligibility requirements, or not entitled to the contributory pension is about 22% of average earnings. But these "First-tier pensions vary in structure from country to country; six percent in countries such as Korea and Turkey to a high of forty percent in New Zealand (OECD Library, ibid). As aforementioned, approximately 82.5% percent of older persons in Sub-Saharan Africa are not entitled to a tripartite or collective bargaining type pension at the time of retirement. This becomes critical for future planning when considering the fact that a high percentage of older persons not entitled to a social pension are residing in countries with high poverty rates, and very low safety net benefits, including adequate access to medical and social services. This cohort of older persons is also being called upon for additional family responsibilities such as childcare duties.

Older retired persons that were not part of a contributory pension system will have to, for the most part, depend on their governments for social protection. The challenge for such governments is to establish a type of social pension, such as what now exist in countries such as Botswana, Liberia, Namibia, C. Verde, Seychelles, South Africa and Swaziland for meeting the needs of individuals who were not part of a contributory pension system (**See Chapter VI**). These public managed programs unless properly and/or efficiently managed, can result in a budget crisis. Zambia is an example of how a budget crisis can occur when funds are not properly managed, especially investments. In Zambia, it was the public Provident Fund decision to invest only in public securities; the results of the decision to invest only in public securities were the loss of approximately 23% per/year on average between the years from 1981 to 1988.

Furthermore, approximately half of the contributions for the year 1988 were used primarily for administrative expenses. If fiscal space for spending on social programs, such as a social pension, is not efficiently planned and implemented, other programs can be jeopardized or eliminated (World Bank, ibid, 1994).

Countries in the developed world, including the OECD countries, will be rethinking their existing systems and making adjustments or creating new models for responding to the growing older population. Pension and retirement systems not only refer to the formal sector tripartite collective bargaining arrangements, including employer, employee, and public, but the greatest challenges may come from older persons who have devoted their working lives within the informal sector. As aforementioned approximately 82.5% of older persons in Sub-Saharan Africa, who for the most part have worked in the informal sector, do not have a social pension. The current estimates are that approximately 75% to 80% of the working population in Sub-Saharan Africa is employed in the informal sector. What this means is that it is highly likely that the current cohort of older persons, unless there are some radical occupational policy changes, will be confronted with a similar reality of not having a social pension.

China is one country that is seriously considering changing or raising the pension age in response to a growing older population. Zhang Yougin writing in the China Daily is recommending a change as a method for increasing the income for the older senior population. "Since an aging population could mean a significant rise in old age pensions, increasing incomes of and reducing social expenditure on senior citizens have become a necessity. One way… of reducing social expenditure on elderly people is to increase the retirement age…raising the retirement age is also an effective way of increasing senior citizens incomes…" (Yougin, Zhang, "Retirement Age Should Be Raised Gradually," The China Daily (Digital), Wednesday, 1/14/2015, 6:19 P.M.).

China is not just addressing the subject of retirement age, also the broad concept of pensions as related to a growing older population. In China recently lawmakers requested from the Vice-Premier a review of the country's pension systems. His first response was that the country had received more than it had paid out. But his second response was not as optimistic indicating that revenues had become slower than expenses. A major concern of the Premier and lawmakers is that China like all countries is an aging society, especially the 60 plus population. China 60 plus population in 2013 was 200 million accounting for approximately 15% of the population. By 2050 it is projected that population 60 plus will be approximately 487 million accounting for a quarter of the world's senior population (Wang Yong, Shanghai Daily, 12/29/2014).

According to the Premier in order for China to cope with these demographic changes the government will need to develop a policy package to boost revenues and streamline the management of pension programs. Other plans being considered is postponing the retirement age, moving more dividends of state owned enterprises to social security funds, and encouraging citizens to explore different types of pension plans. Although these are actions, such as diversifying investments, being considered the government has not come up with plans to implement (Wang Yong, Shanghai Daily, 12/29/2014). It is obvious that in regards to retirement and pension policies in China aging does matter.

Early and Extended Retirement Issues

Globally, there is another critical perspective drawing a great deal of attention related to the concept retirement, the concept of early retirement. More and more countries are now beginning to consider and focus on the subject of early retirement. It has been suggested that by increasing retirement ages it may be necessary for countries to rethink the concept of early retirement. Also, discussions related to increasing the retirement age and/early retirement eventually call attention to the workforce productivity of older workers. "Studies of retirement rules around the globe suggest that increasing workforce participation at older ages will require policy changes in National Social Security Systems. A major ongoing NIA-funded series of studies in 11 industrialized countries (Belgium, Canada, France, Germany, Italy, Japan, The Netherlands, Spain, Sweden, the UK, and the US) documents that in most countries public pensions provide enormous disincentives for continual work at older ages and encourage early retirement. This ongoing research shows that in spite of cultural differences across countries, there is an important relationship between the incentives for workforce participation of older workers and the provisions of social security programs. The study highlights the analytical power of focusing on the design of National Retirement Systems and the importance of incentives" (Department of Health and Human Services, US Department of State: NIH/NIA, Li, Rose Maria (Managing Editor), "Shifting Patterns of Work and Retirement," Why Population Aging Matters, Publication #07-6134, March 2007, pages 19-20).

The United Kingdom, not unlike other countries, is faced with a crisis related to pensions and retirement as the county enters the year 2016. Pension and retirement issues and concerns from all sectors of society resulted in the government requesting a major official review of the state pension age in 2014. Some thoughts expressed by some experts around the time the review was being launched was that those who were now becoming part of the workforce would have to wait until age 75 to receive a pension. Such warnings reminded people that there had been a common expression in the UK not too many generations ago, "one worked until one dropped." The Report established by Labor, the Independent Review of Retirement and Income (IRRI), was completed and published in March 2016. A major conclusion coming from the Report was that workers would need to invest 15% of income into their pension plan; it would require this amount of investing if workers were expecting to have a sufficient amount of pounds available for family survival. The amount 15% would represent three times the current amount of 4.7 % of income (1.8 % of employee pay, 2.9 % from employer). The increase up to 15% will somewhat ensure workers that they will not fall under the category, "pensioner poverty" after retirement. Somewhat coinciding with the IRRI Report was a separate Report from Royal London that workers from some parts of the UK (example Westminster) may have to work into their 80's if they had any desires of having a similar standard of living as their parents following retirement. According to the Report approximately 12% of the population in the UK over the statutory retirement age continues to work. One conclusion could be that workers do not feel that there is sufficient income at this point to meet family needs (Jones, Rupert, the Guardian, (Digital Online), "Workers Need to Put 15% of Income into Pension," Wednesday 2 March 2016; Blake, David, Independent Review of Retirement Income Report, "We Need a Narrative: Building a Consensus Around Retirement Income, UK, March 15 2016).

The IRRI Report recommended that the state pension age be increased to 67 by the year 2028. The IRRI was also recommending the establishment of a permanent, Independent Pensions, Care and Savings Commission. A major charge for the Commission would include reviewing the minimum wage; the minimum wage subject in the UK has come under serious debate in recent years. The minimum wage in the UK refers to the time of employment when a worker may choose to cash in her/his pension. The current minimum wage will rise to age 57 in the year 2028 when the state pension reaches 67. The concern for some is that by allowing workers to have access to their money ten years prior to the statutory retirement age could have a negative ending for workers and their families. In other words, allowing this to happen, 10 year, could create some unrealistic expectations for the workers' concluding they were ready for retirement too early. The IRRI has considered for review by the new Commission, a period of 5 years and not 10, except for workers considered in poor health (Jones, ibid, 2 March 2016; Blake, ibid, 15 March 2016). Pension's Minister Steve Webb in 2014, the year that the IRRI study related to pensions age was launched, reported that workers who left their jobs early had cost the British economy 18 billion pounds in 2013; furthermore workers who left their jobs early could cost those workers more than one-third from their pension (Bachelor, Lisa, "Workers Who Retire 10 years Early Could Lose Third of their Pension," the Guardian, 13 June 2014). Recently a State Pension Poll indicated that one-third of workers, 55 plus, polled indicated their plans were to withdraw money from their pension pot during 2016 (Bachelor, Lisa, "Pensions Freedom: Polls Show Strong Uptake," the Guardian, 14 May 2015).

Without a doubt there are lessons to be learned from countries such as the United States, China and the United Kingdom, including some of the non-OECD countries, in their struggles to resolve issues and challenges of pensions and retirement related to a growing older population. But problems and issues related to retirement now being confronted by countries such as the United Kingdom go beyond the debate of increasing the retirement age. Just raising the retirement age may create more problems than solutions. Current and formers workers in the UK are expressing their views on the subject of raising the retirement age, or "work until you drop." An example follows: One worker expressed that working past 70 may sound very good if you are sitting on a bench in Parliament in either one of the Houses, or working at a job you just really love. But, what if you are standing behind a counter all day? What if your job entails some form of manual labor? (Letters to the Guardian, Subject Pensions, "Time for Some Joined-Up Thinking about the Retirement Age," 3 March 2016)? The aforementioned comments from one letter raise some very relevant concerns and/or issues. The issues and concerns should include health, including the mental health of workers.

The age for retirement has become and will continue to be a major topic for discussion in a number of countries. As aforementioned the United Nations has identified age 60 as old age for the primary purpose of demographic comparisons. The age of 60 was also used in discussions at the Second World Assembly on Aging in Spain. Countries, for the most part are using an arbitrary age of 60, or a range somewhere between the ages of 50 to 65 for determining eligibility for entitlement programs. Yougin (2014), "Countries use this criterion to define 'elderly people,' which means the retirement age could differ from country to country. With social development and advancement of medical technology, people's average life span is increasing… since an aging population could mean a significant rise in old age pensions, increasing incomes of and reducing social expenditure on senior citizens have become a necessity…" (Yougin, Zhang, "Retirement Age Should Be Raised Gradually," The China Daily (Digital), Wednesday, January 14, 2015, p.1, 6:19 A.M). According to Yougin, "…an effective and strategic way of reducing social expenditure on elderly people is to increase the retirement age. Raising the retirement age is also an effective way of increasing senior citizens incomes, which is the established international practice" (Yougin, ibid, 2015, p. 1-2).

One interesting observation related to workforce participation is as life expectancy increases, retirement ages have decreased significantly. For example, "In 1960 men on average could expect to spend 46 years in the workforce and a little more than one year in retirement… By 1995, the number of years in the workforce had decreased to 37 while the number of years in retirement had jumped to 12" (HHS: NIH/NIA, ibid, 2007, p 2). It become obvious that the uncertainties or not been able to rely on some form of social or economic security, especially in old age, is a matter of grave concern globally, including developed and/or OECD countries continue their preparation for a growing older population. Also, there is evidence to support growing concerns regarding the sustainability of pension systems, especially in transitional economies. For example, "…the fate of pensioners during the collapse of Argentina's in 2001, in the high poverty rates among Japanese elderly, and perhaps most vividly in the lack of formal social safety nets for most people in Africa and Asia"(HHS: NIH/NIA, ibid, 2007, p 18).

A major topic of discussion in the United States, not unlike other countries, is focused on the "baby boomers," especially their financial wellbeing in old age. "Baby boomers" refer to those that were born between the years of 1946, following the end of World War II to 1964. It is estimated that approximately 76 million Americans were born during those two decades. A major concern is the financial wellbeing of those individuals projected to retire between the years 2010 and 2030. It is around the year 2030 when the youngest "baby boomers" will reach the age of 66 ("Baby boomers" in Retirement, Congress of the US, Congressional Budget Office (CBO) Study, 1993).

The Lack of Social Protection for the Informal and Self-Employed Workforce

Although Sub-Saharan Africa obviously has many problems and challenges, the one major one that will have to be addressed is the percentage of the population without financial security or a social pension in old age. The fact that so many older persons (app. 82.5 percent) do not have a social pension should be a matter of global concern. Globally, especially with the leadership of organizations such as the United Nations, ILO, ISSA, as well as non-governmental organizations, there is a need to address the lack of coverage of the informal sector workforce. The Action Demand Campaign has been asking that the United Nations to convene a special session on the rights of older people. The lack of pension coverage for older persons should be a priority on the agenda, including the Millennium Development Goals Campaign. The UN Declaration of Human Rights strongly supports the rights of older persons to have a social pension whether workforce participation took place in the formal or informal sector.

Globally, countries are becoming more and more concerned with the challenges of responding to the "Silver Tsunami," the growing older population. The concerns become even more significant in regards to the subjects of retirement and pensions. As the number of older persons grow and their participation in the workforce "...many countries fuel concerns about financial stability of old age pensions...governments with limited resources may find that meeting the needs of the oldest affects their abilities to address needs of other individuals adequately (Lee et al, Population Reference Bureau (PRB), Vol. 71, #2, ibid, 2017, pages 18-19). The aforementioned concerns could confront countries with a major ethical dilemma such as who gets priority the older person with social protection needs or the younger population? **Chapter VII** addresses the subject and provides quality evidence that social pensions are affordable and achievable, including the use of some very innovative strategies for reaching the goal. The evidence is based on lessons learned, case histories from Sub-Saharan Africa and Latin America countries. If a country such as Liberia with a per/capita income of $970.00 (US $) can find fiscal space within its budget to provide a social pension for its older population of former self-employed or informal sector workers, it is possible that other countries can also succeed. Globally, "...labor force participation rates in 2010 for those 65 and older were highest among African men and women, over 50% and 30% respectively, and are projected to remain so at least until 2020 (Lee et al, Population Reference Bureau (PRB), ibid, 2017, p 18). A major issue for the growing older population in Sub-Saharan Africa is that without a social pension, a significant number will continue to work as long as they are able to so in order to carry out family household responsibilities, especially for the children and youth during the "bulge" generation (Lee et al, PRB, ibid). With the growing older population countries in Sub-Saharan Africa are not currently prepared, and there is little evidence that they will be in the near future to provide for this population adequate income support; about equally important is that the countries are not prepared to provide other supports/services such as medical and health care, especially long-term care for this growing older population. A reminder is that as people grow older chronic illnesses such as Alzheimer's and other disabling conditions, become a challenge not only for medical systems, but family caregivers as well.

The major problem that needs to be addressed for the current cohort of older people in retirement in Sub-Saharan Africa was a lack of an opportunity to participate in a formal tripartite or labor collective bargaining system. Now, in old age and retirement they are without a social pension, especially for income support. It has been estimated that less than half, approximately 40%, of the labor force globally participates in a traditional tripartite labor system that ensures income support, including a social pension in retirement. But in Sub-Saharan Africa the percentage is less than 20%. Research points out that the high-income or richer countries, especially the OECD countries, have much higher coverage in the formal systems. The reasons for this conclusion are that "...in part because informal systems no longer function adequately, and in part because richer countries are better able to enforce compliance" (World Bank, Policy and Research Report, Averting the Old Age Crisis, New York: Oxford University Press, p. 39, 1994). The World Bank Report concludes that the informal systems no longer function adequately? There is little or nor data to be found that demonstrates that the informal system ever functioned to a degree that would make a major difference in coverage. Historically, in the developing countries very few workers have been covered, and those who have been covered were employed in the civil services, including school teachers, the military or policemen (World Bank, Policy and Research Report, ibid).

The problem of retirement and/or pension is not just an issue in developing countries' the

United States, a member of the OECD network of countries has major challenges as well. The industrialized cities in the United States are confronted with serious pension system issues, as they continue to transition from an industrialized economy to a more service oriented cybernetic society. Current and future pensioners in recent years have been confronted with the possibility of a loss of or significant reductions in their retirement pensions that were projected to provide a level of economic security following years of dues paying as part of their collective bargaining agreements. The City of Detroit in the State of Michigan is one example of what is happening in some of the more industrialized cities in the country USA). Detroit is commonly referred to as the "Motor City" because of its automobile industry and a long history of automobile manufacturing. The City due to a variety of reasons filed for financial bankruptcy on 7/13/2013. The bankruptcy filing in the city of Detroit was the largest ever in the country, $18-20 Billion. An Emergency City Manager was appointed by the Governor of the State of Michigan oversee the process towards recovery. The process of going into bankruptcy had major implications for the city's pension systems, as well as for the pensioners who obviously were counting on their pensions for their economic security following retirement. A key element as part of labor's collective bargaining (employer, employee, public) is a focus on protections, especially the social pension, workers' compensation, health benefits for the family, and survivor benefits for the family. The pension and survivor benefits are key bargaining tools during the collective bargaining process.

After 15 months in a state of bankruptcy, the City emerged from Bankruptcy status some 15 months later in November 2014. Partial cost to the retirement pension fund as its part in the settlement was pension cuts of 4.5 percent presented on behalf of thousands of retirees to assist in getting out of bankruptcy. Initially, the pension funds had paid $6.2 million in their efforts to fight the bankruptcy case. The State had opposed any attempts to award financial assistance to retirees citing they had received huge financial rewards from the pension annuity program that had significantly harmed the City's pension Fund (Bomey, Nathan, "The Motor City is Counting on the Markets to Keep Its Pension Promises," Detroit Free Press, 11/7/2014; Kadlec, Dan, "Why Detroit Pension Deal is a Warning to Retirement Savers," Time Inc., Network, MONEY, 11/13/2014; Walsh, Mary Williams, "Detroit Emerges from Bankruptcy, Yet Pension Risks Linger, Detroit Free Press, 11/11/2014; and White, Edward, Detroit's Pension Crisis, Crain's Detroit Business, 3/4/2015). Detroit is one example of what can happen in a struggle to find ways to guarantee social protection for retirees following years in the workplace. Although the Detroit case history ends on somewhat of a positive note, one can only imagine the struggles that pensioners' experience during the process of finding solutions that would guarantee some level of social protection in old age.

BANKING/FINANCIAL SYSTEMS: WHY POPULATION AGING MATTERS

Major Challenges Confronting the Banking and Commerce Industries

Population growth, especially global aging will have a significant impact on the banking and financial industries. One scholarly response to the growing older population or "Silver Tsunami" is a new book in circulation, A New Era in Banking. The book addresses some of the unique and/or special needs of an older population related to banking. The authors offer several suggestions to the Banking Industry in preparation for this growing phenomenon. One major suggestion or recommendation from the book is that banks will have to be more flexible in how they go about marketing their products, including what's being sold, and how services will be distributed to each of their client segments, obviously including the population 60 plus. The banks can expect to see a change in customer behaviors, product preferences, and changes in demands with a growing older population. Banks may also see a decline in earnings as well as the savings rate as life expectancy continues to increase. Also, banks may need to locate/ look for opportunities for the purpose of increasing non-interest income, including advisory services, assessment management, including annuities. It is being projected and banks may need to prepare for the fact that a significant segment of the older population will save less, and will have a lower demand for such services as mortgages and consumer credit. According to the authors, once this population is in the retirement category, they will be more inclined to focus on the purchase of annuities, or just spend their savings (Berges, Angel, Moreno, Juan P. and Ontiveros, A New Era In Banking: The Landscape After the Battle, MA: Bibliomotion Books, Inc. 2014).

With life expectancy increasing and as the overall health of people continues to improve, it's expected that the older population will be living in retirement significantly longer than during previous generations. This alone will present a major challenge related to banking needs, especially savings and investments. Not just occupational and/or pension systems, and health and human services, but banking and real estate systems will also need to develop appropriate administrative processes, for responding to the special needs of the older population. For example, long time use of traditional communication symbols, and advertising, may need re-thinking. In other words, there will be a major need for business schools, and other training and other educational entities to develop new curriculums and/or revise older ones in preparing for a growing older population (HHS: NIH/NIA, ibid, 2007). Business schools and other training institutions will have a major challenge in preparing staff personnel for protecting the growing older population from an increasing trend related to scams and other illicit activities. The aforementioned will require that the banking and commerce staffs work closely with other systems, especially law enforcement officials.

Matters related to banking and especially real estate will present major challenges and opportunities for the growing older population. Real estate for example, "The largest component of household wealth…is housing value. This could fall if large numbers of older homeowners try to sell houses to smaller numbers of young buyers." Financial markets will need to be flexible and innovative to meet the needs of aging populations…population aging will create new economic pressures. At the same time create exciting opportunities for expanding our collection of financial tools to accommodate a changing world" (HHS: NIH/NIA, ibid, 2007, p. 24). Yes, aging does matter when it comes to banking and commerce!!!

Globally, countries are beginning to analyze and respond to the demographic trends, especial in the aforementioned areas of banking and finance. Countries are recognizing the potential impact an aging society will have on their economy. Germany, Italy, Japan, as well as other countries across Europe, Greece, Spain, Switzerland, Sweden, to name a few are countries that now have more people age 60 plus than individuals whose age fall below 20. By the year 2025, the projections are that approximately 46 countries will have more people age 60 plus than young people. Other countries expected to join the aforementioned include China and Russia by the year 2030, and India by 2070. The 65 plus population globally is projected to triple by the year 2050 to approximately 1.5 billion, representing approximately 16 percent of the world's population (Moreno, J. P., Chan, A., "Aging Societies Need New Challenges," The China Daily (Digital Newspaper), Wednesday 1/14/2015 – 6:00 A.M.). **NOTE:** Moreno, Accenture Senior Manager and Director of Global Banking; Co-Author of **A New Era in Banking;** Chan, Accenture Managing Director, China Financial Services.

Enhancing Banking Accessibility: Physical Structures, Safety/ Security, Staff/Consumer Communications and Accommodating the Special Needs of the Older Population; including Preventive Measures Against "Scams" and Other Illicit Activities

Does the "Silver Tsunami" or a growing older population matter? The aforementioned trends will undoubtedly have a very significant impact on the global financial institutions and no country will be spared whether developed or developing countries. The aging demographic trends will affect the financial institutions, according to (Moreno and Chan, ibid) in several areas. First, the world will see the wealth distribution shifting more towards the age category 65 plus of the aging population. The process of marketing and developing products for the older generation will become a challenge and opportunity, especially for the banking institutions. Secondly, the institutions can also anticipate that customer behaviors, product preferences, as well as demands will change. This may require new or different staffing patterns, including education and training, in responding to the needs of this population. A very significant implication for banking institutions will be a drop in income as this population retires resulting in a decrease in earnings and savings rate. Moreno and Chan, "…banks will need to find more opportunities to increase non-interest income, including advisory services, asset management and annuities (Moreno and Chan, ibid). Lastly, the fact that women, globally live longer than men, therefore, they will overtime accumulate more wealth. In 2010, approximately 27% of women were in the high net worth category. This factor becomes very significant for banking and/or financial institutions considering that men and women may present different perceptions when it comes to how their savings and investments will be processed. Also, "…larger segments of older customers not only will save less, they will have a lower demand for mortgages and consumer credit, and likely a reduced appetite for risky products" (Moreno and Chan, ibid).

In regards to new consumer demands the "Silver Tsunami" will not only present challenges but great opportunities. Although half of the Continent's population is projected to be younger than 20 years of age, there is another age group to be considered when discussing consumer demands. The growing older population will have their special consumer demands, especially regarding medical and health care. The 21st Century will not just witness a growing older population, but an active aging population. The health needs/issues of the growing older population will be centered on chronic illnesses, such as Dementia, or Alzheimer's; these are health issues requiring specialized medicines and professionals, as well as institutional and/or family support systems. Because of modernization and urbanization the traditional family support systems are changing significantly. Consumer demands for this aging population could very well center around daycare programs for seniors, nursing homes, assisted living facilities, medicine and medications related to the treatment of chronic illnesses. A country's economic planning process cannot ignore the special consumer needs of this population. Western countries have much to share regarding the care of a growing older population; aging does matter!

The attention given to the "generation explosion" regarding consumer demands of the 15-24, 15-30 age groups are extremely important, but consumer demands of the growing older population also has to be seriously considered. If appropriate policies are in place, pension and/or retirement systems, savings and investment opportunities, the older population can contribute significantly to economic growth and transformation. Just imagine the results if and when all retirees, including those from the informal sectors are receiving social pensions in the future.

MEDICAL, HEALTH AND SOCIAL SYSTEMS: WHY POPULATION AGING MATTERS

In an era of chronic illnesses and increasing life expectancy there will be some major challenges for families, medical, health and social service infrastructures, human and physical, as countries prepare for a growing older population. The challenges include ensuring the following:

Need for Financial and Physical Accessibility, esp. Long-Term Care, Meeting the Needs for Occupational and Family Caregiving and Resources that Allow for Aging in Place, the Home in Later Life

In considering all of societal systems' that matters in responding to a growing older population, there is a global consensus that the medical, health, and social systems are extremely critical. Global Population Growth, especially aging or the "Silver Tsunami," is expected to present major challenges for the traditional medical, health and social systems responding to a growing older population, especially those that will be encountering specialized medical and health needs. A major factor contributing greatly to the challenge is that globally, countries are transitioning from communicable diseases to an era where chronic and/or long-term diseases/illnesses will become dominate. Although it is still a major challenge the developed countries have had more time over the years for building the medical, health, and social infrastructures in responding, but the developing world will have a shorter period of time to prepare. "With increasing age, numerous underlying physiological changes occur, and the risk of chronic disease rises. By age 60, the major burdens of disability and death arise from age related losses in hearing, vision, mobility, and non-communicable diseases, including heart disease, stroke, respiratory disorders, cancer and dementia" (WHO: World Report on Ageing and Health 2015, ibid, p 26).

The developed countries for the most part, have been struggling now for years to respond to the challenging special medical, health, and social needs of a growing older population. Now, the developing countries, as life expectancy continues to increase, will also be challenged to modify, introduce new and/or innovative systems, including short and long-term care facilities, for responding to the growing older population. With diseases highly associated with ageing, such as Dementia and Alzheimer's, the need not just for short and long term institutional arrangements, but home based caregiving by professionals, family members, friends and neighbors. As populations increase in age, or life expectancy increases, the world will witness an astronomical increase in physical and mental disabilities. Adding to the challenge is the fact that during the aging process, it is becoming common for an individual to be confronted with not just one but two or more chronic conditions. Research from Germany is a good example of the aforementioned observation; in Germany a cohort of older persons within the age range of 70-85 approximately twenty-four percent were experiencing a minimum of five chronic illnesses at the same time (WHO: World Report on Ageing and Health 2015, ibid).

In the rise of chronic illnesses consumers will be expected to take on a greater responsibility for their health. "The rise of chronic diseases, heart disease, cancer, and diabetes reflects challenges in life style and diet as well as aging. The potential economic and societal costs of non-communicable diseases of this type rise sharply with age and have the ability to affect economic growth. World Health Organization analysis, "In 2002 the projected estimates related to non-communicable diseases were approximately 85% of the burden for diseases such as heart disease, cancer and diabetes in high income countries," (WHO Publication, Why Pop. Aging Matters? Publication #07-6134, March 2007, page 12). Non-communicable diseases during the year 2008 were responsible for approximately 86% of the cost in high-income countries such as the United States; in the middle-income countries the cost was estimated to be 65%, and 37% in low-income countries (WHO: Department of Health and Human Services, NIA/NIH, Global Health and Aging, October 2011, p.10.

Globally, there seems to be a consensus that on the one hand increasing life expectancy is somewhat of a major triumph or victory, but on the other hand there are some negative consequences. One example is the increasing number of those in the older population, who are diagnosed with the chronic illness known as Dementia. The numbers of persons with this diagnosis increases with age, especially those in the category now commonly referred to as the old-old, or the 85 plus group. The estimation is that approximately 25-30 percent of the older population 85 plus has been diagnosed with Dementia/Alzheimer disease. Older people with Dementia will require practically around the clock care and attention with all of their daily living activities. The social, especially the financial costs of caring is without a doubt are and will continue to be a significant component of a country's health and human service budget. The caring components, includes not only the health and human service systems, but families and/or love ones, especially women who normally at this time carry out about 95 percent of the family caregiving duties (WHO: NIA/NIH, Publication #11-7737, ibid, 2011).

Globally, Dementia becomes one of the most challenging of the chronic illnesses as life expectancy increases; the illness as aforementioned has a tremendous impact not only on medical and health systems but family caregiving as well. The fact that reporting systems globally are not standardized and there are significant variations across countries; the disease is extremely difficult to diagnose during early stages. "The memory problems, misunderstandings, and behavior common in the early and immediate stages are often attributed to normal effects of aging, accepted as personality traits, or simply ignored...dementia affected about 10 million people in OECD member countries around 2000, just under 7 % of people aged 65 or older" (WHO: Health and Human Services, Global Health and Aging, NIA/NIH, HIH Publication no. 11-7737, October 2011, p. 14).

The most common form of Dementia is Alzheimer; this particular form of Dementia "... accounted for between two-fifths and four-fifths of all dementia cases...more recent analyses have estimated the worldwide number of people living with AD/dementia at between 27 million and 36 million. The prevalence of AD and other dementias are very low at younger ages, than nearly doubles with every five years of age after age 65" (WHO: HHS, NIA/NIH, ibid, 2011, p. 14). Some research studies have reported that, "...dementia affected fewer than 3 percent of those aged 65 to 69, but almost 30 percent of those aged 85 to 89. More than half of women aged 90 or older had dementia in France and Germany, as did about 40 percent in the United States, and just under 30 percent in Spain" (WHO: HHS, ibid, 2011, p. 14).

These are chronic illnesses demanding long-term care, including specialized health as well as social services. These chronic diseases are becoming the primary cause of morbidity and mortality in developing countries as well. This phenomenon has very serious policy implication, especially as related to long-term care as people live longer. One can readily see the impact a growing ageing population can have on major systems of care, including the family. Chronic diseases have already become a major challenge for health, medical and social systems globally, including long- term care facilities and services. Not just professional caring, but the demands on family systems to provide home care services will increase significantly. In regards to caregiving and the many challenges related to Alzheimer's, an example comes from the State of Ohio (USA): Care Givers in Ohio, "...63.8% of caregivers provide care for at least 2 years...63.3% manage personal care (bathing or feeding)...82.5% who manage household care (cooking or cleaning) Western Reserve Area Agency on Aging, "Spotlight on Dementia and Related Diseases: Alzheimer's and Related Diseases, Fact Sheet," Cleveland, Ohio, Website: www.areaagingsolutions.org, 2018.

The problem is global affecting all corners of the world. There will be tremendous challenges in developing countries, continents or regions, such as Sub-Saharan Africa. Whereas developed or high-income countries have had significantly more time to adapt to a growing older population, including the development of the needed medical infrastructures, the time span, as aforementioned for the developing countries is going to be significantly shorter. France for example has had approximately "...150 years to adapt to a change from 10% to 20% in the proportion of the population that was older than 60 years, places such as Brazil, China, and India will have slightly more than 20 years to make the same adaptation" (WHO: World Report on Ageing and Health 2015, ibid, p 43). Now, just imagine the time span needed for countries in Sub-Saharan Africa; it will need to be done almost overnight.

As population growth and/or ageing continues the world will observe a long list of morbidity and disability issues, including those related to Dementia and Alzheimer that the growing older population will be confronted with. The medical and health issues include '…cardiovascular and circulatory disease, nutritional deficiencies, cirrhosis of the liver, and diabetes as major causes of disability-adjusted life years in Sub-Saharan Africa's older population. Moreover, representative surveys of older adults' health show high rates of hypertension, musculoskeletal disease, visual impairment, functional limitations, and depression' (Aboderin and Beard, Lancet, ibid, 2015, p. 2). As previously discussed, the reality of an individual having more than one disease, the Germany experience, is a high probability.

A major and continuing issue for developed countries, and especially for the developing world will be the cost factor of providing care, including new physical infrastructures, technologies, services, and the need for professional trained providers, requiring new skills. A great deal of attention will be concentrated on an increasing sub- group of the older population now being referred to as the "oldest old" or those in the age category 85 plus. This category is being considered by some demographic experts as the fastest growing in a number of countries, especially the developed ones, such as the United States, France, and Sweden. This particular trend will present major challenges, especially for the medical, health and human service systems (WHO, HHS, NIH/NIA, Oct. 2011, ibid). Because of chronic illnesses such as dementia, the age group referred to, as "oldest-old" will have a major impact, not only medical and institutional arrangements, but family and community caregiving as well. Governments will be confronted with increasing demands on their budgets as they respond to the needs of this ageing category of older persons (World Bank: Policy Research Report, "Averting the Old-Age Crisis: Policies to Protect the Old and Promote growth, New York: Oxford University Press, 1994).

It is anticipated that this age group, 85 plus will probably have a greater need for long-term care support systems, including the family as well as institutional and/or community based services. The projections are that age group 85 plus will triple/quadruple between the time frame 2000 and 2050. Already the currents cost for home care services is approximately 8.6 billion, and will probably grow to around 21,9 billion by the year 2020. Contributing to the aforementioned growth and cost is the increasing episodes of chronic illnesses in the growing older population, especially the 85 plus group. "The process of chronic illnesses and disability is long-term and requires management and coordination of services, by a broad range of parties, including family, informal care givers, poorly paid attendants, and social workers. Long-term care may include supportive social services, respite care, and adult day care (Lynch, Marty and Estes, Carroll, "The Underdevelopment of community Based Services in the United States Long Term Care System: A Structural Analysis," in Estes, Carroll & Associates, Social Policy and Ageing: A Critical Perspective, California: Sage Publications, 2001, pages 201-215).

As aforementioned such chronic illnesses, such as Alzheimer, will require not just family care giving, but professional care in the home as well that can be quite costly. The United Kingdom provides and an excellent example below of some challenges especially the factor of cost, facing the developed countries in responding to the needs of older family members. The developing countries can get a glimpse from experiences in the UK regarding the cost of such care and how overall financial matters can affect the older persons and their families. The Home Health Care Industry, especially in the developed world, is becoming a critical part of caring for older people experiencing chronic illnesses. The Home Care Industry is focused on older persons whose level of illness do not require a nursing home or an assisted living facility, but with adequate home care support an older person can continue to remain in one's home in the community. The home caretakers are either family members, or professional home care assistant. This particular health industry has become a major challenge for the Western countries in responding to a growing older population, especially those with physical and mental disabilities. The United Kingdom is now confronted with serious financial problems within the Home Health Care industry. The following headline appeared recently in Britain's well established newspaper, The Guardian and Observer, "UK's biggest Care Home operator risks running out of cash…Industry expects half of the country's care homes were at risk of closure as the sector faced with a bigger crisis than the steel industry" (Graham Ruddick, Guardian and Observer, November 2, 2015). This private health care industry is known as Four Season Health Care. The industry operates some 470 homes, including more than 20,000 beds in the UK (Ruddick, 2015, ibid).

Approximately one month later following the aforementioned headlines that appeared in The Guardian and Observer, the newspaper reported the latest news regarding the Four Seasons Health Care Industry: "United Kingdom's Biggest Care Home Provider Shuts Loss-Making Homes" (Lisa O'Carroll, Guardian, November 2, 2015). The plan by the industry is to close seven of the loss-making sites that will have a significant effect on "…hundreds of patients" (O'Carroll, ibid). Speaking of the chronic condition dementia approximately 50% of the older population being cared for by Four Seasons have been diagnosed with dementia, including various acute medical conditions.

As life expectancy continues to increase, and the transition to non-communicable illnesses such as dementia and/or chronic illnesses, the problems of caring for the growing older population will have a major impact on a country's budget. Locating fiscal space within the governmental budget becomes more and more difficult. Just as critical will be the daily role of family caregivers in providing care in the homes. The increasing problems for caregivers, especially women, are the daily stressors involved in the caring of love ones. "Ageing in Place," is the new phrase promoting home based services rather than the short and long-term care facilities. More importantly, research findings have concluded that home care is less expensive than institutional care; furthermore, research also concludes that the older population prefers to stay in their home communities. But, if "Ageing in Place" is the country's goal, the legislative leaders, on the national, state, and local levels will have to realize the support services needed to do so; and those programs and services, including long-term home based medial, health and social services have to become a priority in budgets. Home based care and services, especially with diseases such as Dementia and/or Alzheimer are not just provided by paraprofessionals and professionals, but family members as well; there is also evidence to illustrate that friends and neighbors are also involved. A major concern, historically, is the impact caregiving in the home has on health and wellbeing of family members, for the most part women. Speaking of stressors, the emotional and physical impact on female caregivers, a significant number has been classified as part of the "sandwich generation, whereas they are caring not only their immediate families, but older family members, including in-laws as well.

Developing countries can learn from the experiences of developed countries that have been confronted with the challenges of chronic illnesses resulting in the need for long-term care for sometime now. The current experiences in the United States related to family caregiving and the disease Alzheimer's provides a glimpse or what countries can expect in the future as populations continue to age. In regards to caregiving it has been estimated that some 44 million adults have had to provide unpaid care in the home for family members over a twelve-month span of time. Alzheimer's is a disease that at times will require almost around the clock care. The primary caregivers were females, approximately 60%, males 40%. Eight in ten of the caregiving in the home was for one family member. A significant number of caregiving hours, approximately 85%, are provided for relatives, 49% caring for a parent or parent-law, and about one in ten for a spouse (National Alliance for Caregiving and AARP Public Policy Institute (American Association Retired Persons), "Caregiving in the United States 2015," Baltimore Maryland, June 2015).

The cost of caregiving in the home by family members, including neighbors and friends in the United States is extremely high, and illustrates how valuable family members can be in caregiving. But, it should not be overlooked the mental and physical problems that result from being caregivers. During the year 2014 "…15.7 million family and friends provided 17.9 billion hours of unpaid care to those with Alzheimer's and other dementias – care valued at $217. 7 billion…60% of Alzheimer's and dementia caregivers rate the emotional stress of caregiving as high or very high; about 40% suffer from depression…Three-quarters of Alzheimer's and dementia caregivers report they are 'somewhat' to 'very' concerned about maintaining their own health since becoming a caregiver…In fact, due to the physical and emotional toll of caregiving, Alzheimer's and dementia caregivers had $9.7 billion in additional health care costs of their own in 2014 (Alzheimer's Association, aiz.org, Fact Sheet, March, 2015, p. 2). The cost of caring for this special population is not just borne by family members, friends, and neighbors, but also governmental entitlement programs, primarily Medicare. The overall direct costs of caring for those with the diagnosis of Alzheimer's and dementia in 2015 was approximately $226 billion, and half of the costs was billed to the Medicare program (Alzheimer's Association, ibid).

In recognition of the complexities and the tremendous impact chronic illnesses such as Dementia/Alzheimer, are having on the patients and their family systems, Western countries such as the United States are developing non-profit volunteer support organizations. These non-profit organizations are recipients of philanthropic support from the local communities; they are also affiliated with local chapters of the National Alzheimer's Association. One example of such an organization in Ohio, USA, is "The Gathering Place," located in the Northeastern section of Ohio in the City of Beachwood. The "Gathering Place" provides programs and services focusing on the '…social, emotional, physical and spiritual needs of individuals with cancer, their families and friends. The mission of "The Gathering Place" is to support, educate, and empower individuals and families touched by cancer through programs and services provided free' (Brian Albrecht, balbrecht@plaind.com, The Plain Dealer, Thursday November 26, 2015).

Countries, who have not quite reached this stage in the aging process, should be aware of the projections that all countries, at various timelines, will experience what is already happening in some of the more developed ones. Therefore, in preparation for the "Silver Tsunami" countries, not at this stage may want to use some of the Western countries as case histories as they prepare preparation. It is estimated that the costs in the United States in caring for this particular chronic illness population is $226 billion. It is estimated that "...Today, 5.3 million Americans are living with Alzheimer's disease... By 2050, up to 16 million will have the disease... Nearly two-thirds...3.2 million are women. In 2014, 15.7 million family and friends provided 17.9 billion hours of unpaid care to those with Alzheimer's and other Dementias – care valued at $217.7 billion...due to the physical and emotional toll of caregiving, Alzheimer's and dementia caregivers had US$9.7 billion in additional health care costs of their own in 2014" (United States: Alzheimer's Association Fact Sheet, alz.org, March 2015).

These are chronic illnesses demanding long-term care, health as well as social services. These latter diseases are becoming the primary cause of death in developing countries as well. This phenomenon has very serious policy implication, especially as related to long-term care as people live longer.

SUMMARY/CONCLUSION

As discussed in Chapter I for a number of decades globally demographic trends or an astronomical increase in population growth have been occurring at an unprecedented rate; the trends have been referred to as a demographic time bomb or explosion. Not only has the world been witnessing population growth in general, also the "Silver Tsunami," or a growing older population. Most importantly this growth phenomenon is affecting all of societal systems, including medical, health, family, labor, especially pensions and regulatory reforms, banking and family structures. A very important trend the increasing older population has raised one very important question does population aging matters? When one considers the significant impact population aging is having and will continue to have on all critical systems in society the conclusion is yes, aging matters.

Projections are that by the year 2050 there will be more individuals 65 plus than youth under 15. The one trend not expected to change is that women will continue to live longer than men. The age group 85 plus has become the fastest growing of the 60 plus category of the growing older population. The challenges will be issues such as financial wellbeing or more specifically social security, long-term health and social care for the 65 plus as well as the 85 plus group. The question globally what impact will an increasing older population have on family systems, labor and pension systems, banking/financial, medical/health and social systems pension, and health care systems in future years? Chapter II in it narrative attempts to respond to this very critical question.

The Family - The growing ageing population, especially countries in Sub-Saharan Africa, especially the trends towards urbanization and modernization will face some major challenges; the chapter responds to some of those challenges. Developing countries, especially in Africa, will make up the vast majority of people living in urban areas. This factor can have a major impact on family households, especially where children are being housed and cared for by their grandparents. The process of modernization and urbanization will seriously challenge the African extended family network, historically the "safety net" for the older population, children and other vulnerable members.

Chapter II based on lessons learned from some of the more developed countries such as the UK and the United States alert the developing countries that the 60 plus population living longer can have a tremendous impact on families. Research informs that as individuals age chronic illnesses related to dementia and Alzheimer can require almost round the clock caring on the part of family caretakers. One of the biggest growth industries among developed countries is home care for the growing older population not needing institutionalized care. Family members caring for an older population chronic illness related population can have a tremendous impact on family members, not just financial but the health of family members as well.

Retirement/Pensions - The implications or impact of increased life expectancy and/or the growing older population as related to the labor/employment sectors, including retirement and pensions have been addressed in Chapter II. One of the most critical issues discussed is retirement age. Increased life expectancy is presenting major problems, more specifically fiscal, for labor and/or employment sectors globally. Not only problems and issues related to pensions and retirement but such demographic trends will put financial strains and challenges on the traditional labor market tripartite systems, including the informal sectors. The issues are more pronounced, especially in low-income countries where budget issues in general, may find it more difficult to create fiscal space for social programs such as a social pension and or orphan care for vulnerable children.

One major debate addressed in Chapter II had to do with the pros/cons of lowering the retirement age. The discussion also includes the adequacy, cost of living, for current pensions at the time of retirement. Another major discussion was focused on lack of social pensions for the informal sector self employed workers. Globally, approximately 51% of the labor force will not have a pension at the time of retirement; in Sub-Saharan Africa approximately 82.5 of retirees will not have a pension. A major challenge confronted and addressed is the need for a working partnership, not only the two sectors, formal/informal, but a role for governmental and political entities for bringing the parties together with the goal of working towards a solution. Without some radical and/or innovative policy changes beginning immediately there is little evidence that the next older generation of older people will see significant changes in their financial wellbeing.

Banking Changing the Culture - The growing older population will significantly impact banking and banking related institutions. A key factor addressed in Chapter II was the projection of a shift in financial holdings to an older population; also, the fact that women now with increased wealth will continue to live longer than their male counterparts. The "Silver Tsunami" will have implications on policy related issues as they are related to a growing older population. Banks and how they do business with a growing older population will undergo changes in marketing, overall administrative management, including day to day business practices. A major issue addressed was how new and/or different consumer demands of a growing older population will present new challenges and demands resulting a need to change the overall culture of banking. Banks will be challenged to develop new and innovative marketing strategies in responding to the need for new products being demanded by the growing older population; consumer demands will change as the aging process continues. For example, as addressed the older population of consumers may have a preface for purchasing annuities than other types of investments.

Chapter II addressed the need for creating a more age friendly environment for the growing older population. Banking and other financial institutions will have to be more alert to problems and issues related financial abuse, especially scams, a major threat to the growing older population. Financial institutions will be challenged to consider as well as make changes and/or modifications of their physical facilities for enhanced accessibility to services and products; the institutions, not only modifications to physical facilities, but enhanced methods and practices of communications between the institutions, especially employees and consumers. In other words, banking and financial institutions are expected to take advantage of available technology for enhancing the quality of life of a growing older population.

Medical/Health and Social Systems – The unprecedented growth in the aging population, especially the 80 plus group, will have its greatest or most significant impact on the medical, health and social systems globally; not just the caring systems but countries will be challenged to develop and implement innovative social, medical and health policies in response to the aging demographic trends. Although in the narrative Chapter II addresses the human success stories of modern medicine and public health, the narrative also addresses some of the less than positive consequences related to a growing older population. Globally countries, some more so than others, are struggling to cope with the transition from a communicable disease era to one of chronic illnesses. The struggles to cope will be much more difficult for low to middle-income countries than the more developed global economies such as OCED countries. As addressed in Chapter II the more developed or higher income countries have had more time and resources to develop the infrastructures, medical, health and social for responding to this growth phenomenon than the developing countries. Although the "silver tsunami" is happening globally, due to factors such as culture, and social/economic factors contributing to success and/or lack of success will vary from country to country; not just by country as a whole, but in some instances intra-country as well depending on political, social and ethnicity related factors (Population Bulletin, 2005).

A major factor or factors addressed had to do with the physiological changes that are occurring contributing to limitations in mobility, hearing and vision. The risk of medical diseases related Dementia and Alzheimer have a tendency to increase, as the person grows older. The aforementioned is becomes very critical for the fastest growing older population 85 plus. Chapter II addresses two major challenges resulting from chronic illnesses, caring for the older person, and the cost of care. The chapter provides examples of long-term caring in two major countries, the United Kingdom and the United States. Research indicates that it is less expensive caring for the person at home than in an institutional setting. Although there are financial matters related to home caring by professional workers, inadequate salaries and long working hours, home care by family members has become a critical issue. Long-term home care is increasingly becoming 24 hour caring. Home care is provided for the most part by women in addition to other family responsibilities. Research points out that women carrying out these responsibilities are being affected physical and emotional.

Although modernization, the movement from a rural/agricultural oriented economy to a more urban industrialized one, the process and/or timing varies from country to country (Atlas of Global Development, 2013; UN: Population Ageing, 2013). There will be challenges, some very difficult to overcome, especially in the least and less developing countries, to meet the basic needs of a growing older population. The problems/issues of a growing older population related to not having sufficient financial supports, social security and social protection, present major challenges for public officials now and in the future. For the most part the majority of older Africans are a product of the informal labor system without official ties to a system of social security or social protection in retirement. Not only does the current cohort of older persons lack social protection, but are being called on to accept more responsibility for the rearing/ socialization of their grandchildren, especially in an era of HIV AIDS. It is estimated that some 6000 children globally lose one or both parents to HIV AIDS daily, 90% are from Africa.

The challenges or questions are how prepared are the African countries in preparation for the growing "silver tsunami?" What role(s) will the developed countries, especially those that colonized the continent, play as the African countries struggle to provide social protection for a growing older population? Are they, as well as other developed countries, willing to invest, foreign direct investment, not handout or just aid, in Africa's economic transformation?

CHAPTER III

THE WORLD RESPONDS TO UNPRECEDENTED POPULATION GROWTH, INCLUDING THE "SILVER TSUNAMI"

INTRODUCTION

Although there had been an increasing awareness of demographic population growth across all age groups prior to the 1980's, it was the First World Assembly on Aging in 1982 that seemed to bring together the international community around the subject of a growing older population, the "Silver Tsunami" and all of its related implications. Following the 1982 World Assembly the world seemingly became more proactive in responding to the demographic explosion or shock occurring globally. During the years following the First World Assembly on Aging in 1982, global conferences national and regional forums became more common as the world responded to the unprecedented demographic phenomenon occurring. Global organizations, governments, including non-governmental organizations, political and civic groups, have come to recognize a demographic population growth explosion, including that of a growing number of older persons. The aforementioned groups and/or organizations begin recognizing that this global phenomenon would have a significant impact on all societal systems, political, economic, medical, health, occupational and social. All of the aforementioned systems, regardless of country, developed or developing, are in some stage (beginning, advanced) of preparation in order to respond appropriately to these historical demographic trends taking place. Globally, preparations are not just focused on population growth in general, but there has become a very special interest, the human tidal wave or dramatic growth of the aging population or the "Silver Tsunami" occurring as well.

The growing older population has not just caught the attention of international political, governmental and social welfare organizations, but Your Holiness and Most Holy Father Pope and Sovereign of the Vatican City State, has also taken notice. In reference to the "Silver Tsunami" Your Holiness Pope Francis has shared his perspectives on an ageing Europe, including the implications of a growing older population. An Editorial in The New York Times (USA) shared some perspectives from Your Holiness Pope Francis on the subject of "An Aging Europe in Decline." But, prior to Pope Francis observations a brief view of some economic growth patterns in Europe related to population growth is shared. Although some may focus on Europe's economic struggles in recent years (only a 1% growth projected for 2015, and no net growth during the past year) as reason for a declining continent, the problem may be more demographic than economic. From an age perspective, in 2014 one in five Western Europeans was 65 plus, by the year 2030 the ratio is projected to increase from one to four. Now, from a fertility perspective, during the 1970's families in the European Union were experiencing on the average of two children per family; the ratio in 2014 is approximately 1.6. (Brooks, A.C., "An Ageing Europe in Decline," The New York Times, The Opinion Pages, January 6, 2015).

During his visit and address to the European Parliament Your Holiness Pope Francis shared the following observations, "As the European Union has expanded, the world itself has become more complex and ever changing; increasingly interconnected and global, it has as a consequence, become less and less 'Eurocentric'... Europe seems to give the impression of being somewhat elderly and haggard... In my view, one of the most common diseases in Europe today is the loneliness typical of those who have no connection with others... This is especially true of the elderly, who are often abandoned to their fate...This loneliness has become more acute as a result of the economic crisis, whose effects continue to have tragic consequences for the life of society...In many quarters we counter a general impression of weariness and aging, of a Europe which is now a 'grandmother,' no longer fertile and vibrant... Men and women risk being reduced to mere cogs in a machine that treats them as items of consumption to be exploited, with the result that – as is so tragically apparent – whenever a human life no longer proves useful for that machine, it is discarded with few qualms, as in the case of the sick, of the terminally ill, the elderly who are abandoned and uncared for...." (Visit and Address of Your Holiness Pope Francis to the European Parliament and the Council of Europe, Strasbourg, France, Tuesday, 25 November 2014).

Your Holiness Pope Francis provides for the world a perspective in reference to population growth in general as well as the "Silver Tsunami," especially some of the consequences and challenges that will be presented. As so frequently mentioned the occurring "Silver Tsunami" is affecting every corner of the globe. It will have its impact on regions, such as The European Union, who for years has been a symbol of economic wealth and power, as well as regions such as Sub-Saharan Africa, who for so many years have struggled to survive oppression, exploitation, and colonization. Global population growth, including the "silver tsunami" will present not just challenges but opportunities as well. The "Silver Tsunami," if given the opportunities to actively participate in decision making and not pushed aside because of chronological age or ageism, could become a major strength if the global goal is to become a "Society for All Ages." The developing world will experience the most astronomical increase in the older population by the year 2050; the projections are that the African continent alone, the population will increase from 204 million to 210 million by the year 2050 (Help Age International, OAU, African Union, African Union Policy Framework and Plan of Action on Ageing, Durban, South Africa, July 2002).

RESPONDING TO THE GLOBAL DEMOGRAPHIC CRISIS: EVENTS AND ACTIONS PRE-POST FIRST WORLD ASSEMBLY ON AGING 1982

The 26th Session International Labor Organization (ILO), Philadelphia, Pa., USA April-May, 1944

There had been a couple of significant events explicit and implicit with implications related to population growth that had occurred prior to the First World Assembly on Aging in 1982. But, it was the First General Assembly in 1982 that seemed to symbolize a global recognition that the time had come to be proactive in responding to this population growth phenomenon. The aforementioned two events prior to 1982 were the 26th Session, International Labor Organization's (ILO) Labor Conference in 1944, and the Founding of the United Nations in1945; the significance of these two events will be discussed later in the Chapter. In recognition of the demographic explosion occurring globally, international organizations, such as the United Nations decided that the time had come for action and/or proactively to begin responding to a potential global crisis. In addition to the United Nations other International Organizations, such as the International Labor Organization, UNESCO, for a number of years had been exploring with their member organizations, how to become more proactive in efforts to insure that the growing older population will have a quality of life equal to that as any other societal age group. Global advocacy groups, such as Help Age International ((a global non-governmental organization), had been promoting the theme of a "Society for All Ages" for a number of years. The United Nations, UNESCO, Help Age International, The International Labor Organization (ILO), The World Bank, and the International Social Security Administration (ISSA), are some of the global organizations that have been providing leadership during the past several decades in response to the demographic changes that were occurring and the impact those changes would have on the overall quality of life for all age groups, especially the growing older population.

International organizations with a mission focused on human rights, social justice, and social protection of older persons, have been engaged in research activities, and the organization of assemblies and forums searching for answers regarding the most practical strategies and tactics for responding to the growing older population. One major question has focused on the preparedness of countries in the developed and developing worlds for ensuring that the ageing population will have a quality of life with dignity and respect in their later years. The quality of life envisioned for a growing older population would be income security, access to health care, including long-term care, clean drinking water, suitable housing, safety (no physical or psychological abuse), and to live as active citizens in dignity and respect. In other words, to live with dignity and respect include the opportunity to participate with other age groups (active aging), in decision-making regarding the overall welfare of their country as well as themselves (Help Age International/Society for All Ages).

As previously indicated, for decades now, following the First World Assembly, there have been global assemblies, conventions, conferences, and forums, spearheaded by international organizations in pursuit of their mission of ensuring a quality of life for all. In the meantime member countries of international organizations, especially the United Nations, were also beginning to recognize more fully the impact the population growth phenomenon was having on their respective countries. Countries from the developing and developed world, with guidance and support from the various international organizations, were beginning to see the challenges and opportunities being presented by the dramatic demographic changes. It had become the appropriate time for international organizations, including member countries, to begin working together on developing the appropriate plans for actions. The basic question for the various countries, as it was for the international organizations, how prepared were they for a growing older population in the 21st Century?

The following narratives represent some significant actions, events, including assemblies, forums, conferences, that have and continue to play a role in responding to this demographic phenomenon. The World Assemblies, Conferences, and Forums, have resulted in global declarations, and policy briefs providing guidelines for actions. The First World Assembly, 1982, and those that followed, for the most part, were convened specifically in response to the growing older population. There have been organizations, such as the International Labor Organization (ILO) with Conference agendas, pre/1982 and post WWII not specifically related to demographic ageing, but the mission of such organizations was in harmony with such organizations as the United Nations in regards to human rights and social justice for all ages. Historically, a major part of the ILO's mission has focused on social justice and human rights of workers, especially within the labor movement. But, globally the International Labor Organization in recent decades has become a significant partner with other international organizations in focusing on the plight of a growing older population. A very strong beginning for the ILO's advocacy on behalf of workers in Africa can be traced back to the ILO's Conference on Forced Labor in 1930. Considering at the time when colonization, exploitation, forced labor, and all forms of human injustices, a Conference on forced labor on the part of the ILO was exemplary. In regards to social protection, social security/social pension in their future these workers would never have a chance.

Why the inclusion of ILO as a significant event in response to the growing older population? Historically, a major focus of the ILO has been related to labor laws that have become the impetus for a variety of social actions. A major part of the organization's mission and activities since it was founded in 1919 have been around social dialogue. According to the ILO "... social dialogue which builds understanding and expand the common interest and tripartite system, the bedrock of the ILO, which provides for the democratic participation in decisions of the key social and economic actions" (ILO 26th Session, 1944, p 1). The ILO recognizes from its beginning that its mission/mandate for social justice could be constantly challenged by a variety of political and economic forces. In the current struggle for social protection for the old age population those types of challenges continue.

In 1921, twenty-two years after it was founded the organization was struggling to survive. The ongoing war was playing a major part in this struggle. The League of Nations, that the organization was part of, was no longer in operation. The ILO, did spend some time in exile in Canada, with concerns that it would lose it existence like the League of Nations "...declared that it was important to establish that the organization, and all that it stood for should play an important role in the reconstruction of the world after the war." A key player in the survival of the ILO was the President of the United States, FDR, who had supported the ILO and had helped in organizing the Conference in 1919, invited the delegates to the White House following the Convention (ILO 26 Convention, ibid, p. 2). Twenty- eight years later (1969), ILO was awarded the Nobel Peace Prize because of it mission related to peace and social justice. Yes, the social protection/social security/old age pension movement, especially in for Sub-Saharan Africa, is in great need of the ILO.

As aforementioned the Twenty-sixth Session of the International Labor Conference was convened in Philadelphia (USA), April-May, 1944. According to the Resolutions the Conference had been called for the purpose of having dialogue and developing Resolutions that would be presented to the United Nations related to post-war social policies; more specifically "… concerning the social provisions to be inscribed in the various general or special treaties or agreements to which the United Nations will jointly or severally become parties…"(ILO: Resolutions of the 26th Session, Philadelphia, 1944, 1944, p. 1). Quite obviously the 26th Session of the ILO Conference was all about European recovery following World War II, some of the recommendations provide a foundation for action that takes one beyond the Conference agenda. An example from Article III: "Opportunity for useful and regular employment to all persons who want to work, at fair wages or returns and under reasonable conditions, with provision for protection of health and against injury in all occupations (Article III, Item 1)…Provision for a regular flow of income to all those whose employment is interrupted by sickness or injury, by old-age or by lack of employment opportunity (Item 5)" (ILO: ibid, p. 3).

The Conference addressed specifically in "…the present Declaration of the aims and purpose of the International Labor Organization and of the principles which should inspire the policy of its Members;" Item III (f) "…the extension of social security measures to provide a basic income to all in need of such protection and comprehensive medical care" (ILOL ibid, p. 5).

The two examples illustrate how the mission of the International Labor Organization is compatible with the mission, goals, and objectives of those organizations that have engaged in a social and political battle to ensure social protection in old age for all. In recent decades the convening of Conferences such as the Social Security (Minimum Standards) Convention, 1952, No. 102; also the recommendations for National Floors of Social Protection, adopted during the 101st ILC Session, Geneva, 2012. The aforementioned are examples of how the ILO can be a "key player" as the world prepares for a growing older population in the 21st Century.

The Founding of the United Nations – 1945

In discussing global alerts, responses, and actions to the dramatic demographic trends in population growth, including the "Silver Tsunami," it is quite appropriate to include the United Nations. A brief history of the United Nations illustrates why it has become one of the most critical international organizations for providing global leadership in responding to a growing older population although its original mission was primarily focused on global peace keeping. The founding of the United Nations has demonstrated since the beginning of the post-war era (WWII) to be a most significant event as the world began to recognize and respond to the changing demographics of an aging society. As an international organization, the United Nations in collaboration with other global organizations has provided leadership, including research support, and technical assistance to member States as they search for insights, knowledge, and skills in responding to the demographic trends in population growth and aging.

The United Nations succeeded the League of Nations in 1945. The League of Nations had been established in 1919, following the First World War, as a global or international organization with a mission of providing a structure for member states for settling conflicts or disputes. Its primary focus had been to accomplish an "...equitable peace in Europe, but the United States was never a member (The League of Nations, 1920, Department of State, Office of the Historian, page 1). Not only was it extremely difficult to conceive, in the few years of existence was seen as ineffective. The League was the "brainchild" of President Woodrow Wilson (USA), who in his presentation of fourteen points for seeking peace in Europe, called for a "...general association of nations..."(The League of Nations, ibid, p.1).

Following the collapse of the League of Nations The United Nations was born on the 24th of October in 1945. It was in 1945 that representatives came from fifty countries, meeting in San Francisco for the purpose of creating the United Nations Charter. The Charter was completed and signed on the 26th of June 1945 by the 50 members' delegation. The country of Poland not an attendee at the original signing, did so later, resulting in 51 member states. There are currently 193 Member States with a policy and/or decision-making structure, including the General Assembly, the Security Council, the economic and Social Council. The original mission of the United Nations was the maintaining of world peace and cooperation among nations. Although originally known for it peacekeeping activities, the United Nations works globally, on a broad range of issues that "...affect our lives...The Organization works on a broad range of fundamental issues, from sustainable development, environment and refugees protection, disaster relief...to promoting democracy, human rights, gender equality...economic and social development and international health..."(United Nations, History of the United Nations, pp. 1-2).

It is the United Nations commitment to social justice and human rights that makes it relevant in the fight for social protection/social pension as a right of citizenship. It is The Universal Declaration of Human Rights providing a moral frame of reference for advocates in this struggle. It is Article 25 of the Declaration of Human Rights that articulates the basic principal. "Everyone has the right to a standard of living adequate for the health and well-being of himself and of his family, including food, clothing, housing and medical care and necessary social services, and the right to security in the event of unemployment, sickness, disability, widowhood, **old age**, or lack of livelihood in circumstances beyond **his/her** control" (The Universal Declaration of Human Rights, 1948). **Author's Note:** Article 25 requires some editing to meet the current social correct language or "political correct" language, himself/herself and of his/her family, and/or his/her control.

FIRST WORLD ASSEMBLY ON AGEING/VIENNA
AUSTRIA 26 JULY TO 6 AUGUST 1982

The United Nations General Assembly some 36 years ago (1978) recognizing that older people "…in both the developed and developing countries, will increase dramatically during the next two decades…made a decision to convene the First World Assembly on Aging in 1982" (UN A/RES/36/30, 13 Nov. 1981). Not only did the Assembly recognize the population growth factor, but also that the growing older population, represented a very valuable resource, social, cultural (transmission of diverse values and traditions), and economical. It was also recognized that the rapid growth in the aging population would present major challenges globally related to ensuring an adequate income, access to health care, social services, and safety. These challenges could have a major impact on all countries, especially the low and middle-income countries, i.e., Sub-Saharan Africa. The United Nations Fund for Population Activities provided the funding for the First Assembly.

The primary focus of the First World Assembly was to alert the world to the socio/economical/health concerns of a growing older population. A major result or accomplishment of the Assembly was the development of the first International Plan of Action on ageing. The sixty-two items of the Plan requested that specific actions be taken regarding health and nutrition, housing and environment, social welfare, income security, employment, education, as well as protecting old age consumers. The Plan called for humanitarian and developmental approaches in response to the growing older population. For current and future planning, the Assembly called for ongoing collection and analysis of research data (United Nations: Global Issues on Ageing).

The process in the adoption of the International Plan should be noted. One goal of the international bodies over the past several decades was to provide assemblies, forums, utilizing a democratic participatory model for receiving input from all member countries; the model was in place at the First Assembly in Vienna in 1982. The Plan was prepared by an Advisory Committee, and discussed and debated by the Main Committee of the Assembly where all delegations were represented. During the plenary session there was the opportunity for all delegations to provide input, especially regarding the problems and issues related to ageing in their respective countries. Finally, the Assembly adopted the International Plan of Action as amended.

The Assembly's Preamble on Aging

The Preamble to the International Plan included the following: "The countries gathered in the World Assembly on Ageing, Aware that an increasing number of their populations is ageing allow them to enjoy in mind and in body, fully and freely, their advancing years in peace, health and security; and study the impact of ageing populations o development and that of development on ageing, with a view to enabling the potential of the ageing to be fully recognized and to mitigating by appropriate measures, any negative effects resulting from this impact:

1. Do solemnly reaffirm their belief that the fundamental and I alienable rights enshrined in the Universal Declaration of Human Rights apply fully and undiminished to the ageing; and

2. Do solemnly recognize that quality of life is no less important than longevity, and that the ageing should therefore, as far as possible, be enabled to enjoy their own families and communities a life of fulfillment, health, security and contentment, appreciated as an integral part of society.

(The Main Committee Report, World Assembly on Ageing, Australian Journal on Ageing-Wiley Online Library, 2008, pp. 2-3).

Principles Adopted by the First World Assembly on Aging: Human Rights and Social Justice for a Growing Older Population

The formulation and implementation of policies on ageing is the sovereign right and responsibility of each State, to be carried out on the basis of its specific national needs and objectives. However, the promotion of the activities, safety and wellbeing of the elderly should be an essential part of an integrated and concerted development effort within the framework of the new international economic order in both the developed and the developing parts of the world. International and regional cooperation should, however, play an important role.

The aim of development is to improve the wellbeing of the entire population on the basis of its full participation in the process of development and an equitable distribution of the benefits therefrom. The development process must enhance human dignity and ensure equity among age groups in the sharing of society's resources, rights and responsibilities.

Individuals, regardless of age, sex or creed should contribute according to their abilities ..." (Report of Main Committee, World Assembly on Aging, ibid, pp. 2-3).

THE UNITED NATIONS GENERAL ASSEMBLY RESOLUTION 46/9 FOR OLDER PERSONS: SOCIAL JUSTICE AND HUMAN RIGHTS

Approximately one decade from the convening of the First World Assembly on Aging, the United Nations General Assembly presented to the world its principles for older persons. The adoption of the Principles for older persons were preceded by resolution 45/106 in 1990 when the United Nations General Assembly designated the 1st of October as the **International Day of Older Persons.** The initiative to establish an International Day of Older Persons in 1990 confirmed the earlier commitments ensuring the rights of older people to live a life of dignity.

The General Assembly in the adoption of basic principles for older persons recognized the contributions that older people had made and continue to make to their respective communities and to society. The General Assembly called attention to the Charter of the United Nations, "...the peoples of the United Nations declare...their determination to reaffirm faith in the fundamental human rights, in the dignity and worth of the human person, in the equal rights of men and women and of nations large and small and to promote social progress and better standards of life in larger freedom…"(UN General Assembly, A/RES/46/91, 74th Plenary Meeting, 16 December 1991).

The General Assembly in its resolution strongly encouraged Governments to include the principles related to Independence, Participation, Care, Self-fulfillment, and Dignity, within all of their national programs. For example, in regards to **Independence**, older persons should have access to the basic necessities of life, food, water, shelter, clothing, and health care; these items could come through the provision of income, family, community support and self-help. In reference to the aforementioned, the recommendation is not explicit enough. The current thinking is, in reference to income, every older person should be guaranteed an adequate income, such as a social pension.

A commitment to a guaranteed income or at least a basic income is extremely important for countries in Sub-Saharan Africa where less that 20% of the population will not have a social pension at the time of retirement. It would seem appropriate that globally, especially international organizations, as an action plan would commit to ensuring that the older people in Africa would be guaranteed income protection following retirement. One would expect that the leading advocates for such an action plan would come from those European countries, such as England, Belgium, Spain, and France who benefitted from the natural resources from Africa in the development of their economic empires. This era of colonization in Africa, including years of forced labor, contributed significantly to the underdevelopment of Africa.

In regards to **Participation**, the recommendation is that older person should have the opportunity "…to participate actively in the formulation and implementation of policies that directly affect their well-being, and share their knowledge and skills with younger generations" (UN General Assembly, A/RES/1491, ibid).

Another principle had to do with systems of **Care** for the growing older population. According to the resolution, "…Older persons should benefit from family and community care and protection in accordance with each society's system of cultural values" (A/RES/1491, ibid). Specifically, older persons should have access to health care as well as social services, including legal. Legal services will be become vital for "…enhance their autonomy, protection and care. Although it does not say so explicitly, with a growing older population care has to include a variety of long-term care services which could become quite a challenge for the health care system, and the policy commitments to support such services.

The final two principles focus on **Self-fulfillment and Dignity;** Self-fulfillment refers to older persons having the opportunities, including the resources, educational, cultural, spiritual, and recreational, that will allow them to reach their potential. Finally, the resolution has high hopes that the older person, especially if the previous principles become a reality will have the opportunity, "… to live in dignity and security and be free of exploitation and physical or mental abuse" (A/RES/1491, ibid, pp. 4-5).

INTERNATIONAL CONFERENCE POPULATION AND DEVELOPMENT (ICPD)/CAIRO, EGYPT, 5 SEPTEMBER TO 13 SEPTEMBER 1994

Twelve years after the First World Assembly on Aging in 1982, and preceding by eight years the Second World Assembly on Aging in 2002, the ICPD convened in Cairo, Egypt. Considering the fact that declines in fertility and mortality were having an influence on population growth, the Conference, especially its agenda related to reproductive rights, social justice and women's human rights became a significant global event. Some of the major themes emanating from the Conference centered on the accessibility of reproductive and sexual education, including family planning, maternal and child health services; accessibility of primary and secondary education for girls and women globally; and globally, the reduction of infant, child, as well as maternal mortality. The Conference including some 20,000 delegates representing countries/regions from around the World resulted in a Plan of Action that included fourteen Principles. Such a global Conference, population and development, with an agenda emphasizing reproductive rights, could not avoid some controversy. There was opposition to the Conference from segments of the Islamic community, and political conservatives in the United States, expressed strong opposition to then President William Clinton attending and participating. One major issue that fueled debate before and following the Conference had to do with the subject of reproductive rights. The topic within the context of reproductive rights that seemed to generate discussions, debates, and controversy was the concept abortion. For some delegates reproduction rights implied the right for woman to have an abortion. But, there was no reference in the Conference Proceedings, Principles, or Plan of Action, implying that the right to abortion should be part of reproductive rights, including family planning education and services.

Summary of Selective ICPD Conference Principles

The ICPD Conference produced or enacted fifteen Principles. Principle #1 was a declaration that globally "…all human beings, are born free and equal in dignity and rights and freedoms set forth in Universal Declaration of Human Rights, without distinction of any kind, such as race, color, sex, language, religion, political or other opinion, national or social origin, property, birth of other status. Everyone has the right to life, liberty, and security of person" (Report of the ICPD, 94/10/18, pages 14 - 17).

In Principle #4, the delegates became more specific in regards to women; "…ensuring women's ability to control their own fertility, are cornerstones of population and development… the human rights of women and the girl are an inalienable, integral and indivisible part of universal human rights" (Report of the ICPD, ibid).

The responsibility of Countries/States, globally, in ensuring that the aforementioned human rights are addressed in Principle #8. It was the consensus of delegates at the ICPD Conference that "States should take all appropriate measures to ensure, on a basis of equality of men and women, universal access to health care services, including those related to reproductive health care, which includes family planning and sexual health…Reproductive health care programs should provide the widest range of services without any form of coercion. All couples and individuals have the right to decide freely and responsibly the number and spacing of their children and to have the information, education and means to do so" (Report of the ICPD, ibid).

The ICPD delegates in Principle #9 explicitly stated, "The family is the basic unit of society and as such should be strengthened. It is entitled to receive comprehensive protection and support" (Report of the ICPD, ibid).

In Principle #15, the Conference concluded that "Sustained economic growth, in the context of sustainable development and social progress require that growth be broadly based, offering equal opportunities to all people (Report of the ICPD, ibid, pages 14 -17).

A Program of Action and Member States Commitment

The ICPD concluded its Conference in 1994 with a plan of action, including goals and objectives to be implemented by delegates and/or all member States. The delegates representing some 179 global governments agreed to a 20 Year Program and Action Plan that hopefully would result in improving the quality of life for all. All member governments at the Cairo Conference made a commitment to implement the Plan. Furthermore, they made a commitment to reaffirm this commitment over the next twenty years (UN: FPA. Org., ICPD Beyond 2014, Population and Development: The 5 Pillar Breakdowns 2012, New York, N.Y.).

There is documentation that the member states, over the past twenty years have followed through on their commitments. One example of reaffirmation by member States was the African Regional Conference (Representing 53 African Countries) on Population and Development that convened in Addis Ababa, Ethiopia in 2013. The purpose of the gathering was to review the progress of the African Regional Conference on the ICPD Beyond 2014. Furthermore, to reaffirm the African Union Commission commitment "...periodically review the outcomes of the African Regional Conference on ICPD beyond 2014" (UN: Economic Commission for Africa, African Union Commission, African Regional Conference on Population and Development, Addis Ababa, Ethiopia, 3-4 October 2013).

Anne C Richards, The United States Secretary of State, at a Special Session of the United Nations to reaffirm support for the ICPD agenda adopted at the Cairo Conference, "Mr. President it is an honor to speak on behalf of the United States, and to join other member States, United Nations Agencies and Civil Society, in renewing our full support for the ICPD Program of Action first adopted nearly 20 years ago..." (UN: Special Session on the ICPD Beyond 2014, September 22, 2014, New York, NY).

THE SECOND WORLD ASSEMBLY ON AGEING/ MADRID, SPAIN 8 APRIL TO 12 APRIL 2002

The Second World Assembly convened twenty-years following the First Assembly that had taken place in Vienna, Austria in 1982. The major goal of the second was to evaluate the successes and/or failures of the International Plan of Action adopted at the First Assembly. A key program factor during the Second Assembly was the role to be played by Non-Governmental Organizations (NGO's). Observer status was granted to the NGO's representing States throughout the world, including international NGO's.

The Second Assembly provided a Forum for the NGO's that convened over six days during the Assembly. The Forum was an opportunity for the NGO's to meet, interact, "…exchange global ideas and experiences, highlight their role in advocacy and awareness-raising, and discuss ways to put the strategy into effect."

(UN: Jenni Nana, Ministry of Social Development), (UN: Global Action on Ageing), (UN: Department of Public Information, DPI/2264, March 2002)

In addition to the assessment of progress that had been made by States during the past twenty-years, the Second Assembly's proposal included the adoption of a Political Declaration as well as an International Plan of Action on Ageing. The overall goal was to have member States to agree/confirm an international commitment to accept and respond to the challenges and opportunities confronting a growing older population; furthermore, "…to accept a moral obligation to strive for agreed objectives.

Another significant element of the Second World Assembly was the plenary sessions. These sessions not only provided an opportunity for member states, including the NGO's to exchange ideas, but out of the presentations various themes emerged. These discussions allowed for representatives to address particular concerns/issues/challenges facing the "silver tsunami" in their respective States. For example, an occurring theme and/or issue for Africa, and some of the other developing countries, the impact HIV/AIDS was having on the older population. Not only was the concern regarding the number of persons who had and continue to die, especially at a younger age, but the increasing role of older people in caring for the children left behind by the victims (Grandparents Raising Grandchildren).

Although the primary goal of the Second World Assembly was to finalize an International Plan of Action, some of the major actions from the 1982 Plan was brought forward. Some of the 1982 actions included and/or expanded on were:

1. The debit relief and other financial mechanisms put forward to address population ageing in developing countries.
2. A global approach to ageing and development guided by a commitment to Human Rights
3. Designed options for an ageing labor force, including the rights to pensions and/or Social protection
4. Older persons access to health care, including care services. (UN: SWAA 2002/PRKIT)

The 2002 Plan focused on changes in attitudes in State and International policies. Also, the Plan called for attitudinal changes in communities, corporate structures, as well as organizational missions/goals and practices to ensure that the overall potential of ageing is fulfilled. More specifically some of the goals (selective with paraphrasing by author) include:

1. The reaffirmation of the goal of eradicating poverty in old age.
2. Empowerment of older persons to participate fully and effectively in all forms of decision-making, social, economic, and political processes of their societies.

3. The providing of provisions of opportunities that will allow for individual development, self-fulfillment, and wellbeing.
4. The guaranteeing of economic, social and cultural rights of older people, civil and Political.
5. A commitment to gender equality; the elimination of gender-based discrimination.
6. The recognition of the importance of inter-generational interdependency solidarity and reciprocity for social development.
7. The access to health-care and care supports for older people.
8. Private sector, non-governmental organizations, and the full participation of older.
9. The facilitation/harnessing of scientific research and expertise (scholars and human services practitioners, to focus on the individual, social and health implications of ageing. (UN: DPI/2264, March 2002)

UN: ECONOMIC COMMUNITY FOR EUROPE MINISTERIAL CONFERENCE, ENSURING A SOCIETY FOR ALL AGES, SEPTEMBER 18-20, 2012, VIENNA, AUSTRIA

Approximately thirty years, or three decades following the First Assembly on Ageing, and approximately one decade from the convening of the Second World Assembly in Madrid, Spain in 2002, the Ministerial Conference convened in Vienna, Austria in 2012. The Conference theme, "Ensuring a Society for All Ages." The major focus of the Conference was the promotion of quality of life for older persons and active ageing. The 2012 Conference was to build on concepts/themes established during the First and Second Assemblies, as well as the United Nations Principles for Older Persons in 1991. The First Assembly addressed the strengths possessed by the growing older population and suggested that the global society could benefit from the dividends. The First Assembly recognized, "...ageing represented a very valuable resource social/economical as well as the transmission of cultural heritage..." especially from an intergenerational perspective.

In 1991, The General Assembly adopted the United Nations Principles for older persons, including the principle on active participation. The older persons in society should have the opportunity, "... share their knowledge and skills with younger generations." During the Second World Assembly, the major theme continues, "Building a Society for All Ages." The Plan of Action recommendations included, "Empowerment of older persons to participate fully and effectively in the social, economic and political lives of their societies." A major focus was on the high level of importance related to intergenerational solidarity, and reciprocity regarding social development for all.

Although the World Assemblies focused on a number of issues, concerns, challenges, one of the common threads linking them all was on active ageing. The 2012 Conference paid tribute in marking the 30th Anniversary of the First World Conference in 1982. A major part of its agenda was "...review progress in implementing the Madrid International Plan of Action on Ageing...and its Regional Implementation Strategy (RIS), both adopted in 2002, and define the post-2012 agenda on ageing" (United Nations Social Development Network, Posted by UNSDN September 19, 2012, p. 1).

Those taking part in the 3 day discussions, debates, decision-making, included some 450 participants, Ministers, Deputy Ministers or State Secretaries, officials from UNECE member States; also, the participants included European as well as international organization, the scientific or scientists community, older persons, and representatives from non-governmental organizations (UNSDN, ibid, p. 1).

Discussion topics included the promotion of longer working lives and how to maintain work ability, non-discrimination and social inclusion of older persons, creating an enabling environment for older persons to grow to their maximum capacity. The outcomes or declarations, or the final "…document shall highlight the future priorities for the Third Implementation of the Madrid International Plan of Action on Ageing and it Regional implementation Strategy 2013 – 2017" (UNSDN, ibid, p. 1).

The 2012 Conference worked in partnership with the 2012 European Year for "Active Ageing and Solidarity between Generations." The Conference as well as all of the activities related to the year for active ageing and solidarity between generations, seems to highlight the fact that solidarity between generations provided opportunities for significant future dividends. The focus, it seems, for UNECE, has been, "…encouraging member states to exchange experiences on good practices and to agree on new and promising strategies and approaches" (UNSDN, ibid, p.1).

The 2012 Ministerial Declaration, "Ensuring a society for all ages: promoting quality of life and active ageing" expressed determination to reach by the year 2017 the following policy goals:

1. Longer working life is encouraged and ability to work is maintained (6 methods/activities are included for reaching this goal);
2. Participation, non-discrimination and social inclusion of older persons are promoted (10 methods/activities are included for reaching this goal);
3. Dignity, health and independence in older age are promoted and safeguarded (13 methods/activities are included for reaching this goal);
4. Intergenerational solidarity is maintained and enhanced (6 methods/activities Included for reaching this goal);

(UN: Economic Commission for Europe, Working Group on Ageing, Ministerial Conference on Ageing, ECE/AC.30/2012/3, Vienna, 19 and 20 September 2012, pp. 1-6).

AGEING IN THE TWENTY-FIRST CENTURY: A CELEBRATION AND A CHALLENGE - 2012

The United Nations Population Fund in collaboration with Help Age International published in 2012 what is being described by one gerontologists as a landmark document, Ageing in the 21st Century: A Celebration and Challenge. "A landmark document by Help Age and the United Nations paves a way forward for human rights for older persons" (Hokenstad,

M. C., Roberts, Amy R., "The United Nations Plans for a Future Free of Ageism and Elder Invisibility," Journal of the American Society on Aging, Vol. 7, No. 1, Spring 2013, p. 76).

The importance of the document is highlighted by the fact that the research, analysis and final publication were a three-year process. The two organizations, the United Nations Population Fund, and Help Age International (Non-governmental organization) began the process by developing "...and overview of available policies and legislation, data and research, and institutional arrangements relating to older persons...This report is the product of a collaboration of over twenty United Nations entities and major international organizations working in the area of population ageing" (Ageing in the Twenty-First Century: A Celebration and Challenge, 2012, p. 11).

Ageing in the 21st Century focuses on several critical areas, such as an evaluative process that takes a look at the current state of affairs, plight or quality of life of older persons globally. A second focus was to assess the policies, as well as actions that have been initiated and/ or implemented by government entities and other stakeholders following the Second World Assembly on Ageing. The critical analysis was focused on the success and/or lack of the implementation of the International Plan of Action on Ageing that was adopted at the Second World Assembly. A very important component of the overall analysis is the identification of the gaps, or lack of progress or success in reaching desired goals. In regards to the aforementioned the document provides very explicit recommendations for ensuring or enhancing the quality of life for older persons (Ageing in the 21st Century...ibid, 2012, p. 12).

A great deal of credit has to be given to the collaborative team for including in the process, the voices or input from the older population. So often in data collection and analysis, the voices or input of those who are the victims of the problems are not normally heard from. The UN: ECE Conference had as its overall theme "Active Ageing." The theme advocates for the inclusion of the older population globally in all forms of decision-making affecting their lives. Also, in Chapter I, reference is made to the "Silver Tsunami" as a growing number of older persons who can bring to the process of decision-making years of experience, knowledge and skills, including a value foundation related to social justice and human rights.

Ageing in the Twenty-First Century identified several major concerns that were most expressed from the older population, globally. The number one concern of this population had to do with a lack of income security. In reference to income security the fact that less than twenty percent of retired older persons in Sub-Saharan Africa lack basic income security, or no pension at the time of retirement. A major goal of any post-2015 Millennium goals has to focus on encouraging countries to invest in the older population; research has shown that investments in older persons not only reduce the level of poverty for this population, it also represents an investment in the socialization of children, their growth and development (Ageing in the 21st Century, ibid, 2012)

Another concern that was expressed focused on a lack of access to affordable quality health care, including long-term care. As life expectancy increases, older persons will be greatly impacted by the transition to chronic illnesses, such as Alzheimer's and dementia. Ageing in the 21st Century in response to health concerns is recommending "...preventive, curative and long-term care" (Ageing in the 21st Century, ibid, p. 14). A very important recommendation from the document has to do with "Training of caregivers and health professionals to ensure that those who work with older persons have access to information and basic training in the care of older people. Better support must be provided to all caregivers, including family members, community based {caretakers}, particularly for long-term care for frail older persons, and older people who care for others" (Ageing in the 21st Century, ibid, p. 14).

The document strongly recommends that enabling environments become a top priority, especially eliminating all forms of abuse and violence directed towards older persons. A key recommendation in this area relates to the promotion "...development and use of innovative technologies that encourage active aging...especially important as people grow older and experience diminished mobility and visual and hearing impairments. Affordable housing and easily accessible transportation that encourage aging in place are essential to maintain independence, facilitate social contacts and permit older persons to remain active members of society" (Ageing in the 21st Century, ibid, p. 14).

Ageing in the twenty-first Century is recommending ten top priority actions that would ensure that older persons will be able to live in dignity with adequate or basic income supports, affordable access to health and social support systems, and enabling environments. In summary they are: (1) Recognize the inevitability of population ageing and the need to adequately prepare all stakeholders (government; civil society, private sector, communities, and families for the growing number of older persons; (2) Ensure that all older persons can live with dignity and security, enjoying access to essential health and social services and a minimum income through the implementation of national social protection floors; (3) Support communities and families to develop support systems which ensure that frail older persons receive the long-term care they need and promote active and healthy ageing at the local level to facilitate ageing in place; (4) Invest in young people today by promoting healthy habits, and ensuring education and employment opportunities, access to social security coverage for all workers as the best investment to improve the lives of future generations of older persons; (5) Support international and national efforts to develop comparative research on ageing, and ensure that gender-and culture-sensitive data and evidence from the research are available to inform policy makers; (6) Mainstream ageing into all gender policies and gender into ageing policies, taking into account the specific requirements of older women and men; (7) Ensure inclusion of ageing and the needs of older persons in all national development policies and programs; (8) Ensure that ageing issues are adequately reflected in the post-2015 development agenda, including through the development of specific goals and indicators; (9) Ensure inclusion of ageing and the needs of older persons in national humanitarian response, climate change mitigation and adaptation plans, and disaster management and preparedness programs; (10) Develop a new rights–based culture of ageing and a change of mindset and societal attitudes towards ageing and older persons, from welfare recipients to active, contributing members of society. This requires, among others, working towards the development of international human rights instruments and their translation into national laws and regulations and affirmative measures that challenge age discrimination and recognize older people as autonomous subjects (Ten priority actions to maximize the opportunity of ageing populations, Ageing in the Twenty-First Century, p.15).

UNITED NATIONS MILLENNIUM DEVELOPMENT GOALS: 2000-2015

A major and most significant policy activity by global leadership in recent years was the development of the United Nations, <u>Millennium Development Goals: 2000 to 2015.</u> The United Nations and the Member countries agreed on MDG goals approximately one decade ago. Also as part of the democratic process, organizations (private sector, non-governmental), including leaders representing social development institutions were part of the consensus agreement.

The MDGs included eight (8) goals that were scheduled to reach their final outcomes by the year 2015:

1. Eradicate extreme poverty and hunger
2. Achieve universal primary education
3. Promote gender equality and empower women
4. Reduce child mortality
5. Improve maternal health
6. Combat HIV/AIDS, malaria and other diseases
7. Ensure environmental sustainability
8. Develop a global partnership for development

(United Nations Millennium Declaration A/55/L.2)

The MDG goals included measurable outcomes related to specific targets (who will be doing what, by when, how much, how measured). Although the target date has been established for 2015, progress/achievements are being reported annually in the form of, <u>Millennium Development Goals Report (Year).</u> An example is the <u>Millennium Goals Development Report 2012.</u> The 2012 Report highlights progress and/or no progress in each of the eight areas:

1. Extreme poverty – The 2012 Report shared that the poverty rates for people living in extreme poverty were reduced (not reached) in both developing and developed countries, especial Sub-Saharan Africa. The number of people living on less than $1.25 day dropped from (47%) percent in 1990 to twenty-four (24%) percent in 2008. (UN: The Millennium Development Report 2012)
2. Primary Education – As of 2012 there have been a significant increase in the number of children enrolled in primary education since 2000. Significant progress was reported between the enrollment ratio of girls and boys in primary education for all developing regions.
3. Gender Equality and Women Empowerment – Gender inequality has shown little progress. Women, continue to confront problems related to access to education, work and economic assets, as well as participation in government.
4. Maternal Health – Although some progress has been made in maternal and child health, the reduction in maternal deaths continues to lag behind. The use of contraceptive methods has shown little progress since 2000.

5. Child Mortality - Some significant progress has been shown in the reduction of under-five deaths worldwide, especially in the developing countries. In Sub-Saharan Africa that historically has reported high rates in under-five deaths the reduction rates have doubled.

6. HIV/AIDS and other diseases – Although there had been significant progress of persons receiving the antiretroviral therapy for HIV in the developing countries, the 2010 target of universal access was not yet reached. T.B. rates have been falling significantly since 2002. The projections are that the 1990 death rate from tuberculosis will be statistically cut in half by the year 2015. Malaria has decreased significantly globally, including malaria-specific mortality rates.

7. Environmental Sustainability – Although some progress has been made, approximately half of the population in developing countries still do not have adequate access to improved sanitation conditions. The number of people living in slums continue to grow, from a base of approximately 650 million in 1990 to 863 million presently.

8. Global partnership for development – "The MDG goals have been a fundamental framework for global development. A clear agenda, with measurable goals and targets, and a common vision have been crucial for this success…There is now an expectation around the world that sooner, rather than later, all these goals can and must be achieved…" (Zukang, Sha, Under-Secretary-General for Economic and Social Affairs, UN: Millennium Development Report 2012).

A review of the 2014 Report indicates that extreme poverty globally had decreased by half; although not quite reached in 2014, there have been significant results in the fight against malaria and TB; significant progress has also been made in improving the quality of water for some 2.3 billion people; there has also been success in closing the gap and/or disparities in primary school attendance between boys and girls; one could also add that women's participation in the political process has significantly improved; some success in reducing threats to environmental sustainability have seen progress; although hunger and chronic nutrition haves declined, approximately one in four children need assistance in this area and continuous work is needed; one good sign of progress was that child mortality had dropped by 50% between 1990 and 2013.

The general consensus is "Much has been accomplished through the concerted efforts of all, saving and improving the lives of many people, but the agenda remains unfinished. The post-2015 development agenda is slated to carry on the work of the MDGs and integrate the social, economic and environmental dimensions of sustainable development" (Hongbo, Wu, Under-Secretary-General for Economic and Social Affairs, UN: Millennium Development Report 2014, pages 8-9).

As seen in the 2012 and the 2014 Reports significant progress had been made in some areas but additional work, some areas more so than others, need to be done by the 2015 deadline. According to one UN representative "The Millennium Goals (MDGs) 2012 have been the most successful global anti-poverty push in history…" (UN: Ban Ki-moon, Secretary-General, United Nations, The MDG Report, 2014).

A Social/Civic Pension For All

Although the 2015 Millennium Development Goals (MDGs) could be considered an excellent global planning document, especially for the developing world, a major problem area had been overlooked and excluded from the discussion. The missing component was an explicit goal with measurable objectives/outcomes focused on reducing the number or percentage of older persons globally without a social pension following retirement. As aforementioned in Chapter I, in Sub-Saharan Africa approximately 82.5% of the older population does not have a social pension at the time of retirement. Considering the fact that so many older persons, globally, are living in poverty, and so many, especially in Sub-Saharan Africa without a social pension, it would have been appropriate to include the aforementioned as part of the Millennium Development Goals. In other words, the addition of an Area related to a social pension for all in accordance with the United Nations Declaration of Human Rights would have been quite appropriate for inclusion as part of the MDG goals 2015.

UN/TRANSFORMING OUR WORLD: THE 2030 AGENDA FOR SUSTAINABLE DEVELOPMENT, GENERAL ASSEMBLY (70TH SESSION) SEPTEMBER 25, 2015

United Nations Sustainable Development Goals 2020-2030

As indicated in the conclusion of the 2014 Progress Report the post-2015 agenda is expected to complete the original task set out some fifteen years ago; the 2030 agenda is now ready for action. Although additional goals have been added to the 2030 agenda it should be noted that there is still no explicit goal related to old age social protection/social security. Although omitted from the 2030 Agenda, the subject of social protection for the growing older population was addressed in the recent published document, Ageing in the Twenty-First Century: A Celebration and a Challenge.

Fifteen years ago the leadership of the United Nations, including 189 countries convened to explore some of the problems confronting the world. At that time they expressed concern about continuous famines, droughts, wars, plaques, and poverty that were having a significant impact on the lives of people. It was from this dialogue that the decision was made to develop an action plan consisting of eight goals to be implemented and completed by the year 2015, Millennium Development Goals. The UNDP has concluded that although there has been progress in most of the eight areas, there is still work to be done. Therefore the UNDP has committed to continuing the work that began during the year 2000.

The United Nations General Assembly adopted a Resolution during its 70th Session put forward the theme, Transforming Our World: the 2030 Agenda for Sustainable Development. The Resolution identified seventeen (17) Sustainable Development Goals focused on 169 targets; referred to as the new universal agenda. The Preamble: "The agenda is a plan of action for people, planet, and prosperity. All countries are stakeholders acting in collaborative partnership will implement the plan" (UN General Assembly, 70th Session (A/Res/70/10, 21 October 2015, p. 1).

Goal one (1) is a commitment to end extreme poverty, globally in all forms by the year 2030; (2) to see zero (0) hunger by 2030; (3) goal three calls for good health and well being. It is more implicit than explicit or specific details lacking; (4) the fourth goal focus on quality education. In past years very little progress in this area, for the poorest households globally children are four times more likely to leave school before completing basic education requirements; (5) gender equality is the focus of goal five; progress made doing the MDG timeline, girls and women continue to lag behind; (6) clean water and sanitation for everyone by 2030; (7) affordable and clean energy by the year 2030; (8) decent work and economic growth is the focus for goal 8. There is a need for a very explicit goal and measurable outcomes for this very important area. There is a very strong correlation between decent jobs, social protection and/or social security for workers; (9) industry, innovation and infrastructure are key features of goal nine; (10) reduced inequalities for goal 10; (11) sustainable cities and communities, a great challenge considering that more than half of the global population now live in cities and two/thirds by the year 2050; (12) responsible consumption and production; (13) climate actions a major challenge; (14) Life below water or the use of the oceans, and sea resources for sustainable development; (15) life on land, halting biodiversity losses; (16) peace and justice; and (17) global partnerships for sustainable development (UN: General Assembly, 70th Session, ibid).

The Exclusion of a Social/Civic Pension for the Older Population

For the United Nations and all of the member countries, the 2030 agenda is a very ambitious undertaking. Once again a key goal has been omitted, social protection for the older population. Goal five (5) calls for good health and wellbeing can be considered a mission or goal, but it lacks measurable objectives (outcome measures), as well as methods for achieving the objectives. The document Ageing in the twenty-first century in discussing health and well being, especially for the older population, is a little more explicit. "In order to realize their right to enjoy the highest attainable standard of physical and mental health, older persons must have access to age-friendly and affordable health care information and services that meet their needs. This includes preventive, curative and long-term care. A life course perspective should include health promotion and disease prevention activities that focus on maintaining independence, preventing and delaying diseases and disability, and providing treatment. Policies are needed to promote healthy lifestyles, assistive technology, medical research and rehabilitative care. Training of caregivers and health professionals is essential to ensure that those who work with older persons have access to the information and basic training in the care of older people. Better support must be provided to all caregivers, including family members, community based {caretakers}, particularly for long-term care for frail older persons, and older people who care for others" (UN: Population Fund/Help Age International, Ageing in the Twenty-First Century: A Celebration and A Challenge, 2014, p. 14).

In Sub-Saharan Africa less than twenty (20%) or more specifically only 16.9 percent of the older population receives a basic pension, or a minimum income in old age or at the time of retirement. Despite global assemblies and conferences resulting in declarations expounding on the rights of older persons to live in dignity, the percentages remain constant. Current data indicates little hope for the next generation of older persons. The special needs, especially an income, continue to be ignored. The Millennium Development Goals 2015 did not address the issue; the 2030 Sustainable Development Goals focusing on Sustainable Development did not include among the seventeen (17) goals explicit language related to social protection, especially income security or social pensions in old age.

Although most of the attention reference social protection has focused on the informal entrepreneurs in countries such as Sub-Saharan Africa, some global concerns in countries such as Great Britain are beginning to surface. With a growing older population, increasing life expectancy, and dramatic changes in dependency ratios, the self-employed in countries such as Great Britain, maybe facing similar concerns related to social protection following retirement. For example, the dramatic increase in the self-employed population has begun to raise questions regarding the availability of pensions/social protection following retirement; it is estimated that approximately 4.5 million individuals, in the United Kingdom, an increase of 1.5 million in the past thirteen years. A significant number of the self-employed are engaged in low-income jobs that result in many not paying into any form of a pension. It has been reported that globally only about one in ten self-employed individuals are making regular contributions to a pension fund. The reason given is can't afford it. The issue of lack of social protection in old age is becoming more of a global issue beyond Sub Saharan Africa, even among the middle and high-income countries (Collinson, Patrick, "British Workers will have Worst Pension of any Economy and the Oldest," Guardian, 12/1/2015). (**NOTE: See Chapter II Section 2, "Retirement and Pensions" for discussion on Pensions in the United Kingdom**).

Three in ten workers worldwide are now self-employed. Approximately eighteen percent of self-employed of adults worldwide represent twenty-nine percent of the global workforce. The estimation is that the global self-employed workforce are about three times as those who are employed full-time by a company and/or employer to be living on less than $2.00 p/day, and that amount borders on extreme poverty (Ryan, Ben, "Nearly Three in Ten Workers Worldwide Self-Employed," Gallup Daily, World, 8/22/2014; The Pew Research Center (USA), "Social and Demographic Trends," 10/22/2015).

SELECTIVE HISTORICAL DECLARATIONS IN RESPONSE TO THE GROWING OLDER POPULATION, THE "SILVER TSUNAMI"

There have been some very significant Declarations issued by some of the International Organizations in responding to a growing older population. At the time of adoption of these Declarations there was the hope that they would eventually become fully implemented. The goal of the Declarations is that they will create awareness of the plight of the growing older population, especially their special needs: income security, access to health and social services, as well as a safe environment. Furthermore, the days of observance could present a great opportunity for mobilizing around the issues affecting the older population, and planning for action.

The United Nations Declaration of International Day of Older persons (UN: Resolution 45/106, December 14, 1990).

The United Nations Adoption of Principles for Older People: (UN: Resolution 46/91).

The United Nations Declaration of World Day for Social Justice/ Human Rights 1948

The International Labor Organization (ILO) Call for Gender Protection in Social Security and the Establishment of Social Protection Floors for Older People: (ILO Social Protection Floors, No. 202, 2012)

The International Social Security Association Declaration that Social Security is a fundamental right, "...there can be no social justice without social security" (sustainable and effective social security)

The Founding of Help Age International, Non-governmental Advocacy Agency on Behalf of Older Person Globally

NOTE: There is no Declaration calling for the development of goals, objectives, and implementation strategies and tactics, for increasing the number of older persons globally with a social pension. Such a specific Declaration did not emerge from any of the World Assemblies, including the International Plan of Action, or the 2015 and the 2030 Millennium Development Goals. On a positive note The United Nations has agreed to work closely with international organizations such as Help Age International in addressing the needs of a growing older population during future General Assembly Sessions.

SUMMARY AND CONCLUSION

More than three decades ago, international organizations, such as the United Nations, concluded that it was time for working together proactively as a team in responding to the growing older population, or the "Silver Tsunami." Over the years, there have been global assemblies providing a forum for countries and their delegates to come together for discussions, debates, resulting in preambles, new and revised concepts, principles and/or action plans focused on how to appropriately respond to this population growth phenomenon. International organizations, such as the World Bank, the International Labor Organization, International Social Security Administration, non-governmental organizations (Help Age International), have provided research and technical assistance to countries as they struggled with ways to develop a plan of action. Despite all of the world assemblies and forums more than half of the older population globally will retire from their years in the workforce without basic income security; in Sub-Saharan Africa approximately 80% will not be privy to such income.

The United Nations during the past decade introduced two major plans of action (Minimum Development Goals 2015 and Sustainable Development Goals 2020) for enhancing the overall quality of life for most age groups. The Goals included problem/goal statements, measurable objectives, and implementation and evaluative strategies. The problem of a lack of social pensions and/or social protection for the current and future populations of older persons were was not explicitly or implicitly included among the plans for countries to follow. More than half of the global population of older persons currently does not have basic social security income at the time of retirement; in Sub-Saharan Africa, less than 20%, more specifically 16.9% of older persons will have basic income security at the time of retirement.

There are possibilities for global actions that may draw attention to the plight of the growing older population. For several years now there has been a global movement, Age Demand Campaign, calling attention to the plight, including social pensions, issues of social justice and human rights for older persons globally. The campaign has been organized by non-governmental organizations, specifically Help Age International. A major spokesperson for the movement has been Bishop Desmond Tutu of South Africa, an international leader for social justice and human rights. The movement continues to call on the United Nations to convene a special session for addressing the plight of older persons globally. The Age Demand Campaign had an opportunity for some action items to be addressed during the month of July 2017 when the Eight Open Ended Working Group (OEWG) convenes at the United Nations in New York, USA. The major agenda items for the group will be focused on: "…Rights to non-discrimination and equality and to freedom from violence, abuse and neglect" (Jaskiran K. Marway, Campaign and Communication Administrator, Help Age International, "Older People Take the Fight for their Rights to the United Nations!" (Help Age Global Network, campaign@helpage.org, July/5/2017). Hopefully, the OEWG will add explicit language to the agenda items, especially related to social protection in general, but specifically social pensions or basic income security, access to health care, including long-term care.

Globally, the time is now for ensuring that the older population will have income security, access to health and social care, including long-term care for living out final years in a state of dignity and respect. From lessons learned from countries such as Botswana, Liberia, Namibia, Swaziland, Kenya including low to middle income countries, a social pension for those who have worked outside of the traditional tripartite collective bargaining system, a social pension is affordable and achievable. Not only is it affordable there is evidence to illustrate that a social pension contributes to a reduction in poverty, unemployment as well as social and economic development.

CHAPTER IV

SOCIAL WELFARE PROTECTION PRACTICES IN TRADITIONAL AFRICAN SOCIETIES: IMPLICATIONS FOR THE "SILVER TSUNAMI"

INTRODUCTION

What global scholars, political and civic leaders are referring too as a world demographic population explosion across all age groups, including the "Silver Tsunami," will have a significant societal impact especially in the developing countries such as in Sub-Saharan Africa. The developed world and/or the countries labeled as OECD such as the United States, Germany, France, United Kingdom and Japan will be affected as well **(OECD history and mission, See Appendix B: Definitions, Concepts and Special Notes)**. It is anticipated that Sub-Saharan African countries will become part of the global preparation in responding to the unprecedented demographic trends occurring including the growing older population. In responding to this global demographic phenomenon countries in Sub-Saharan Africa will be confronted with some of the greatest challenges since the era of the "Scramble for Africa" followed by years of colonization. The era of colonization on the continent, approximately three quarters of a century, included all forms of social injustices such as taking over and controlling the continent's land resources, the separation of families and/or tribal groupings and the use of forced labor which contributed significantly to overall underdevelopment across the continent of Africa.

Sub-Saharan Africa currently is also witnessing not just a growing older population, the "Silver Tsunami," also the demographic phenomenon being referred to as the "youth bulge" generation, an increasing number of youth throughout the continent. Both demographic trends will require much attention and astute decision making from a variety of societal systems. The key systems as aforementioned include the family, educational, economical, medical, health, social and political. The overall goal for Sub-Saharan Africa should be to become proactive in preparing not just for the "youth bulge" generation, also the growing older population. The growing older population should be ensured that they will have a quality of life living in dignity and respect in their later years. In Sub-Saharan Africa, considering the "youth bulge" generation there has to be a need to ensure that the youth will be provided with opportunities, especially educational, that will prepare them to live and contribute to social and economic development within a modern and cybernetic society.

A caring society, especially in the caring for the older population, children and other vulnerable members is not something new within African cultures. Sub-Saharan Africa has a lengthy history of caring, well entrenched in the rich traditions, culture and customs of the continent. Although the growing older population will present many challenges it is not that the continent has not faced challenges in its past history. Despite the many past challenges, especially the era of colonization, the continent and it varies by country, has continued to carry out the tradition of caring for its vulnerable members. It should be noted that although some aspects of the "youth bulge" generation will be addressed in the overall manuscript, especially the relationship to the overall demographic growth phenomenon, the major focus of attention will be on the growth and implications of the "Silver Tsunami," or the growing older population.

Therefore, regardless of what is currently described negatively as political and military conflicts and corruption practices, to some extent, and it varies by country, these descriptors represent some level of reality. But, within the midst of the aforementioned negative descriptors Africa is also being described as a continent on the rise, including one of the fastest growing economies globally and there is a new spirit on the continent, especially among the youth. No, "Tarzan" does not live there anymore. Yes, there are major problems and challenges, for example only 16.9% of older persons currently have a social pension or income security at the time of retirement. Yes, the continent has been there before and the hopes are that the continent will carry out whatever responsibilities required in preparing for the next generation, including the "Silver Tsunami" or the growing older population.

Global organizations, governments including non-governmental organizations, political and civic leaders have begun to recognize the impact and/or implications of a growing older population. Most importantly, as aforementioned, is the recognition of the impact this historical demographic phenomenon will have on various systems, economic, political, medical/health, social and cultural. The question is how prepared are the countries, developed and developing, to respond in a manner that will ensure the current and future populations of those described as older persons will live in dignity and respect following retirement from the workplace? Not just from the traditional workplace, but other increasing family and citizenry responsibilities, including child caring duties as well as caring for other vulnerable members of the extended family system.

The coming of the "Silver Tsunami" will present major global challenges, especially for low income, as well as low to middle income countries in making sure that this growing population will have at least basic income security, access to medical, health and social care, including long-term care. Current statistics from global organization, such as the International Social Security Association, illustrate that countries in Sub-Saharan Africa are not currently prepared for the task. As often repeated throughout the manuscript, less than 20%, more specifically 16.9% of older citizens or retirees in Sub-Saharan Africa do not have a social pension or income security; also a significant number of older citizens in Sub-Saharan Africa are currently living in poverty. For the current cohort of older persons the future does not look very bright and there is little evidence to project that the next cohort/generation of older citizens in Africa will not live under similar circumstances, the lack of social protection or income security.

In Sub-Saharan Africa there is a very positive historical note when it comes to caring for the older population and other vulnerable members in society. African societies have a very rich historical tradition of caring for family members across all age groups, especially children and the older populations. This long and effective tradition of caring gives some hope that as the "Silver Tsunami" becomes more and more a significant part of the fabric of African societies, policy makers, governments and citizen organizations will be reminded of this history of caring. As aforementioned the "Silver Tsunami" or the growing older population will present some very unique challenges. A major challenge for policy makers will be the recognition of the reality that a "carbon copy" of the traditional extended family system will not necessarily suffice in an urban modernized society. Preparation will require that conceptualization and planning for meeting the needs of a growing older population should first of all begin with the identification and evaluation of those strengths from the past that may be appropriate in the development of a future master plan of action. Any future comprehensive plan for caring has to involve all relevant systems, medical, health, social, political and economical. It is highly unlikely that any identifiable specific problem such as education or lack of income security for the older population or the "youth bulge" generation can have a successful outcome if treated in isolation from other systems, especially political in society. Leadership on the continent has to remember that a social pension, according to research, contributes to reductions in unemployment, poverty, overall positive socialization of children and youth, as well as the countries' economic growth and development.

AFRICA'S TRADITIONAL SOCIAL WELFARE SYSTEM: THE EXTENDED FAMILY NETWORK

Without much debate the global consensus is what has become known as a social welfare system in the Western world in countries such as the United States and other European countries probably had its origins on the continent of Africa. First of all, caring for vulnerable members of society, especially the older population and children have been carried out in many different forms for centuries on the continent of Africa. The current demographic shocks sweeping the globe should not have to alert Africans to their historical roles and responsibilities of caring for society's vulnerable populations. Prior to the European invasion and colonization, there existed in African societies a broad range of systems in place, family kinship, tribes, clans, economic, medical/health, with the primary interest focused on the overall wellbeing of all population groups across all age brackets. Traditional African societies had in place a well-defined holistic social welfare system for social protection that included provisions for food, shelter, housing and medical care, including maternal and childcare. A basic principle underlying traditional African societies was based on collective involvement or participation, or what was in the best interest of the family, or the village. Based on the principle or concept collectivity, traditional African societies placed emphasis on the 'we' first. The concept 'I' was not part of the thought and/or helping or caring process in traditional society. In accordance with the 'we' concept, the basic principle of reciprocity or the intergenerational contract between generations, older family members who had cared for the young were now supported and cared for in old age by the younger population (Blau, 1967).

Within the family group all needs were met and reciprocity was the guiding principle underlying the system. When older members of the family became less and less productive, it was the duty of the younger members to take over just as the older members had met their needs as young children. A major factor contributing to the success of such a system was "... paternal ownership of family assets, land and homes reinforced these arrangements. Mutual Aid societies extended the informal insurance-redistribution system beyond the family to the broader ethnic or cultural group" (World Bank Policy Paper, ibid, p. 33). Mutual aid systems provided reciprocal assistance in the construction of bridges, religious places of worship, as well as contributing to various agricultural tasks. The underling principle of mutual aid was families helping other family members around tasks such as the planting of crops, raising a storage facility or home. The possession and/or ownership of land were a critical element, especially in decision-making in African society; as indicated above land ownership helped to reinforce the system of reciprocity. The "Scramble for Africa," or the forceful taking over of land and resources by European colonizers was a devastating blow within African society. The take over and the control of land and other resources began the era of underdevelopment of African society (Rodney, Walter, "How Europe Underdeveloped Africa," Baltimore: Black Classic Press, 2011, pages 149-150).

It was the intergenerational contract or reciprocity that was the basis of the commitment to care for each other. In traditional African societies age was greatly respected, especially by the young who assumed that older members of the extended family had mystical powers over their descendants. Therefore, the young treated the older members well, believing that when they died, their spirits would be kind to them. It was in such cultural tradition that the older individuals in the villages were taken care of (Nyerere, 1967; Ondego, 1999; and Cohen, et al, 2006). The aforementioned responsibilities had been "...institutionalized in most cultures in patterns of kin and clan obligations which specified what help should be given, by whom, and under what conditions" (Midgley, J., 1984, p. 103).

Africans, says Kaseke (2008, p. 4), historically have been bound together by 'traditional values.' These traditional values "...are all about solidarity, collective responsibility, compassion, equality, unity, self-determination, human respect and human dignity" (Kaseke, ibid, p. 4). As a result of this very strong value orientation "...individuals subsist as families and families become closely interlaced communities which form a large society. The uniqueness of African societies is that this value orientation transcends the "... social, political and economic activities." Obviously, based on the aforementioned this values orientation permeates "...the social security context as well" (Kaseke, ibid, p. 4). Because of these deeply rooted traditions, no wonder that despite all of the cruelties and injustices that took place during an era of colonization the family kinship system, although culturally "bruised" was never totally destroyed.

The extended family system in Africa was similar in principles and structure to other countries such as Thailand, Asia, and India, but "Africa's support systems are based on a broader definition of family than Asia" (World Bank: Policy Research Report 1914, pages

52-53). One major difference is that "Households are often extended in many directions ...adult brothers and sisters may live together, as well as parents and children. Likewise, old age support from siblings is far more common than in Asia. The definition of children is also much more inclusive – adoption, fosterage, and borrowing offspring of other family members are common. In some cases, grandparents raise and are eventually cared for by their children's children" (World Bank: Policy Research Report, ibid, pages 52-53).

The Western concept of social security/social protection as applied in the more developed countries represented a framework, primarily out of governmental or public origins, and a body of principles somewhat similar to the extended family kinship network system in Africa. There were a couple of basic differences between the two systems, first of all, in Africa the principles and practices of caring emerged out of the historical traditions, culture, and customs of the African society. Whereas, in Western societies or the more developed countries, the concept social security originated for the most part from statutory or legislative initiatives that emerged from a process of collective bargaining between employer and worker. The aforementioned was especially true during the era referred to as the Industrial Revolution or the transition from an agricultural to an industrial economy. It was during this era that witnessed the birth and growth of a tripartite labor or collective bargaining systems (employer, employee, public) that provided the leadership in the creation or development of social protection/social security systems of caring. The tripartite labor systems focused primarily on caring for workers and their families within the formal labor sector. The self-employed workers and/or those working in the informal sectors, as many are today, were and continue to be excluded. Also, the fact cannot be overlooked that some major religious organizations in response to biblical teachings committed to meeting some of the basic needs of the poor but not guaranteeing or ensuring such as a social pension during retirement.

The concept social security as applied in Western societies had little meaning or usefulness in traditional African Societies. Although the concept social security has been widely used in the developed world, there continues to be a lack of consensus on a universal definition as well as what services are to be provided and to whom. As pointed out by (Midgley (1984) experts in the field often differ when it comes to efforts at arriving at a universal definition of social security and/or social protection. Although the focus for some view the concept in terms of governments and/or private sectors ensuring some limited forms of financial supports at a time of need, others have broaden its meaning to include basic services such as health, medical care, and housing (Midgley, 1984, p. 79). Although the Western concept of social security was not well defined or without a universal consensus of it's meaning, the basic principles, roles and responsibilities of the traditional African social welfare system, or the extended family system for the purpose of caring for societal members were not just clearly defined, also it was universal.

Yes, the basic principles, roles and responsibilities of caring for all members of society, and not including some form of a "means test," (process of determining eligibility for services) especially the older population and children, were well defined in traditional African societies. To some extent despite years of colonization, including forced labor, some of those basic principles, roles and responsibilities of caring, although weakened by various forces, continue to exist today for meeting the basic needs of families. The extended family system, historically from an African perspective included the tribe, clan, as well as mutual-aid societies for meeting the needs of all family members. According to one African scholar, "The oldest institution of social security in the history of mankind is the family" (Keizi, 2006).

As aforementioned despite the many human injustices brought on by colonization, including forced labor, the family systems although weakened by those external forces, continued to function in some form. Although the aforementioned traditional systems to some extent survived the era of colonization, they are now threatened by an era of modernization, industrialization and urbanization. The traditional African version of a social welfare system was obviously impacted during the era of colonization, but some elements survived; the systems continued to survive in some form(s) primarily because historically the family systems had been so deeply entrenched in the traditions, culture and customs of African society.

During the long era of colonization native Africans had no other viable options. The European colonizers had little or no interest in sharing social, medical, health and economic resources, unless there was something to be gained that would satisfy their economic needs back home in return. There is no evidence that a spirit of reciprocity existed among the parties, the colonizers and the native populations residing within the colonies. The Europeans were in control of the land, the people, and the natural resources that were being extracted from the rich African lands, as well as how those resources would eventually be utilized. Therefore, there was no interest in the sharing of any knowledge, resources, especially economic development and labor practices, related to that era of history especially in regards to social protection, including social pensions. Labor and/or occupational systems, including resources for future social protection, especially related to retirement, were reserved for the wellbeing of the expatriate families. There were no thoughts or initiatives coming from the colonizers addressing any forms of social protection for the workers under forced labor mandates addressing issues related to social protection of the workers and their families.

In regards to the survival of some elements of the traditional family system, some African scholars have provided examples of post-colonial experiences that illustrate the ongoing relevancy of the strong family ties that still exist. An example of the strong family links could be seen within the Mashona family kinship group in Zimbabwe. "… If the mother dies leaving young children, one of her sisters should care for them; the grandparents rear older children who are orphaned or dependent because of divorce. Elderly people live with their sons who are responsible for their welfare" (Mbanje, 1979). Family kinship obligations as described could extend beyond the immediate family structure reaching outward to a particular clan (Clan a larger grouping of households that could make the claim of descent from a common ancestor). The Clan family system '… among the Akan people of Ghana is so highly organized that individuals can travel hundreds of miles and receive help from clansmen they have never met' (Rodney, in Midgley, 1984, p. 103).

The traditional extended family system was never perfect, there were factors when some members of the village were not protected, or as seen currently in the well-developed protection systems of developed countries. In Africa, "…some people fall through the cracks—those who never had children, those who children have died or moved away, and those whose children do not earn enough to support less productive household members. These cracks widen as urbanization and mobility increase, nuclear families replace extended families, medical progress extends life expectancy for the old, and the formalization of jobs makes it difficult for people to continue working as they age and their productivity declines (World Bank: Averting the Old Age Crisis, World Bank Policy Report, New York Oxford University Press, 1994, p. 33). In addition to the aforementioned factors in more recent decades, diseases such as HIV/ AIDS, military and political conflicts, have significantly reduced the working age population. This factor will become even more important in the future as fertility rates decline and as the population ages, or people living longer (World Bank Policy Report, ibid).

The Matriarchs' of Mthatha Village, South Africa

A recent story from South Africa's Eastern Cape provides an excellent example of the struggles and challenges confronted by caring and/or extended family groups in meeting basic needs of family and other vulnerable members of the village. The story centers around a group of 30 women who come together in the village of Mthatha to share stories of the roles they carry out daily as the primary breadwinners and parents to grandchildren. It should be noted that the Village of Mthatha has been the home of some of South Africa's greatest heroes, including Nelson Mandela, Steve Biko, Walter, Sisulu, and Thabo Mbeki. Now, approximately three decades following the end of Apartheid, the Village Mthatha the birthplace of such heroic figures from the Eastern Cape, "…remains one of the poorest regions in the country (Harrisburg, Kim, Reporter, "The Matriarch of Mthatha," Story product - Code for South Africa – Data Journalism Academy, Al Jazeera Media Network, 2017, p 1).

The Matriarch shared how they had become breadwinners and parents for a second time in their lives because the children's parents, their children had gone to the cities seeking employment opportunities or jobs. As addressed in Chapter V this is one of the contributing factors when families are making the transition from the rural to urban areas. In the Eastern Cape employment opportunities are not very good and the village of Mthatha has a very high unemployment rate. In keeping with the traditions and customs of the extended family network, "In addition to regular childrearing, they operate a Disabled Children Centre, where they look after children with disabilities. Since unemployment is so high on the Eastern Cape, Social grants are often used to support entire extended families and communities" (Harrisburg, Kim, ibid, 2017).

The major problem shared by the women, not unlike many of the countries in Sub-Saharan Africa has to do with social pensions or income security. The problem is not just a matter of the lack of a social pension but even when there is a social grant including provisions for children, such as received by grandparents in the Eastern Cape, it is not adequate for meeting the basic needs of the family. Keep in mind more than 80% of older persons, unlike those in Mthatha, do not receive a social grant. The major problem expressed by the women in the village of Mthatha was "…their grants are not sufficient…61% of elderly female breadwinners South Africa feel they do not receive enough financial benefits…For many households the state pension is the only formal and reliable source of income" (Harrisburg, K., ibid, 2017). The women also addressed the issue of poverty. "We want to fight poverty but it is difficult…we are hungry…(Harrisburg, K, ibid, 2017). To the women of the village poverty "…means a life of living from hand to mouth surviving on social grants and what they can produce through gardening, beading and baking bread…"(Harrisburg, K., ibid). Some years ago the government provided the women of the village sewing machines and equipment for baking bread (bread making tins); the problem is that most of the families in the village do not have electricity and/or running water.

Within the nine Provinces of South Africa, women represent the majority of breadwinners. Women, as the case exist throughout Sub-Saharan Africa have a longer or higher life expectancy than men; therefore not surprising women normally end up with much of the child caring responsibilities over the years. According to women in Mthatha, "The changeover from male dominance normally occur around age 60" (Harrisburg, K., ibid, 2017). This is the timetable when women begin the takeover as the primary breadwinner. There are other factors related to women becoming the primary breadwinner; for example, "…husbands are dying from Silicosis, a lung disease from inhaling Silica in the mines, or becoming slaves to alcohol or unemployment…Grandmothers are often left to support their children. Fifty-eight percent of elderly female breadwinners look after a child under 17…Essentially, grandmothers are becoming parents twice, using their meager income (monthly pension) approximately $113 and child support $27 to support both their children, who are unable to find work, as well as their grandchildren" (Harrisburg, K., ibid, 2017).

The historical caring traditions of the African extended family network, including clans, tribes, mutual aid societies, are globally well documented. As the expression goes, it has and continues to stand the test of time; the Matriarchs of Mthatha on the Eastern Cape in South Africa, is a current example how the caring traditions have survived centuries and are alive and well in Africa. Not only has the culture, traditions and customs survived on the Continent of Africa, also the Diasporas, including the era of slavery in the United States.

When discussing their hardships and struggles with limited financial and other supports as parents and grandparents of the children, the Matriarchs of Mthatha from the Eastern Cape of South Africa expressed that the major challenges were preparing their grandchildren for the future (Harrisburg, K., Ibid, 2017). Can the concept intergenerational reciprocity be expressed more appropriately within the context of what's happening on the Eastern Cape?

THE AFRICAN TRADITIONAL MEDICAL SYSTEM OF CARING FOR FAMILIES

Medicine and Medical Practitioners

African societies not only had systems for meeting the social welfare needs, food, shelter, clothing and housing of the populations but systems caring for their medical and health needs as well. In contemporary Africa and in the future, systems for the caring for the medical and health needs of a growing older population is and will continue to be very critical; as life expectancy of the older population increases, medical and psychological needs intensify, especially for chronic conditions such as Dementia and Alzheimer's. Also, as the older population increases in chronological age requiring more complex and specialized medical care, there will be a growing need for long-term care in the home environment or public or private institutions.

The medical system for caring included herbal medicine and maternal and childcare.

Scholars have used such headings as "Traditional Medicine," Traditional Midwives," and "herbal medicine," in describing a system focusing on the health/medical needs of families across all age groups. "Traditional medical treatment has existed in all cultures as an independent health care system…with a history perhaps as old as man himself" (Staugard, 1985, p. 1). It cannot be overlooked that traditional medical practices, including herbal medicine in Africa did play a key role as part of the system of social protection for all. It is obvious that Africa like other continents and member countries of the United Nations have begun the transition towards what is considered as an era of modern medicine.

In recent decades countries have also witnessed a major shift from infectious diseases to chronic illnesses. There has been a significant decline in infectious diseases resulting from factors such as improved sanitary measures, the development of vaccines to fight off or defend against infectious/communicable diseases; diseases that can be treated with various antibiotics (Technology and Aging in America, ibid, p 7, 1985/See Chapter I). Globally, as population growth continues, especially with a growing older population, the onset of chronic illnesses such as Dementia, Alzheimer's, coronary heart diseases, strokes will become major challenges for countries, not only in the so-called developed world, but the developing world as well. The aforementioned becomes critical as countries continue to respond to the "Silver Tsunami."

The growing older population will have a tremendous impact on the current medical, health, social, economic and social systems in Africa. As life expectancy increases not only will medical problems become more complex, the cost of caring, including long-term care becomes extremely costly or expensive. The current struggles and challenges of caring for a growing older population have been illustrated in developing countries such as the United States and the United Kingdom. As the world observes not only a growing older population that brings along new and more complex medical issues, also the continuing transition from a communicable disease concept to one of chronic illness, the challenges become greater.

Historically, especially in the Western world or the more developed countries, modern medical practitioners until more recent times had not given proper respect to traditional medical practitioners including the use of herbal medicine. Some scholars have used the word skepticism in describing how modern medical practitioners have viewed and discussed traditional medicine (Staugard, ibid, 1985 p. 1). A great deal of the skepticism regarding traditional African medicine can be traced to the views of those who colonized the continent. The negatives somewhat evolved from the perspective, "…that all healers are witch healers practicing 'black magic… (Quoted in Traditional Medicine in Africa, p.17, from Thairu, K. The African Civilization, Nairobi: East African Literature Bureau, 1975). "Witchcraft refers to all the aspects of the use of mystical power to harm others in society in which case, witchcraft, sorcery, evil eye, or whatever terminology it may be given, is evil" (Quoted in Traditional Medicine in Africa, p.17, from Mbiti, J.S., Africans Religion and Philosophy, London: Heinemann, 1969).

The skepticism and or negative attitudes are changing, especially in the developed world thanks to some extent from the works of the World Health Organization (WHO). There has been increasing cooperation between the WHO and the various Health Ministries in the developing countries. The two critical entities with the goal of improving health of the populations, are being confronted with the reality, "…that a system of health care built on the Western and predominantly curative model, represents a fast growing and very heavy burden on the poorer nations under-developed economies and seem to have very little positive effect on the majority of diseases threatening the populations in the Third World" (Staugard, Frants, 1985, ibid, p.1).

There is little evidence that the African natives living in the colonized countries had access to Western medicine and practices during the era of colonization. The European settlers or expatriates were the primary beneficiaries of what Western medicine existed in the colonies. Therefore, the native populations had practically no choice other than to rely on their traditional medical systems. A good example is Botswana, formerly Bechuanaland prior to Independence (1966); the country of Bechuanaland "…had no access to western medicine until the third decade of the century…it can be assumed that the majority of the efforts of the qualified medical staff up to, and probably far beyond this time were devoted to the health care of the European immigrants…the Tswana population had no option but the services of the traditional healers in the case of disease or ill health up to the pre-Independence period, and in fact not until the first part of the decade following Independence (Staugard, 1985, ibid, p.34). It can be concluded that Botswana, never traditionally colonized in the sense of other African countries (A protectorate country under the British) was not unique in medical practice experiences. It can be assumed that whether classified as a Protectorate country, or a traditional colonized country, most countries continued to depend on traditional medical systems.

Maternal and Child Health

The traditional medical/health system included maternal and childcare and the system of midwifery. Traditional (midwives) carried out their child-care responsibilities within the villages where they resided. A major strength of this system was that the practitioner (midwife) was always accessible. Not only accessible, but "They speak the local language and understand and adhere to the local system of health beliefs." Traditional midwives, normally, were older women past the menopause state, who had given birth to children of their own. Although the focus has been on females, in some countries, such as Ghana, there were male midwives. A female midwife normally accompanied the male in some countries, such as Nigeria, during the delivery process. In traditional African societies, there were no educational or training institutions for midwives. The knowledge and skills utilized by midwives came from their experiences of working with kin or the local expert (Anderson, Sandra and Staugard, Frants, Traditional Midwives: Traditional Medicine in Botswana, Ipelegeng Publishers – Gaborone, 1986).

In reference to herbal medicines it is interesting to note the use of such practices in maternal and child health. Traditional midwives did not just make an appearance at the home for the birth event, for the most part midwives were available to the mother during pregnancy, childbirth, and followed her during the neonatal period. An important aspect of this relationship was the sharing of health information/education during this time. There were times when herbal medicines, and practices or techniques such as a massage may be applied to "ease pains, to 'heat,' fortify and protect her…"(Anderson and Staugard, ibid, p. 136). Anderson and Staugard quote is from, (Cosminsky, S, Traditional Midwifery and Contraception, In: Bannerman, R et al, Traditional Medicine and Health Care Coverage, WHO, Geneva, 1983).

Some examples of the use of herbal medicines in Botswana during childbirth are: Motsisidi

(BMP 266), the midwife prescribes a cup of water boiled with fresh roots one time a day. The purpose is for easing stomach pains during pregnancy. Morolwane (BMP 525) is prescribed for the treatment of constipation. Seretlwane is used for the treatment of abdominal pain in pregnant women, and is also used for treatment of diarrhea. The roots are boiled in water in water, and the woman drinks ½ cup per/day. Seswagadi (BMP 718) is used for the treatment of pain in the uterus, as well as irregular menstruation. The purpose here is to make the fetus strong, but also to treat pain in the feet and lower legs. The dose and the regimen for this treatment require two pieces of tuber (2x5 cm) boiled in ½ cup of water. The pregnant woman is required to drink this dosage twice a day until she has fully recovered (Anderson and Staugard, ibid, pp. 136-138).

Herbal Medicine

Herbal medicine has historically played a major role in Africa for maintaining the health of the population. There was and to some extent and even today, a reliance on herbal medicine. The saying is that herbal medicine can be dated to a time in history when "…early man became conscious of his surrounding…thousands of years of experience by trial and error must have taught him to distinguish between their properties as healing agents dawning on him much later" Baquar, S R, The Role of Traditional Medicine in a Rural Environment in (Sindiga, I, Nyaigotti-Chacha, C, and Kanunah, M P (Editors), Traditional Medicine in Africa, East African Educational Publishers, Nairobi, 1995, pp. 141-143).

Many years ago even before the introduction of farming; it was the nomadic tribes who possessed a knowledge base regarding plant life and it healing potential. "The earliest reference to the use of medicinal herbs as a cure for diseases is found in the manuscript of 'Eber Papyrus' in about the 16th century B.C. which recorded the use of poppy (Papaver somnifera), castor oil (Ricinus communis), squills (Urginea sp) and aloes (Aloe sp)" (Baquar, ibid, p. 141). Any study of the importance of herbal medicine reveals that it represented supernatural powers, and those who possessed the knowledge and use of plant life, such as the "shamans," the "Witchdoctors" became very important individuals in their respective villages (Baquar, ibid, p. 142). "Plants have provided man with a storehouse of various drugs where he can search for medicines for practically all ailments" (Baquar, ibid, p. 143).

Now, even in the developing countries, the major drug companies have included research in their planning in an attempt to identify plants with a therapeutic value for inclusion in the practice of modern medicine. **(PERSONAL NOTE OF AUTHOR:** While living in Botswana in the late 1980's (Fulbright Professor, University of Botswana – 1987-88), the Author was introduced to a plant, Kalahari Devil's Claw that grew in the vast Kalahari Desert. The Kalahari makes up approximately 70% of the country's 2 million population, the majority living in the Eastern part of the country. Author was informed of the common knowledge shared that the plant had many uses, including the health of the internal body system, especially enhanced energy levels. The author recalls brewing the plant for tea, couple of glasses a day, no condiments, sugar, etc. Over a period of time the author did appear to have more energy. Anyway, on returning to the United States, and not having a supply of "devil's claw," the author went back to his western dosages of energy vitamins. He noted one day while visiting one of the local health stores specializing in vitamins, and noted a product that included "devil's claw" in a powder form. Initially the author was surprised and after doing some research discovered that some of the pharmaceutical companies had discovered the plant in the Kalahari Desert and had contracted to export the plant for use in vitamins' supplements to the Western world. The aforementioned personal note reminds one that "The discovery of Penicillin, was derived from the Penicillium, a common fungus…chloromycetin from a common actinomycetes, belonging to a group of lower plants" (Baquar, ibid, p. 144). We are all now aware of the importance of these plants as antibiotics universally.

UTILIZING THE STRENGTHS OF TRADITIONAL AND MODERN MEDICINE

Over the years, in developed and developing countries, the concept of traditional medicine is changing. The concept "alternative medicine" is now in vogue or being utilized in many countries, such as the United States to describe non-Western medical practices. The World Health Organization in an effort to distinguish between modern medical practice and traditional medicine recommended that the term doctor be used in describing scientifically trained physicians. Furthermore the term doctor should not be used in describing such practitioners as "traditional healers," including the Ngaka and the Baprofiti of Botswana. But, several decades later the WHO begin a campaign promoting as well the use of traditional medicine especially in developing countries. The WHO concluded that there were valuable elements in traditional medical practices that could be properly incorporated into the scientifically based health care system (Akerele, 1987).

The potential for the utilization of traditional medical practices emerged from the World Health Assembly (WHA) around 1977. It recognized the potential of "…of its human power reserve in national health care." It was at this time that this very important global organization begins a campaign of encouraging its member countries to consider the use of traditional medical practices (Akerele, 1987, Nakajima, 1987). Two very significant declarations followed. First, the WHA pointed to the role of herbs becoming part of the health care system in developing countries; secondly, it was strongly recommended that governments, especially in developed countries, begin using "…traditional medicines in their national drug policies and regulations. (Nakajima, 1987)

Pillsbury (1979) presented a major case for the use of traditional medical practitioners, or the incorporation into modern health care practices. Her argument was that official health care teams could only reach the majority of the populations residing in rural and/or remote areas. Therefore, the reality of this geographical situation would strongly recommend the use of local practitioners. Furthermore, Many of those living in the rural areas were not making use of the official services and/or were suspicious of western medicine. The perception of local people was that the western practitioners had a very low tolerance for local beliefs.

According to (WHO, 1978, Pillsbury, 1979, Phillips, 1986,) traditional medical practices have been promoted for a number of reasons:

1. It is an integral part of every culture developed over many years. Thus, it is effective in curing certain cultural health problems.
2. It is socially acceptable.
3. It has the widest spatial coverage; each community has its own healers. It is thus the surest way of moving towards attaining health for all by the turn of the century.
4. It is holistic in approach. It views disease and illness to be disequilibrium of social groups with the total environment.
5. It is efficacious.
6. Traditional healers charge affordable fees.

In considering a plan for meeting the needs of a growing older population planners should consider as part of the conceptualization process the above six areas from The World Health Organization (WHO).

THE EXTENDED FAMILY KINSHIP NETWORK: THE CHANCES OF SURVIVAL IN A MODERN, URBANIZED AND INDUSTRIALIZED SOCIETY

Despite memories of the European powers carving up the natives' land, separation of family and tribal extended networks, and all for the purpose of building economic empires in Europe, African countries in the Post-Independence era were ready to move forward. One conclusion of the newly Independent countries following approximately 75 years of occupation, domination and exploitation, was that so much of the historical cultural traditions, customs, including the extended family network system had been somewhat weakened. But, entrenched in rich historical traditions the extended family network system, although somewhat weakened continued to survive; not just in Africa, also among the former slaves in America and the Diaspora. To illustrate the strength of these strong African cultural traditions many of the slaves captured in Africa in earlier centuries and brought to America, not only survived the rough waters of the Atlantic in crowded slave ships, continued to cling to some of the traditions on American soil; those who arrived in the United States continued to carry on some of the cultural traditions, extended family network, and especially the concept of mutual aid societies from the "mother country." The mutual aid society movement in the United States following a very lengthy period of slavery provided a system for families working together and caring for each other. In other words a type of social welfare system similar to the extended family network of tribal groups and clans that were common within African culture and traditions. The Mutual Aid Societies in America provided financial foundations that helped to develop some of the most successful Black businessmen and women, including some of the first American Black millionaires. Charles Spaulding is an example of how a small Mutual Aid Society became the very successful North Carolina Mutual Life Insurance Company with current headquarters in North Carolina with an office complex that stands out prominently in Durham, North Carolina. It has been assumed by so many that those traditions and customs were lost in the Atlantic Ocean, or beaten or "whipped" out of the slaves by their masters (Byrd, Alicia, (Ed.),

"Philanthropy of the Black Church," in <u>Philanthropy and the Black Church</u>, Washington, D.C., 1990; Davis, Alan et.al, <u>The People of Philadelphia</u>, Temple University Press, 1973; Frazier, F. <u>The Negro Church in America</u>, New York: Schoker Booker Publishers, 1964; Herskovits, Melville, <u>The Myth of the Negro Past</u>, Boston: Beacon Press, 1958; Kessel, Felicia, "Black Foundations Meeting Vital Needs," <u>CRISIS</u>, VOLUME 96, No. 10, December 1989; McKinney, Edward, "A School of Social Work Trains Indigenous Leadership in Cleveland, <u>Journal of Community Development: London</u>, Vol. 15, No 3, 1980).

SUMMARY AND CONCLUSION

Globally, it is well established that historically the Continent of Africa possessed a very well defined institution or system of caring commonly referred to as the Extended Family Network. Family members, including tribes, clans from "cradle to grave" were well cared for by the extended family network including financial support, housing, medical, health needs and companionship. Globally, it is also recognized that factors such as colonization slowed down the process or social and economic development on the continent for decades. In other words, there is little doubt that the era of colonization had a tremendous impact on the culture, customs, and traditions on the continent, including the traditional extended family network and medical systems. Despite the long era of colonization that weakened the aforementioned caring system, some of the customs and traditions survived even until current times. Current examples are the Mashona family kinship group in Zimbabwe and the Matriarches Mthatha kinship group on the Eastern Cape of South Africa. As aforementioned one should not forget the roles played by mutual aid societies in the Southern part of the United States and throughout the Diaspora. In other words, some of the customs and traditions arrived safely in America and the Diaspora after a stormy journal across the Atlantic; as aforementioned although many humans/slaves were lost at sea some customs and traditions such as mutual aid societies survived the stormy seas.

The historic success of Africa's rich caring traditions is no guarantee of success in preparing for the growing older population, the "Silver Tsunami" in Sub-Saharan Africa. Preparations for meeting the basic needs of a growing older population, not unlike other continents including the developed world, will be confronted with major challenges. Currently in Sub-Saharan Africa approximately 82.5% of older or retired persons do not have a statutory social pension or basic income security. Continents and/or countries will have to prepare for the future within a context of a modern, urban, industrialized and cybernetic world. There are no appropriate "carbon copies" from past generations to bring forward. The conceptualization of a plan in preparing for a growing older population should consider all relevant strengths from past successes, customs and traditions that may apply within the context of a modern society. Most importantly, there will be the challenge of developing innovative and/or new and different strategies within the context, as aforementioned of a modern society for meeting the basic needs not only of a growing older population also across all age groups.

End of Chapter IV

✳✳✳

ADDENDUM INFORMATION FOR POTENTIAL USE IN CHAPTER

Forced Labor Era

The colonizers possessed all of the political and military power to maintain obedience from the native workers. Furthermore, they had strategically located and/or dispersed the workers, and closely watched by the military would make it difficult organize; the Europeans with the help of the missionaries always used the racist theory of inferiority to justify lower wages and forced labor.

Shortly before the end of WWII, "The International Labor Organization elevated human rights to a position of fundamental importance in it work…" The Philadelphia Conference 1944 a milestone in the history of human rights…from this point at the latest the ILO norms provided a clear point of reference for political and social for the most part, it began during the Berlin Conference in 1884-85 resulting in what is now commonly referred to as the "The Scramble for Africa." The Conference does not mean that attempts and some successes to exploit the continent did not occur prior to 1884-85. Threats to the traditional systems of care caring began to take hold when the European powers made a political, and for the most part, an economical decision to divide or split the African continent into geographical boundaries/colonies. Not only did the actions from the European powers threaten the existence of the traditional social welfare system, but all the deeply rooted traditions, culture, and customs as well. The European powers, scramble for Africa, illustrated no respect for the traditions, culture, and traditions of Africa. In other words, no consideration, appreciation or respect to the historical family kinship, tribal, or clan system ties that were essential for the survival of the traditional social welfare system. As a result, the tribal and/or kinship groups so essential for social in all forms were separated and left struggling to survive. The carving up or dividing the native land was crucial for the European powers in their efforts to develop the financial/economic empires back home in Europe.

The "scramble for Africa" was great timing for the economies of Europe. The scramble and eventually the geographical carving up of a great continent was taking place in the midst of or during the industrial revolution in Europe and the West. Once the European powers, now possessing the necessary political and military power, gained control over the land and the people, were in a position to seize the natural resources needed for the development of their economic empires in Europe. Labor or native workers needed for achieving their goals were simply no major problem for the Europeans; the powers of Europe had the political and military powers for achieving their goals. Native workers, especially during the forced labor era, were moved out of the villages and into the cities as manufacturing centers emerged for processing resources back to Europe. It was during the industrial revolution that European states became the center of financial power and influence **(GLOBAL HISTORY/BARRON SERIES, PP. 407-409)**.

It is important to note that the primary recipient of the benefits, especially the wealth derived from the industrial revolution, especially phase one was Great Britain. But, as the revolution moved into the second phase, there were more competition from other European countries. During the early years Great Britain was the center of manufacturing, shipping, banking, and transportation for the world. But other European countries, including the United States began to become imitators of the British technology, as well as the use of British capital for moving forward. By the mid-70's, approximately one decade prior to the Berlin Conference, that many considered the coming of the second phase of the Revolution, Britain, had begun to lose some of its industrial dominance held during the first phase. The second phase was now focusing on steel, electricity, and petro chemicals, not being demanded globally. Now, Great Britain was operating in a very competitive world, especially with Germany and the United States. The U.S. had fast become not only the number one steel producer in the world, but a major world competitor with Britain and other European powers. These are possible factors that influenced the European powers to begin thinking about new natural resources, such as minerals for maintaining, not just their economic power but ways to expand it (Rand McNally: Atlas of World History, Chicago: Rand McNally and Company, 1987). The question, to what extent the aforementioned factors influenced the need for the Berlin Conference and the beginning of the "scramble for Africa?"

The European powers, during deliberations and negotiations among themselves, concluded that there was a need to develop a written document or contract that would regulate the anticipated competition that would eventually emerge from their actions. The concept put forward was referred to as "effective occupation;" the criteria underlying the recognition of territory claim on a global level. "The importance of direct rule in terms of "effective recourse to armed force against indigenous states and people" (Pakenham, Thomas, The Scramble for Africa: The White Man's Conquest of the Dark Continent from 1876-1912, New York: Random House, 1991). The principle of "effective occupation" stated that "…powers could acquire rights over colonial lands only if they possessed them or had "effective occupation:" In other words, if they had treaties with local leaders, if they flew their flags there, and if they established an administrative territory to govern it with a police force to keep order. The colonial powers could also make use of the colony economically…" (Pakenham, ibid,1991).

The final Berlin document was signed on the 26th of February 1885. The General Act included some thirty-eight inexplicit clauses; therefore there was a crucial need for the Principles of effective occupation. It has been suggested, "The race to grab a slice of the African cake had started long before the first day of the conference. And none of the thirty-eight clauses of the General Act had any teeth. It had set no rules for dividing, let alone eating, the cake. In one sense…the Berlin conference marked a turning point in the history of Africa and Europe. There was something that came to be called 'the spirit of Berlin.' For the first time great men like Bismarck had linked their names at an international conference to Livingston's lofty ideals: to introduce the '3 c's – commerce, Christianity, civilization – into the dark places of Africa. Of course, the main policy of the Powers was directed to strategic and economic objectives such as protecting old markets or exploiting new ones" (Pakenham, Thomas, The Scramble for Africa: The White Man's Conquest of the Dark Continent from 1876-1912, New York: Random House, 1991, pages 254-255).

During the "scramble for Africa," including the negotiations among the European powers, an extremely peculiar happening was taking place in Belgium that would have implications for what initially was called The Congo Free State. Other than advisors the only participant or decision maker regarding this very wealthy geographical area in Africa was King Leopold II of Belgium. The European powers seated at the negotiating table in Berlin seemed to have no interest in this part of Africa. Could it have been that the Congo Free State, later to become the Belgian Colony, did not have the natural resources, minerals, diamonds, and gold thought to be in other African colonies? King Leopold II had ascended to the throne of Belgium in 1865. As the story unfolds of how the King's acquisition of the Congo, becoming its sole ruler, provides another demonstration of the disrespect the Europeans had for the African continent and it people. Well, there is a piece of land in Africa that looks promising let's just grab it? Operating externally from the negotiations taking place among the power brokers from countries, such as England, France, and Spain, King Leopold II, on his own terms, became the sole ruler of the Congo Free State (Gondola, CH. Didier, The History of the Congo, London: Greenwood Press, 2002).

The King's actions that eventually, and without any serious opposition from the other European powers have been described, "Leopold's acquisition of so much power, incidentally, took place almost by sleight of hand. The European powers had not recognized him, but his Association Internationale du Congo, as sovereign administrator over the Congo basin…no one seemed to protest. People saw him as a great philanthropist with a great many ideals and even more means at his disposal" (Reybrouck, David Van, Congo: The Epic History of a People, New York, HarperCollins Publishers, 2014, p. 58).

Operating behind the scenes, King Leopold II successfully acquired for himself a territory, naming it the Congo Free State, eighty times larger than his home country of Belgium (Didier, ibid, 2002). What became known as the Congo Free State had been regarded as one of Africa's richest geographical areas for its natural resources that were located in the Congo Basin. The area possessed approximately a third of the rainforests in Africa. Also, the Congo Basin was known to possess numerous species of trees known for the production of ebony, mahogany and teak; the basin is considered to be the "…second largest river in the world in terms of volume flowing water, exceeded only by the Amazon River of South America…Africa's most extensive network of navigable waterways and sources of hundreds of different species of fish" (Didier, ibid, 2002, p. 2). Just imagine all of the aforementioned, and obviously much more, "fell in the lap" of King Leopold II. No, not just by accident this happened, "On April 30 1885, the Berlin Conference, devoted to the peaceful partitioning of those parts of Africa not yet claimed by a European power, accorded him personal control of the Congo" (Edgerton, Robert B., The Troubled Heart of Africa: A History of the Congo, New York: St. Martin's Press, 2002).

It is interesting to note that the people of Belgium historically had opposed colonialism; furthermore, there was no history of ties with the African continent, including any business interests, or contacts of any kind. "Yet it was Leopold, rather than the head of any European trading or mining company, who several years earlier paid Sir Henry Morton Stanley, African Explorer, to supervise the building of the road that opened the Congo River to navigation… And it was Leopold…who convinced thirteen European powers and the United States at the Berlin Conference that he would improve the moral and material conditions of the Congolese and moreover, put an end to slave trading" (Edgerton, ibid, 2002, pages 78-79. His intent to free all of the Africans in the Congo played a part in the name, Congo Free State (Edgerton, ibid, 2002).

King Leopold remained the sole ruler of the Congo Free State for 23 years not as a colony but a state; after 23 years the Congo Free State became a Belgian colony. Speaking of peculiarities King Leopold II was considered an absentee but sole ruler of the Congo; furthermore, King Leopold II never visited the Congo. His residence was approximately 3,700 miles to the North, and it would have taken approximately a four-week journey to reach the borders of the Congo Free State (Reybrouck, ibid, 2014).

In regards to inhumane treatment or social injustices, consider the fact that the native population had no input in the design or mapping of their native states, including the Congo Free State, and later a Belgian colony. The final physical boundaries of each area drawn on maps, without input from the native population, were actually completed by Europeans who had never been to Africa (Dowden, Richard, "The End of Colonialism, New States, Old Societies," Africa-Altered States, Ordinary Miracles (1st Edition), NY: Public Affairs, 2009). In the process of gaining complete control over the land, resources, and the people, any aspects of culture, customs, traditions, including the foundations of the traditional social welfare system were completely ignored or despised. "Europeans had claimed racial superiority to justify slavery and imperialism…African dignity and self worth eroded. They were forced to abandon their own beliefs, identities and values…"(Dowden, Richard ibid, p. 62). One can imagine how devastating the seizure of land was to the people of Africa. Land ownership and the authority and decision-making surrounding it in the villages were critical in maintaining the traditional social welfare system, but also all of the customs and traditions of society.

What other factors, other than the aforementioned legislative initiatives, that gave the settlers their power to oppress? For one, "… the alien colonial state had a monopoly of political power, after crushing all opposition by superior armed force. Secondly, the African working class was small, very dispersed, and very unstable owing migratory practices. Thirdly… European capitalists in Africa had additional racial justification for dealing unjustly with the African worker. The racist theory that the black man was inferior led to the conclusion that he deserved lower wages…The combination of the above factors made it extremely difficult for African Workers to organize themselves" (Rodney, Walter, How Europe Underdeveloped Africa, Baltimore: Black Classic Press, 2011, pp. 149-150).

The social injustices and inhuman treatment toward Africans were deeply rooted in "… the racist principal that barbarism pervaded Africa and there was no culture to be salvaged" (Maloba, 1995, p. 11). The European powers had strong allies in various religious denominations/congregations of missionaries who had come to Africa in their attempts to civilize and save the savages from the fires of hell. The missionaries sought to replace African religious and cultural practices with strong civilized Western cultures. The goal for the French during a process of assimilation was to change African men, women, and children into good civilized French models (Maloba, 1995 ibid).

In was from this colonized and oppressed world that the colonizers were in need of very cheap labor and would not be able to carry out their mission with the supply of African workers. The colonizers or settlers had come into the possession of huge plots of agriculture land, estimated to be on average some 2400 acres per/family. And, obviously the only solution was to create a system whereas the Africans had to work for the. In order to carry out their goals it became necessary for the settlers to create or enact labor as well as economic legislation that would allow them to recruit laborers. Also the legislation included provisions that would prevent the colonized the opportunity to have access to opportunities to engage in profitable cash crop production, as well as having access to fresh land. Furthermore, to make things more difficult for the natives the legislation enacted provided the settlers with the opportunity to impose such provisions as poll and hut taxes. These legislative initiatives gave the natives just option, give their labor and services to the foreign settlers (Ogot, B.A. & Ochieng, W.R., Decolonization and Independence in Kenya 1940-93, Ohio University Press, 1995 p. xv).

One major concern of the European powers had to do with what strategies could be used in forcing the native population to engage in seeking employment away from their homesteads or villages. They concluded that some form of taxation was the answer. The settlers "… taxation is the only possible method of compelling the natives to leave his reserve for the purpose of seeking work. Only in this way can the cost of living be increased for the native… and it is on this that the supply of labor and the price of laborer depends" (Ogot and Ochieng, Ibid, p. xvi – Quote is from, Leys, C., Underdevelopment in Kenya: The Political Economy of Neo-Colonialism, London, Heinemann, 1975, p. 29). The European settlers had the power to enforce any policies that would benefit or achieve their economic goals.

Also, in countries such as Kenya, Rhodesia (now Zimbabwe), the settlers put forth special efforts to prevent the natives from growing their own cash crops; the goal being to make sure that their labor would be made available only to the settlers. One of the great settlers by the name of Colonial Grogan speaking specifically of the Kikuyu, the largest tribal group currently in Kenya, and the tribe of Jomo Kenyatta, First President of Kenya, "… 'We stolen his land. Now we must steal his limbs. Compulsory labor is the corollary of our occupation of the country' (Rodney, Walter, ibid, p. 165-166). One of the key principles of the European forced labor campaign.

The European conquest of Africa took place beginning around 1884 and continued for approximately three-quarters of a century. The major powers carrying out the conquest represented, for the most part the countries of France, Germany, British, and Portugal; only approximately 10% of Africa was in the powers of Europe around 1870, at the time of the Berlin Conference, but by the year 1914, the territory under European control had reached 90% (Pakenham, ibid).

In slightly more than a Century from the convening of the Berlin Conference in 1884-85, approximately 110 years, scholars were expounding on the current social, political, and economic conditions in Africa that linked with the era of colonization. The purpose of the scholarly presentation was "…to show how the present conditions in Africa could be ideologically and institutionally linked to the colonial and imperial past. Without comprehending this tragic linkage, Africa's poverty and misery become the results of ill-fortune, a curse or some inexplicable haunting set of circumstances (Maloba, 1995) in Ogot and Ochieng, <u>Decolonization and Independence in Kenya: 1940-1993, p. 7).</u>

The Traditional Social Welfare System's cultural traditions, and linguistic borders that had been created over thousands of years, were extremely important, especially for social protection and/or mutual aid. But, these concepts, including the concept of "we" were of no relevance to the invaders. The primary agenda of the invaders was one of conquest that would allow them to extract the needed resources for the development of Europe during the era of the Industrial Revolution as Western societies moved from an agricultural economy to one centered around industrialization.

One scholar, activist once described the world of colonization as divided into two worlds. The line that divided the two worlds, the colonizers and the victims or natives, was the border "... represented by the barracks and the police stations. In the colonies, the official legitimate agent, the spokesperson for the colonizers and the regime of oppression, is the police officer or the soldier...the colonist sector is a sector built to last, all stone and steel, lights, paved roads... colonized sector, famished sector, hungry for bread, meats, shoes, coal and light...sector that crouches and covers, a sector on its knees, a sector that is prostrate. It's a sector of niggers, a sector of towel heads" (Fanon, Frantz, The Wretched of the Earth, Grove Press, NY, 1963, pp. 3-5).

The Traditional African Social Welfare System, or Extended Family System for providing social protection/social caring/health care for its members continued to do so in spite of limitations during the era of European invasion, and colonization. The Berlin Conference 1884-1885 began what became known as the "Scramble for Africa," the invasion, forced occupation, colonization, and the forceful annexing of African land masses and/or territory by the invading, militarily, politically powers of Europe. The final results of the Berlin Conference were the division of Africa into some 50 colonies; each major European power being delegated its share of the redistricted territory that it would have control or dominance over (Pakenham, 1990). In addition to the 50 colonies, King Leopold II had his own Congo Free State, not a colony but a state.

The Forced Labor Era: No Chance for Social Protection in Old Age

It was in this world of colonization, domination by superior powers resulting in all forms of social injustices that the International Labor Organization convened the Forced Labor Convention. The Convention took place in 1930 a half century following the Berlin Conference and the "Scramble for Africa." During this time millions of Africans were part of a system of colonization, and being denied the opportunity to benefit from all of the medical advances, economic and social development, and a tripartite labor system; a system that would ensure social protection in old age. Furthermore, instead of benefitting economically from the ongoing industrial revolution at the time, native Africans were providing the labor and resources for the establishment of European economic empires. How many children did not survive to reach old age at the time? Now, many of the off springs, 84%, of the forced labor generations in Sub-Saharan Africa, do not have social protection (basic income, access to healthcare and social services) in old age.

During the many years of underdevelopment in Africa as the Western world was building massive industrial systems, including tripartite labor structures, Sub-Saharan Africa was struggling to just survive. Post-Independence have provided some opportunities and the countries have made tremendous progress, but in many respects still struggling to catch up, especially in the areas of economic development. The hopes are as the countries continue to develop their industrial sectors, accompanied by a strong labor movement, one can expect more and more workers to move away from the dominant informal labor sector and more towards a tripartite labor market. The 1930 Convention, in regards to labor, workers' rights, although not highly successful in its mission at the time, began to raise questions, mobilize the global community, and knowingly recognizing or not, playing a role in preparing the world for the "Silver Tsunami."

It was almost three decades following the 1930 Convention that the first African country Ghana, 1957, was granted Independence. Following 1957, many countries in received or were granted Independence after so may years of colonization. The long era of colonization did not end with the Declaration of Independence and the raising of the country's flag. Decolonization, especially in the areas related to work, and labor issues in general would remain on the agendas of organizations, such as the ILO. The ILO with its mission of enhancing the overall working conditions of the human workforce, began to recognize following WWI, somewhat of a positive political environment that would become favorable enough for carrying out its mission (Human Rights, Development, and Decolonization p. 4). Also, it was following the 1930 Convention that the mission and work of the ILO began to expand from a primary focus on the physical requirement of work towards more and more emphasis on areas such as social security, as well as issues and concerns related to human rights (HRDD, ibid. p.4).

In was from this colonized and oppressed world that the colonizers were in need of very cheap labor and would not be able to carry out their mission without a steady supply of native workers. The colonizers or settlers had come into the possession of huge plots of agriculture land, estimated to be on average some 2400 acres per/family. And, obviously the only solution was to create a system whereas the Africans had to work for the settlers. In order to carry out their goals it became necessary for the settlers to create or enact labor as well as economic legislation that would allow them to recruit laborers. Also the legislation included provisions that would prevent the colonized the opportunity to have access to opportunities to engage in profitable cash crop production, as well as having access to fresh land. Furthermore, to make things more difficult for the natives the legislation enacted provided the settlers with the opportunity to impose such provisions as poll and hut taxes. These legislative initiatives gave the natives one option give their labor and services to the foreign settlers (Ogot, B.A. & Ochieng, W.R., Decolonization and Independence in Kenya 1940-93, Ohio University Press, 1995 p. xv).

The settlers "… taxation is the only possible method of compelling the natives to leave his reserve for the purpose of seeking work. Only in this way can the cost of living be increased for the native… and it is on this that the supply of labor and the price of laborer depends" (Ogot and Ochieng, Ibid, p. xvi – Quote is from, Leys, C., Underdevelopment in Kenya: The Political Economy of Neo-Colonialism, London, Heinemann, 1975, p. 29).

Also, in countries such as Kenya, Rhodesia (now Zimbabwe), the settlers put forth special efforts to prevent the natives from growing cash crops the goal being to make sure that their labor would be made available to the settlers. One of the great settlers by the name of Colonial Grogan speaking specifically of the Kikuyu, the largest tribal group currently in Kenya, and the tribe of Jomo Kenyatta, First President of Kenya, "… 'We stolen his land. Now we must steal his limbs. Compulsory labor is the corollary of our occupation of the country' (Rodney, Walter, ibid, p. 165-166).

What other factors, other than the aforementioned legislative initiatives, that gave the settlers their power to oppress? For one, "... the alien colonial state had a monopoly of political power, after crushing all opposition by superior armed force. Secondly, the African working class was small, very dispersed, and very unstable owing migratory practices. Thirdly... European capitalists in Africa had additional racial justification for dealing unjustly with the African worker. The racist theory that the black man was inferior led to the conclusion that he deserved lower wages...The combination of the above factors made it extremely difficult for African Workers to organize themselves" (Rodney, Walter, How Europe Underdeveloped Africa, Baltimore: Black Classic Press, 2011, pp. 149-150).

It was in this world that the Forced Labor Convention of 1930 was convened. The global population reached one billion in 1800 and it occurred after some 50,000 years. Between 1800 and 1930 it only took 130 years to reach the two billion mark. It is obvious in reviewing this accelerated timeframe, that the world was experiencing rapid population growth. Some contributing factors for this growth in over just 130 years were medical advances, including public health education, prevention, and improvements in the quality of life (growth and development) as a results of social and economic development. During this time millions of Africans were part of a system of colonization, and denied the opportunity to benefit from all of the medical advancements, and social developments taking place around them. How many children did not survive to reach old age at the time? Now, many of the off springs, 84%, of the forced labor generations, in Sub-Saharan Africa, do not have social protection (basic income, access to healthcare and services) in old age. During the many years of underdevelopment in Africa as the Western world was building massive industrial systems, including tripartite labor structures, Sub-Saharan Africa was struggling to just survive. Post-Independence have provided opportunities and the countries have made tremendous progress, but in many respects still struggling to catch up, especially in the areas of economic development. The hopes are as the countries continue to develop their industrial sectors, accompanied by a strong labor movement, one can expect more and more workers to move away from an informal labor sector and towards a more tripartite labor market.

For the generations of Africans born about one generation prior to the period of colonization, and those born during the period, roughly from around 1885 to approximately 1957 (Ghana' Independence), there would be no opportunities for social pensions or social security. In other words, these cohorts would not have the opportunity to engage in any form of a tripartite labor mechanism (collective bargaining) that would ensure social security/social protection or a traditional social pension. During this era there was no such opportunity to organize as workers. Attempts to engage in such practices would have been a definite threat to the European powers, especially governments in the colonies" (HRDD, ibid, p. 6).

The Introduction of Social Protection in the Colonies: For Expatriates Only

As illustrated African societies established their own system of social security/social protection for responding to the social and medical needs for all, including the elderly, children, as well as vulnerable members of the population. Traditional forms of social security/social protection were very much part of the social/cultural fabric of African societies when the conquering Europeans arrived.

The African traditional forms of social security/protection for the purpose of responding to human needs remained somewhat in tact for the most part during the era of colonization. Despite the fact that the extended family network systems, including medical and health were deeply entrenched in the culture, to some extent the systems had to have been challenged and weakened during an era of colonization and accompanying exploitation and social injustices. The foreign occupiers by this time were well aware of the need for social protection/social security for workers and their families. As aforementioned the foreign occupiers made no efforts to provide any forms of social protection for the forced laborers who were contributing so greatly to empire building back home in Europe. It says a great deal about the involved countries and their leaders that when their concept of social security, the precursor to the modern schemes, was introduced in the colonies during colonization, they were for expatriates only. These schemes were not targeted for the local populations; the primary targets were Europeans, or the expatriates employed in government or public service positions. The social security schemes, such as employer liability, social insurance, old-age assistance, Widows' pensions, poor relief and public assistance, were targeted primarily to the expatriate population. Exclusionary provisions, excluding Africans, were explicitly pointed out in the legislative policy of the occupying country (Midgley, 1984 p.106).

One example of an exclusionary provision in a social policy document was in South Africa. In 1928 an old age non-contributory pension scheme was introduced in the Republic of South Africa. This provision was explicit in stating that Africans and Asians were excluded from the old age pension scheme. A similar old age pension scheme was introduced in what was then known as Southern and Northern Rhodesia (presently known as Zimbabwe) around 1936 with similar provisions, as the one aforementioned reference South Africa, of exclusions (Midgley, 1984).

The Freedom Charter of South Africa: A Response to the Forced Labor Era

The Freedom Charter (Adopted at the Congress of the people at Kliptown, Johannesburg, June 25-26, 1955) speaks loudly to the injustices that existed in South Africa during the era of colonization or Apartheid:

"We the People of South Africa, declare for all our country and the world to know: South Africa belongs to all who live in it, black and white, and that no government can justly claim authority unless it is based on the will of all the people;

That our people have been robbed of their birthright to land, liberty and peace by a form of government founded on injustice and inequality;

That our country will never be prosperous or free until all our people live in brotherhood, enjoying equal rights and opportunities; that only a democratic state, based on the will of all the people, can secure to all their birthright without distinction of colour, race, sex or beliefs…"

The Charter included a section related to the general subject of this manuscript: "THERE SHALL BE WORK AND SECURITY!"

"All who work shall be free to form trade unions, to elect their officers and to make wage agreements with their employers.

The state shall recognize the right and duty of all to work, and to draw full unemployment benefits.

Men and women of all races shall receive equal pay for equal work.

There shall be a forty-hour working week, a national minimum wage, paid annual leave, and sick leave for all workers, and maternity leave on full pay for all working mothers.

Miners, domestic workers, farm workers and civil servants shall have the rights as all others who work.

Child labour, compound labour, the total system and contract labour shall be abolished."

The Introduction of Western Programs of Social Protection: Post Colonial Era

Social Security Schemes for African Civil Servants

Social protection and/or social security schemes, including employer liability, poor relief, old-age pension, widows and orphan funds, had been introduced into the African colonies during colonization, but Africans were excluded. But, following Independence Africans who took over the public and/or government jobs once occupied by expatriates now became the employees in the employer/worker insurance schemes. The International Labor Organization (ILO) played a major role in ensuring that the employment rights and privileges once held by the expatriates should now be passed on to the Africans now occupying these civil service and/ or government positions (ILO, 1961).

Although a small segment of African civil service workers were now protected to some extent by the passed on social security schemes, the vast majority of Africans were unprotected. Therefore, traditional systems of social security/social protection continued to be the major sources of protection. Historically, and even until contemporary times, the majority of those in the workforce in African countries were and continue to be employed in the informal sector of the workforce. This is a major factor why only 16.9 % of retirees are without social protection. This sector of the workforce, for the most part, is not connected to contributory and/or non-contributory social insurance schemes; therefore, not only are they not protective from employer liability, lack of access to medical care, including disability, this vast informal sector remains un-protective following retirement without income security. Therefore, a major challenge facing developing countries in the 21st Century is how to include this growing population of workers from the informal sector into some system of social security/social protection, or tripartite collective bargaining system.

Summary and Conclusion: Caring for a Growing older Population in Africa

Without a doubt, when considering the role(s) played historically by the extended family network, including the medical and health components, the conclusion is that an incredible job has been done in caring for the needs of family members, especially the older population. Now, with a growing older population with more complex and special needs, the current and future challenges will become greater. Speaking of historical challenges the various systems of caring survived the era of colonization that included the forceful takeover of land, the separation of families, forced labor as well as other forms of human injustices. There is no reason not to believe, although with major challenges, that the caring tradition will continue.

There are major questions emerging as policy makers, researchers, and human service professionals, consider the challenges accompanying a growing older population and how Africa will respond. During an era of urbanization and modernization and all of the implications, is there a role for the traditional extended family kinship tradition, including health and medical, in preparation/planning for meeting the needs of a growing population? Those needs include income security, housing, environmental safety, access to health and social caring, including long-term care. Secondly, not only what the specific role(s) of those traditional systems could play in responding to the "Silver Tsunami," how can the strengths of those systems be incorporated utilizing creative/innovative methods become part of the advanced model(s) for implementation?

Planners will need to be realistic that a carbon copy of the principles, roles and responsibilities may not suffice in an urbanized modernized society in caring for the older population; with this thought in mind, responsible leaders will have to be innovative and creative. In other words one cannot expect a "cookie cutter" model during the problem solving process. A major challenge has to be addressed by political, economic, medical, health and social systems, what legislative mandates/policies are needed for planning and implementation to ensure the goal of social protection? Is there a relationship between social protection/social pensions and social/economic development? If yes, how would advocacy and planning strategies/tactics be formulated and implemented to convince the citizenry to become part of the movement for ensuring social protection? The questions become extremely critical when countries begin to confront the realities associated with a growing older population, the "Silver Tsunami," and the transition of traditional societies to a more modernized and urbanized society. Keeping in mind the growing older population will bring more complex and special needs, including the transition from a communicable disease model to one of chronic diseases.

The transition from a traditional society to a more urban modernized society for all age groups is and will continue to present major challenges for all systems, educational, medical, health, political and economical in meeting the needs of all citizens. Now, comes the demographic shock of a growing older population in the midst of urbanization and modernization. The sociologist Toennis (See Chapter IV) projected that all societies would eventually begin the transition from a traditional to a modern society. It was even suggested by one theorist that a major threat in achieving modernization was the extended family system and its lack of mobility principles. The sociologist presents an interesting observation when considering that a major strength, especially in caring for the needs of others has been the family. Historically, within this extended family system, the elderly lived with or near younger members of the family. Although weakened during the era of colonization, and now by the processes of modernization and urbanization, the extended family, to some extent continues to play some important roles in most African countries, especially in caring for the elderly, children, and other vulnerable members of the family. The question can the extended family, or some selective strengths brought forward play a role in a modern society?

Is there a role for public/social policy to play during the innovative process of the inclusion of strengths from the extended family system? It is obvious that social policies especially in regards to social pensions and other areas of social protection are needed immediately. In reference to the current crisis, lack of social pensions and other social protections, there are traditional principles and practices that could be considered in preparation for models to be utilized in the caring process, especially for the older population. One potential example relates to one of the basic principles embodied within the extended family kinship system of caring, namely the concept of intergenerational reciprocity. The concept refers to commitment of the grandparents seeing after or taking care of the younger children; in carrying out the aforementioned commitment it was expected that as the older person grows into old age the younger generation would be committed to caring for the older family members. Now, how could this traditional consult of sharing be applicable to the "Silver Tsunami?" Global research, data and information from medical and health practices, including professional caregivers, have pointed out that as persons' age they become at risk for chronic illnesses/diseases such as Dementia. Because of the current "demographic shock" of a growing older population, caring becomes more of a challenge to all systems, especially the family as well as other medical/health institutions and professionals. Long-term care responsibilities, especially caring for the older populations in facilities are becoming more and costly. Research in the United States is now demonstrating that it is significantly more costly maintaining older persons in institutions than in their homes and communities. Long-term home care cost significantly less but can also have a negative impact on home caregivers, mostly women and their health. If countries are committed to ensuring that the older generation should have the opportunity to live in dignity and respect in later life why not commit to social policies in addition to a social pension that would provide support for the concept intergenerational reciprocity become operational within the home. Not only will it be less expensive that building and maintaining expensive care facilities, but play a major role in keeping families together. Social and public policies could support tax deductible incentives for keeping families together, such as home renovations providing additional space for family members, including plans for making the home more accessible for the older person; those plans could include the construction of ramps for a wheelchair, handles and bars for bathroom use for improved accessibility.

History says that the extended family network system contributed greatly to the overall quality of life across all age group. Why not give some of the strengths of this traditional system the opportunity to operate in a modern society? A review of Africa's traditional history of caring, especially the extended family system network, could be of some importance in responding to a growing older population living in dignity and respect. For the older populations the time is now for action; to just wait for legislative initiatives to take place without other meaningful actions presents a serious threat to the quality of life expected for these warriors of many years. Let's not forget that the current population of older persons represents the grandchildren and great grandchildren of the working or laboring parents from the era of colonization, including their "forced labor" participation without any promises and/or guarantees of social protection. Shouldn't they have the right to live in dignity and respect? It was their hard labor and the natural resources of their native lands that helped to build the economic empires of Europe.

ADDENDUM-POST CHAPTER FUTURE CONSIDERATIONS

The Era of Colonization/Forced Labor: Impact on Culture, Customs and Traditions

The colonizers possessed all of the political and military power to maintain obedience from the native workers. Furthermore, they had strategically located and/or dispersed the workers, and closely watched by the military would make it difficult organize; the Europeans with the help of the missionaries always used the racist theory of inferiority to justify lower wages and forced labor.

Shortly before the end of WWII, "The International Labor Organization elevated human rights to a position of fundamental importance in it work…" The Philadelphia Conference 1944 a milestone in the history of human rights…from this point at the latest the ILO norms provided a clear point of reference for political and social mFor the most part, it began during the Berlin Conference in 1884-85 resulting in what is now commonly referred to as the "The Scramble for Africa." The Conference does not mean that attempts and some successes to exploit the continent did not occur prior to 1884-85. Threats to the traditional systems of care caring began to take hold when the European powers made a political, and for the most part, an economical decision to divide or split the African continent into geographical boundaries/ colonies. Not only did the actions from the European powers threaten the existence of the traditional social welfare system, but all the deeply rooted traditions, culture, and customs as well. The European powers, scramble for Africa, illustrated no respect for the traditions, culture, and traditions of Africa. In other words, no consideration, appreciation or respect to the historical family kinship, tribal, or clan system ties that were essential for the survival of the traditional social welfare system. As a result, the tribal and/or kinship groups so essential for social in all forms were separated and left struggling to survive. The carving up or dividing the native land was crucial for the European powers in their efforts to develop the financial/ economic empires back home in Europe.

The "scramble for Africa" was great timing for the economies of Europe. The scramble and eventually the geographical carving up of a great continent was taking place in the midst of or during the industrial revolution in Europe and the West. Once the European powers, now possessing the necessary political and military power, gained control over the land and the people, were in a position to seize the natural resources needed for the development of their economic empires in Europe. Labor or native workers needed for achieving their goals were simply no major problem for the Europeans; the powers of Europe had the political and military powers for achieving their goals. Native workers, especially during the forced labor era, were moved out of the villages and into the cities as manufacturing centers emerged for processing resources back to Europe. It was during the industrial revolution that European states became the center of financial power and influence **(GLOBAL HISTORY/BARRON SERIES, PP. 407-409)**.

It is important to note that the primary recipient of the benefits, especially the wealth derived from the industrial revolution, especially phase one was Great Britain. But, as the revolution moved into the second phase, there were more competition from other European countries. During the early years Great Britain was the center of manufacturing, shipping, banking, and transportation for the world. But other European countries, including the United States began to become imitators of the British technology, as well as the use of British capital for moving forward. By the mid-70's, approximately one decade prior to the Berlin Conference, that many considered the coming of the second phase of the Revolution, Britain, had begun to lose some of its industrial dominance held during the first phase. The second phase was now focusing on steel, electricity, and petro chemicals, not being demanded globally. Now, Great Britain was operating in a very competitive world, especially with Germany and the United

States. The U.S. had fast become not only the number one steel producer in the world, but a major world competitor with Britain and other European powers. These are possible factors that influenced the European powers to begin thinking about new natural resources, such as minerals for maintaining, not just their economic power but ways to expand it (<u>Rand McNally: Atlas of World History</u>, Chicago: Rand McNally and Company, 1987). The question, to what extent the aforementioned factors influenced the need for the Berlin Conference and the beginning of the "scramble for Africa?"

The European powers, during deliberations and negotiations among themselves, concluded that there was a need to develop a written document or contract that would regulate the anticipated competition that would eventually emerge from their actions. The concept put forward was referred to as "effective occupation;" the criteria underlying the recognition of territory claim on a global level. "The importance of direct rule in terms of "effective recourse to armed force against indigenous states and people" (Pakenham, Thomas, <u>The Scramble for Africa: The White Man's Conquest of the Dark Continent from 1876-1912</u>, New York: Random House, 1991). The principle of "effective occupation" stated that "…powers could acquire rights over colonial lands only if they possessed them or had "effective occupation:" In other words, if they had treaties with local leaders, if they flew their flags there, and if they established an administrative territory to govern it with a police force to keep order. The colonial powers could also make use of the colony economically…" (Pakenham, ibid,1991).

The final Berlin document was signed on the 26th of February 1885. The General Act included some thirty-eight inexplicit clauses; therefore there was a crucial need for the Principles of effective occupation. It has been suggested, "The race to grab a slice of the African cake had started long before the first day of the conference. And none of the thirty-eight clauses of the General Act had any teeth. It had set no rules for dividing, let alone eating, the cake. In one sense…the Berlin conference marked a turning point in the history of Africa and Europe. There was something that came to be called 'the spirit of Berlin.' For the first time great men like Bismarck had linked their names at an international conference to Livingston's lofty ideals: to introduce the '3 c's – commerce, Christianity, civilization – into the dark places of Africa. Of course, the main policy of the Powers was directed to strategic and economic objectives such as protecting old markets or exploiting new ones" (Pakenham, Thomas, <u>The Scramble for Africa: The White Man's Conquest of the Dark Continent from 1876-1912</u>, New York: Random House, 1991, pages 254-255).

During the "scramble for Africa," including the negotiations among the European powers, an extremely peculiar happening was taking place in Belgium that would have implications for what initially was called The Congo Free State. Other than advisors the only participant or decision maker regarding this very wealthy geographical area in Africa was King Leopold II of Belgium. The European powers seated at the negotiating table in Berlin seemed to have no interest in this part of Africa. Could it have been that the Congo Free State, later to become the Belgian Colony, did not have the natural resources, minerals, diamonds, and gold thought to be in other African colonies? King Leopold II had ascended to the throne of Belgium in 1865. As the story unfolds of how the King's acquisition of the Congo, becoming its sole ruler, provides another demonstration of the disrespect the Europeans had for the African continent and it people. Well, there is a piece of land in Africa that looks promising let's just grab it? Operating externally from the negotiations taking place among the power brokers from countries, such as England, France, and Spain, King Leopold II, on his own terms, became the sole ruler of the Congo Free State (Gondola, CH. Didier, The History of the Congo, London: Greenwood Press, 2002).

The King's actions that eventually, and without any serious opposition from the other European powers have been described, "Leopold's acquisition of so much power, incidentally, took place almost by sleight of hand. The European powers had not recognized him, but his Association Internationale du Congo, as sovereign administrator over the Congo basin…no one seemed to protest. People saw him as a great philanthropist with a great many ideals and even more means at his disposal" (Reybrouck, David Van, Congo: The Epic History of a People, New York, HarperCollins Publishers, 2014, p. 58).

Operating behind the scenes, King Leopold II successfully acquired for himself a territory, naming it the Congo Free State, eighty times larger than his home country of Belgium (Didier, ibid, 2002). What became known as the Congo Free State had been regarded as one of Africa's richest geographical areas for its natural resources that were located in the Congo Basin. The area possessed approximately a third of the rainforests in Africa. Also, the Congo Basin was known to possess numerous species of trees known for the production of ebony, mahogany and teak; the basin is considered to be the "…second largest river in the world in terms of volume flowing water, exceeded only by the Amazon River of South America…Africa's most extensive network of navigable waterways and sources of hundreds of different species of fish" (Didier, ibid, 2002, p. 2). Just imagine all of the aforementioned, and obviously much more, "fell in the lap" of King Leopold II. No, not just by accident this happened, "On April 30 1885, the Berlin Conference, devoted to the peaceful partitioning of those parts of Africa not yet claimed by a European power, accorded him personal control of the Congo" (Edgerton, Robert B., The Troubled Heart of Africa: A History of the Congo, New York: St. Martin's Press, 2002).

It is interesting to note that the people of Belgium historically had opposed colonialism; furthermore, there was no history of ties with the African continent, including any business interests, or contacts of any kind. "Yet it was Leopold, rather than the head of any European trading or mining company, who several years earlier paid Sir Henry Morton Stanley, African Explorer, to supervise the building of the road that opened the Congo River to navigation… And it was Leopold…who convinced thirteen European powers and the United States at the Berlin Conference that he would improve the moral and material conditions of the Congolese and moreover, put an end to slave trading" (Edgerton, ibid, 2002, pages 78-79. His intent to free all of the Africans in the Congo played a part in the name, Congo Free State (Edgerton, ibid, 2002).

King Leopold remained the sole ruler of the Congo Free State for 23 years not as a colony but a state; after 23 years the Congo Free State became a Belgian colony. Speaking of peculiarities King Leopold II was considered an absentee but sole ruler of the Congo; furthermore, King Leopold II never visited the Congo. His residence was approximately 3,700 miles to the North, and it would have taken approximately a four-week journey to reach the borders of the Congo Free State (Reybrouck, ibid, 2014).

In regards to inhumane treatment or social injustices, consider the fact that the native population had no input in the design or mapping of their native states, including the Congo

Free State, and later a Belgian colony. The final physical boundaries of each area drawn on maps, without input from the native population, were actually completed by Europeans who had never been to Africa (Dowden, Richard, "The End of Colonialism, New States, Old Societies," Africa-Altered States, Ordinary Miracles (1st Edition), NY: Public Affairs, 2009). In the process of gaining complete control over the land, resources, and the people, any aspects of culture, customs, traditions, including the foundations of the traditional social welfare system were completely ignored or despised. "Europeans had claimed racial superiority to justify slavery and imperialism…African dignity and self worth eroded. They were forced to abandon their own beliefs, identities and values…"(Dowden, Richard ibid, p. 62). One can imagine how devastating the seizure of land was to the people of Africa. Land ownership and the authority and decision-making surrounding it in the villages were critical in maintaining the traditional social welfare system, but also all of the customs and traditions of society.

What other factors, other than the aforementioned legislative initiatives, that gave the settlers their power to oppress? For one, "… the alien colonial state had a monopoly of political power, after crushing all opposition by superior armed force. Secondly, the African working class was small, very dispersed, and very unstable owing migratory practices. Thirdly… European capitalists in Africa had additional racial justification for dealing unjustly with the African worker. The racist theory that the black man was inferior led to the conclusion that he deserved lower wages…The combination of the above factors made it extremely difficult for African Workers to organize themselves" (Rodney, Walter, How Europe Underdeveloped Africa, Baltimore: Black Classic Press, 2011, pp. 149-150).

The social injustices and inhuman treatment toward Africans were deeply rooted in "… the racist principal that barbarism pervaded Africa and there was no culture to be salvaged" (Maloba, 1995, p. 11). The European powers had strong allies in various religious denominations/congregations of missionaries who had come to Africa in their attempts to civilize and save the savages from the fires of hell. The missionaries sought to replace African religious and cultural practices with strong civilized Western cultures. The goal for the French during a process of assimilation was to change African men, women, and children into good civilized French models (Maloba, 1995 ibid).

In was from this colonized and oppressed world that the colonizers were in need of very cheap labor and would not be able to carry out their mission with the supply of African workers. The colonizers or settlers had come into the possession of huge plots of agriculture land, estimated to be on average some 2400 acres per/family. And, obviously the only solution was to create a system whereas the Africans had to work for the. In order to carry out their goals it became necessary for the settlers to create or enact labor as well as economic legislation that would allow them to recruit laborers. Also the legislation included provisions that would prevent the colonized the opportunity to have access to opportunities to engage in profitable cash crop production, as well as having access to fresh land. Furthermore, to make things more difficult for the natives the legislation enacted provided the settlers with the opportunity to impose such provisions as poll and hut taxes. These legislative initiatives gave the natives just option, give their labor and services to the foreign settlers (Ogot, B.A. & Ochieng, W.R., Decolonization and Independence in Kenya 1940-93, Ohio University Press, 1995 p. xv).

One major concern of the European powers had to do with what strategies could be used in forcing the native population to engage in seeking employment away from their homesteads or villages. They concluded that some form of taxation was the answer. The settlers "… taxation is the only possible method of compelling the natives to leave his reserve for the purpose of seeking work. Only in this way can the cost of living be increased for the native… and it is on this that the supply of labor and the price of laborer depends" (Ogot and Ochieng, Ibid, p. xvi – Quote is from, Leys, C., Underdevelopment in Kenya: The Political Economy of Neo-Colonialism, London, Heinemann, 1975, p. 29). The European settlers had the power to enforce any policies that would benefit or achieve their economic goals.

Also, in countries such as Kenya, Rhodesia (now Zimbabwe), the settlers put forth special efforts to prevent the natives from growing their own cash crops; the goal being to make sure that their labor would be made available only to the settlers. One of the great settlers by the name of Colonial Grogan speaking specifically of the Kikuyu, the largest tribal group currently in Kenya, and the tribe of Jomo Kenyatta, First President of Kenya, "… 'We stolen his land. Now we must steal his limbs. Compulsory labor is the corollary of our occupation of the country' (Rodney, Walter, ibid, p. 165-166). One of the key principles of the European forced labor campaign.

The European conquest of Africa took place beginning around 1884 and continued for approximately three-quarters of a century. The major powers carrying out the conquest represented, for the most part the countries of France, Germany, British, and Portugal; only approximately 10% of Africa was in the powers of Europe around 1870, at the time of the Berlin Conference, but by the year 1914, the territory under European control had reached 90% (Pakenham, ibid).

In slightly more than a Century from the convening of the Berlin Conference in 1884-85, approximately 110 years, scholars were expounding on the current social, political, and economic conditions in Africa that linked with the era of colonization. The purpose of the scholarly presentation was "…to show how the present conditions in Africa could be ideologically and institutionally linked to the colonial and imperial past. Without comprehending this tragic linkage, Africa's poverty and misery become the results of ill-fortune, a curse or some inexplicable haunting set of circumstances (Maloba, 1995) in Ogot and Ochieng, Decolonization and Independence in Kenya: 1940-1993, p. 7).

The Traditional Social Welfare System's cultural traditions, and linguistic borders that had been created over thousands of years, were extremely important, especially for social protection and/or mutual aid. But, these concepts, including the concept of "we" were of no relevance to the invaders. The primary agenda of the invaders was one of conquest that would allow them to extract the needed resources for the development of Europe during the era of the Industrial Revolution as Western societies moved from an agricultural economy to one centered around industrialization.

One scholar, activist once described the world of colonization as divided into two worlds. The line that divided the two worlds, the colonizers and the victims or natives, was the border "… represented by the barracks and the police stations. In the colonies, the official legitimate agent, the spokesperson for the colonizers and the regime of oppression, is the police officer or the soldier…the colonist sector is a sector built to last, all stone and steel, lights, paved roads… colonized sector, famished sector, hungry for bread, meats, shoes, coal and light…sector that crouches and covers, a sector on its knees, a sector that is prostrate. It's a sector of niggers, a sector of towel heads" (Fanon, Frantz, The Wretched of the Earth, Grove Press, NY, 1963, pp. 3-5).

The Traditional African Social Welfare System, or Extended Family System for providing social protection/social caring/health care for its members continued to do so in spite of limitations during the era of European invasion, and colonization. The Berlin Conference 1884-1885 began what became known as the "Scramble for Africa," the invasion, forced occupation, colonization, and the forceful annexing of African land masses and/or territory by the invading, militarily, politically powers of Europe. The final results of the Berlin Conference were the division of Africa into some 50 colonies; each major European power being delegated its share of the redistricted territory that it would have control or dominance over (Pakenham, 1990). In addition to the 50 colonies, King Leopold II had his own Congo Free State, not a colony but a state.

The Forced Labor Era: No Chance for Social Protection in Old Age

It was in this world of colonization, domination by superior powers resulting in all forms of social injustices that the International Labor Organization convened the Forced Labor Convention. The Convention took place in 1930 a half century following the Berlin Conference and the "Scramble for Africa." During this time millions of Africans were part of a system of colonization, and being denied the opportunity to benefit from all of the medical advances, economic and social development, and a tripartite labor system; a system that would ensure social protection in old age. Furthermore, instead of benefitting economically from the ongoing industrial revolution at the time, native Africans were providing the labor and resources for the establishment of European economic empires. How many children did not survive to reach old age at the time? Now, many of the off springs, 84%, of the forced labor generations in Sub-Saharan Africa, do not have social protection (basic income, access to healthcare and social services) in old age.

During the many years of underdevelopment in Africa as the Western world was building massive industrial systems, including tripartite labor structures, Sub-Saharan Africa was struggling to just survive. Post-Independence have provided some opportunities and the countries have made tremendous progress, but in many respects still struggling to catch up, especially in the areas of economic development. The hopes are as the countries continue to develop their industrial sectors, accompanied by a strong labor movement, one can expect more and more workers to move away from the dominant informal labor sector and more towards a tripartite labor market. The 1930 Convention, in regards to labor, workers' rights, although not highly successful in its mission at the time, began to raise questions, mobilize the global community, and knowingly recognizing or not, playing a role in preparing the world for the "Silver Tsunami."

It was almost three decades following the 1930 Convention that the first African country Ghana, 1957, was granted Independence. Following 1957, many countries in received or were granted Independence after so may years of colonization. The long era of colonization did not end with the Declaration of Independence and the raising of the country's flag. Decolonization, especially in the areas related to work, and labor issues in general would remain on the agendas of organizations, such as the ILO. The ILO with its mission of enhancing the overall working conditions of the human workforce, began to recognize following WWI, somewhat of a positive political environment that would become favorable enough for carrying out its mission (Human Rights, Development, and Decolonization p. 4). Also, it was following the 1930 Convention that the mission and work of the ILO began to expand from a primary focus on the physical requirement of work towards more and more emphasis on areas such as social security, as well as issues and concerns related to human rights (HRDD, ibid. p.4).

In was from this colonized and oppressed world that the colonizers were in need of very cheap labor and would not be able to carry out their mission without a steady supply of native workers. The colonizers or settlers had come into the possession of huge plots of agriculture land, estimated to be on average some 2400 acres per/family. And, obviously the only solution was to create a system whereas the Africans had to work for the settlers. In order to carry out their goals it became necessary for the settlers to create or enact labor as well as economic legislation that would allow them to recruit laborers. Also the legislation included provisions that would prevent the colonized the opportunity to have access to opportunities to engage in profitable cash crop production, as well as having access to fresh land. Furthermore, to make things more difficult for the natives the legislation enacted provided the settlers with the opportunity to impose such provisions as poll and hut taxes. These legislative initiatives gave the natives one option give their labor and services to the foreign settlers (Ogot, B.A. & Ochieng, W.R., Decolonization and Independence in Kenya 1940-93, Ohio University Press, 1995 p. xv).

The settlers "... taxation is the only possible method of compelling the natives to leave his reserve for the purpose of seeking work. Only in this way can the cost of living be increased for the native... and it is on this that the supply of labor and the price of laborer depends" (Ogot and Ochieng, Ibid, p. xvi – Quote is from, Leys, C., Underdevelopment in Kenya: The Political Economy of Neo-Colonialism, London, Heinemann, 1975, p. 29).

Also, in countries such as Kenya, Rhodesia (now Zimbabwe), the settlers put forth special efforts to prevent the natives from growing cash crops the goal being to make sure that their labor would be made available to the settlers. One of the great settlers by the name of Colonial Grogan speaking specifically of the Kikuyu, the largest tribal group currently in Kenya, and the tribe of Jomo Kenyatta, First President of Kenya, "... 'We stolen his land. Now we must steal his limbs. Compulsory labor is the corollary of our occupation of the country' (Rodney, Walter, ibid, p. 165-166).

What other factors, other than the aforementioned legislative initiatives, that gave the settlers their power to oppress? For one, "... the alien colonial state had a monopoly of political power, after crushing all opposition by superior armed force. Secondly, the African working class was small, very dispersed, and very unstable owing migratory practices. Thirdly... European capitalists in Africa had additional racial justification for dealing unjustly with the African worker. The racist theory that the black man was inferior led to the conclusion that he deserved lower wages...The combination of the above factors made it extremely difficult for African Workers to organize themselves" (Rodney, Walter, How Europe Underdeveloped Africa, Baltimore: Black Classic Press, 2011, pp. 149-150).

It was in this world that the Forced Labor Convention of 1930 was convened. The global population reached one billion in 1800 and it occurred after some 50,000 years. Between

1800 and 1930 it only took 130 years to reach the two billion mark. It is obvious in reviewing this accelerated timeframe, that the world was experiencing rapid population growth. Some contributing factors for this growth in over just 130 years were medical advances, including public health education, prevention, and improvements in the quality of life (growth and development) as a results of social and economic development. During this time millions of Africans were part of a system of colonization, and denied the opportunity to benefit from all of the medical advancements, and social developments taking place around them. How many children did not survive to reach old age at the time? Now, many of the off springs, 84%, of the forced labor generations, in Sub-Saharan Africa, do not have social protection (basic income, access to healthcare and services) in old age. During the many years of underdevelopment in Africa as the Western world was building massive industrial systems, including tripartite labor structures, Sub-Saharan Africa was struggling to just survive. Post-Independence have provided opportunities and the countries have made tremendous progress, but in many respects still struggling to catch up, especially in the areas of economic development. The hopes are as the countries continue to develop their industrial sectors, accompanied by a strong labor movement, one can expect more and more workers to move away from the informal labor sectors or self-employed and towards a more formal tripartite labor market.

For the generations of Africans born about one generation prior to the period of colonization, and those born during the period, roughly from around 1885 to approximately 1957 (Ghana' Independence), there would be no opportunities for social pensions or social security. In other words, these cohorts would not have the opportunity to engage in any form of a tripartite labor mechanism (collective bargaining) that would ensure social security/social protection or a traditional social pension. During this era there was no such opportunity to organize as workers. Attempts to engage in such practices would have been a definite threat to the European powers, especially governments in the colonies" (HRDD, ibid, p. 6).

CHAPTER V

Pre-Post Independence Sub-Saharan Africa: Challenges of Modernization, Industrialization, and Urbanization

INTRODUCTION

The continent of Africa and its people, including cultural traditions and customs survived the colonization era, although significantly weakened from years of European injustices, was now ready to assume its rightful place in a global and competitive world. During the early years of what was referred to as "African Independence" the question frequently asked was, has the era of Independence really begin? Also, will the European powers, following three quarters of a Century in control of the continent, finally realize that the Post-independence era was beginning? The world needs to remember that prior to the Berlin Conference in 1984-85 resulting in the "Scramble for Africa," Africa was not only rich in social and cultural traditions, but also very rich in natural resources, including vast mineral sources; in some respects the continent of Africa was the envy of the world, especially at the beginning and during the early stages of the Industrial Revolution. The eventual "Scramble for Africa" era was not a great surprise. The historical rich culture, customs and traditions of Africa, especially the family network kinship system was highly responsible for the overall survival of the people during the lengthy period of colonization. The Berlin Conference came to symbolize one of the most evil forms of social injustices known in world history. The continent survived with Ghana becoming the first "Independent" African country in 1957. The countries in Sub-Saharan Africa following years of colonization were now ready to confront other societal challenges such as the demographic population explosion, including the "Silver Tsunami," modernization, industrialization and urbanization. In other words, it was time for the newly and future independent countries to move on!!!

THE PRE-INDEPENDENCE/COLONIZATION ERA: IMPACT ON ECONOMIC, SOCIAL DEVELOPMENT, CULTURE AND TRADITIONS

The major focus of the historical period referred to as Pre-Independence, highlights some of the most significant events/actions, political, militarily and economically and their impact on the Continent occurring after the 1884/85 Berlin Conference. The resulting decisions of the Berlin Conference had a tremendous negative impact on the culture, customs and traditions on the continent for three-quarters of a century; the impact on the Continent's economic and social development were tremendous. The self-rewarding actions, especially economical, undertaken by the European powers following the Berlin Conference played a major role in Africa's efforts to succeed towards social, economic growth and development in the 21st Century. Globally, it is well established that historically the continent of Africa possessed, not just vast natural resources, but very well defined institutions or systems of caring, commonly referred to as the Extended Family Network. It could be debated that the extended family network in Africa was a model for social welfare globally, especially in the Western world. Family members, including tribes, clans from "cradle to grave" were well cared for, including financial, housing, medical and health needs and companionship (**Chapter IV**). Globally, it is also recognized that colonization, including the domination and control of the land, the separation of families from their land, and forced labor slowed down the process and/or progress towards social and economic development on the continent for decades to come. Also, there is little doubt that the era of colonization had a tremendous impact on the culture, customs, and traditions on the continent, including the traditional extended family network for caring for families, especially the older populations and children, including clans and tribal groups.

For the most part, the underdevelopment of Africa began during the Berlin Conference in 1884/85 resulting in what is now commonly referred to as the "The Scramble for Africa." The convening of the Conference at that time does not mean that attempts and successes to exploit the Continent did not occur prior to 1884/85. Threats to the traditional systems of caring began to take hold when the European powers made a political, and for the most part an economical decision, to divide or split the African continent into geographical boundaries/colonies. Not only did the actions from the European powers threaten the existence of the traditional social welfare system, but all the deeply rooted traditions, culture, and customs as well. The European powers, scramble for Africa, illustrated no respect for the traditions, culture, and traditions of Africa and its people. In other words, there was no consideration, appreciation or respect for the historical family kinship, tribal, or clan system ties that were essential for the survival of the traditional social welfare system as well as other customs and traditions. As a result, the tribal and/or kinship groups so essential for meeting social needs of the people were separated and left struggling to survive. The carving up or dividing the natives' land was crucial for the European powers in their efforts to develop their financial/economic empires back home in Europe and other parts of the Western world.

The Berlin Conference and the "scramble for Africa" began deliberations in 1884/85 and ended some three decades later around 1914. It took the significant European powers, including countries such as Britain, France, Germany and Portugal to complete the carving up or the complete partitioning of the African continent. The United States of America also had a seat at the decision making table. The deliberations were at times extremely difficult considering that each country had a special interest in a particular geographical region or area of the continent. For example, "…British and German agents were very interested in the Lake Victoria region because of it access to the Nile River, and Leopold II of Belgium also sought to extend his Congo Free State to the river" (Kasule, Samuel, The History Atlas of Africa, New York: Macmillan Company, 1998, p. 63). It should be noted that African leaders were not invited to participate during the years of deliberations.

Initially, the carving up and/or occupation of the continent focused primarily around the coastal areas, but beginning around 1901 the Europeans were in complete control of the African continent (Kasule, ibid, 1998). The carving up of Africa and taking complete control of the entire continent, including resources and forced labor policies had a devastating effect on the native population. The aforementioned actions "…stripped Africans of independence, freedom and civil rights and often subjected them to harsh European rule. European racism, rooted in the scientific principles of the period, dictated that white people had a duty to govern and civilize Africans, whom they saw as children, but bloody wars of pacification frequently destroyed whole communities, like the Ashanti of Ghana (Kasule, ibid, 1998, p. 64).

The "scramble for Africa" was great timing for the economies of Europe. The scramble and eventually the geographical carving up of a great continent was taking place in the midst of or during the industrial revolution in Europe and the West. Once the European powers, now possessing the necessary political and military power, gained control over the land and the people, were now in a position to seize the natural resources needed for the development of their economic empires in Europe. Labor or native workers needed for achieving their goals were simply no major problem for the Europeans; the powers of Europe had the political and military powers for achieving their goals. Native workers, especially during the forced labor era, were moved out of their villages and into the cities as manufacturing centers emerged for processing resources back to Europe. It was during the industrial revolution that European states became the center of financial power and influence (GLOBAL History/Barron Educational Series: Global History and Geography, New York, 2017, page. 407-409).

The European powers, during deliberations and negotiations among themselves, concluded that there was a need to develop a written document or contract that would regulate the anticipated competition that would eventually emerge from their actions. The concept put forward was referred to as "effective occupation;" the criteria underlying the recognition of territory claim on a global level" (Pakenham, Thomas, The Scramble for Africa: The White Man's Conquest of the Dark Continent from 1876-1912, New York: Random House, 1991). The principle of "effective occupation" stated that "…powers could acquire rights over colonial lands only if they possessed them or had "effective occupation:" In other words, if they had treaties with local leaders, if they flew their flags there, and if they established an administrative territory to govern it with a police force to keep order. The colonial powers could also make use of the colony economically…"(Pakenham, ibid, 1991).

The final Berlin document was signed on the 26th of February 1885. The General Act included some thirty-eight inexplicit clauses; therefore there was a crucial need for the Principles of effective occupation. It has been suggested, "The race to grab a slice of the African cake had started long before the first day of the conference. And none of the thirty-eight clauses of the General Act had any teeth. It had set no rules for dividing, let alone eating, the cake. In one sense…the Berlin conference marked a turning point in the history of Africa and Europe. There was something that came to be called 'the spirit of Berlin.' For the first time great men like Bismarck had linked their names at an international conference to Livingston's lofty ideals: to introduce the '3 c's – commerce, Christianity, civilization – into the dark places of Africa. Of course, the main policy of the Powers was directed to strategic and economic objectives such as protecting old markets or exploiting new ones" (Pakenham, Thomas, The Scramble for Africa: The White Man's Conquest of the Dark Continent from 1876-1912, New York: Random House, 1991, pages 254-255).

The European powers had strong allies in various religious denominations/congregations of missionaries who had come to Africa in their attempts to civilize and save the savages from the fires of hell. The goal for the French during a process of assimilation was to change African men, women, and children into good civilized French models (Maloba, ibid, 1995, p. 11). "The Portuguese 'civilizing mission' was propagated in spite of the fact that by 1970 about 30% of the population of Portugal was officially classified as illiterate, and therefore could not have qualified to be Portuguese!" (Gibson, Richard, African Liberation Movements, London: Oxford University Press, 1972, p. 195), cited in Ogot and Ochieng, "Decolonization: A Theoretical Perspective," Maloba, 1995, p. 11).

According to Fanon the Colonial powers, including the missionaries, did not just hate the natives but made every attempt to destroy their cultures and traditions with numerous unjust obstacles, such as carving up and taking away their land and resources preventing them from planning for the future generations (Fanon, Frantz, The Wretched of the Earth, New York: Grove Press, 1963). The era of colonization was happening in the midst of the industrialization and emerging or growth of Western Capitalism. Rodney's perspective is this was a time for Capitalist Western, especially European domination and control over the Continent of Africa. It was all about domination, the scramble, and carving up of the land and control, and not about Africa's long-term development. The results were the building of economic empires in Europe (Rodney, ibid, 2011).

One major concern of the European powers had to do with what strategies could be used in forcing the native population to engage in seeking employment away from their homesteads or villages. They concluded that some form of taxation was the answer. The settlers "… taxation is the only possible method of compelling the natives to leave his reserve for the purpose of seeking work. Only in this way can the cost of living be increased for the native… and it is on this that the supply of labor and the price of laborer depends" (Ogot and Ochieng, Ibid, 1995, p. xvi – Quote is from, Leys, C., Underdevelopment in Kenya: The Political Economy of Neo-Colonialism, London, Heinemann, 1975, p. 29). The European settlers had the power to enforce any policies that would benefit or achieve their economic goals.

Also, in countries such as Kenya and Rhodesia (now Zimbabwe), the settlers put forth special efforts to prevent the natives from growing their own cash crops. The primary goal of the settlers was to ensure that natives' labor would be made available only to the settlers or colonizers. One of the great settlers by the name of Colonial Grogan speaking specifically of the Kikuyu, the largest tribal group currently in Kenya, and the tribe of Jomo Kenyatta, First

President of Kenya, "We have stolen his land. Now we must steal his limbs. Compulsory labor is the corollary of our occupation of the country" (Rodney, Walter, ibid, 2011, p. 165-166).

In 1870, fifteen years prior to the Conference, 1884/85, only 10% of Africa was in the powerful hands of Europe; but, by the year 1914, the territory under European control had reached 90% (Pakenham, 1991, ibid). In slightly more than a Century from the convening of the Berlin Conference in 1884/85, approximately 110 years, scholars were expounding on the current social, political, and economic conditions in Africa that linked with the era of colonization. The purpose of the scholarly presentation was "...to show how the present conditions in Africa could be ideologically and institutionally linked to the colonial and imperial past. Without comprehending this tragic linkage, Africa's poverty and misery become the results of ill-fortune, a curse or some inexplicable haunting set of circumstances (Maloba, "Decolonization: A Theoretical Perspective," ibid, in Ogot and Ochieng, 1995), p. 7).

One scholar, activist once described the world of colonization as divided into two worlds. The line that divided the two worlds, the colonizers and the victims or natives, was the border "... represented by the barracks and the police stations. In the colonies, the official legitimate agent, the spokesperson for the colonizers and the regime of oppression, is the police officer or the soldier...the colonist sector is a sector built to last, all stone and steel, lights, paved roads... colonized sector, famished sector, hungry for bread, meats, shoes, coal and light...sector that crouches and covers, a sector on its knees, a sector that is prostrate. It's a sector of niggers, a sector of towel heads" (Fanon, Frantz, The Wretched of the Earth, Grove Press, NY, 1963, pp. 3-5). The colonizers possessed all of the political and military power to maintain obedience from the native workers. Furthermore, they had strategically located and/or dispersed the workers, and closely watched by the military would make it difficult organize; the Europeans with the help of the missionaries always used the racist theory of inferiority to justify lower wages and forced labor.

It is important to note that the primary recipient of the benefits, especially the wealth derived from the industrial revolution, especially phase one was Great Britain. But, as the revolution moved into the second phase, there were more competition from other European countries. During the early years Great Britain was the center of manufacturing, shipping, banking, and transportation for the world. But other European countries, including the United States began to become imitators of the British technology, as well as the use of British capital for moving forward. By the mid-70's, approximately one decade prior to the Berlin Conference, that many considered the coming of the second phase of the Revolution, Britain, had begun to lose some of its industrial dominance held during the first phase. The second phase was now focusing on steel, electricity, and petro chemicals, not being demanded globally. Now, Great Britain was operating in a very competitive world, especially with Germany and the United States. The U.S. had fast become not only the number one steel producer in the world, but a major world competitor with Britain and other European powers. These are possible factors that influenced the European powers to begin thinking about new natural resources, such as minerals for maintaining, not just their economic power but ways to expand it (Rand McNally: Atlas of World History, Chicago: Rand McNally and Company, 1987). The question, to what extent the aforementioned factors influenced the need for the Berlin Conference and the beginning of the "scramble for Africa?"

During the "scramble for Africa," including the negotiations among the European powers, an extremely peculiar happening was taking place in Belgium that would have implications for what initially was called The Congo Free State. Other than advisors the only participant or decision maker regarding this very wealthy geographical area in Africa was King Leopold II of Belgium. The European powers seated at the negotiating table in Berlin seemed to have no interest in this part of Africa. Could it have been that the Congo Free State, later to become the Belgian Colony, did not have the natural resources, minerals, diamonds, and gold thought to be in other African colonies? King Leopold II had ascended to the throne of Belgium in 1865. As the story unfolds of how the King's acquisition of the Congo, becoming its sole ruler, provides another demonstration of the disrespect the Europeans had for the African continent and it people. Well, there is a piece of land in Africa that looks promising let's just grab it? Operating externally from the negotiations taking place among the power brokers from countries, such as England, France, and Spain, King Leopold II, on his own terms, became the sole ruler of the Congo Free State (Gondola, CH. Didier, The History of the Congo, London: Greenwood Press, 2002).

The King's actions that eventually, and without any serious opposition from the other European powers have been described, "Leopold's acquisition of so much power, incidentally, took place almost by sleight of hand. The European powers had not recognized him, but his Association International du Congo, as sovereign administrator over the Congo basin…no one seemed to protest. People saw him as a great philanthropist with a great many ideals and even more means at his disposal" (Reybrouck, David Van, Congo: The Epic History of a People, New York, HarperCollins Publishers, 2014, p. 58).

Operating behind the scenes, King Leopold II successfully acquired for himself a territory, naming it the Congo Free State, eighty times larger than his home country of Belgium (Didier, ibid, 2002). What became known as the Congo Free State had been regarded as one of Africa's richest geographical areas for its natural resources that were located in the Congo Basin. The area possessed approximately a third of the rainforests in Africa. Also, the Congo Basin was known to possess numerous species of trees known for the production of ebony, mahogany and teak; the basin is considered to be the "…second largest river in the world in terms of volume flowing water, exceeded only by the Amazon River of South America…Africa's most extensive network of navigable waterways and sources of hundreds of different species of fish" (Didier, ibid, 2002, p. 2). Just imagine all of the aforementioned, and obviously much more, "fell in the lap" of King Leopold II. No, not just by accident this happened, "On April 30 1885, the Berlin Conference, devoted to the peaceful partitioning of those parts of Africa not yet claimed by a European power, accorded him personal control of the Congo" (Edgerton, Robert B., The Troubled Heart of Africa: A History of the Congo, New York: St. Martin's Press, 2002).

King Leopold remained the sole ruler of the Congo Free State for 23 years not as a colony but a state; after 23 years the Congo Free State became a Belgian colony. Speaking of peculiarities King Leopold II was considered an absentee but sole ruler of the Congo; furthermore, King Leopold II never visited the Congo. His residence was approximately 3,700 miles to the North, and it would have taken approximately a four-week journey to reach the borders of the Congo Free State (Reybrouck, ibid, 2014).

In regards to inhumane treatment or social injustices, consider the fact that the native population had no input in the design or mapping of their native states, including the Congo Free State, and later a Belgian colony. The final physical boundaries of each area drawn on maps, without input from the native population, were actually completed by Europeans who had never been to Africa (Dowden, Richard, "The End of Colonialism, New States, Old Societies," Africa-Altered States, Ordinary Miracles (1st Edition), NY: Public Affairs, 2009). In the process of gaining complete control over the land, resources, and the people, any aspects of culture, customs, traditions, including the foundations of the traditional social welfare system were completely ignored or despised. "Europeans had claimed racial superiority to justify slavery and imperialism…African dignity and self worth eroded. They were forced to abandon their own beliefs, identities and values…"(Dowden, Richard ibid, p. 62). One can imagine how devastating the seizure of land was to the people of Africa. Land ownership and the authority and decision-making surrounding it in the villages were critical in maintaining the traditional social welfare system, but also all of the customs and traditions of society.

What other factors, other than the aforementioned legislative initiatives, that gave the settlers their power to oppress? For one, "… the alien colonial state had a monopoly of political power, after crushing all opposition by superior armed force. Secondly, the African working class was small, very dispersed, and very unstable owing migratory practices. Thirdly… European capitalists in Africa had additional racial justification for dealing unjustly with the African worker. The racist theory that the black man was inferior led to the conclusion that he deserved lower wages…The combination of the above factors made it extremely difficult for African Workers to organize themselves" (Rodney, Walter, How Europe Underdeveloped Africa, Baltimore: Black Classic Press, 2011, pp. 149-150).

The social injustices and inhuman treatment toward Africans were deeply rooted in "… the racist principal that barbarism pervaded Africa and there was no culture to be salvaged" (Maloba, 1995, p. 11). The European powers had strong allies in various religious denominations/ congregations of missionaries who had come to Africa in their attempts to civilize and save the savages from the fires of hell. The missionaries sought to replace African religious and cultural practices with strong civilized Western cultures. The goal for the French during a process of assimilation was to change African men, women, and children into good civilized French models (Maloba, 1995 ibid).

In was from this colonized and oppressed world that the colonizers were in need of very cheap labor and would not be able to carry out their mission with the supply of African workers. The colonizers or settlers had come into the possession of huge plots of agriculture land, estimated to be on average some 2400 acres per/family. And, obviously the only solution was to create a system whereas the Africans had to work for the. In order to carry out their goals it became necessary for the settlers to create or enact labor as well as economic legislation that would allow them to recruit laborers. Also the legislation included provisions that would prevent the colonized the opportunity to have access to opportunities to engage in profitable cash crop production, as well as having access to fresh land. Furthermore, to make things more difficult for the natives the legislation enacted provided the settlers with the opportunity to impose such provisions as poll and hut taxes. These legislative initiatives gave the natives just option; give their labor and services to the foreign settlers (Ogot, B.A. & Ochieng, W.R., Decolonization and Independence in Kenya 1940-93, Ohio University Press, 1995 p. xv).

One major concern of the European powers had to do with what strategies could be used in forcing the native population to engage in seeking employment away from their homesteads or villages. They concluded that some form of taxation was the answer. The settlers "… taxation is the only possible method of compelling the natives to leave his reserve for the purpose of seeking work. Only in this way can the cost of living be increased for the native… and it is on this that the supply of labor and the price of laborer depends" (Ogot and Ochieng, Ibid, p. xvi – Quote is from, Leys, C., Underdevelopment in Kenya: The Political Economy of Neo-Colonialism, London, Heinemann, 1975, p. 29). The European settlers had the power to enforce any policies that would benefit or achieve their economic goals.

The Traditional African Social Welfare System, or Extended Family System for providing social protection/social caring/health care for its members continued to do so in spite of limitations during the era of European invasion, and colonization. The Berlin Conference 1884/85 began what became known as the "Scramble for Africa," the invasion, forced occupation, colonization, and the forceful annexing of African land masses and/or territory by the invading, militarily, politically powers of Europe. The final results of the Berlin Conference were the division of Africa into some 50 colonies; each major European power being delegated its share of the redistricted territory that it would have control or dominance over (Pakenham, 1990). In addition to the 50 colonies, King Leopold II had his own Congo Free State, not a colony but a state.

In slightly more than a Century from the convening of the Berlin Conference in 1884-85, approximately 110 years, scholars were expounding on the current social, political, and economic conditions in Africa that linked with the era of colonization. The purpose of the scholarly presentation was "…to show how the present conditions in Africa could be ideologically and institutionally linked to the colonial and imperial past. Without comprehending this tragic linkage, Africa's poverty and misery become the results of ill-fortune, a curse or some inexplicable haunting set of circumstances (Maloba, 1995) in Ogot and Ochieng, Decolonization and Independence in Kenya: 1940-1993, p. 7).

The Forced Labor Era: No Chance for Social Protection in Old Age

It was within the world of colonization and domination by superior powers resulting in all forms of social injustices that the International Labor Organization convened its Forced Labor Convention. The Convention took place in 1930 almost a half-century following the Berlin Conference and the beginning of what has become known as the "Scramble for Africa." During this time millions of Africans were part of a system of colonization, and being denied the opportunity to benefit from all of the medical advances, economic and social development, and a tripartite collective bargaining labor system that would ensure social protection in old age. Furthermore, instead of benefitting economically from the ongoing industrial revolution at the time, native Africans were providing the labor and resources for the establishment of European economic empires. How many children did not survive to reach old age at the time? Now, many of the off springs, 82.5%, of the forced labor generations in Sub-Saharan Africa, do not have social protection (basic income, access to healthcare and social services) in old age.

During the many years of underdevelopment in Africa as the Western world was building massive industrial systems, including tripartite labor structures, Sub-Saharan Africa was struggling to just survive. The Post-Independent era has provided some opportunities and the countries have made tremendous progress, but in many respects still struggling to catch up, especially in the areas of economic and social development. The hopes are as the countries continue to develop their industrial sectors, accompanied by a strong labor movement, one can expect more and more workers to move away from the dominant informal labor sector and more towards a tripartite labor market. The 1930 Convention, in regards to labor, workers' rights, although not highly successful in its mission at the time, began to raise questions, mobilize the global community, and knowingly recognizing or not, playing a role in preparing the world for the "Silver Tsunami."

It was almost three decades following the 1930 Convention that the first African country Ghana, 1957, was granted Independence. Following 1957, over a period of time most countries received or were granted Independence. The long era of colonization did not end with the Declaration of Independence and the raising of the country's flag. Decolonization, especially in the areas related to work, and labor issues in general would remain on the agenda of organizations, such as the ILO. The ILO with its mission of enhancing the overall working conditions of the human workforce, began to recognize following WWI, somewhat of a positive political environment that would become favorable enough for carrying out its mission (Human Rights, Development, and Decolonization p. 4). Also, it was following the 1930 Convention that the mission and work of the ILO began to expand from a primary focus on the physical requirement of work towards more and more emphasis on areas such as social security, as well as issues and concerns related to human rights (HRDD, ibid. p.4).

What other factors, other than the aforementioned legislative initiatives, that gave the settlers their power to oppress? For one, "... the alien colonial state had a monopoly of political power, after crushing all opposition by superior armed force. Secondly, the African working class was small, very dispersed, and very unstable owing migratory practices. Thirdly... European capitalists in Africa had additional racial justification for dealing unjustly with the African worker. The racist theory that the black man was inferior led to the conclusion that he deserved lower wages...The combination of the above factors made it extremely difficult for African Workers to organize themselves" (Rodney, Walter, How Europe Underdeveloped Africa, Baltimore: Black Classic Press, 2011, pp. 149-150).

It was in this world that the Forced Labor Convention of 1930 was convened. The global population reached one billion in 1800 and it occurred after approximately 50,000 years or longer. Between 1800 and 1930 it only took 130 years to reach the two billion mark. It is obvious in reviewing this accelerated timeframe, that the world was experiencing rapid population growth. Some contributing factors for this growth in over just 130 years were medical advances, including public health education, prevention, and improvements in the quality of life (growth and development) as a results of social and economic development. During this time millions of Africans were part of a system of colonization, and denied the opportunity to benefit from all of the medical advancements, and social developments taking place around them. How many children did not survive to reach old age at the time? Now, many of the off springs, 82.5%, of the forced labor generations, in Sub-Saharan Africa, do not have social protection (basic income, access to healthcare and services) in old age.

For the generations of Africans born about one generation prior to the period of colonization, and those born during the period, roughly from around 1885 to approximately 1957 (Ghana' Independence), there would be no opportunities for social pensions or social security. In other words, these cohorts would not have the opportunity to engage in any form of a tripartite labor mechanism (collective bargaining) that would ensure social security/social protection or a traditional social pension. During this era there was no such opportunity to organize as workers. Attempts to engage in such practices would have been a definite threat to the European powers, especially governments in the colonies" (HRDD, ibid, p. 6).

EUROPEAN AND WESTERN PERCEPTIONS OF AFRICA AND AFRICANS: IMPLICATIONS FOR FUTURE COLLABORATIONS IN ECONOMIC GROWTH AND DEVELOPMENT

The European and/or Western views of the African Continent and its people have historically been under serious question or scrutiny for a very long time. This is especially the situation when the European powers attempted to justify the reasons for the "scramble for Africa" resulting in decades of domination and exploitation. During an era of unheard of human injustices whereas the colonizers geographically carved up the natives' land, the rich cultural traditions and customs of the continent were ignored. Views and perspectives from representatives from Europe and the Western world were extremely negative, including all forms of stereotypical connotations. It was not just the sociological and anthropological theorists whose perceptions of Africa were seen in such negative ways, but the leaders representing the European Empire as well as well as the Christian missionaries. Africa was viewed or seen by Europeans as a backward and savage like country, lacking a respectful western type culture, mobility, and the ambitions and competitiveness to succeed in a modern society. The fact that the sociologists and anthropologists were viewed as scholarly and "learned men," the leaders of the European Empire were not only willing to accept these views, but used them to justify why it was necessary to colonize and bring a level of civilization within the colonies. But, the European powers, including some of the social scientists, failed to recognize that Africa was not an underdeveloped Continent prior to the European invasion. Although stereotypical and racist views existed globally, the European powers utilized such views with the help of the missionaries to justify the unjust and inhumane invasion and treatment of Africa's people during the period of colonization. During an era of colonization the Europeans discovered that it was convenient to attack and denigrate Africa's traditions, culture and customs (Midgley, James, Professional Imperialism: Social Work in the Third World, London: Heinemann Educational Books Ltd, p. 45).

As aforementioned above Africa and Africans were viewed by Europeans, including the missionaries, as a backward and savage like country; it's citizens not viewed as being capable of participation, economically and socially in a global and modern society. Now, as the world enters the 21ˢᵗ Century some full Century and three decades from the time of the Berlin Conference with an agenda of geographically carving up the African Continent, have the perceptions of Europeans, especially political leaders changed? Let's not forget that one of the major reasons for invading the continent was to bring civilization to the savage and uncivilized natives. Recently, July 11, 2017 the newly elected President of France Emmanuel Macron was asked during a global news conference convening in Hamburg, Germany, why there was no European type Marshal Plan for Africa? As the world recalls, following World War II some European countries had been devastated, especially infrastructures, during years of bombings, including fighting by various military units. Following the war a comprehensive document which became known as the Marshal Plan was introduced to the world by an American George Marshall with the goal of rebuilding Europe; the Plan, included the rebuilding of cities, especially infrastructures, and resources available for economic growth and development. In responding to the reporter's question the current President of France seemed to have gone back in time for his answer, "…Africa had civilizational problems." The President followed up by stating that the African countries still have seven to eight children p/women (Eliza Anyangwe, the Guardian, UK, Tuesday 11/July/2017).

In essence the European countries that benefitted from the Marshal Plan symbolized a civilized society or an advanced state with a high level of culture, science, government, industry had been reached; also, the countries did not have eight children p/female. An additional question for the President, colonization took place over one-quarter of a Century from the date of the Berlin Conference (Scramble for Africa) to 1957 when Ghana received its Independence. The world is now aware that during the era of colonization that countries such as France benefitted from the natural resources extracted from the rich natives' land, including the use of forced labor for carrying out the tasks that contributed to the building of the economic empires back home in Europe. The question needing a response is what contributions did France and the other colonizing countries make in helping to prepare the so-called "backward" and "savage" countries for a modernized and industrialized global society? As the President's statement or response to the question is shared globally, there are some lyrics used by an American Rock Band, from Sayreville, New Jersey, Ban Jovi: "The More Things Change The More They Remain The Same." Yes, a great deal has changed over almost a Century, but the response from the current President of France is probably identical to what the President of France would say years ago during the Berlin Conference; Africa has civilization issues.

One could debate that the failure of the European powers to form some kind of a economic partnership with the African countries during the more than seven decades of colonization had to do with a belief that the Continent and its people was not capable of moving forward towards modernization. But, the general consensus seem to be that the European powers in preparing for the "scramble for Africa," had only one primary goal in mind, not to form economic development partnerships, but the domination and exploitation of the continent for the purpose of developing an economic empire back home in Europe. Therefore their negative views were more related to a need to justify the reason for invasion than what factual knowledge and information were available for their perusal in articulating such negative views of the Continent and its people. An unbiased scholarly review or study of African culture, history and traditions would have challenged the negative perspectives; or, some scholarly verbal gymnastics with scholars from the Dependency School may have provided other insights and perspectives to consider.

But, once again, if the European powers only interests were in expropriating the valuable resources for social and economic development back home in Europe and the West, the total negative perspectives served their purposes. Some modernization theorists viewed traditional

African societies, including the extended family kinship system, as a symbol of backwardness and parochial tribalism. The European powers used such a negative view of Africa to help justify the reason behind the "Scramble for Africa." The perception of the native populations of Africa being viewed as uncivilized "savages," was one of the main justifications for the Europeans invading the continent for the purpose of contributing to the development of a civilized society. Their way of thinking was in line with many of the early missionaries who went to Africa for the purpose of carrying out God's will, with the assumption and/or beliefs that Christianity was in the best interest of the native population.

There were social scientists, not members of the Modernization School who viewed the European take over of Africa as socially racist and a dictatorship (Wunyabari, Maloba, "Decolonization: A Theoretical Perspective," in Ogot, B.A., Decolonization & Independence in Kenya, 1940-93, London: James Currey, East African Educational Publishers (EAEP), Nairobi, Athens (USA) Ohio University Press, 1995). As a dictatorship, "It was imposed by violence and maintained by violence. Ruling with utter indifference to the opinions of the governed-the Africans-colonialism perfected a reign of terror by silencing its opponents through detention, exile, even outright extermination..." "Culturally, colonialism operated from the racist principle that barbarism pervaded Africa and therefore there was no culture to be salvaged. Missionaries in their evangelical duties championed this outlook, condemning centuries-old African religions and cultures, seeking to replace and in some cases succeeding in replacing them with Western European culture" (Maloba, W., ibid, pages 9-11).

The aforementioned perceptions of African society were just the opposite of how some theorists and the Western World viewed the modern and developed societies. Modern societies were viewed as forward looking, and the future image of social and economic progress. The modernization theorists viewed the modern society as a symbol of rugged individualism, mobility, and small and large groups bound together by written contracts. The individuals and groups maintained a focus of producing goods and services for global markets, not just for the purpose of caring for kinship groups. It should not be surprising that the blueprint for economic and social development in developing countries, such as Africa, would be centered on the theory of modernization. After all, modernization theory and practice were conceptualized in the European and/or Western world, the former colonial powers. There is little or no evidence that the former European colonial powers, pre-post-independence, made any efforts to contribute to social and economic development of their former colonies. But, with the beginning of the modernization movement, their focus became how to assist the newly independent countries in modernizing their economies. There was the introduction of social development Aid programs to countries, and academic scholarships, especially to Economic Departments in African universities, receiving or rewarded with financial assistance and grants for the purpose of training students, economists, and macro/micro planners. It would appear that theories related to socialism, would have a very difficult time surviving in this academic and policy planning environment (Midgley, J. Social Security, Inequality, and the Poor of the Third World, New York: John Wiley and Sons, 1984).

It would appear, and there is no evidence to the contrary, that the modernization movement focused primarily on social and economic growth in developing countries. One can assume that if the process of modernization were to be achieved, problems related to social protection, poverty, access to health care and services, housing, illiteracy, and plans for a growing older population, would have been properly addressed. Also, there is little evidence that the former colonizers contributed or invested significantly in direct foreign investments; the major investments on the part the European and Western powers were the paternalistic Foreign Aid Programs. There were little or no significant investments in direct foreign assistance in the development of Africa into a strong industrialized, manufacturing formal sector. Western and European countries are slowly beginning to consider Direct Foreign Investments in Africa. It is interesting to note that currently (2014-15), the major foreign direct investor in Africa, has been and continue to be China, not one of the former colonizing countries that participated in the Berlin Conference **(NOTE: See Chapter VII).**

It was also the view of the European powers that developing countries in Africa had too much reliance on subsistence farming, and the technology utilized was still identified with a primitive stage of development. There was a very strong belief system among the Europeans that the native traditions, culture, customs would get in the way of accepting modern ideas in order to enhance their methods of productivity. It was concluded by the powers of Europe that major investments, especially in the area of manufacturing would be needed by the developing countries to begin the steps towards economic modernization. It was the belief of some that with significant investments, the building of strong infrastructures, resulting the development of a strong industrialized manufacturing and service sector, would provide for Africans the opportunity to leave the poor agriculture or subsistence sectors; they would find work and an improved standard of living in a modernized wage labor sector of society. One would-would surmise that eventually workers would become part of labor's tripartite system, including collective bargaining that would ensure medical and social benefits for families as well as social security/social protection for the future.

History will tell us that the non-contributory insurance scheme would confront challenges and obstacles, even until today, because in subsequent or succeeding years the informal sector of the workforce in most developing countries have been and continue to be dominant. In other words, workers outside of the formal sector have been and continue to be excluded from contributory insurance schemes; this fact explains why some *77 %* of older people ds not have a social pension following retirement from the informal, not the formal labor sector.

The aforementioned scenario could be operationalized by the European powers if there only interest in invading Africa had been for the purpose of investing in the continent and providing the assistance needed for becoming a contributing partner in global economic development. Or, was the only interest of the Europeans the extrapolation or extraction of rich raw materials, minerals, for the purpose of building the massive economic empires in Europe? Some scholars have concluded that the scramble was all about becoming wealthy in a short period of time. According to Fanon, for the most part, "Europeans set off for the colonies because they could get rich over there in a very short time, and that, with rare exceptions, the colonial is a trader, a trafficker, you will have grasped the psychology of the man who produces the 'feeling of inferiority' in the native" (Fanon, Frantz, <u>Black Skin, White Masks</u>, New York: Grove Press, 1952, p 88).

One could very well conclude considering the views of Africa by European and other Westerners that with all of the existing deficits cited the Continent would have very limited chances of succeeding in the future. Based on all of the deficits the possibility of succeeding along the linear lines towards modernization as prescribed by the social theorists would have to be under the guiding leadership and hands of their former colonizers. In such a scenario, to some extent the newly Independent countries and the citizens' of those countries would have to first of all accept those negative views.

The world now knows that five decades post-Independence the aforementioned scenario never became a reality, nor was there serious thought given to the possibility. Currently, five decades later Africa has one of the fastest growing modern economies in the world. Some scholars are describing the current era, "Africa's Renaissance" and this is "Africa's time in history." Not that there have not been struggles, political/economical/social, the Continent continues to move towards a modern industrialized economy with some of the elements of modernization theory.

EUROPEAN AND WESTERN POWERS: ZERO CONTRIBUTIONS TO AFRICA'S SOCIAL AND ECONOMIC DEVELOPMENT

Social Security/Protection Schemes in the Colonies: Expatriates Only

Although native Africans did not have access to the European and Western tripartite labor systems for workers, including the forced labor population, those systems did exist on native land for the benefits of expatriates and their families. The foreign occupiers were well aware of the need for social protection/social security for expatriates and their families, but they made no efforts to provide any forms of social protection for the native workers, especially the forced laborers who were contributing so greatly to empire building for the invaders back home in Europe. It says a great deal about the involved countries and their leaders that when their concept of social security, the precursor to the modern day global schemes, was introduced in the colonies during colonization, they were for expatriates only. These schemes were not targeted for the local populations; the primary targets were Europeans, or the expatriates employed in government or public service positions. The social security schemes, such as employer liability, social insurance, old-age assistance, widows' pensions, poor relief and public assistance, were targeted primarily to the expatriate population. Exclusionary provisions, excluding Africans, were explicitly pointed out in the legislative policy of the occupying country (Midgley, 1984 p.106).

One example of an exclusionary provision in a social policy document was in South Africa. In 1928 an old age non-contributory pension scheme was introduced in the Republic of South Africa. This provision was explicit in stating that Africans and Asians were excluded from the old age pension scheme. A similar old age pension scheme was introduced in what was then known as Southern and Northern Rhodesia (presently known as Zimbabwe) around 1936 with similar provisions, as the one aforementioned reference South Africa, of exclusions (Midgley, 1984).

Social Welfare, Social Protection and Economic Growth: On Behalf of European Powers Only

As frequently mentioned in this manuscript there is little or no scholarly evidence that significantly demonstrate an interest by the European invaders in the social welfare of the African people residing in the various colonies. Also, there was no interest shown, especially during the forced labor era, in the future welfare or social protection of the workers and their families. Although various social welfare policies were introduced during the era of colonialism, the targets were the expatriate populations; these programs included health care (medical facilities) and the introduction of social protection and/or social insurance programs. Historically, in response to the aforementioned some may claim that the colonial powers built railroads, schools, and hospitals, but less so for the benefits of Africans than for the expatriates. In order to carry out their goals on the continent it was necessary that the European governments would provide an array of services, including housing, health and social services for the expatriates and their families.

Gradually over a period of time, hospitals on a very limited basis were available for Africans. Secondly, there was little or no interest in the sharing of knowledge, or technology in Africa's economic growth and development beyond what benefitted the building of the economic empires in the Europe and the Western world. Therefore, for the most part, medical and social services during the era of colonization, despite all of the restrictions and barriers remained a primary responsibility of the traditional social welfare system. To make it more difficult the extended family, including tribes, clans had been strategically separated during carving and/ or slicing up the territory during the scramble. What limited sharing of any social welfare or economic benefits on the part of the European countries, were done to satisfy their own needs. It has been argued by some scholars, such as Rodney (1972) from the Dependency school, that nothing was done during the era of colonization for social and economic development of Africa (Rodney, Walter, How Europe Underdeveloped Africa, Baltimore, Maryland: Black Classic Press, 2011).

The historical evidence seems to indicate that there was very little done for Africans from the beginning of colonialism up to the time of WWII. It was the period following WWII that some limited health and social services were made available or shared. For some limited comparison purposes it has been noted or statistically shown that service areas such as health, housing, and education, were several times higher than similar statistics at the end of the colonial era. It would seem from the aforementioned that some service areas begin to improve for Africans post-Independence (Rodney, ibid, 2011).

Although, obviously restricted in many ways, especially with the separation of kinship groups, the extended family continued to be the dominant social welfare system during the era of colonization. Furthermore, the European powers primary interest in the provisions of medical, health, and other forms of services were introduced and maintained primarily for the benefit of the expatriates. "…Limited social services within Africa during colonial times were distributed in a manner that reflected the pattern of domination and exploitation…In British East Africa there were groups: firstly, the Europeans, who got the most; then, the Indians, who took most of what was left, and thirdly, the Africans, who came last in their own country" (Rodney, ibid, 2011, pages 206-207).

Another example of domination, exploitation, and racist practices in regards to social welfare can be seen in the way medical and hospital services were shared in Nigeria. Rodney, "…In predominantly black countries, it was also true that the bulk of the social services went to whites" (Rodney, W., ibid, p 2011. In Nigeria, the City of Ibadan was statistically one of the most highly populated cities in all of Africa. Prior to WWII Ibadan had a population of 50 Europeans. As was the practice or custom, the British made available services in a segregated hospital; for the population of 50 Europeans there were a total of eleven beds. But, for the Africans in the City of Ibadan, total population half-million, the British provided 34 beds (Rodney, ibid, 2011).

The mining industry and their geographical locations, especially South Africa, clearly demonstrated the disparities in health and social services between blacks and whites. Obviously, the mining industry was a key factor in regards to economic development and profiteering. It was a good example of how profits and institutional racism, domination and exploitation can have a serious impact on morbidity and mortality, especially a disease such as tuberculosis. Speaking of forced labor as related to the distribution of social services one continues to see the domination and exploitation when it came to the profit motive in the mining industry. The very limited distribution of the social services would only be provided to the workers and their families if it could be proven that they were producing surplus that could be exported for economic growth of the powerbrokers (Rodney, ibid, 2011).

It was around the late 1860's when diamonds were discovered near Kimberely South Africa; and gold was discovered on the Witwatersrand around 1886. TB became an epidemic between the years 1895-1910. Prior to the diamonds and gold discoveries the primary economic activities in South Africa were herding and agriculture. The first African minister to be ordained in the Presbyterian Church of South Africa died of TB in 1871; he was the first Christian leader in South Africa to advocate for freedom and equality in South Africa (TB FACTS.ORG, GLOBAL HEALTH EDUCATION (GHE), a.kanabus@btinternet.com (Author), England: West Sussex PH13 8GHI).

During the colonial period in Africa, industries related to mining, diamonds, gold, took their toll on workers. The health of the workers was a major issue. During the era of colonization, "…The exploitation of miners was entirely without responsibility… In 1930 scurvy and other epidemics broke out in the lupa goldfields of Tanganyika. Hundreds of workers died. One should not wonder that they had no facilities which would have saved some lives, because in the first place they were not being paid enough to eat properly" (Rodney, ibid, p 207). Observations from the TB Commission Report of 1912 was that at least one member of any family at the time was suffering from tuberculosis. Also, because are the terrible conditions of services and caring in the hospitals the practice was to just send people home to die. And, by sending infected persons home to die, obviously the infections are more likely to be passed on to others. In some geographical areas the patient to doctor ratio was like 1 to 40,000. What could have been seen as a screening out financial mechanism, all patients had to pay a fee, no exceptions. It was estimated that approximately 65% of the children died before reaching the age of two (Rodney, ibid, Quoting from the 1912 TB Commission Report, p 207).

As aforementioned there were few initiatives on behalf of Africans and their social welfare and economic development from the European or Western Empires prior to post War II. Dependency school thinkers such as Rodney (1982) "…argued convincingly that the sum total of benefits accruing from the colonial relationship was amazingly small for Africa (Rodney, 1982, p 205). Another scholar described that what actually happened during the era of colonialism "…was selective investment by European and other foreign capitalists in those enterprises that promised immediate profit with little risk…These enterprises had not been conceived as part of a coherent national economic plan for development but rather for their profitability to foreign investors (Molaba, Wunybarai, ibid, p 9).

One significant initiative that emerged at the conclusion of WWII was the establishment of development studies and/or institutes. The incentives promoting such development centers were brought about in response to great interest in research related to an enhanced understanding of the economic, political, and social problems that the newly independent countries would face in a post-independent environment. Prior to this initiative, the European powers as already addressed articulated very little interest and very few if any action steps had been taken toward a coherent plan of social development for the former colonies. The primary goal of this initiative, that took place more than a half-century following the scramble for Africa, the political and military control of the land, extraction of mineral resources for exportation, and forced labor, was to assist in the modernization of the countries' economies. The European and Western countries begin to provide aid programs, but not investments; they sent technical advisors, including academics to the various countries to assist in policy formulation and implementation on behalf of the European powers. This was the beginning and the advancement of development centers and/or institutes within the universities; there were scholarships for students to study the science of social development (Midgley, 1984, pages 54-56). Therefore, it was not difficult, as discussed under the section on the modernization school, that planning for economic development, when it did happen, would be based on Western style models (Midgley, 1984, ibid). Aid programs, not direct investments, seemed to become the top method for assisting African countries, especially during the post-Independent era. It was during the 2014 African Development Forum where the delegates articulated that Aid was not what the African countries needed; the delegates to the Forum made the point during the discussions that direct investments, were what the countries needed for social and economic transformation.

Although Aid Programs became somewhat fashionable serious investments in Africa were not. There was little or no economic development planning, especially in partnership with the colonies taking place. One scholar describes an experiment that took place around 1920, known as 'The Guggisberg Plan' that took place on the Gold Coast, that became Ghana following Independence. The Plan was an attempt at economic planning that yielded no positive outcomes for future countries to follow (Watherston, A., "Development Planning: Lessons from Experience," Baltimore: Johns Hopkins University Press, 1965). But, it was the period of the 1960's, approximately three years after Ghana's Independence, and fifteen years following the end of WWII, when national development planning begin to be seen as a mechanism for social and economic development planning (Watherston, ibid, 1965).

It was following WWII, especially during the 1950's, when global leadership decided that it was necessary to change the way developing countries were viewed or perceived. It was decided that a new phrasing, "Third World," a geopolitical concept could better describe the nonaligned countries of the world. Although the concept was "…designed to promote the nonaligned status of the nations of Africa, Asia, Central and South America…The term subsequently acquired an economic and social welfare connotation implying that these nations were impoverished and economically underdeveloped. Many were engaged in subsistence agriculture, the modern economic sector was often quite small, incomes were low; and health, education, housing, and other social conditions were unsatisfactory (Midgley, 1984, p 53). But, despite economic shortcomings, it was noted that the countries continued to express a very strong interest in economic growth as the solution for enhancing the welfare of their citizens (Midgley, 1984, ibid).

THEORIES OF SOCIAL AND ECONOMIC DEVELOPMENT: MODERNIZATION, DEPENDENCY, AND SOCIAL DEVELOPMENT SCHOOLS OF THOUGHT

Projections, according to social science theorists are that Africa like other societies in the past and present would eventually begin the transition from a traditional to a modern urbanized and industrialized society. Obviously, following all of the social and economic deficits brought forward from years of colonization, domination, and exploitation, the challenges would be great. The various global scholarly schools of thought, including Social development, modernization, and dependency, have provided forums for critical thinking centered around possible directions that the newly Independent countries of Africa may or may not pursue. One major question Pre-Post Independence was what global economic model or combination of models would the Independent countries of Africa select to follow? Would the free and Independent countries move toward a Western Capitalist type model, or a Socialist, or Communist type model? Or, would some countries choose to adopt a model for future social and economic development more related to the culture and traditions of historical African societies?

Some scholars, political, and civic leaders may have expected the transition from an era of colonization to whatever political/economical model chosen to use as a blueprint for social/economic development, would be somewhat of a smooth and uninterrupted process. But, as each country proceeded in the process it was soon realized that the challenges and obstacles would be great; the time immediately following Independence was probably the most challenging. The European powers had become so entrenched politically and economically in the colonies for more than three-quarters of a Century in positions of power and decision-making, it should have been expected that they would have some serious separation issues. It should not be difficult to understand how European leaders who through military power carved up and dominated a Continent for so many years to build economic empires back home, would find it easy to just let go. What would make it more difficult was the fact that the European countries in the second phase of the industrial revolution and the increasing competition among themselves in maintaining their separate empires would need Africa more than in the past. In other words, sustainable economic growth at home in Europe to some extent still needed the resources from the former colonies for their continuing survival, economically.

Once again, following the lengthy period of colonization the continent, as it would be expected, was quite ready to move forward and ready for the challenges. Despite all of the questions regarding the separation or obstacles to separation, it was time for the Continent to move forward taking its place globally, especially economical, in a competitive technological and industrialized world. The continent approximately five decades ago, the beginning of the post-colonial era, began to seek its place, especially economically, in a world where the developed countries had already a very significant "head start" in reference to social and economic development. Whereas, the newly independent African countries at the time, like so many other economically struggling countries would be labeled as "third world" countries. The phrase "third world" would eventually be removed and a new label or phrase, "developing countries," would take its place referring to countries at the beginning stage of social and economic development.

The newly independent African countries would not just be confronting the challenges of social and economic development, but also the challenges of responding to an unprecedented growth in population, including the "Silver Tsunami;" at the time Ghana received its Independence in 1957 the crisis that the world was slowly beginning to recognize, the growing older population was barely mentioned globally. Now, as countries develop socio/economic plans for the future the increasing growth of the older population cannot be ignored during the planning process. As repeatedly mentioned this demographic phenomenon will have a major impact on practically all systems, political, medical, health and the family.

Whereas some developed countries had 100 years to prepare for a growing older population, it probably appeared to leaders of the developing countries that they would have a very short time period for preparation, and not 100 years. The working agenda among countries is not just the transition from a traditional to a modern society with all of the implications, but also a growing older population in the midst of a transition from a communicable disease era to one of chronic illnesses. This latter transition will have major implications, especially on the medical/health and social systems. Once again, some six decades following Ghana's Independence, it appeared that the goal of most African countries were to become an industrialized modern society. The fact that Africa currently has one of the fastest growing global economies is some indication of what path of social and economic development the countries chose to follow.

Modernization School

Social theorists, such as Comte (1964), Levy (1967), Tonnies (1957), projected that traditional societies, including Africa, would eventually follow a similar path that had occurred in the now more industrialized western countries leading to modernization and industrialization. To these theorists the general trend of all societies was to move in a linear direction; the linear movement was strongly believed by theorists, such as Ferdinand Tonnies to be deterministic and irreversible. Tonnies, one of the more scholarly social change theorists, viewed all societies as moving over a period of time (not each at the same pace due to each country's uniqueness) in a linear direction from a traditional to a modern society. He described or labeled the traditional society as Gemeinschaft, a society with very strong kinship groups, or groups with strong reciprocal bonds of sentiment that operated or function within a common code of traditions and customs, with an emphasis on "we." Within this strong kinship system there were no need for formal contracts as are known in the developed or modern western world. In contrast Tonnies coined the concept Gesellschaft that represented a modern society. In a Gesellschaft society Tonnies saw a larger and more complex society, that was highly mobile, individualistic, and structured around formal contracts and industrialization. Furthermore, relationships between members of society, unlike in a traditional society, was governed by very impersonal and contractual relationships between individuals and/or groups.

It should be quite obvious that for an African society that had been deeply entrenched for centuries in a society with strong kinship ties would find the transition to the more Western industrialized modern society somewhat challenging. They would be leaving behind a society focused on reciprocal relationships and obligations, with an emphasis on "we" and not "I" especially in areas of social protection for its members. One would assume that such traditional systems, especially the extended family system, possessed strengths that could possibly become part of family units in a modern society? One of the more challenging debates, dialogues, and/ or discussions may focus on what strengths from the traditional society may be incorporated into a Gesellschaft or modern type society; or, the basic question could be, how will significant components of the traditional system, especially in the caring of vulnerable members of society, and mutual aid support systems be maintained? Finally, would the developing countries continue to see the maintaining of critical elements of the traditional system, as a realistic goal as they moved toward a more modern urbanized society? Or, eventually, will the forces of modernization and urbanization become so overwhelming that traditional ties, family kinship systems, reciprocity, eventually be abandoned? The aforementioned questions become very critical for a country's leadership during the process of conceptualization and planning for a growing older population that brings "to the table" more complex problems and issues to be considered.

Some social science theorists from the Modernization School were very explicit in stating that traditional societies moving towards a modern and urbanized society would have to abandon some of their cultural traditions and customs. One such theorist expressed, "… traditional cultural institutions such as the extended family with its extensive networks of dependents, duties, and obligations was inimical to individualism and the mobility of labor required in an industrialized economy" (Goode, W.J., World Revolutions and Family Patterns, ibid, 1970). Another scholar came to a similar conclusion, "…traditional patterns of authority hindered the emergence of an open, free enterprise economy" (Hoselitz, B.F., 'Social Stratification and Economic Development,' International Social Science Journal, 16, 1964, pages 237-251). There was also the view expressed by some scholars as well as European leaders that within the culture and traditions of Africa was the lack of a desire to excel or succeed at anything challenging. According to Hagan, Africans did not have what it would take to succeed in a modern industrialized society. Personal as well as group attributes, such as ambition, acquisitiveness, and especially a strong sense of competitiveness were needed, but were lacking within the culture and traditions of Africa (Hagan, E., On the Theory of Social Change, Homewood, Dorsey, 1962). Wow, speaking of global racism that became so entrenched prior to and during the "scramble for Africa" and the period of colonization. One would hope that those social science theorists articulating such racist perspectives have been observing what have been happening on the African Continent, especially during recent decades in regards to economic growth and development.

Social science scholars and leaders of the developed world seemed to have been saying to the developing world, especially following Independence, we have been "in your shoes" and we can share with you former colonies the grand formula(s) for your success into a world of modernization. We have followed a blueprint to reach our current state defined as a developed society and you may find the blueprint useful. One scholar and policy analyst concluded, "It was, therefore perhaps inevitable that proposals for the economic development of the underdeveloped countries would be abstracted from the experience of the industrialized countries. These proposals were subsequently formulated into a coherent approach to development which became known as modernization theory" (Midgley, 1984, ibid, p. 56).

During the early 1950's there were others, including the International Labor Organization (ILO) by no means associated with the "scramble for Africa" and colonization, who concluded that the developing countries would eventually move into phase one or the first step towards a modern urbanized society as predicted by the social science theorists and scholars. The process would eventually lead to a modern industrialized wage oriented society, including benefits of social protection for workers and their families. The aforementioned conclusions emerged during the ILO's Convention in 1952. The International Labor Organization (ILO) known historically as strong advocates of social justice and human rights for workers had a similar view of what could eventually happen on behalf of workers in Sub-Saharan Africa; the transition of the labor force from traditional subsistence agriculture, informal sector employment, to more of a modernized formal wage labor sector of social protection, including workers' benefits such as social pensions. Some six decades later, following the ILO's Convention in 1952, countries in Sub-Saharan Africa continue to be dominated by workers in the informal labor sector and/or self-employed without adequate social protection for employees and their families.

The ILO Convention that took place approximately three decades, 1952, prior to the United Nations First World Assembly in 1982 on Aging, was a very important Global Convention. The Convention that was planned and implemented by the International Labor Organization (ILO) set the tone for Social Security conceptualization and/or future policy discussions related to social justice, human rights, and social protection. The social security/social protection scheme that emerged from the Convention was one of contributory social insurance (based on a long standing tradition of a Tripartite managed social insurance), which was strongly favored by the ILO (ILO, p. 159). In considering some of the difficulties and challenges developing countries would have with the contributory system initially, the Convention included some qualifying exemptions for developing countries. For example, developing countries would be allowed a longer period of transition in the country's implementation process. The proportion of the population covered was not to exceed more than (50%) percent of the industrial workforce rather than the total workforce. (ILO and the Quest for Social Justice, 1919-2009).

A major highlight, other than the social insurance scheme, that emerged from the Convention was the focus on Modernization, or the path to a modern society where issues, such as social security would be achieved. The ILO's very strong belief was that "Modernization by industrialization and democratization..." was the blueprint for developing countries to follow (ILO, p.159). It should be noted that the International Labor Organization is not on record expressing that to achieve the goal of modernization they would have to abandon the cultural traditions and customs as expressed by some of the scholars from the modernization school. The ILO known historically as strong advocates of social justice and human rights would undoubtedly search for other means or methods that would enable the transition to become a reality.

As aforementioned some of the theorists offered guidelines and/or blueprints that could be used in the transition from a traditional to a modern society. One example was the blueprint suggested or recommended by the well-known social theorist W.W. Rostow, "The Five Stages of Economic Growth, Tradition to Modern Society." In regards to a conceptual framework or blueprint for developing countries to follow towards modernization and economic growth, the social science theorist W.W. Rostow offered one very explicit model; the model included specific goals, objectives, and methods of implementation and evaluation. It was Rostow's extensive research related to the economic history of Europe that provided him with the intellectual tools to conceptualize "…an evolutionary process involving a series of stages in which progression from one stage to the next depended on whether or not certain preconditions had been met… For example, these included economic factors such as investment, which Rostow claimed must reach between 5 and 10 per cent of national income before a society could experience what he described as economic an take off, "… As capital accumulation increased, developing countries would progress to higher evolutionary levels until they reached the final stage of 'high mass consumption' when between 10 and 20 per cent of national income would be invested in productive enterprises" (Midgley, James, Professional Imperialism: Social Work in the Third World, London: Heinemann Educational Books, Ltd, 1981, p 46).

Some social theorist, have described Rostow as one of the most influential theorists of modernization of all times (So, 1990, p.30). According to Rostow all societies in regards to their economic dimensions can be identified within one of five categories referred to as (1) the traditional society (2) the pre-conditioning for take off, (3) the take off, (4) the drive to maturity, and (5), the age of high mass-consumption. According to Rostow, the first stage "… the traditional society is, however, in no sense of static; ad it would not exclude increases in output. Acreage could be expanded; some ad hoc technical innovations…could be introduced in trade, industry and agriculture; productivity could rise with, for example, the improvement of irrigation works or the discovery and diffusion of a new crop… "The second stage of growth embraces societies in the process of transition; that is, the period when the pre-conditions for take off are developed; for it takes time to transfer a traditional society in the ways necessary for it to exploit the fruits of modern society, to fend off diminishing returns an thus enjoy the blessings and choices opened up by the march of compound interests… We come now to the great watershed in the life of modern societies: the third stage in this sequence, the take off. The take off is the interval when the old blocks and resistance to steady growth are finally overcome. The forces making economic progress, which yielded limited bursts and enclaves of modern activity, expand and come to dominate. The society's growth becomes its normal condition…After take off there follows a long interval of sustained if fluctuating progress, as the now regularly growing economy drives to extend modern technology over the whole front of its economic activity. Some 10-20% of the national income is steadily invested, permitting output regularly to outstrip the increase in population…We now come to the age of high-mass consumption, where in time, the leading sectors shift toward durable consumers' goods and services" (Rostow, WW, The Stages of Economic Growth: A Non-Communist Manifesto, Cambridge University Press, Chapter 2, 1960, pages 4-16).

Dependency School

The Modernization school was not without strong opposition; the intellectual and theoretical opposition came primarily from the Dependency School that was highly represented by scholars such as Rodney, Frank, and Amin. The primary theoretical objection from the Dependency School was in response to the hypothesis that all societies over time would pass through a series of stages and eventually reach a final stage of social development. According to Tonnies, the process would follow a linear path and would be deterministic and irreversible. Rostow's Five Stages of Development is one example of this linear model. Therefore, one can surmise that the modernization theorists would suggest that underdeveloped countries are currently in a similar position or stage of development that the now developed countries were in at some point in the past.

First of all, social theorist such as Frank (1975), Rodney (1972), Amin (1974), rejected the aforementioned premises from the Modernization School. The Dependency School seriously questions the assumptions that the current state, or level of development in developing countries is similar to the past history of current Western developed countries. According to some scholars representing the Dependency School such as Frank, Rodney and Amin, there is no evidence to illustrate concrete similarities between the current underdeveloped countries and the structure and development of the now developed Western countries from the past. Frank, "The now developed countries was never underdeveloped though may have been undeveloped" (1975 p 4). The consensus of the Dependency School was that the developing countries, if considered by some to be economically backward, it was not due to culture traditions and customs but "...was caused by European colonial penetration" (Frank, 1975, ibid). In other words let's not just "blame the victim."

Also, from a Marxist perspective the primary factor for invading a continent, the use of military force after the invasion, followed by ongoing domination and exploitation, had little to do with culture traditions in Africa, but with the economic motives of the colonizers. The European economic empires needed new and more natural resources, as well as markets for their products. They were experiencing a need for new markets as a result of the domestic markets been saturated and the countries were witnessing a significant decline in profits; the aforementioned issues of declining domestic market and profits, expansion was badly needed and encouraged. Therefore, decisions made during the Berlin Conference in 1884-5 (Scramble for Africa) provided the opportunities for the European Empires to acquire the sources of capital needed for domestic investments, resulting in increased wealth for maintaining the economic empires back home (Midgley, James, <u>Social Welfare in Global Context,</u> California: Sage Publications, 1997, p 28).

Also, some Dependency scholars expressed that developing countries needed to break away from capitalism if they were going to achieve their development objectives (Amin, S., <u>Unequal Development</u>, New York: Monthly Review Press, 1976). But some scholars expressed that this may not be a good idea when considering or exploring global economies. But, there were others who offered a different perspective on how developing countries should proceed. One recommendation was that it was very crucial that governments and countries developed an understanding of how various economic systems in countries actually worked. It was pointed out that some countries had been able to somewhat excel in regards to sustainable economic development and may become a model for other countries trying to achieve the same. An example to consider was East Asia who seemingly grasped how the global economic forces operated its government's capacity to influence capital flows. The East Asia experience demonstrated how a country can develop development strategies and take advantage of the opportunities that became available through the global economy (Wallerstein, I., "The Capitalism World Economy," New York: Cambridge University Press".

Is there anymore evidence-based research needed to support the hypothesis presented by Frank in regards to what happened over some seven decades in Africa following the Berlin Conference? How else can the modernization school explain the forced labor, domination, and exploitation in the unjust acquisition of raw materials from the land such as gold and diamonds, for purpose of building economic empires in Europe?

The developing countries of Africa were never underdeveloped, nor were they primitive, savages, lacked ambition, or a competitive spirit prior to the Berlin Conference in 1885 and the beginning of the Scramble for Africa. 'All the countries named as underdeveloped in the world are exploited by others and the underdevelopment with which the world is now preoccupied is a product of capitalist, imperialist and colonialist exploitation' (Rodney, 1972, p 22). The expropriation of wealth (raw materials, minerals, including goal and diamonds), from many of the developing countries over a span of time left many in an extended state of social and economic stagnation.

Not unlike the Modernization School, the Dependency School had some scholarly critics as well. Some of the critics, including orthodox Marxists, have argued the point that scholars representing the Dependency school have in their problem conceptualization and analysis drifted way from classical Marxist framework. But, beyond the criticism, they give credit to the scholars from the Dependency school by stating "...they succeeded in radicalizing development studies and putting the problem of underdevelopment into its global perspective. In doing this, they highlighted the problem of international inequality and the way in which international economic processes create differentials in living standards between the world's people (Midgley, J, ibid, 1984, p 58). The Dependency school also came under criticism for not devoting more attention to issues of poverty (...the problem of domestic inequality and the appalling conditions of poverty and deprivation in which the majority of the world's population lives" (Midgley, ibid, 1984, p 58). A significant part of the criticism directed towards the Dependency school was related to problem solution. The Dependency school did not go far enough in providing guidelines toward problem solving, especially related to poverty and economic disparities. A major issue with some scholars was that the Dependency school only solution was the call for a World Revolutionary approach (Midgley, ibid, 1984). Global problems of poverty, inequalities, and global disparities were major problems for people living in developing or Third World countries. Furthermore, poverty and inequality are major obstacles to economic development (Myrdal, G., 1968, "Asian Drama: An Enquiry into the Poverty of Nations," Penguin Publishers).

Development School

Some of the major contributions addressing issues such as poverty, inequalities and/ or disparities in economic development have come from scholars representing what may be described as the development writers; their scholarly works on development issues are shared in the literature of development studies. A primary focus articulated is that the reduction or elimination of the problems confronted by people in Third World countries such as poverty, food insecurity, health, housing, as well as other social disparities and inequalities, should be a primary concern when discussing development issues. These issues will require a strong advocacy approach with a mission of direct policy interventions (Midgley, ibid, 1984, p 59).

Based on available research the data indicate that when considering plans for economic growth and development, issues related to poverty and inequalities have to be included in the discussions. A lesson to be learned from the development scholars, such as (Myrdal, 1968), is that a focus only on economic growth is not the answer to all of the social problems, such as poverty inequalities, hunger, education, housing, and income deficiencies. Serious planning, including policy formulation and implementation, will need to address the issues of inequalities as well (Myrdal, 1968, ibid), (Seers, Dudley, "The Meaning of Development," Institute of Development Studies (IDS), IDS Communications 44, 1969).

Scholars (Chenery, 1974) and others working in a scholarly collaboration with the World Bank have addressed the subject of poverty and inequalities as well as a need for egalitarian development. These scholars, especially emphasizes the relationship between equity and growth; they are not according to Chenery, 1974 antithetical but there exist a significant degree of commonality. Hollis (2006) another World Bank Scholar has also addressed the subject. Commenting on research conducted in East Asia Hollis makes the point "It is clear…from the World Banks's work on sustained poverty reduction…that economic growth must be balanced with measures that ensure equity and sustainability. These include agrarian reform, heavy investments in education, and strategic protection of key industries until they are competitive in world markets" (Hobbs, Jeremy, "Global Inequalities: What can be done to reduce international inequities," in Equity and Development, (Ed.) Gudrun Kochendorfur, The World Bank: Berlin Workshop Series, 35918, 2006, The World Bank, Washington, DC).

POST-INDEPENDENCE ERA: DEVELOPMENTAL PERSPECTIVES OF AFRICAN LEADERS

Although there were scholarly perspectives, for the most part from the Western world, on what may be the best strategies and tactics for African countries to follow for achieving social and economic success post- independence, more importantly the question is what did African leaders have to say? Several African leaders, such as Nyerere of Nigeria (1962), Mboya, Kenya (1963), and Nkrumah, Ghana (1963), articulated a socialist approach to economic growth and development following Independence. The interest on the part of some African leaders in a Communist/Socialist approach to development could be traced back to the 1920's some three decades following the Berlin Conference, and almost four decades prior to Ghana's

Independence in the year 1957 (Drew, 2014). According to Drew, linkages between African Socialism/Communism can be viewed from two historical timelines; the period between the 1920's and into the post WWII era witnessed African leaders reaching out "...in attempts to forge links with trade unions, anti-colonial and national movements (Drew, 2014, ibid, p 285). The next critical era or period came about following Independence of African countries from their European colonizers. It was during this time period that witnessed a number of Independent countries beginning to articulate Communist/Socialist ideological perspectives. The adoption of the Communist philosophy and ideology helped in promoting international alliances for the purpose of carving out a model of social and economic development for meeting the needs of the people. The newly independent countries that embraced the ideology of Communism were classified as 'one party states.' So, it was the African one party states following Independence that gravitated towards Communism as a relevant social/economical and developmental model for the future. In both the Colonial and post-Colonial periods, Communism depended on alliances where communists were few in numbers or there movements extremely weak; they generally merged into national liberation movements or left wing one party systems. The success of these African countries in maintaining a significant level of political autonomy depended on the strength of their independent social bases (Drew, 2014, ibid, pages 285-286). (Drew, Allison, "Communism in Africa," Chapter 16, in <u>The Oxford Handbook of the History of Communism</u>, (Ed.) S. A. Smith, Oxford University Press, 2014).

In considering a Socialist model for development following Independence the role of the former colonizers should not be overlooked. A Socialist approach to social and economic development was not part of the former colonizers agenda. The Modernization theory of development continued to be the dominant model; development institutes became part of the newly formed universities. European and Western experts now were providing technical supports as well as curriculums to study the problems being confronted by the newly developed countries and how those problems could best be resolved. Then, there were the foreign aid packages, not investments, to countries to assist in their social development efforts. Students, especially graduate students were now being sent to European and other Western countries for study. The Modernization theory of social and economic development was obviously a major curriculum item on the agenda. In other words, the African leaders may not have lost completely their sentiments for a Socialist/Communist model for social and economic development, but the ideological competition became quite a challenge, especially with the growth of multi-political parties. It could be concluded that the movement away from a single or one party system, to multi-party systems was a major factor shifting politics away from socialist ideology.

African leaders and first Presidents of countries, Nyerere, Mboya, and Nkrumah, did articulate a Socialist or Communist ideology as a model for development but they were confronted with a reality they could not control. It was when they were confronted with the trend towards multi-parties, not a single party state that witnessed less activism related to Communist/Socialist ideology as the model for development. The Neo-Marxist Scholars were advancing a socialist approach to development during the early Post-Independent era and obviously caught the attention of future leaders. According to one African Scholar, "Some of them might mouth the rhetoric of socialism, but the reality was the modernization of the economy by developing industries" (Brown, 1995, p.38). Leaders such as Nyerere were probably greatly torn with conflicting views and interests regarding strategies that would move their respective countries forward. After decades of European exploitation, domination, and control, it was decision time for the leaders as they struggled to find the most credible approach for social and economic development. One example of the aforementioned observation by Brown was the development of a National Development Plan in Kenya several decades following independence. In Kenya the 8th National Development Plan (NDP) was to focus "...attention on industrialization as a strategy for achieving rapid and sustained economic growth" (National Development Plan (NDP) of Kenya, 1997-2001). Obviously the primary goal of Kenya, as articulated in the 8th Development Plan, was to become an industrialized modern society.

President Nkrumah of Ghana, first African President following Independence, was commonly referred to as the 'father of African socialism.' He possessed very strong beliefs that only socialism would be the solution that would bring quickly to Ghana rapid economic growth to the country and its people. Whereas on the other hand Nyerere, the President of Tanzania was not a friend of Western capitalism. Capitalism, according to President Nyerere would encourage 'individual acquisitiveness and economic competition.' He viewed a money economy as being uncommon in Africa and would destroy the traditional African family network or system. Furthermore, he advocated for Tanzania becoming a nation of small communities (Ayittey, George B.N., Africa Betrayed, New York: St. Martin's Press 1992, p 3).

The African leaders following Independence considering an economic model to follow may have been influenced by the perspective of one scholar who recommended "...Skipping the Capitalist Stage" (Shivji, Issa G., Class Struggles in Tanzania, New York and London, Monthly Review Press, 1976, p. 14). The newly elected leaders no doubt considered a number of economic blueprints for moving their countries forward following decades of colonization. As aforementioned by (Brown, 1995, p. 38) it seemed that a primary focus was on industrial development. Furthermore, African countries as they emerged following Independence were considered, like many other countries globally, as underdeveloped. In the countries classified as underdeveloped at the time the perspective was, "...Capitalism has not developed to its advanced stage in these countries. The dominant mode of production is pre-capitalist or feudalist...Hence the task of the progressives...is to support the national bourgeoisie to build capitalism" (Shivji, ibid, 1976, pp. 14-15).

During the early stages of development following Independence, there was not yet developed a high level of capitalist development, and to be greatly influenced by Marxist Theory at the time. The reality would be for such countries to first develop capitalism. The real struggle at the time would be "...against natural conditions and not social between men and men. The question is not one of distribution since there is not much to distribute but one of producing more" (Shivji, ibid, 1976, pp. 14-15). The newly Independent countries if Africa of course had a very low stage of economic development that would take some time to get going. But, the world should recognize that all of the negative conditions existing at the time, poverty, diseases, political and military conflicts, "...are the results of the history of exploitation of the African people by the advanced capitalist countries (Shivji, ibid, 1976, pp. 14-18).

The following example from Kenya illustrates some of the cultural conflicts that may have existed among some of the leadership. Approximately three decades (30 years) prior to the 8th National Development Plan in Kenya (1997), the Vice-President of Kenya, D. T. arap

Moi made the following observation reference modernization during a presentation at a social welfare conference in Kenya, "The process of modernization, technological development and the consequent urbanization have drastically affected our traditions and customs. The extended family system through which the less fortunate members of the community were protected and cared for by the family group, clan or tribe, is undergoing a very drastic change, if not in the process of breaking down completely. The consequences of all this are manifested in the increasing cases of social maladjustment, of stresses and strains of family life, of lonely and needy old people and children and young people requiring care and protection" (Moi, Speech, Social Welfare Conference, Nairobi, Kenya, 1967).

In regards to views or perspectives of political leaders related to modernization, industrialization and urbanization it had been suggested by one social theorist several decades ago that the economic and social plans of African leaders would not focus on strengthening traditional family values and traditions. The reasoning behind such suggestion, "...partly because their tribal core or foundation would hinder the desired intensification of loyalties to the nation, made up of many tribes. The ideologies of economic growth and family 'modernism' will continue to shape the next decade of change in Sub-Saharan Africa. The removal of European administrators will not remove the effects of ideas and socioeconomic processes, originally European, which is now integrally part of the African world (Goode, William, J., World Revolution and Family Patterns, "World Changes in Family Patterns," New York: The Free Press, 1970, p. 202).

A very significant observation expressed by one Scholar regarding African leadership following Independence was, "...most African leaders did not value their own heritage and the significance of their indigenous systems. The new leadership stripped the traditional chiefs of their authority and actually set out to destroy indigenous systems through various government policies and civil wars...new leaders acted as if Africa had no history, no culture, no native institutions...The same African leaders who railed against Western denial of the intellectual capabilities of Africans placed more faith in expatriates and foreign systems than in their own African peoples (Ayittey, George, Ibid 1992 pages 110-111).

It would appear that African countries, for the most part, had chosen following Independence, the goal of transitioning towards a modern, urban and industrialized society. Current research and during recent decades an appropriate decision was made by some if not all. Although there have been many challenges since Ghana became an Independent country in 1957 as the slogan goes, "Rising Africa" referring to positive economic growth. The continent currently has one of the fastest growing economies in the world, being referred to as the "African Renaissance." **(NOTE: Chapter VII addresses Africa's current economic successes).**

Selective Contemporary Views on Modernization and Colonization

Dr. Chigozie Obioma

As aforementioned some scholars such as Frank and Rodney from the Dependency School have challenged some of the basic principles embracing the concept of modernization. The two scholars' major criticism is in response to the modernization school's assumption that not unlike the now developed worlds, the current developing worlds were beginning their transition or beginning to modernization from similar circumstances. The scholars, Rodney and Frank have observed, based on historical research, that the now developed countries globally were never underdeveloped. One contemporary scholar, Chigozie Obioma, questions if the goal of African societies is to focus on the transition of reaching what has been described as a modern society (Obioma, Chigozie, "Africa has been failed by Westernization," The Guardian, African Opinion, November 12, 2017: 13:50 EST). He questions the global notion, including Africans that to become, according to the Western interpretation, "...civilized and modern is simply 'aping' the behaviors and manners of the Western world" (Obioma, ibid, 2017, p. 1). Obioma also takes very serious exception to the notion that the only criteria for defining and measuring modern is sole responsibility of the Western world. Furthermore, the countries of Africa should not be referred to as the nations of Africa but "...Western African Nations... African nations have a total dependency on foreign political philosophies and ideas, and their shifts and movements. Africa is being slowly emptied of its essence and becoming a relic..." (Obioma, Ibid, 2017, p.1).

According to Obioma African countries or nations instead of becoming a Western relic need to conceptualize and pursue a different pathway for the future. "The most viable pathway would be for African's elite to look within the vast political and ideological resources on which successful civilizations, the Zulu, the Igbo, the Malian dynasties of Timbuktu, the Oyo empires were built...In most Igbo states, for instance, there was an equalitarian system where an elder member of a clan represented his people in the Elders' Council. There were no Kings or Presidents. Perhaps there could be a way to adapt this unique political structure to replace the Western one which has so far failed" (Obioma, ibid, 2017). The major challenge becomes who and how this tremendous proposal being put forward will be operationalized in the midst of such 21st Century environment?

Dr. Bruce Gilley

In regards to the subject of failed African nations and/or countries following Independence Gilley has been advocating for what has been viewed by scholars globally to be a very radical and divisive solution to the problem from his scholarly perspective. A very controversial article that appeared in the Third World Quarterly, "The Case for Colonialism (Bring Back Colonialism), 08/September/2017, File Preview 09/12/2017: 10.1080/01436597.2017, has now been withdrawn by journal's Editorial Board (**See Note of Withdrawal Below**). In the article 'Bruce Gilley sparked a storm of protest by claiming colonialism had been a good thing. He stated bluntly-for the last 100 years, Western Colonialism has had a bad name...Western colonialism, he claimed, was, as a general rule, both objectively beneficial and subjectively legitimate in most of the places it was found. The countries that embraced their colonial inheritance by and large did better than those that spurned it (Lusher, Adam, "Bring Back Colonialism," Independent, 10/12/2017: 11:11, BST).

From Gilley's perspective for more than 100 years of disasters on the continent of Africa, '...it is time to make the case for colonialism again. Alien rule has been legitimate because it has provided better governance than the indigenous alternatives...Millions of people moved closer to areas of more intensive colonial rule, sent their children to colonial schools and hospitals, went beyond the call of duty in positions in colonial governments, fought for colonial armies' (Lusher, ibid, 2017). Dr. Gilley suggested several proposals for "bringing back colonialism," including the replication of colonial governments on the continent; secondly, the developed or Western countries '...should be encouraged to hold power in specific governmental areas, such as public finances and criminal justice; thirdly, build new Western Colonies' (Lusher, ibid, 2017).

One can only imagine the response globally to Dr. Gilley's published article appearing in a "peer reviewed" scholarly Journal. Following only a few weeks of discussions, debates, death threats and violent acts targeting the author, the Third World Quarterly Editorial Board withdrew the article. A general consensus was that academic freedom did not apply to such comments reference colonialism' (Lusher, ibid, 2017).

The <u>Third World Quarterly</u> Withdrawal Notice: "Bring Back Colonialism,"
Dr. Bruce Gilley, Portland State University, Oregon

"This viewpoint essay has been withdrawn at the request of the academic journal Editor, and in agreement with the author of the essay. Following a number of complaints, Taylor & Francis, conducted a thorough investigation into the peer review process on the article...The journal Editor has subsequently received serious and credible threats of personal violence. These threats are linked to the publication of this essay. As a publisher we must take this seriously. Taylor & Francis has a strong and supportive duty of care to all of our academic editorial teams, and this is why we are withdrawing this essay" (Third World Quarterly – File Preview, 9/12/2017 – 10.1080/01436597-2017).

THE POST INDEPENDENCE ERA ON THE AFRICAN CONTINENT BEGINS

It was almost three decades following the 1930 ILO Labor Convention that Ghana, considered by some as the first African country 1957, to be granted Independence. Several other countries should also be noted. Prior to Ghana's Independence other African countries had previously received the honor for a variety of different reasons.

Selective Chronological List of African Independence Before 1957

<u>COUNTRY</u>	<u>YEAR OF INDEPENDENCE</u>
Liberia, Republic of	July 1847
South Africa, Republic	May 1910
Egypt (North Africa), Republic of	February 1922

Ethiopia, People's Democratic Republic of Libya, (North Africa) Socialist People's	May 1941
Libyan Arab Jamahiriya	December 1951
Sudan, Democratic Republic (North Africa)	January 1956
Morocco, (North Africa), Kingdom of	March 1956
Tunisia, (North Africa), Republic of Morocco, (North Africa), Spanish Northern	March 1956
Zone, Marruecos	April 1956
Morocco, (North Africa), International Zone, Tangiers	October 1956
Ghana, Republic of	**March 1957**

Reference: (Boddy-Evans, Alistair, "Chronological List of African Independence," **Thought Co,** - www.thoughtco.com, Updated 12/18/2017, page 1).

Following Ghana's Independence in 1957, it would not be long before practically all countries in Africa, various timelines, were granted Independence after more than three-quarters of a century of colonization. The long era of colonization did not end with the Declaration of Independence and the raising of the country's flag. Decolonization, especially in the areas related to work, and labor issues in general would remain on the agendas of organizations, such as the ILO. The ILO with its mission of enhancing the overall working conditions of the global human workforce, began to recognize following WWI, somewhat of a positive political environment that would become favorable enough for carrying out its mission (Human Rights, Development, and Decolonization p. 4). Also, it was following the 1930 Convention that the mission and work of the ILO began to expand from a primary focus on the physical requirement of work towards more and more emphasis on areas such as social protection/social security, as well as issues and concerns related to human rights and social justices (HRDD, ibid. p.4).

For most African countries following Independence the challenges would be great and the journey long. Despite the challenges the leadership was ready to move on. It is interesting to note that when the Republic of the Congo finally became an Independent Country in 1960, Premier Patrice Lumumba had this message for the former colonizers of the his country: "We are no longer your monkeys…no Congolese worthy of the name will ever be able to forget that this Independence has been won through a struggle…in which we did not spare our energy and our blood. The Republic of the Congo has been proclaimed and our country is now in the hands of its own children…"(Ayittey, Ibid 1992, p. 98).

The Introduction of Western Programs/Schemes of Social Protection For African Civil Servants

Social protection and/or social security schemes, including employer liability, poor relief, old-age pension, widows and orphan funds, had been introduced into the African colonies during colonization, but Africans were excluded. But, following Independence Africans who took over the public and/or government jobs once occupied by expatriates now became the employees in the employer/worker insurance schemes. The International Labor Organization (ILO) played a major role in ensuring that the employment rights and privileges once held by the expatriates should now be passed on to the Africans now occupying these civil service and/or government positions (ILO, 1961).

Although a small segment of African civil service workers were now protected to some extent by the passed on social security schemes, the vast majority of Africans were unprotected. Therefore, traditional systems of social security/social protection continued to be the major sources of protection. Historically, and even until contemporary times, the majority of those in the workforce in African countries were and continue to be employed in the informal sector of the workforce. This is a major factor why only 16.9 % of retirees are without social protection. This sector of the workforce, for the most part, is not connected to contributory and/or non-contributory social insurance schemes; therefore, not only are they not protective from employer liability, lack of access to medical care, including disability, this vast informal sector remains un-protective following retirement without income security. Therefore, a major challenge facing developing countries in the New Millennium is how to include this growing population of workers from the informal sector into some system of social security/social protection.

The Time For Moving Forward

Following three-quarters of a Century, or approximately 73 years of colonization by the European powers, and following Ghana's Independence in 1957, African countries were ready to move forward and take its place as a new member in the global constellation of productive nations. The three-quarters of a Century time frame refers to the era of colonization using the beginning date (1884-85) of the Berlin Conference commonly referred to as 'The Scramble for Africa,' and the official date or year of Ghana's Independence in 1957. Some scholars use the year 1960, not 1957, referred to as the "stylized" date of Independence for the reasons that it was the end of colonial rule in the French colonies, geographically South of the Sahara as well as in the most populous British and Belgian occupied colonies (Austin, G., "African Economic Development and Colonial Legacies," International Development Policy, Graduate Institute of International Studies, Geneva, 2010, pages 11-32).

Despite all of the injustices resulting from the "Scramble for Africa," the extended family network system in some form has continued its tradition of caring, especially for the children, older family members, including other vulnerable members of the population. Post-Independence research, addressed in **Chapter IV** provides an example of how the strong cultural traditions continue to survive on African soil. Within the Mashona family of Zimbabwe, older members or grandparents continue the tradition of caring and/or rearing dependent grandchildren and/or orphans. Also, older or elderly family members continue to live with their sons who are responsible for their care (Mbanje, ibid, 1979). Yes, to some extent intergenerational reciprocity, and a commitment to "We" and not "I" continues. The aforementioned examples raise the hopes and expectations that African countries will respond positively in confronting the challenges of a growing older population, or the "Silver Tsunami." Chapter IV also provides a more current example of how the culture and traditions of family caring, "The Matriarchs of Mthatha" on South Africa's Eastern Cape.

The current and future focus in Africa will probably be less on the concepts of Post-Independence and Colonization and more on the challenges as well as opportunities presented by an urban modernized and cybernetic society. According to some Economist, "Africa is Rising;" globally, not only is Africa one of the fastest growing economies, but over the next several decades some major cities in Africa will continue to experience growth rates comparable to other regions of the world. "Economic growth and a rapidly growing population of about 1 billion mean more urbanization in Africa than any other continent, with major cities in Africa currently contributing about $700 billion to the continent's GDP. This figure is set to grow to $1.7 trillion by 2030" (Bafana, Busani, "Africa's cities of the Future," United Nations Department of Public Information: Africa Renewal, page 4, 2016). Sustained economic growth will contribute significantly to more and more urbanization and modernization resulting in major challenges, including the need for job opportunities, especially in the formal sectors, educational accessibility especially for the "bulge generation," across gender lines, housing, medical, health and social services.

In considering all of the major challenges accompanying a growing population, including the "Silver Tsunami," one major question of many is, are there elements of the traditional system of caring, example, intergenerational reciprocity, that has the potential of being part of the planning process in responding to current and future demographic trends, youth "bulge" and the "silver tsunami?" It is obvious that in transitioning from a traditional and informal society with strong kinship ties, geographically and interpersonal, to a more modern technological/cybernetic and formal society, the challenges will become more complicated. Yet, despite the fact that centuries and decades have passed, and some evidence exist that elements of the extended family network continue to be preserved. Well, considering the growing older population and the concept of intergenerational reciprocity, wouldn't" it be wise to think about some innovative social policies, such as housing incentives for example, for keeping families, especially older members closer?

THE TRANSITION FROM A TRADITIONAL TO A MODERN SOCIETY: IMPLICATIONS FOR POPULATION GROWTH, INCLUDING THE "SILVER TSUNAMI"

It is now more than six decades since Ghana was crowned an independent and sovereign country. Since that time in 1957 Africa has been moving forward confronting new challenges. Considering the trials and tribulations of the past, especially surviving a quarter-century of colonization despite the naysayers, the Continent despite struggles continues to move on. In addition to the negative insights there are now positive observations such as one of the fastest growing economies globally, The Fastest Billion: The Story Behind Africa's Economic Revolution, and "Tarzan doesn't live here anymore." The current challenges are the unprecedented growth in population across all age groups, especially the "Silver Tsunami," and the "youth Bulge" generation.

Population Growth: The Urban Challenge

The projections are the world's population will grow to approximately 7 billion people by calendar year 2015. Ten years later, 2025, the population will reach approximately 8 billion. The largest proportional increase in population will take place in Sub-Saharan Africa; the percentage increase will go from 12% today to approximately 21% by the year 2050. It is interesting to note that between the years 2008 and 2030 practically all population growth will happen in urban areas; the majority in developing countries (Atlas: Global Development, 4th Edition, 2013). In other words millions of people making the transition from rural and village life to urban areas, will be taking place in Sub-Saharan Africa.

Population scholars project that 90% percent of the global growth will take place in developing countries. Furthermore, 90 percent of the population growth in developing countries will be living in urban areas. By the year 2025, 9 percent of the population will be 65 or older. The 9 percent represents a 42 percent increase of those 65 plus since 2010. It is projected that in Sub-Saharan Africa approximately 60% of the population will live within the slums of the cities or urban areas. Individuals and/or families living in these slums (Such as the Mathare Slum in Nairobi, Kenya) will be surrounded by poverty stricken conditions, including the lack of access to clean drinking water and sanitation, basic health and social services, and poor housing (Atlas: Global Development, ibid).

Kenya is one of eleven countries in the Eastern African Region, including Burundi, Comoros, Djibouti, Eritrea, Ethiopia, Madagascar, Malawi, Mauritius, Reunion, Rwanda, Seychelles, Somalia, Tanzania, and Uganda (UN-HABITAT: The State of African Cities, 2010). Estimation is that approximately 200 million people are living in slum areas in Sub-Saharan Africa. Globally, Africa has the reputation of having some of the largest slums, including the aforementioned Mathare, and the most talked about being the Kibera slum in Nairobi, Kenya, considered the largest in Africa with a population of more than 2 million people (UN-HABITAT: 2010, ibid). Speaking of challenges, just imagine a slum area housing two million people. This example is not unlike what will be experienced by many others making the transition from rural to urban areas, including members of the growing older population.

Approximately 40% of all Africans were living in cities in 2010; the population of those living in the Eastern African Region in 2010 was 23.6 %. "Urban demographic growth across the continent remained the strongest worldwide at an annual 3.3% average, compared with a global 2.5% rate." There were variations in growth patterns across the sub-regions between 2005-2010; the strongest sub-region during this time span was Central Africa, 4.3%, Western Africa, 4.05%, and Eastern Africa, 3.86%. The regions in Northern (2.45) and Southern Africa (1.88) dropped below the global average (UN-HABITAT, ibid, p. 136).

Between 1960 and 2010 the urban population of the Eastern African Region increased from 6 million to 77 million. "Eastern Africa's urban population is projected to increase by another 38.9 million to 116.1 million in 2020, a 50.4% growth rate. Between 2020 and 2030, the region's urban population is expected to increase by a further 56.6 million to 172.7 million; this would signal a slight slowdown compared with the previous decade, but still a significant 48.7% increase over the projected 2020 urban population...By 2050, Eastern Africa's urban population is projected at 337.4 million which, with a 47.4% urbanization rate, will still leave it short of the

50% "tipping point" which the world as a whole experienced in 2008 (UN: HABITAT, IBID, p. 136). The three major connections between poverty, inequality, and slum incidence in the Eastern African Region are, (a) "…a lack of access to affordable and adequate land for the predominantly poor urban populations; (b) severe inequality in domestic wealth sharing, and (c) unequal access to basic (including social) infrastructures (UN: HABITAT, ibid, p. 138).

Employment Opportunities in an Urban Industrialized Society

Globally, regardless of Region, access to jobs will continue to be a major challenge for anyone living within the slums of urban areas. Within the slum areas of the growing or emerging cities the problem of finding a job can be the most challenging. This is especially the case where the birth and growth of urban areas are not accompanied by any levels of industrial and/or manufacturing activities. Most individuals seeking jobs normally will end up in the informal sector of the labor market. This only adds to the issues surrounding social protection and/or social security, including not having a social pension in old age. The major challenge will be providing jobs in a tripartite labor arrangement that provide social protection/social pensions for the future populations, especially the older population; not just income security, also access to health and social services during the working years for families and social protection for the growing older population.

In Nairobi, Kenya the unskilled workers are competing on a daily basis for a job. The worker will incur on a daily basis transportation expenses and no doubt disappointment and frustration as he/she searches for some kind of job; in this desperate search the worker is probably not thinking too much regarding benefits, such as hours, hourly pay rates or vacation times. The worker is probably more concerned about just landing a job (Metcalfe, V and Pavanello, with Mishra, P. HPG Humanitarian Policy Group, HPG Report 33, "Sanctuary in the City," Urban Displacement and Vulnerability, Final Report, June, 2013 – QUOTED by Haysom, S, in "Urban Displacement and Vulnerability in Nairobi, HGP Working Paper, London: HGP).

The Urban Challenge: Traditional System of Caring in a Modern urbanized Society

What About the Elderly and the Children

As global population growth, including the "Silver Tsunami," continues the transformation of people from rural to urban areas or the process of urbanization, will present some opportunities, but on the other hand overwhelming challenges; this is especially true for traditional family/kinship caring systems, as well as political, social (including health and human services), and economic institutions preparing for a growing older population. Although modernization and/or urbanization have been viewed historically as a positive phenomenon, there are also some very negative consequences as the aforementioned systems attempt to respond to all of the challenges accompanying urbanization and modernization.

A review of data informs in regards to urbanization that globally approximately 500 million individuals 65+ are currently living in cities; that is more than half or 58% of all older people. This population, including those 60+ represents the fastest-growing group of urbanized populations. It should be noted that approximately half, or 289 million of those are living in low-and middle-income countries. Furthermore, approximately 250 million of those 65+ are living in cities in Asia, 23 million are in Africa and 57 million of those 65+ are residing in Latin American cities (Jones, Sion Eryl et al, "Ageing and the City: Mking Urban Spaces Work for Older People," Help Age International, London, 2016). No, the older population for whatever the reason will not be staying in the villages, therefore the challenge of responding to the "Silver Tsunami" will be even greater.

The older population transitioning to urban areas will be confronted by major challenges that will threaten their day-to-day survival, especially overall quality of life. The dream of the older people to live their later lives in safety, dignity and respect could go very well unfilled in an urbanized modern society. In the so called modern urban society, "Many people are marginalized and excluded – socially, economically and spatially – particularly in old age, due to ageist attitudes and behavior and the lack of inclusive planning and development decisions" (Jones, S., ibid, 2016, p. 3). In all of the cities globally, the marginalization and exclusion, including social and economical are major threats to the quality of life of the older population. Other significant issues faced by the older population include, "Traffic dominated streets and air pollution, limited public transport, unsafe green spaces, social isolation, insecure incomes, poor health, inaccessible buildings, and insecure or inappropriate housing can all deny older persons their right to lead, dignified and independent lives" (Jones, S., ibid, 2016).

At this point in time it seems that globally, especially the low-to middle-income countries preparation for a growing older population is not on time; obviously, there is a great deal of work to be done. It can not expected that the developing countries, including those in Sub-Saharan Africa, will be capable of responding to this demographic phenomenon without assistance from the international community. Globally, it should be expected that international organizations would be line to support a movement such as the "Age Demand Campaign," and it petition to the United Nations. The Campaign with leadership coming from advocate non-governmental organizations such as Help Age International, calling on the United Nations to convene a Special Session to address major issues of older people. The Campaign has received support from Bishop Tutu of South Africa a long-time leader around issues of human rights and social justice.

As social science theorists, such as Tonnies projected countries in Africa would eventually follow the path of other countries in transitioning from a traditional to a modern and urbanized society. Some major issues or concerns of this transition for the African countries, especially the growing older population, would be the potential loss or of some treasured traditions, cultures and customs, in caring for some of the most vulnerable members of society. One example would be the extended family system as described at the beginning of the Chapter. Some of the theorists expressed that the traditional extended family system would be an obstacle to African countries seeking to become part of a modern society. It was suggested by some of the theorists that for the countries to achieve success in a modern society they would have to abandon some of the cultural traditions and customs. It was even suggested by some that the celebrated extended family with a strong emphasis on "we," and "...its very extensive networks of dependents, duties, and obligations was inimical to individualism and the mobility of labor required in an industrialized economy (Goode, W.J., World Revolutions and Family Patterns, New York: Free Press, pages 1-10, 164-200, 1970).

A major challenge in the transition would be how the newly Independent African countries will maintain, if chosen to do so, some of the strengths of the traditional family system, such as the concept of "We," not "I," and the very important tradition of intergenerational reciprocity? The transition to a modern urban and industrialized society could have major implications for a growing older population. As aforementioned numerous times, currently less than twenty percent of older persons in Sub-Saharan Africa do not have basic income security or a social pension at the time of retirement. The problem of a lack of social pensions for the growing older population has been addressed for several decades, beginning with the United Nations First World Assembly in 1982. One such international organization addressing the problem of income security, globally, for the growing older population is the World Bank.

The World Bank expresses the perspective that "Income security in old age is a worldwide problem, but its manifestations differ in different parts of the world. In Africa and parts of Asia, the older population includes a small percentage of the general population. Historically, the older population has been cared for by extended family arrangements, including mutual aid societies, and other informal mechanisms (A World Bank Policy Research Report, "Averting the Old Age Crisis," New York, Oxford University Press, 1994, p. 3). But, the era of modernization, including urbanization, are making some of the traditional ways of providing financial and other supports for older people in regions such as Sub-Saharan Africa obsolete (See Chapter IV of Text, Modernization). The extended family system, especially in the Sub-Saharan region of Africa, that historically has been the primary caregivers for the older population, as well as other vulnerable members of the family, has been and will continually be significantly challenged in the 21st Century. Beyond modernization and urbanization, other factors have also curtailed traditional family roles such as the HIV epidemic, droughts/famine, wars, mobility, and political instability (A World Bank Policy Research Report, Ibid, 1994).

But, as aforementioned, globally the problem of financial wellbeing is not just a crisis in Sub-Saharan Africa, but in "…Latin America, Eastern Europe, and the formal Soviet Union, which can no longer afford the formal programs of old age security they introduced long ago…."(A World Bank Policy Research Report, Ibid, 1994, p. 4). Furthermore, even the developed World or OECD countries, including the United States, Belgium, Canada, Spain, United Kingdom, have been and/or recently have had social security problems related to a growing older population.

According to social theorists, modernization, industrialization, and urbanization symbolize the "promised land," or the "land of milk and honey," "where the streets are paved with gold" {Author's comments describing the Northern U.S. encouraging African-Americans to move North from the South during the era of industrialization in the United States}. Social change theorists, such as Comte, Tonnies, tell us that the process from a traditional society to a modern society is inevitable. The process symbolizes the road to modernization and industrialization. The process may be viewed on the one hand as a technological success story, but modernization presents new challenges, especially the negative consequences. Once again, the major question in response to the transition from a rural to an urban industrialized society is, what are the implications for a growing older population? Will they need new support groups, especially those without social security/social protection? What will life be like if they remain in the village or rural area? **{A colleague from Kenya who works for SADC, stationed in Ethiopia; on a recent visit shares with me that his father is upset because the family does not seem like family anymore. Nobody can come home anymore}** What happens to Africa greatest social welfare system, the extended family kinship group? How does the concept reciprocity survive in an individualistic, complex, contract oriented modern society? The timetable has already been set. Raymond B. Cattell (1993, p. 13) raises several very important several very important questions, "… it is only reasonable to ask what can be done to meet the needs of elderly Africans now, the millions who are already old or will become old in the next decade; specifically what can be done for those who require long-term care." These are some of the questions where answers are needed, and action immediately taken as an increasing number of young Africans trek towards urban areas in search of new opportunities in a cybernetic society.

The transition from a traditional to a modern urbanized cybernetic society began shortly following Independence, or during the Post-Independence Era. The transition has and will continue to present major challenges, such as increasing urbanization, migration in all forms, housing shortages, unemployment, crime and poverty. There have been, since Independence and will continue in the future, several major challenges that will confront all of the countries in Sub-Saharan Africa. First of all, finding ways to maintain a level of sustained economic growth; secondly, preparing for the "Silver Tsunami," or the demographic shock of a growing older population, including all of their special needs; thirdly, the development of partnerships and/or collaborations in the labor sector that will bring together the formal and informal sectors that will reduce the number of retirees without basic income security, or a social pension at the time of retirement. In this area there is a need for a comprehensive plan involving the public/private sectors, including government in efforts to guarantee future generations of older people can live in respect and dignity in later years. Currently, only about eleven countries, approximately 16.9 % of the total population has a statutory pension system for those retirees who did not work in the formal sector. But, in this area there is hope considering the fact that approximately a third of the countries in Sub-Saharan Africa currently without a social pension, have initiated arrangements to include workers from the informal sector and/or the self-employed **(SEE CHAPTER VI: Country by Country Analysis)**. Finally and most importantly will be planning for the "bulge," or growing youth generation. Preparation and planning have to include all levels of education, job preparation and political participation with a focus on human rights, social justice and the avoidance of all forms of corruption activities.

The Informal Economy

A key factor or focus during the transition has to be on the workforce or labor sector. A major concern, especially in the developing countries has to be on the increasing growth of the informal labor sector, especially the implications for social protection. First of all, "…rural to urbanization in developing countries is accompanied by growth in the informal economies" (Elgin, C., and Oyvat, C., "Lurking in the Cities: Urbanization and the informal Economy," <u>Structural Change and Economic Dynamics,</u> 2013 p 27, 36-37 – Cited in Habitat III, "Issue

Paper on the Informal Sector," UN: 31/May/2015, p 2). The primary living and working centers for those in transition will be the secondary cities or the major cities "outer circles." As aforementioned a very large number of individuals, families, including the older population will end up in these secondary cities and/or slums. It will be in these secondary centers where the most significant population growth will take place. As aforementioned, it will be in these secondary towns, centers or slums where the informal labor sectors will continue to grow and dominate the employment statistics (UN: DESA, World Urbanization Prospects, 2014 – Cited in Habitat III).

The continuing or increasing growth of the informal sector is a critical issue as countries in Sub-Saharan Africa prepare for the "Silver Tsunami." In Sub-Saharan Africa the primary reason so many older persons lack income security or a social pension at the time of retirement is that their work history in the labor sector was primarily self-employed or they worked in the informal sector. There is no indication that reality will change at any point in the near future. The continuing challenge during the rural to urban transition is forming a partnership between the informal and formal sectors. "Among the push and pull factors that drive rural-urban migration are the prospects for better paying jobs. However, limited availability of such jobs means the informal economy is the main option for work" (Elgin and Oyvat, ibid, 2013 – Cited in Habitat, ibid, p 2). Some examples provide a glimpse of the current non-agricultural informal labor/employment sector. The West African City Niamey (pop. 800,000) in Niger comprises 76% of the non-agricultural, informal urban labor sector; the City of Lome (pop. 837,437) in Togo comprises 83% of the labor sector (Elgin and Oyvat, ibid, 2013 – Cited in Habitat, ibid).

From a gender perspective women represent a more significant portion of the non-agricultural/informal workforce than men. For example, in Sub-Saharan Africa the percentage is 74 % women to 61% men; in Abidjan, Cote d'Ivoire, 9 out of every 10 women are employed in the informal sector compared to 7 out of 10 for men (Herrera, J., et.al, "Informed Sector and Informal Employment: Overview of Data for 11 Cities in 10 Developing Countries," Working Paper #9, Cambridge, MA, "Women in Informal Employment: Globalizing and Organizing" (WIEGO), 2012 - ILO, Geneva, "Women in Informal Employment," ILO, Geneva, 2013 – Cited in Habitat, ibid, 2013). Another factor is the role played by youth in the informal employment sector. Research from a 10 Country study has pointed out that approximately 8 of 10 young workers are represented in the informal sector (ILO, "Global Employment Trends for Youth: A Generation at Risk," ILO, Geneva, 2013 – Cited in Habitat, ibid, 2013).

The "Youth Bulge" Generation: Challenges/Opportunities

Authors of the recently published Global Development Index (GDI) expressed the importance of the global youth population, "…From ending poverty to tackling climate change, the world's future lies in the hands of the young. So why are we failing to give theme a descent shot at life?" (Abhik Sen and Rafiullah Kakar, "Why are we failing 75% of the world's youth at a time of unique opportunity?" The Guardian: Global Development, February 20, 2017 p 1, 02: EST). The authors utilizing some 18 indicators covering areas such as health, education, employment and political participation, shared some insights regarding the plight of youth globally. The report concluded that for a majority of youth globally their future prospects were not good. For comparative purposes the 183 countries participating in the GDI study for some analysis were ranked according to lowest and highest income countries. For example, "...youth mortality rate is on average 5 times higher in the lowest ranked countries of the index in comparison with countries where young people have the best shot at living a descent life. Equally shocking is the gap in secondary education enrollment for the highest and lowest ranked countries...only 40% of countries have achieved something close to parity in secondary education rates. In tertiary education that figure drops to 4%...young females are on average twice as likely as young males to be out of education, employment or training" (Sen and Kakar, 2017, ibid, p 1). Youth that are experiencing the greatest difficulties and challenges are those surrounded by on-going country violence, especially armed conflict; country examples from the Index (bottom of the index) were the Central African Republic, Democratic Republic of the Congo, Chad and Afghanistan. The study concluded that the most likely indicators of youths' growth and development were countries experiencing a large bulge, such as most African countries, income status and the type of regime existing in her/his country (Sen and Kakar, 2017, ibid).

Although Sub-Saharan Africa has been viewed, based on data analysis, at the very bottom of the 183 countries under review, there is a very positive note coming from the Inaugural presentation; during the past 5 years the country who has demonstrated the greatest improvements in regards to young people is Kenya. "Together with 4 other Sub-Saharan countries: South Africa, Niger, Togo and Malawi, Kenya made the largest gains globally across a range of criteria, from health to political participation (Quinn, Ben, The Guardian: Global Development, "Kenya Lights the Way for Beleaguered Youth of Sub-Saharan Africa," October 21, 2017, p 1).

Time to Alter the Course of History: Informal to a More Formal Labor Sector

A very sad scholarly note has to do with the continuing increase in the informal sector in practically all of the countries within Sub-Saharan Africa. The Informal sector is a major factor why 82.5% of older persons do not have a social pension. In Kenya as an example "...it is evident that the share of the urban population in informal employment...has hugely increased since the 1980s and continues to do so" (UN: HABITAT, ibid, p.143). One question that has been raised has to do with how do the slum dwellers survive considering all of the challenges, especially the lack of job opportunities? In urban/slum areas all across the continent there will be found "...a large pool of unemployed and underemployed city dwellers keeps labor costs low and therefore can make Eastern Africa increasingly competitive, the consequences of massive urban poverty almost inevitably include increased urban violence, crime, insecurity and social unrest that are in no one's interest and can scare away foreign capital" (UN: HABITAT, ibid, p.144).

Scholars have written books and journal articles about the informal sector in countries such as Kenya. There are those who view the informal labor sector as strength in countries such as Kenya; there are others who see the informal sector as a problem without a short or long-range solution. "The informal sector acts not as a savior but as a predator for the poor, often extending the most hostile and brutal labor conditions on disfranchised people who are in no position to fight back" (UN: ibid, p.145).

In Kenya the concept, "informal sector" (Also the jua Kali is used and has become popular not only in Kenya but globally) became very popularized following a study by the ILO in its 1972 study of Kenya (ILO, "Employment, Incomes and Equity: A Strategy for Increasing Productive Employment in Kenya," Geneva: ILO 1972). The informal sector becomes critical when in discussions around the fact the vast majority of older persons are without a social pension in old age had worked in the labor sector.

In a Chamber of Commerce publication (US based organization- The Center for International Private Enterprise) there were discussions relevant to the numerous challenges that the informal sectors had to endure in Kenya. Primarily the discussion focused on "…cumbersome laws and regulations remain out of step with current realities and are hostile to the growth of the informal sector. The by-laws applied by many local authorities are not standardized and appear to be punitive instead of facilitative in most cases…The bureaucratic, lengthy process of transacting business with government agencies adversely impacts informal traders by diverting their scarce resources from production to sheer housekeeping (Orwa, Bani, Jua Kali Association in Kenya: A Force for Development and Reform, Center for International Private Enterprise, Washington, DC, Reform Case Study No. 0701, 2007, p. 1).

The Case Study addressed a number of challenges confronting the informal sector, including the aforementioned, previous paragraph, and others were the difficulty in gaining ownership over their businesses and land, and "…their workshops and stands lack electricity and running water (Orwa, ibid, p. 2). Also, there were references to the health care services being inadequate, lack of suitable information on marketing, and having access to training and technology (Orwa, ibid, p.2).

The Case Study makes the point that most Kenyans recognize jua kali "…as the most important economic sector in Kenya, the one in which they all work" (Orwa, ibid, p. 1). At the time of the Case Study the informal sector accounted for approximately 74% of total employment" (Orwa, ibid). The everyday saying in Kenya is 'We're all jua kali nowadays' (Quote from Kenneth King, Jua Kali Kenya: Change and Development in an Informal Economy, 1970-95 (London: James Curry, 1996) 25.

What was missing from the Case Study document, especially the challenges, was any discussion regarding social security and/or social pensions. There was a lack of discussion around any level of negotiation underway or planned to involve the informal sector in any way within the formal sector for the purpose of acquiring family health and social service benefits, including retirement benefits for a growing older population. It is interesting and "mind boggling" that at this time scholars and community advocates were not addressing issues related to pillars of social protection for the informal sector (**See Appendix A: Tables/Charts, Chapter V, Tables 1 and 2**).

A POST-INDEPENDENCE INITIATIVE, STRUCTURAL READJUSTMENT PROGRAMS (SAP): IMPLICATIONS FOR SOCIAL AND ECONOMIC DEVELOPMENT?

As discussed in the previous section there was not a coherent social/economic comprehensive planning initiative for Africa prior to Independence. The one attempt or initiative that never fully materialized was the 1920 Guggisberg Plan on the Gold Coast now the country of Ghana. Following the granting of Independence to African countries beginning with Ghana in 1957, there was no such initiative such as the Marshal Plan for recovery and development that occurred in Europe following World War II. The Marshall Plan was an initiative that was introduced by General George C. Marshall of the United States with the goal of rebuilding the destruction of Europe. After the war the world took notice that some of the European countries, especially the cities, had been partially or totally destroyed during the war years. The physical destruction of the infrastructure of cities, and their economies had been devastated as a result of the military encounters, including air raids or aerial bombings. Globally, it was felt that Europe needed to be rebuilt, and the initiative was the "Marshall Plan" requiring billions of dollars.

Now, following decades of underdevelopment in Africa, including taking over and control of the land, forced labor, the extraction and exportation of valuable raw resources, with the goal of developing the economic empires in Europe, there was no global Marshall Plan for Africa. Once again the lack of a coherent initiative, such as a Marshall Plan, further demonstrates the lack of respect for the Continent. There is no concrete evidence to illustrate how the European powers expressed thanks to the colonies for the overall development of the European economies. Some may say that the Europeans left infrastructures, including buildings, roads, educational facilities, educational partnerships with universities, and the beginning of foreign aid. Also, there was the passing on to African public and/or government employees a tripartite labor system that included a system of social protection, including social pensions. It is interesting that some of the most innovative initiatives related to social protection, including workers rights to bargain collectively, were drafted and implemented in Europe. The original concept and program referred to as social security came out of Germany under the leadership of Bismarck. Also, Conferences such as the Forced Labor Conference in 1930, three decades prior to Ghana's Independence, and the Conference on Minimum Standards for workers in 1952 were significant global events on behalf of workers. The question is why none of the Western powers could conceptualize and put forward a plan that would ensure social protection for the future older population. Once again after more than a half a century less than twenty percent of retirees in Sub-Saharan Africa do not have a social pension. They have worked but were never part of a formal labor system that could ensure social protection.

Based on the aforementioned discussion related to the plight of Europe following the war, and the introduction of a recovery program initiated by the United States, there is a second question for discussion. Why didn't the European leaders or their successors representing their respective countries, who had sit around the table at the Berlin Conference during the "Scramble for Africa" negotiations in 1884, consider a recovery plan or program for Sub-Saharan Africa? After all, it was those European countries that had colonized a continent, introduced forced labor, divided families, kinship groups, and tribes, and purposely underdeveloped the continent in meeting their own economic needs back home.

Structural Readjustment Programs (SAPs)

The Structural Readjustment Programs (SAP) may have been the closest to an initiative for some kind of a coherent plan of action for Africa. The International Monetary Fund (IMF) and the World Bank were the "brainchild" behind the concept and initiative of the Structural Readjustment Programs. This was to be a major initiative affecting developing countries globally, especially Sub-Saharan Africa. The concept emerged from the leadership of two Heads of State, Margaret Thatcher, England, and President George Bush, Sr., of the United States. It was under their leadership that the World Bank and the International Monetary Fund were created. It should be noted that the SAP concept and initiative was the "brainchild" of European and Western leaders, specifically George Bush, United States, and Margaret Thatcher, England. There is no evidence of significant solicitation of ideas or input from the leadership or Heads of State from the developing or target countries, including Sub-Saharan Africa, in the conceptualization of the overall plan. It was if the European and Western leaders came to a realization, we know what's best for the developing countries and more importantly how the goals should best be achieved. There is evidence to suggest that the major goal was to impose or pressure the developing countries to adopt Western economic values of economic development. The initiative was introduced at a time of vulnerability or weakness within the developing countries. Considering the oil and debt crisis, and the global recession confronting the developing countries, they were left with one option, The World Bank, and the International Monetary Fund.

The impetus for such an initiative goes back to the global economic crisis, especially in developing countries, around the 1970s. Prior to the latter part of the 1960's and up to the mid-1970s there was evidence of significant economic growth in a number of developing countries including some countries in Sub-Saharan Africa. Developing countries began to achieve increasing levels of social and economic success especially in the 1960s (Midgley, 1960, p. 53). It was in the 1970's when a reversal in economic fortunes began to become a reality. Several significant global factors contributed to the reversal, the oil crisis, debt crisis, and the global recession that took place between the latter part of the 1970s and to about mid 1980. The international recession had a major impact on developing countries, especially Sub-Saharan Africa. There were factors in Sub-Saharan Africa that exacerbated the problem, such as a significant increase in the growth of the population, repeated droughts, as well as political conflicts contributing to instability within a country.

It was during the global recession, and more specifically the economic crisis occurring in the member states, that countries such as Sub-Saharan Africa began to experience a significant decline in export earnings, resulting from a decrease in commodity prices, as well as increasing interest rates in the OECD countries. The rise in interest rates automatically increased the debt crisis, especially in the lower income or poor countries. Although countries were committed to carrying out necessary reform programs, the recurring economic crisis made it extremely difficult to obtain adjustment loans because by that time they are faced with increasing high deficits, inflation, as well as capital flight. Being somewhat overwhelmed they became open to ideas for assistance (WASAPS, ibid, pages 2-3).

Somewhat related to the crisis was a concept that had emerged prior to the beginning of the global crisis in the 1970s. The concept "Third World Countries," included the following continents, Sub-Saharan Africa, Asia, Central and South America. The thinking behind the concept was that a geopolitical framework for the aforementioned continents were needed for the purpose of categorizing as well as promoting the status of the nonaligned continents. Once established as "Third World" continents, not only were they part of a geopolitical framework, were now being viewed as having economic and social welfare implications. Now, they were part of a group of continents that were socially and economically underdeveloped (Midgley, ibid 1984).

Because of the global economic crisis, and now their own domestic issues, including huge debt obligations, unwillingness on the part of capitalist countries to finance their loans, countries had no options but to form a contractual relationship with the IMF/World Bank. Since the commercial loan market or the granting of loans needed by the developing countries to support economic reforms had been significantly curtailed, the only option for the developing world was to turn to the SAPs. In accepting a SAP loan from the World Bank developing countries would have to agree to a number of conditions. Those conditions would require that the developing countries would have to and based on conditions set forth by the Bank included the stabilization of their economies within a very short timeframe. Furthermore, countries would be asked to devalue their currencies, lift export and import restrictions on goods, removes price controls, as well as state subsidies. Although the Bank did like the method of raising taxes for budget balancing, it strongly recommended the cutting of government programs. The results of cutting government programs eventually had very negative impact on the quality of life on the citizenry; this was especially the case when programs in education, social welfare, and health were cut or eliminated (What are SAPs? and Whirlead Bank Group, SAP, p. 1).

To some structural adjustment policies and programs' primary goal is to achieve in a very short period of time, Western standards, is the overall restructuring of the economy and significantly reduce government interventions in the day to day as well as the long-term operations of countries in the developing world. A good example related to the role of government was the focus on the privatization of public sectors, such as the health sector. By so doing it provides an opportunity for foreign competition in those sectors.

Structural Adjustment Programs evolved around the time when the world's system of communism was in a downfall. Some was referring to the era as the end of communism and the rise of capitalism, and/or the growth in a free market economy. So, when structural adjustment programs emerged their main features focused on policies related to free market systems, including privatization of state owned entities, controlling inflation, fiscal austerity, free trade and deregulations for the purposes of encouraging competition. With the downfall of communism the Western world appeared to be telling the developing world, including the "Third World countries" that if you want to succeed economically the free enterprise capitalist countries have a blueprint (SAP) for you to follow. With the introduction of the SAPs, the newly independent countries of Africa, and their leaders, who were devoted to African Socialism as the blueprint for the future now would have some competition.

The overall conceptualization of the Structural Adjustment Program, since its introduction and implementation, has demonstrated a lack of insightfulness by the World Bank and the International Monetary Fund. A very significant part of the problem was the single-mindedness of these two global organizations whose primary goal it seemed was offer only to the developing countries a capitalist and/or Western style model for economic growth. There is an old axiom sometimes used in problem solving discussions that sees a relationship between how one perceives a problem should determine the methods to be used for a positive outcome. In other words if the perception of a problem is off base one cannot expect a positive outcome. Considering years of critical analysis of the SAP concept, there are some serious questions regarding the perception of the economic realities in Africa following the global and domestic economic crisis and the solution put forth by the IMF and World Bank. "The incorrect perception of a problem can lead to the development of poor theories to solve it…The objectives of a SAP are largely the same for most African nations, because the world bodies presume that African economies are at the same level of development and are experiencing similar problems (Ogbimi, Structural Adjustment is the Wrong Policy, Forum: African Technology Forum, Vol. 8, #1). Nigeria has been used as an African Country that following approximately ten years of implementing SAP, not one of the contractual objectives as set forth by the World Bank, and there have been similar, or the same results in countries such as Ghana, Zambia, as well as other countries that have introduced SAPs (Ogbibi, ibid).

Carlos Lopes (Think Africa Press, 25/13/2013) challenges the premise put forth by Shantayanan Devarajan, Chief Economist, World Bank's Africa's Division, who credited Africa's robust economic success to the introduction and implementation of SAPs. According to Lopes "The main theoretical premise of SAPs was that government interventions were inefficient because they distorted market signals. Long-term development planning was therefore abandoned and industrial policies became neglected in most African countries. In their place, governments focused on macroeconomic stability and institutional reforms to protect property rights and ensure contract enforcement. These policies however, lacked coherent strategies to address inherent market failures and externalities, and these actions ended up constraining investment, growth and economic diversification" (Lopes, ibid, p. 2-3).

Although there are some, especially from the ranks of the World Bank, that SAPs have had an impact on African economies, there are other scholars, Heidhues and Obare (2011, p. 60) who suggest that the impact of SAPs "…on economic development and food and nutrition security is debatable." The lack of success and/or the failures of SAPs have caused the World Bank and the IMF to do some re-thinking of the original conceptualization and approach (In the 1990s some relief from health fees were removed, Stock, Robert, Africa South of the Sahara: A Geographical Interpretation, 1989). Although there have been some re-thinking of the original approach it has not been completely discarded (Heidhues and Obare, ibid).

"The neoliberal approach, on which SAPs were poorly founded, while theoretically sound, was fraught with pitfalls and failures to effectively address challenges to economic development in Africa…It is most doubtful that a development strategy which is purely designed…can be effective in addressing the poverty and underdevelopment prevalent in the region" (Heidhues, F and Obare, G., "Lessons from SAPs and their Effect on Africa," in Quarterly Journal of International Agriculture, 50 (2011), No. 1:55-64).

Strong Resistance to Structural Readjustment Programs

The Structural Readjustment Programs had a very significant impact mostly negative throughout their existence. Those affected represent citizens in general, especially consumers, students and/or community activists who have expressed their reactions to SAP in a variety of ways. The Committee for Academic Freedom in Africa has detailed a long list of resistance to SAPs activities over two decades. Some examples from the protests as well as mass movements follow:

Algeria – Some 200 killed in rioting in response to high prices/unemployment related to the implementation of SAP (1988).

Benin – Students' strike protesting the intention of government to discontinue their pay as part of SAP reforms (1989).

Bolivia – General strike by labor unions and agricultural workers in response to government's increase in food and gasoline prices related to SAP (1985).

Ecuador – Students clash with policemen during protests against the government's SAP; workers firebomb a bank during a one-day general strike against SAPS (1999).

Jamaica – Demonstrators protest the government's decision to raise fuel prices in accordance with a SAP directive (1985).

Niger – Students boycott classes protesting reductions in educational funding mandated by SAP (1990).

Nigeria – Security forces massacred twenty students' in Zaria after staging peaceful protests over the impending introduction of SAP (1986); Students carry out demonstrations at 33 universities protesting an increase in fuel prices demanded by SAP (1988); Students and faculty on campuses nationwide protest the government's decision to accept a $150 million university restructuring loan from the World Bank (1990).

Uganda – Students at Makerere University stage protest in response to the cutting of stationary and travel allowances from a World Bank SAP directive (1990).

Venezuela – Approximately 600 people were killed and approximately 1000 wounded during rioting in response to sharp increases in fuel and public transport prices as a result of a SAP directive (1989).

Zambia – Food price riots occurred in a copper mining district in response to the introduction of a SAP in 1986. The riots led to the suspension of the program.

(The Whirled Bank Group, Structural Adjustment Program, 2003)

For a program designed to assist countries with economic recovery following a global and domestic crisis, obviously created more problems than it was been able to resolve. Not only have the world witnessed debates regarding success or lack of SAPs, in the academic and public arenas, but has resulted in protests, riots, and killings in a number of countries. People have responded in a variety of ways to decreases in their standards of living, job losses, decreases in public services, as well as decreases in healthcare and social services (The Whirled Bank Group, ibid).

Once again, the failure of an initiative such as SAPs to assist developing countries in their economic development goals only delays the progress needed that could eventually reduce the number of old age citizens without a basic social pension.

SUMMARY AND CONCLUSIONS

Modernization and/or the transition of traditional African societies to, as social science theorist projected, modern industrialized societies, presented opportunities and challenges. With the evolution of a technological and industrialized society resulting in social and economic development, there would be new opportunities, especially for a growing youth population for education and jobs. As a result the latter would contribute to an enhanced quality of life for all. Also, with sustainable economic growth and development countries would have an opportunity to share and compete on a global stage. But, on the other hand the transition can present challenges. For example, how does a country or Continent maintain some of it historical strengths such as caring for the older population, as well as other vulnerable family members? The question is critical considering, not unlike other countries globally Sub-Saharan Africa is experiencing a growing older population, and are beginning to see some significant changes in the potential support ratio. Another major challenge to be addressed is ensuring that measures, public and private, be taken allowing the dominant informal labor sector to become part of the tripartite collective bargaining process so future generations of older persons have a social pension on retirement. Not just a social pension (income), additional benefits such as social, health, and medical, including long-term care benefits and services.

The modern and urban industrialized areas will have to prepare for a growing older and aging population that will present new challenges, demands, and needs impacting social, health, and medical systems. For the growing older and aging population, the health and medical attention will be centered around chronic illnesses, such as dementia, heart disease, cancer, and strokes; also, the demands for medical/health and social services will include the needs for home based services, and institutional care. There will be the need for different levels of care, such as care for those unable to remain at home, or with family members. "Aging populations bring their own burden of chronic and non-communicable diseases such a heart disease and stroke, cancer, and diabetes. Such diseases currently account for 60% of all deaths, and they are rapidly increasing in developing countries, putting additional pressure on health budgets" (The World Bank: ATLAS Of Global Development, Fourth Edition, 2013, p. 33).

END OF CHAPTER V

CHAPTER VI

THE CURRENT AND FUTURE STATE OF SOCIAL PENSIONS: SUB-SAHARAN AFRICA

INTRODUCTION

The current state of social pensions and/or basic income security among the growing older population in Sub-Saharan Africa is a cause for global concern, alarm and urgent action. Africa, a continent that provided vast natural resources and labor (forced labor) for the development of economic empires in Europe, post 1884/85 Berlin Conference (The Scramble for Africa), now has millions of persons without income security in old age. The problem is especially critical in Sub Saharan Africa, forty-seven countries, where only 16.9% of the current older population is eligible to receive a social pension. North Africa that includes seven countries, the percentage of those receiving a social pension is 36.7%. Globally or worldwide the percentage of those with a social pension following retirement is 51%, three times the percentage of those in Sub-Saharan Africa (**See Appendix A: Tables/Charts, Chapter VI, Table 1**).

The concept social pension/social security is one component listed by the International Social Security Association (ISSA) under the category of Old Age Disability and Survivor Insurance (OADSI). According to the ISSA a statutory social pension should provide basic income security for the worker and her/his family following retirement from the workplace. The other components of the OASDI are sickness and health, including temporary or permanent disability protection for the worker and family, including maternal and child health. Access to these programs during the employee's work history or tenure is extremely critical for meeting the medical, health, social and economic needs of working families. Also, such protection increases the possibility that following retirement there will be income security, social, health, and medical care availability. The aforementioned types of social protection programs will ensure that former employees and their families can live during the aging process in respect and dignity. It is obvious that the majority of retirees in Sub-Saharan Africa, specifically those who have worked in the informal sector or were self-employed, do not have such social protection during pre-post retirement.

Globally, and especially in Sub-Saharan Africa where native citizens suffered years of colonization, including forced labor as well as other social injustices, the goal should be that all older persons have at least basic income security. The current cohort of older persons in Sub-Saharan Africa without social protection represent the great/great grandchildren and/or grandchildren of those who made the sacrifices that helped to build the economic empires in Europe and the Western world, especially during the industrial revolution. Therefore, the crisis of so many older persons without basic income security should be a global concern and not just the problem(s) of a continent or specific countries. Although a major focus of the book beyond global population growth is to address social protection/pensions, the plight of older populations should not be limited to social pensions and/or social security; the focus should also include access to total medical, health and social welfare services, and with increasing life expectancy, long-term care within the aforementioned areas.

THE SOCIAL PENSION CRISIS IN SUB-SAHARAN AFRICA

Chapter III highlighted the global response to the "Silver Tsunami," the growing older population, beginning especially with the First World Assembly on Aging in 1982. For several decades now global organizations have taken on a more assertive or proactive role in responding to the special needs of a growing older population, including all of their accompanying health, medical and social conditions. Also, during recent decades The United Nations (UN) has put forward what has been referred to as the 2015 Minimum Development Goals (MDG) as well as the 2020 Sustainable Development Goals (SDG). The goals for 2015 and 2020 include problem statements, goals, objectives and methods for improving the overall quality of life for all globally. But, surprisingly missing from the MDG/SDG goals for the global projects, was the lack of an explicit problem statement regarding the lack of social pensions globally. Also, in reference to the aforementioned was the lack of explicit goals, objectives and methods for reducing the number of older persons globally, especially Sub-Saharan Africa, without a social pension and/or basic income security.

For several decades now international organizations such as The International Labor Organization (ILO), The International Social Security Association (ISSA), Help Age International, a Non-governmental organization (NGO), have been facilitating and organizing World Assemblies, Regional Forums and Conferences, that provided opportunities for member States to discuss, debate and develop strategies for responding to the global challenges of the "Silver Tsunami." The results of such global participatory Assemblies and Conferences have been on-going research, declarations, policies and action statements for responding globally, as well as by continents and member countries. The organizations should be applauded for their efforts but there has been little change that significantly improved the quality of life related to social pensions/basic income security, of the "Silver Tsunami," especially in Sub-Saharan Africa. The major question remains, how prepared are countries globally and especially in Sub-Saharan Africa and other low and middle-income countries, to meet the special needs, social, economical, medical, health and long-term care of this growing older population? The question takes on greater significance and urgency when the focus is on the low and middle-income countries, especially those in Sub-Saharan Africa where 82.5% of the older population does not have a social pension or basic income security.

SUB-SAHARAN AFRICA: SOCIAL PROTECTION CHALLENGES AND OPPORTUNITIES

Chapter VI has selectively addressed, based on research findings, some major areas related to factors regarding the current state of social protection, specifically social pensions in Sub-Saharan Africa. Most importantly, the Chapter focuses on the current status and/or level of progress regarding the enactment of statutory laws governing social pensions throughout the Sub-Saharan Region. Also, of importance the Chapter shares some findings and/or results not only reference the current state of social pensions, but some of the other quality of life measures affecting the populations across all age groups. Although the Chapter makes mention of the lack of access to health and medical care, especially long-term care, the primary focus is on the lack of basic income security for the growing older population in Sub-Saharan Africa. These results or findings are based on global annual surveys conducted by organizations/social agencies such as The International Social Security Association (ISSA) and Help Age International, a global non-governmental advocacy organization. Also, research findings from other global organizations such as the United Nations, World Bank, International Labor Organization, Transparency International (focus on corruption/illicit business practices) and the Ibrahim Foundation (countries' governance practices) are shared that provide for an expanded social, economic and/or quality of life profile for countries under review.

Although the major focus of the Chapter is on the state of social protection, especially social pensions, the readers' should also have a glimpse of some of the quality of life factors surrounding the population of older persons under review. The Chapter provides a geographical and/or Regional perspective of Sub-Saharan Africa, with limited references to the region of North Africa. Also, the Chapter takes a look at the sub-region of Sub-Saharan Africa, specifically the Southern Africa Development Corporation (SADC). A brief history of this sub-region is shared as well as its mission, goals and its relationship to the other countries within the overall Sub-Saharan African continent. It should be noted that the highest percentage of countries with a statutory social pension resides within the SADC Region. Also, from a geographical perspective, the Chapter attempts to share some reasoning or explanations why some global leaders, academics, political as well as global organizations, continue to view North Africa as a separate region from Sub-Saharan Africa.

As aforementioned the Chapter's goal is to provide an overview or country profile of the forty-seven countries within Sub-Saharan Africa. The country profile for each country include factors such as its total population, and more importantly in reference to population size, the percentage represented by what each country considers to be its old-age population, or those eligible for a social pension. Other factors include life expectancy from birth for male and female populations, and some of the social, economical (country GDP/Income), political and overall quality of life or wellbeing (Human Development Index) of the population of each country. For an expanded view of each country, beyond the "Silver Tsunami" and especially related to the overall welfare of the people in general, the following factors will also be included in the overview: age dependency and potential support ratios (**See Appendix B: Concepts, Definitions and Special Notes**). Globally, considering all of the discussions/debates focused on corruption and/or government illicit practices, as aforementioned included in the country profile are two global indexes related to the subject matter: First, the Ibrahim Index of African Governance (IIAG), and secondly the Transparency International Corruption Perception index (CPI). The IIAG Index, prepared by the Mo Ibrahim Foundation, is more of a comprehensive perspective focusing on a country's overall governance including four categories: Safety and the Rule of Law, Citizen Participation and Human Rights, Sustainable Economic Development and Human Development. The Corruption Perception Index is prepared annually by the organization Transparency International with a defined or specific focus on the level of corruption practices in each country (**See Appendix A: Tables/Charts, Chapter VI, Tables 6, 10 and 11; For Clarification of concepts reference IIAG and CPI, See Appendix B: Concepts, Definitions and Special Notes**).

Most importantly, the primary focus of the Chapter centers around factors more specifically related to the status and/or progress being made towards a social pension in each country. A key question of the profile is does the country have a statutory non-contributory social pension for the older population? If the country has a social pension the key questions become, the age of eligibility, life expectancy (male/female) and statutory pension age (male/female). Also, if a tripartite type collective bargaining system does exist in a country, is there ongoing communication or collaboration between the formal and informal sectors underway with the goal of inclusion or partnership of the latter into a traditional tripartite collective bargaining system?

Chapter VI is critical in regards to highlighting the current state of social pensions in Sub-Saharan Africa. It has been pointed out repeatedly that a significant number of older persons in Sub-Saharan Africa do not have basic income security or a social pension at the time of retirement. It is obvious that most of the current population of retirees does not and there is a strong probability that the next generation of retirees will be confronted with a similar reality of not having income security or a social pension in their advanced age. Although the percentage of current coverage is rather small, the fact is that beyond income security the growing older populations will also need access to health/medical and social services. This comprehensive goal will require collaboration on the part of political, governmental and labor systems, formal and informal. A most critical question to be addressed is the relationship between the traditional tripartite labor or collective bargaining sectors and the informal sectors of the labor market; the traditional labor sectors could play a major role along with the governmental and political systems in reducing the number of older persons without social pensions in the future. Current data from the ISSA survey provides some information regarding the extent traditional labor systems are beginning to take the initiative to provide opportunities for the self-employed or informal sector employees to participate in the formal collecting bargaining or tripartite systems (**See Appendix A: Tables/Charts, Chapter VI, Tables 2-3**).

As global population growth, especially among the growing older population continues, continents and/or countries are becoming more and more aware of the impact this demographic explosion will have on all essential societal systems. A major challenge for countries will be locating fiscal space within their budgets to meet the increasing demands and obligations for statutory social programs to respond to this phenomenon. But, countries, especially the politicians, governmental and civic leaders should recognize some of the strengths accompanying the demographic population growth as well; a major strength is the "Silver Tsunami," the growing older population. The "Silver Tsunami" is unlike the traditional destructive "tsunami," but a growing number of older persons who bring to the decision-making tables years of experience, knowledge and skills from years of struggle and survival, waiting to become involved in decision-making with other social activists and political leaders. If given the opportunity this growing older population will help to develop outstanding economic, political, social, medical and health caring systems across continents, countries and regions globally. The foundation for this movement will be built on basic concepts of human rights and social justice for all regardless of age.

NORTH AFRICA/SUB-SAHARAN AFRICA: SEPARATE AND UNEQUAL?

In reference to the geographical perspective of Africa it is appropriate at this point that the question often raised by some academic scholars and others, why the region of North Africa is considered a separate region and not included with the vast region of Sub-Saharan Africa (Amrani, Iman, the Guardian, Wednesday, September 9, 2015, page 1)? Some political leaders, Heads of State, individuals/groups with wealth and International Organizations, see a need especially during social, economic, and policy analysis to separate North Africa and Sub-Saharan Africa into two separate regions. One example, The Library of Congress identifies some 51 countries comprising Sub-Saharan Africa (The United States Library of Congress, African Collection, November 15, 2010). The World Bank identifies forty-seven (47) countries within the Region of Sub-Saharan Africa. For the purpose of this book The World Bank geographical definition of Sub-Saharan Africa will be used. There does not seem to be a consensual geographical definition of North Africa. The United Nations sub-region of North Africa includes Algeria, Egypt, Libya, Morocco, Sudan, Tunisia and Western Sahara (The World Bank Group: Working for a World Free of Poverty, DATA, Country Lending Groups, 2016).

The countries comprising North Africa as aforementioned has been grouped with the Middle East under the geographical umbrella referred to as MENA, Middle East and North Africa (Amrani, Iman, ibid, 2015). Why the separation of the regions although both are situated within the African Continent? One perspective is that the motive of the economic and political self-interest groups to separate or distance North Africa from 'Black Africa' is very much related to the region's vast amount of resources, specifically oil, gas, political and economic power; for some experts there is the 'elephant in the room,' known as racism (Amrani, ibid, 2015).

North Africa does have somewhat of an interesting history and background that some scholars use to justify its separate geographical existence. Speaking of resources and power the MENA region has an incredible amount of natural gas and petroleum reserves; the Oil and Gas Journal January 1, 2009 - Cited in The Guardian, 2015, reported that MENA possesses 60% of the global oil reserves, and 45% of the global natural gas reserves within the sub-region. When one considers that of the 12 OPEC (Organization of the Petroleum Exporting Countries)

countries, 8 exist within the MENA region. There are significant benefits for some countries in developing partnerships with the Middle East when considering the vast resources for social and economic developments. One example is that Saudi Arabia happens to be a major trading partner, imports and exports, with Egypt, situated economically as a top five trading partner with Egypt (Armani, Ibid, 2015).

Colonial history tells the world of a time when war, the Second World War in particular, was the glue that brought the regions together. Maybe the current population of Northern Africa has forgotten the historical wartime or military past. The colonial troops from France included soldiers from North and Southern Africa: Algeria, Senegal, Ivory Coast, Niger, and the Republic of Congo. The British Colonial forces included troops from Egypt, Nigeria, South Africa and Kenya (Amrani, ibid, 2015). "The story is told that in 1962 both North Africa and South Africa were both struggling against colonialism and apartheid when Nelson Mandela received military training with the Algerian forces in Morocco" (Amrani, ibid, 2015, p.1). But currently, more than a half-century post-World War II, for some the continent is viewed as North Africa and Sub-Saharan Africa.

COUNTRY PROFILE: SUB-SAHARAN AFRICA

Population Characteristics: Sub-Saharan Africa

A UNICEF Report, "The future of humanity is increasingly African" projects that by the end of the 21st Century Africa will be home for approximately forty percent of people globally. Currently the population is approximately 1.2 billion, and projected to reach 4 billion by the year 2100, approximately eighty-five years from the present; eighty-five years currently represents the life expectancy from birth of persons in the high-income countries. In 2100, Nigeria, currently, the most populous country in Sub-Saharan Africa will be home for nearly twenty-five percent or 1 billion of the 4 billion (Research Report Author David Anthony, UNICEF, Interview with National Public Radio (NPR) Melissa Block, Staff, NPR, "UNICEF Report: Africa's Population Could Hit 4 Billion By 2100," All Things Considered, August 13, 2014). Although fertility rates have declined significantly in Africa in comparison with countries globally, the rates are continuing to be significantly higher than other countries of the world. Also of significance related to fertility rates, the number of African women of reproductive age is projected to double over the next three decades (Block, ibid, 2014).

Sub-Saharan Africa (SSA) has the world's fastest growing population. Population growth in SSA is estimated at about 2.7% a year compared to approximately 2% in Asia. Approximately 60% of the population in SSA depends on Agriculture representing approximately 29% of the Region's GDP. The agriculture sector of Sub-Saharan Africa represents Sixty percent of the work force. Agricultural production in SSA is extremely dependent on rainfall. The lack of adequate rainfall is considered a major constraint in regards to agricultural production; only 4% of the arable land is irrigated compared to approximately 35% in Asia. Women in SSA play a key role not only in agricultural production but caregiving in the home as well. It has been estimated that women contribute approximately 50 hours per/week, especially in caring for children and older family members. Also, women have been the gender mostly affected by HIV/ AIDS, Structural Adjustment Programs, and all forms of civil strife (IAASTD: SSA Report, Vol. V, 2009). The countries with the largest populations in SSA are Nigeria at 136.5 million, Ethiopia 68.6 million, and the Democratic Republic of Congo 53.2 million. The population of the continent is extremely diverse, the most diverse language population in the world. In Sub-Saharan Africa there are more than 2000 indigenous languages (IAASTD: ibid, 2009 **(See Appendix A: Tables/Charts, Chapter VI, Table 4).**

Medical, Health and Social Service Medical Issues

Despite the fact the 60 plus population is increasing at an unprecedented rate and pace, currently doubling the number of the 60 plus group, or older adults in Northern Europe, there is some concern that little attention has been given globally to ageing in Sub-Saharan Africa. From an intergenerational perspective it appears that most of the attention has been giving to the younger age groups than the growing older population. This seems to be an accurate assessment when discussing issues such as social pensions, and matters related to health. Globally, 'Sub-Saharan Africa…remains the world's poorest and youngest region. Development and health agendas for that region, including those being discussed in relation to targets to succeed the Millennium Development Goals, understandably center on how to increase the capacity of and opportunities for the region's young people. Yet strong arguments exist for why the health of older people (aged 60 years and older, more appropriately 50 plus) should not be overlooked' (Aboderin, Isabella, A G, Beard, John R, "Older People's Health in Sub-Saharan Africa," The Lancet, Vol. 385, No 9968, 14 February 2015, p e9-e11 On-line Publication p 1, 05/November, 2014). It should be noted, in discussions around the concept older person, that life expectancy in Sub-Saharan Africa for females is around 59 years and for males 52. In comparison with the United States, life expectancy for females is age 81 and 76 for males. Although more than eighty percent of the older population in Sub-Saharan Africa and 51% globally does not have a social pension at the time of retirement, the matter was not included as part of the 2015 MDGs; nor was the matter addressed in 2020 SDGs.

For the growing older population in Sub-Saharan Africa, the problem of lack of attention goes beyond income security in the form of a social pension, but also is related to the overall health of the ageing population. It has been recommended that in order "To make healthy ageing a reality, radical changes are required in the education, organization, and delivery of health care (Editorial, The Lancet, "Ageing in health—an agenda half completed," Volume 386, No. 10003, 17 October 2015, p 1509, On-line publication p 1). There is somewhat of a global consensus, based on the evidence that the older population in Sub-Saharan Africa is confronted with major medical/health issues. This is a critical era for the ageing population as the continent, not unlike other developing countries, transition from communicable to chronic diseases.

As the reality of chronic illnesses become dominant a major challenge for the medical/ health systems, including the role of family members, are instituting provisions for long-term care that will become part of everyday life for an ageing population. Scholars are projecting that the growing older population will be confronted with serious problems related to morbidity and disabilities (Aboderin and Beard, <u>The Lancet,</u> ibid). Some of the medical/health issues affecting this ageing population include cardiovascular and circulatory illnesses, cirrhosis of the liver, and '…diabetes as major causes of disability adjusted life years in Sub-Saharan Africa's older population…Moreover, representative surveys of older adults' health shows high rates of hypertension, musculoskeletal disease, visual impairment, functional limitations, and depression…Yet a large proportion of even most, older Africans lack the requisite care…in Ghana, for example, showed 96% of those with hypertension to have no adequate treatment for the disorder' (Aboderin and Beard, <u>The Lancet</u>, ibid, 2015).

It has been suggested that medical and health care systems in the past has been prepared to manage acute illnesses, more specifically communicable diseases, that are quite common as populations age. The problem of systems responding to chronic illnesses is happening not just in low-income countries but high-income countries as well. One example is shared from the WHO's World Report on Ageing and Health (Editorial, The Lancet ibid) of an experience of an older population of consumers, chronic illness, seeking care in a high-income country. The consumers were so disappointed that approximately twenty-five percent decided against a follow-up appointment. Globally, an alert is needed for all countries, including the high-income countries that preparation and actions are needed in planning and preparing for a growing older population.

Social, Income and/or Economics

The per/capita income of the population in Sub-Saharan Africa is $1966.00. Forty-Eight percent, about half of the population in Sub-Saharan Africa lives in poverty. Projections are that 250 million could face water shortages by the year 2020. Politically, a very progressive or positive note in regards to gender equality is that women in Sub-Saharan Africa represent twenty percent of the seats in Parliament (UNDP in Sub-Saharan Africa, Supporting a Region on the Move, June 30, 2013).

Of the forty-seven countries in Sub-Saharan Africa identified by the World Bank, twenty-six, or approximately two-thirds are considered to be Low-Income ($1,045 or less), fifteen countries are identified as Low-Middle Income ($1,046 - $4,125), six are considered Upper-Middle Income ($4,126 - $12,735), and two identified as High – Income ($12,736) and above (The World Bank, ibid, 2016; The Kaiser Family Foundation: Country Income Classification, USA 2014).

Four of the countries with some form of a statutory social pension for the older population are listed in the Upper Middle Income category, Botswana, Mauritius, Namibia and South Africa; four are in the Low Middle Income category, Kenya, C. Verde, Lesotho and Swaziland; two are listed in the Low Income category, Liberia and Mozambique; one country with a statutory social pension is listed in the High Income category, Seychelles. It should be noted that one country in Sub-Saharan Africa Equatorial Guinea, is listed in the High Income category but not a member of OECD countries (World Bank Report). Also, Equatorial Guinea, with a GDP p/capita of $32,000 does not have a statutory pension plan for older persons compared to Liberia and Mozambique listed in the Low Income category, $1,045 or less. Equatorial Guinea not only does not have a statutory social pension, it is not one of the countries currently reaching out to the informal sector or self-employed with an invitation to become part of the country's tripartite system. Furthermore, Equatorial Guinea in its response to the ISSA Survey section Coverage, the self-employed was listed as excluded. In other words, the self-employed and/ or informal sector workers living in the country is excluded from participation in the formal tripartite system (International Social Security Association (ISSA" Annual Survey, 2015).

Sub Saharan Africa in recent years, especially since the economic crisis, has contributed significantly to the now popular slogans, "Africa Rising," and it is "Africa's Time." The past couple of years have witnessed a slowing down of the economy. Overall, economic growth in 2015 slowed to 3.4% in comparison to 4.6% in 2014, a decline of approximately 1% in Sub-Saharan Africa. The aforementioned decline in growth demonstrated the most significant negative performance since the year 2009. The drop or slowdown was best demonstrated by Nigeria, the country representing the largest economy in Sub-Saharan Africa, as well as it largest oil economy and exporter. Nigeria's growth in 2015 went from 6.3% in 2014 to 3.3% in 2015. The decline was contributed to several factors, including a significant drop in commodity prices, a tightening of global borrowing conditions, as well as a slowdown among Sub-Saharan Africa's major trading partners. Also, the "elephant in the room" phrase commonly used to draw attention to factors such as a country's corruption, or political unrest that contributes to conflicts and instability. There was also the factor of a major shortage in electricity a reminder of a weakness in infrastructure development in this vital area for economic growth (World Bank: Global Economic Prospects, Sub Saharan Africa, Gerard Kambou (Author), January, 2016, page 153).

The economic system on the continent was looking better for 2016. Growth is expected to reach 4.2%, 0.8% growth from 2015. A major factor contributing to this almost 1% in growth is the expectations that commodities prices will begin to stabilize in 2016. Despite this positive note there will continue to exist a concern about the possibility of another drop in commodity prices, and most importantly a concern about the continuing slowdown in China's economy (World Bank: Global Economic Prospects, ibid, pages 156-157, 2016).

An important projection for the Region beginning in 2016 is that prices of commodities will stabilize but continue at a steady low level during 2017. The projections were that recovery during 2016 was going to be slower than anticipated. The expectations are that economic activities in Sub Saharan Africa should reach 4.7% during the year 2017 into 2018. The positive projections depend on the possibilities of stabilization in commodity prices, and less rigidity regarding constraints on electricity. Overall, economic growth in the Region's three largest economies, Nigeria, South Africa and Angola are expected to remain at somewhat of a steady level without a very significant increase in activities. The problem in Angola is related to rising inflation that has kept consumer spending down. The problem in South Africa is related to a lack of sufficient electricity and/or other power supplies, and lack of confidence in business practices. Nigeria problems are similar to those in South Africa, power and fuel shortages, which point to the need for further infrastructure development (World Bank, ibid, 2016).

Ghana, another major economic player in Sub Saharan Africa can expect, according to projections, see an increase in oil production that should increase economic growth in Ghana. There is some optimism in Kenya as a result of major investments in major infrastructural projects, especially in collaboration with China. The building of the railroad across Kenya should result in increased domestic trade. Another country, Zambia, will have some major economic challenges due to the low prices in copper, as well as power and electricity shortages. The latter will not be very helpful as far as copper production and could be a significant set back as far as investments and exports (World Bank: ibid, 2016). A note of optimism reference social pensions is Kenya introduced a universal statutory social pension in 2018.

Some countries in Sub-Saharan Africa described as low-income, Cote d'Ivoire, Ethiopia, Mozambique, Rwanda and Tanzania, are projected to continue their high GDP growth during the next couple of years. Also, ongoing public investments, consumer spending, and mining production are areas that should help these countries to maintain their high level of economic growth, not only in 2016-2017 and beyond or future years (World Bank: ibid, p 157).

Despite the positive observations, including the slogan "Rising Africa," many challenges remain in reducing poverty. Estimates are that there are "more people are poor today than in 1990…two in five adults are still illiterate, and violence is on the rise" (The World Bank: Working for a World Free of Poverty, <u>Poverty in a Rising Africa: Africa Poverty Report</u>," "While Poverty in Africa Has Declined, Number of Poor Has Increased" March 2016, page 1). Current estimates may be lower than the estimates; the percentage of people now living in what is considered extreme poverty has increased significantly.

The current Report from the World Bank "…estimates, the share of Africans who are poor fell from 56% in 1990 to 43% in 2012… However, because of population growth many more people are poor, the report says. The most optimistic scenario shows about 330 million poor in 2012, up from about 280 million in 1990. Poverty reduction has been slowed in fragile countries…and rural areas remain much poorer, although the urban-rural gap has narrowed" (World Bank, ibid, page 2, 2016).

Some positive news from the Report emphasizes that there have been improvements in various nonmonetary areas of poverty. Some examples are adult literacy rates have increased upward by four percentage points, and there is evidence that the gender gap has and continues to decrease. Also, "… chronic malnutrition among under five-year olds is down six percentage points…" But, on the other hand, "…despite substantial improvement in school enrollment, the quality of schooling is often low and more than two in five adults are still illiterate" (World Bank, Africa Poverty Report, ibid, p. 2).

These findings point to the importance of commitment on the part of countries in Sub-Saharan Africa to successfully meeting the goals set forth in the Millennium Development Goals 2015, especially in the areas of education and poverty. Although there is major emphasis as well as commitment on the part of Sub-Saharan countries to economic growth and development, one conclusion or observation from the Africa Report is extremely important, "The findings underscores that while economic growth is critical for poverty reduction, it is not sufficient" (World Bank, Africa Poverty Report, ibid, p. 2). In other words, the planning for economic growth should include strategies for reducing all forms of inequality, especially in the area of income insecurity **(See Appendix: Tables/Charts, Chapter VI, Tables 6, 10-11)**.

SOUTHERN AFRICA DEVELOPMENT COMMUNITY (SADC)

Within the geographical, political boundaries of Sub-Saharan Africa is the sub-region known as the Southern Africa Development Community. The SADC is a regional economic community, established in 1992, consisting of fifteen Member States; the Member States include Angola, Botswana (Location of SADC Headquarters), The Democratic Republic of Congo, Lesotho, Madagascar, Malawi, Mauritius, Mozambique, Namibia, Seychelles, South Africa, Swaziland, The United Republic of Tanzania, Zambia, and Zimbabwe. The SADC Region represents two-thirds of the countries in Sub-Saharan Africa (SADC: Towards a Common Future). Of the fifteen Member States/Countries in SADC, eight has a Statutory Social Pension (ISSA, Annual Survey, 2015/**See Appendix A: Tables/Charts, Chapter VI, Tables, 2-3).**

A major incentive for the creation of SADC was achieving peace and unity within the Region. Overall, the establishment of SADC was based on the realization that if the Region was to achieve significant economic growth and peace on the African Continent, the Member States would have to commit to working together. To achieve the aforementioned goals the Member States established the SADC Tribunal. The Tribunal primary goal was to ensure compliance to the provisions contained in the SADC Treaty, and especially in the adjudication of disputes brought forward by Member States (SADC, ibid).

Economic development is one of the goals cited in the SADC Treaty that requires cooperation among the Member States. One example related to economic development considered productive strength in the Region is its sugar production. Sub-Saharan Africa is a global hot spot for sugar production, especially for 10 of the 15 Member States; the States include Tanzania, South Africa (World leader in sugar cost production), Swaziland (Production has increased from 165,000 tons time of independence to 658,000 in 2013), Malawi, Mauritius (Sugar production in the country represents 2% of GDP, and 28,000 employees), Zambia, and Zimbabwe (SADC Annual Sugar Digest, Issue 1, 2014).

THE CURRENT AND FUTURE STATE OF SOCIAL PENSIONS IN SUB-SAHARAN AFRICA

Chapter VI provides somewhat of a statistical as well as an analytical perspective, especially related to social protection and overall quality of life of older persons in Sub-Saharan Africa. Keeping in mind as the narrative proceeds that the concept social protection normally will include not only income security/social pension, but other factors such as access to social services, medical and/or health care, including long-term care, and environmental safety. The fact that so many older persons are without basic income security or a social pension (82.5%) in Sub-Saharan Africa should be an indication of how much additional political advocacy and policy actions are urgently needed. The goal should be to ensure that the continent as a whole has all of the appropriate programs and services for the older population to experience an enhanced quality of life in old age. Even in North Africa, the region with the vast resources of oil as an example, approximately 62.5% of older persons are without a social/civic pension following retirement.

Once again or as aforementioned, the major factor why so many older persons in sub-Saharan Africa are without a social pension is that they were employed in the informal labor sector or were self-employed. In other words, the current cohort of older persons were not part of a contributory tripartite labor system (employer/employee/public partnership); the tripartite type of collective bargaining system to a great extent ensures a level of social protection at the time of retirement. Such a system also provides a level of protection against job related disabilities (temporary and permanent), as well as maternal and family health protection during employment. The informal labor sector that continues to represent the major share of the labor market in Sub-Saharan Africa does not provide these types of protections for workers and their families.

Globally, slightly more than half, approximately 51%, of older persons throughout the world now receive what is commonly referred to as an old age pension, or regular cash benefits. But, in Sub-Saharan Africa only about 16.9% of older persons are beneficiaries of an old age pension or regular monthly cash benefits during retirement (ILO: World Social Protection Report 2014/15, Building Economic Recovery, inclusive development and social justice, Geneva: ILO, 2014). The social pension for those who receive such benefit somewhat ensures meeting some of their basic financial needs, especially for food and shelter. Also, the monthly benefit in so many instances provides the support to grandparents who are helping to meet the needs of their grandchildren. There are an increasing number of children, for a variety of reasons, HIV/AIDS, war and other political conflicts, unemployment, and urbanization, now living with grandparents. The aforementioned factors are a major reason that a social pension has become so critical (See Chapter II, Section Why Population Ages Matter).

The countries in Sub-Saharan Africa are at the bottom tier when considering most of the recognizable and acceptable international indexes, including social pension coverage. Examples, in the Middle East the pension coverage for older persons is 29.5 percent, almost double the rate for Sub-Saharan Africa (16.9%); North Africa 36.7%, twice the rate for Sub-Saharan Africa; Asia and the Pacific 47%; Latin America and the Caribbean 56%, and North America and Europe 90% (ILO: World Social Protection Report 2014/15, Section 4.4.1, pp. 83-84, 2015). Although extremely low at 16.9 %, other regions of the world, especially North Africa, Asia and the Pacific, Latin America and the Caribbean, should also be very concerned regarding the lack of social protection for older people following retirement from the workforce.

Not only is Sub-Saharan Africa currently listed on the bottom tier in regards to social pensions globally, a major concern for the future older generation is that, according to current statistics, it appears that little change will occur within the next generation. In other words unless there are major policy initiatives very soon it appears that little change will occur to ensure social protection for the growing older population. For example, "Effective old-age pension coverage of the working age-population...5.9 per cent of the working –age population in sub-Saharan Africa and 23.9 per cent in North Africa, compared to 66.7 per cent in Western Europe and 77.5 per cent in North America" (ISSA: Developing Trends, "Africa: Strategic Approaches to Improve Social Security 2014, pp. 1-3). When considering factors such as effective coverage under unemployment protection schemes the situation is even more discouraging; in considering both contributory as well as non-contributory type schemes, the coverage rate in Africa is less than 3 per cent compared to 5 per cent for Latin America, 7 per cent for Asia and Pacific and 64 per cent in the region of Western Europe (ISSA, ibid, 2014). In regards to social protection schemes for workers the crisis is not just in Sub-Saharan Africa, although not as severe, but globally.

As aforementioned, the problem lack of social pensions is not just in Sub-Saharan Africa, although most severe, but globally. Furthermore, the problem of social protection extends beyond just a lack of social pensions but other forms of social protection. The latest Social Protection Report addresses some of the issues. Currently, only "…45% of the global population is now covered by at least one social benefit…55% are still left unprotected" (World Social Protection Report 2017-2019, International Labor Organization (ILO), Geneva Switzerland, 29/11/2017). According to the ILO approximately 4 Billion people globally are currently without social protection. "New research 29% of the global population enjoys access to comprehensive social security…small increase compared to 27th % in 2014-2015…while the other 71%, or 5.2 Billion people are not or only partially protected" (ILO Report 2017-2019, ibid, 2015).

The most serious concern globally continues to be a lack of income security for the older population reaching retirement age. The ILO reports that, "…globally 68% of people above retirement age receive an old age pension…associated with the expansion of both non-contributory and contributory pensions in many middle-and low-income countries. With expenditure on pensions and other benefits for older people accounting for 69% of GDP on average with large regional variations, the report underlines that benefit levels are often low and not enough to push older people out of poverty. This trend is often fueled by austerity measures" (ILO 2017-2019, ibid, 2015)

Another major area of concern is related to legal coverage under mandatory work injury schemes. The story remains the same for Sub-Saharan African countries; "…less than 20 percent of the total labor force in Africa, compared to nearly 30 percent in Asia and the Pacific, over 50 per cent in Latin America, and between 70 and 80 per cent in Europe and North America…In Sub-Saharan Africa, some 80 per cent of the population have no access to legal health coverage, a coverage gap that is twice a high as the global figure (38.9 percent)" (ISSA, ibid, 2014, pp. 1-2). Social protection for workers and their families should extend beyond basic income security or a social pension, but should also include protection related to sickness and health, temporary or permanent disability, and maternal and child health. The concept social pension is just one component listed by the ISSA under the very broad category of Old Age Disability and Survivor Insurance (OASDI). As aforementioned the other very critical components of OASDI should include access to protection and support during the times of sickness and health issues, disability, temporary or permanent and especially maternal and child health. The lack of coverage for the aforementioned components on behalf of workers and their families is critical, especially in Sub-Saharan Africa; in other words the crisis is similar to that of the social pension crisis.

Tanzania one of the forty-seven countries in Sub-Saharan Africa, identified by the World Bank, as a good example of the lack of income security (social pension), confronting the current and future older populations. Less than 1 % of the eligible population is currently covered with a social pension and only about 6.5 % of the current formal working population. Furthermore, in

Tanzania almost the entire informal labor sector is currently not covered by a social protection/ social security scheme. The informal non-contributory social assistance programs are expected to meet only some of the basic needs of the elderly, disabled as well as vulnerable children. But funding such programs are a major problem. The government of Tanzania currently funding for social assistance programs represent only about 0.5 % of the country's GDP. These social assistance programs with such limited funding are only capable of covering a very small segment of these vulnerable populations (ISSA Country Profiles, Annual Survey of Countries, Section Overview: United Republic of Tanzania, 1/1/2015).

On a much brighter side the country is somewhat preoccupied with preparing for a growing older population. There is evidence that the country has been giving serious thoughts to how to utilize its fiscal space and/or financing strategically and effectively for areas such as health care, education, and social protection. With the assistance of the United Kingdom, Department of International Development providing the funding, Tanzania, Zambia and Zanzibar working collaboratively, have carried out a social protection, expenditure and performance review (SPER). This review has resulted in a Social Budget that will provide some guidelines for budgeting in response to meeting social protection needs (ISSA Country Profiles, ibid 1/1/2015).

It is interesting to note that one of the three countries, Tanzania, Zambia and Zanzibar that participated in the aforementioned Social Protection, Expenditure and performance Review (SPEPR) Project Zanzibar has introduced a universal social pension scheme for older persons. Zanzibar is still considered by some to be somewhat of a semi-autonomous country within the geographical and political boundaries of Tanzania. The government of Zanzibar announced globally on April 16, 2017 that the country had introduced a universal social pension scheme (ZUPS) for older people. The country highlighted the point that the scheme was the first universal social pension fully funded by a government in East Africa. Eligibility enrollment for the scheme targeted all citizens of Zanzibar age 70 and above; each eligible person would receive a monthly non-contributory pension of 20,000 Tanzanian Shillings the equivalent of $9.00 monthly in American currency. The government of Zanzibar has allocated 6.5 billion Tanzanian Shillings in support of the scheme.

Not only was the scheme being promoted as the first universal pension fully supported by the government in East Africa, it was the cheapest in regards to GDP among other African countries who had enacted a social pension for their older populations. The percentage of GDP for the scheme in Zanzibar is 0.24 compared to 0.3 in Swaziland, 0.3 Botswana, 1.2 Namibia, 1.3 Lesotho, and 2.9 in Mauritius. The government in adopting the scheme was responding to survey research indicating that approximately 30% of the population was living below the poverty line; approximately 79% of citizens of the older population over the age of 70 indicated that their economic status was worse than average. Country surveys also pointed out that approximately 63% of those over 70 had to rely on family members for support.

Although Zanzibar should be applauded for taking such a significant step on behalf of older persons, some clarifications are appropriate in regards to the country's state of sovereignty, and the scheme meeting the definition of a social pension. First is the question of sovereignty, or is Zanzibar a fully autonomous State? It has been referred to as a semi-autonomous State or part of Tanzania. Approximately one decade ago, the then Prime Minister of Tanzania, expressed there was no sovereignty of Zanzibar within the Union government unless the Constitution was going to be changed. Does the relationship, semi-autonomous or not, has any implications for the pension scheme in Zanzibar? Tanzania at the time of the announcement did not have a statutory law providing a social pension for its older citizen. Also to consider, according to the government of Zanzibar, the pension scheme announced in April 2017 does not currently have a statutory or law designation, or a legal framework; it has been announced by the government of Zanzibar that legislation related to the welfare of older persons was currently being discussed. It was also pointed out that the 6.5 billion Tanzanian Shillings was financed through the National Budget and will be distributed by the Ministry responsible for the elderly population in Zanzibar. The aforementioned, according to the government, should guarantee that the budget expenditures are only allocated to the universal pension scheme.

Secondly, one has to consider the definition of a social pension; the global consensus is that a social or civic pension is a non-contributory cash transfer paid regularly to older people by their government; it is the result of a legislative action by government which <u>becomes a statute or law within a particular country</u>. One can assume that part of the current legislative discussions regarding the welfare of older persons the scheme eventually will become a statutory law. Finally, another question regarding the scheme centers on the statutory pension age of 70; the life expectancy in the country is 66. The issue here is not unlike the majority of African countries where the age of eligibility is significantly higher than a country's life expectancy, including Botswana considered to have a model pension scheme (Gillam, Sarah, "Zanzibar's New Universal Social Pension The First of its Kind," Help Age International, April 14, 2016.

SOCIAL PENSIONS AND THE SURVIVAL OF FAMILIES

The goal of a statutory social pension should be to ensure that older persons have income security for meeting their daily needs; it should also include access to other needed social services including medical and health care as well as support for children and orphans. Globally, international organizations, public and private, including member countries, have to not only recognize but become more proactive in ensuring provisions for children being cared for by grandparents. Due to a variety of circumstances, the HIV/AIDS epidemic, political and military conflicts, and more and more young mothers and fathers transitioning to major cities in search of job opportunities and leaving children with grandparents. One can imagine older persons attempting to survive from a pension that is inadequate, financially in amount in the first place, just imagine if a grandparent have to take care of the children without basic income security.

An excellent example of how a social pension(s) contributes to the survival of families was addressed in Chapter IV, the Matriarches of Mthatha. The thirty women and their families living on the Eastern Coast of South Africa have come together combining their resources, especially from their pensions to ensure that the basic needs of the families, especially the children are being met. They have become the breadwinners and grandparents of the children, including those with developmental disabilities. One can imagine the consequences for these children as well and other vulnerable families without the help of a social pension.

COUNTRY PROFILE: OLD AGE PENSION SCHEMES (OLD AGE SURVIVOR AND DISABILITY INSURANCE - OASDI)

The profiles of the countries in Sub-Saharan Africa were analyzed within the category, Old Age Disability and Survivor Insurance (OASDI). The OASDI concept includes coverage of workers in the following areas: sickness and maternal and child-care, occupational or work injuries, unemployment, and family benefits. The goal of the OASDI programs are to ensure social protection for families in the event of old age, sickness and maternity, death, and disability. There are several very broad approaches or program types for providing social protection for workers and their families, including employment-related, universal, and means-tested systems. As reported in the ISSA, SSA, and the Help Age International surveys, all of the countries have managed or within the framework of their respective countries, created nine (9) program types (ISSA, January 15, 2015/January 15, 2017).

Keeping in mind that the primary focus of this manuscript is focused on non-contributory social pensions, as defined within the Section on Definitions and Concepts. Within the program types, a social pension program is normally identified or listed as universal, social assistance or provident fund. Considering the fact that less than 20% of older persons in Sub Saharan Africa do not have a social pension, the global goal should be that all older persons eventually be assured of having all of the benefits, beginning with income security, now provided for the contributory or formal occupational sectors.

The International Social Security Administration (ISSA) in its annual country profile survey (January 1, 2017) asked countries to identify under the category Old Age, Disability and Survivors, a Program Type or Type of Program that best describe its contributory and/or non-contributory social pension schemes or systems. In response to the question the countries identified or described Program Types as aforementioned using nine different categories: (1) Social Insurance System (2) Universal System (3) Social Insurance and Social Assistance (4) Social Insurance and Mandatory Occupational System (5) Mandatory Individual Accounts and Provident Fund (6) Social Insurance and Provident Fund (7) Universal and Social Insurance System (8) Mandatory Individual Accounts and (9) Provident Fund. The nine categories represent fifty-five countries including seven from North Africa. Thirty-two of the categories listed Social Insurance as the only Program Type an indication that most countries do not include the informal work sector as part of its tripartite collecting bargaining system. Countries that were not included were due to a lack of sufficient data or information, examples, Eritrea, Somalia, and South Sudan (Sudan is now considered geographically part of North Africa (**See Appendix A: Tables/Charts, Chapter VI, Tables 2-3).**

REFERENCE NOTE: Several data sources were used for the country profile section: One major document used for research and analysis, <u>Social Security Throughout the World</u> (survey and analysis of 178 countries) a collaborative effort with The United States Social Security Administration, and the International Social Security Association (ISSA). Also, the Annual Country Profile Survey of the global Non-Profit organization Help Age International was also used for research and analysis.

SOCIAL PENSION PROFILE: SUB-SAHARAN AFRICA

Currently (2017) eleven countries have established some form of a statutory pension for the older population who worked in the informal sector or were self-employed during their work tenure. A review of the aforementioned data sources (**Reference Notes**) revealed that five of the 47 countries in Sub-Saharan Africa have been identified as having a statutory social pension with age as the only eligibility requirement. The five countries have instituted statutory provisions that provide basic income security, a civic or social pension, for former self-employed workers, or those who worked in the informal sector. The five countries are Botswana, Lesotho, Mauritius, Namibia and Seychelles. Six of the eleven countries including Cape Verde, Kenya, Liberia, Mozambique, South Africa, and Swaziland, in addition to age as an eligibility requirement, utilize additional forms of a means or pension test to determine the level of need (**See Appendix B: Concepts, Definitions and Special Notes**).

The five countries with age as the only eligibility criteria for a social pension use the following phrases in describing their programs or program types: Botswana, Universal System, Lesotho, Universal System, Mauritius, Universal/Social Insurance, Namibia, Social Insurance/ Social Assistance, and Seychelles, Universal/Social Insurance. The six countries using some form of a means or pension test to assist in determining eligibility describe their programs in the following manner: C. Verde, Social Insurance/Social Assistance, Kenya, Social Insurance/ Social Assistance, Liberia, Social Insurance/Social Assistance, South Africa, Social Insurance and Social Assistance, Mozambique, Social Insurance and Social Assistance and Swaziland, Provident Fund/Social Assistance. In reference to program type some countries with a social pension use the combination social insurance and social assistance. What is now happening globally, a very positive movement, is that governments are beginning to institute statutory social assistance programs/social pensions for those who had previously worked or currently working in the informal labor sector and/or self-employed.

Clarification/Interpretation of Selective Program Types

In reference to program type, some countries list Provident Fund and/or a combination of Provident Fund and Social Insurance or Social Assistance. Gambia has a social insurance system for public and civil employees, but also a voluntary Provident Fund. Uganda has a Provident Fund for employed workers only and Swaziland has a Provident Fund but also a social assistance plan for old-age social protection.

A major concern regarding the concept Provident Fund is that at retirement there is an option in most instances for a "lump sum" payment at the time of retirement. Some countries with a Provident Fund will allow for an early withdrawal from the fund. Also, the early withdrawal in some countries will allow the pensioner to convert savings into some form of an annuity. The Provident Fund concept does raise some questions regarding future social protection in later years following retirement; for example, how does a Provident Fund manage to protect someone during the complete retirement years if the lump sum payment or other forms of savings have been exhausted? In such instances if a country does have a statutory pension for older person the aforementioned example (s) may not become a problem. These are questions that countries need to consider in discussing or deciding on a particular program type, such as the Provident Fund (**See Appendix B: Concepts, Definitions and Special Notes**)

Means or Pension Test

The concept means test (**See Appendix B: Concepts, Definitions and Special Notes**) has been used globally for years to separate the needy from the non-needy; one country in the survey Liberia for example, uses the phrase the needy elderly indicating that there are older persons who may have sufficient resources and do not need governmental assistance. The purpose of the process involving the means test is to separate the needy from the non-needy. As previously discussed, countries such as Brazil and Mauritius have challenged this method for determining program eligibility. The government of Mauritius concluded that the administrative costs of employing or carrying out a means test were significantly more expensive than a universal program type as being used in a country such as Botswana. Brazil reached similar conclusions following years of utilizing a means test in addition to age in determining eligibility.

The majority of the countries that responded to the ISSA survey identified social insurance as the method or scheme for providing social protection. But, the system described as social insurance has been established primarily for the contributory tripartite (employer/employee/public) framework for the formal public and private sectors of employment. Historically in Africa there has been a significant separation or lack of collaboration between the formal and informal sectors of labor; the informal sector continues to be the primary or dominant source of employment in developing countries, especially Sub-Saharan Africa. On a more positive note reference the two sectors, formal and informal, some fourteen countries with social insurance type programs or schemes are now reaching out to the informal sectors and/or self employed to encourage levels of collaboration and participation. Those fourteen countries in the survey have moved toward providing a special provision among their levels or pillars for the self-employed or those who are employed in the informal sector. These provisions are voluntary and the worker is required to contribute a percentage of her/his "declared income" on a weekly or monthly basis to receive benefits such as a social pension. But, an indication of the challenges ahead for reducing the high number of older persons without social pensions, slightly more than half of the countries in Sub-Saharan Africa are not currently involved in any collaborative efforts with the informal sector or the self-employed; they have stated in the survey in response to the question coverage, that informal sector or self-employed workers are excluded from their traditional tripartite systems (**See Appendix A: Tables/Charts, Chapter VI, Table 5**).

The required contributions from the voluntary informal sector workers, depending on the country, can be significantly different from the amount being contributed by those representing the formal sector. Some examples are, in Ethiopia the self-employed individuals contribute 18 percent of salary monthly, but the formal sector employees contribute only 7 percent; Rwanda 6 percent self- employed, 3 percent for the formal sector; Sierra Leone, 15 percent self-employed, 5 percent formal sector, and Angola, 11 percent self-employed, 3 percent for the formal sector employees. The fact that these cooperative arrangements are voluntary one major question is what percentage of the informal sector voluntarily participates? And, for those who don't, why?

Is the difference in contributions between the formal and informal sector employees, especially since the arrangement is voluntary, a significant factor for a low rate of participation among the informal sector employees? Most importantly, should the formal tripartite sectors evaluate their approach in reaching out to the informal sectors, including the involvement of governmental and/or political entities in the process? Should they reconsider the defined contributions and benefits component? Should governmental entities contribute a small percentage of their GDP as an incentive for voluntary enrollment?

PROPOSED METHODS FOR EVALUATING A COUNTRY'S CURRENT STATUS AND PROGRESS TOWARDS A SOCIAL PENSION

The challenge is to develop some criteria, based on the aforementioned definition of a social pension, to provide a framework that can assist in determining the progress of each country towards the goal of a social/civic pension; the ultimate goal would be a social pension with age, as defined by each country, as the primary criteria for eligibility.

Five distinct frameworks/categories are being proposed for the purpose of determining the status of a social pension, including some indication of the level of progress towards the goal in each country. The categories are scored from five (5) highest level of progress to one (1) lowest level of progress. The basic rationale for each category or level follows: Category five (5) the country has a statutory social pension for older citizens who were employed for the most part in the informal labor sector or self employed, and do not qualify for a pension from a traditional tripartite employment scheme; most importantly in this category age is the only eligibility requirement. In Category four (4) the country has a statutory social pension targeting the group aforementioned in Category five (5) but in addition to age the country also utilizes an administrative process, including a means or pension test for determining eligibility; for Category three (3) unlike countries in Categories (5) and (4), the country does not have a statutory social pension for older persons who worked primarily in the informal sector or self-employed. The country does have traditional tripartite collective bargaining systems, and some of those systems have taken the initiative to reach out to those in the informal sector with an invitation to join or become part of their tripartite system. The results are a number of countries, with tripartite systems, approximately fourteen at this point, are now open to the self-employed and/or those working in the informal sector. Considering the importance of bringing the two sectors, formal and informal, together in an effort to reduce the number of older persons without a social pension, these initiatives are considered an extremely positive step. In Category two (2) traditional tripartite systems have begin the discussion regarding an invitation to participate toward a formal arrangement(s), but at this point there is no evidence of any contractual arrangements such as a specified monthly salary contribution to the scheme or defined benefits. In other words, Category (2) activities are primarily in the talking phase. In Category one (1), the lowest level of progress, there is no evidence of any initiatives at this time to invite participants from the informal sector to become part of the country's tripartite system. Furthermore, in responding to the ISSA survey question related to coverage, the country states explicitly that those who are self-employed or work within the informal sector is excluded. (**The data/information used for the country profile analysis is from the following sources: Annual Survey of Countries, Country Profiles, ISSA, Social Security Programs Throughout the World (Collaborative Effort: US Social Security Association, and the ISSA), Help Age International Country Fact Sheet, and the ISSA World Social Protection Report).**

Sub-Saharan African Country Scoring Results

High Score – Category 5 - Based on the criteria (Definition of a Social Pension) only five countries meet the criteria of having a statutory social pension whereas age is the only eligibility requirement. What does this mean? This means that the five countries have reached the goal of having a universal social pension whereas age is the only eligibility factor, and the policy is imbedded in the law or country's statue.

Medium High Score – Category 4 - Based on the definition of a social pension six countries are in this category, or have been placed in the category of Medium High. Each country has a statutory social pension targeting the older population who do not meet the eligibility criteria of a traditional tripartite collective bargaining system. Unlike Category (5) the five countries in addition to age utilizes a means or pension test for eligibility determination. A means test is a targeting method for determining eligibility for a particular program based primarily on income. The process includes the collection of comprehensive household data/information related to family income and/or resources. Some countries, such as Brazil (Latin America) and Mauritius (Sub-Saharan Africa), have been opposed to the targeting process beyond the variable age in determining eligibility for a social pension. A couple of potential problems have emerged in the utilization of the means test. First, is the omission of a significant number of needy persons during the administrative process, and secondly, the high administrative cost for implementing the process. The country of Mauritius concluded that the use of such a method for determining who is needy or not could have excluded approximately 20% of the older people in need of a cash transfer. The country also concluded that the overall administrative costs in the end would surpass any savings accumulated in the staffs' attempt to eliminate the un-needy from the needy. <u>Therefore, a major concern in the use of a means test is the administrative cost for implementation as well as the possible exclusion of a significant number of older persons in need of income security.</u> The use of a means test could become problematic or somewhat of a barrier in ensuring that the entire older population in a country will be ensured a social pension. Therefore a country with a scheme for providing a social pension for older persons, but utilizes the "means test" as part of the eligibility criteria, is placed in the category of Medium High Coverage. The goal for a county under this category is to move toward a system where age would become the primary category.

Low Medium Score – Category 3 Not unlike the countries listed in the previous two categories, each country has contributory schemes for formal sector workers employed in the labor workforce. Also, similar to the previous two categories, the majority of workers in the country are employed in the informal sector or self-employed. As aforementioned the informal sector lacks a tripartite system, employer, employee, and public participation for collective bargaining purposes. But a major positive for category three is the willingness and commitment

193

on the part of the tripartite network to reach out or extend an invitation, although voluntarily, to the workers in the informal sector or self-employed; the goal is to become part of a collective bargaining arrangement including monthly contributory defined payments that will result in defined benefits for workers and their families. In other words, such an arrangement could lead to social protection for the worker and family during the working years and a social pension at the time of retirement. In Category (3) countries utilize a voluntary invitation, including a payment system for participation, i.e. 8% of monthly wages that could result in social protection, especially a social pension for worker and/or family. The formal sector should be applauded considering the fact that historically there has not been a comprehensive plan on the part of the formal sector, international leaders and organizations to conceptualize and implement a plan to include informal sector employees. Although a positive approach, a major concern with the volunteer approach is how many of the self-employed workers in the informal sector will participate? What is the percentage of voluntary participation? Also, what research has been carried out by the formal sector, as well as the international organizations in determining the barriers to voluntary participation? Also, what efforts have been made to reduce the barriers that may exist? And, and what incentives will it take for encouraging voluntary participation? So, for grading purposes the voluntary system seems to carry more risk for ensuring that all persons at the time of retirement will have a social pension.

Low Minimal Score – Category 2 - Countries placed in Category (2) represent those countries who have been considering the possibility of inviting workers from the informal sector or self employed to become part of a tripartite system or scheme; unlike the countries in Category (3) countries in Category (2) have not finalized specific contractual arrangements such as defined contributory monthly or weekly payments and defined benefits. In other words, the countries at this point have not moved beyond the talking or negotiating phase that would eventually result in identifying the specific contributions for the worker and resulting benefits.

Low Score – Category 1 - Once again, not unlike the countries identified in the four (4) previous categories, the countries in Category (1) have traditional contributory type systems for workers in the formal sectors. But, beyond the contributory scheme each of the countries explicitly states that the self-employed workers are excluded. Finally, unlike Categories (5) and (4), there is no statutory pension for the older population who worked in the informal sector or was self- employed. Also, unlike the countries in Categories (3) and (2), the countries indicate no evidence of beginning the discussions such as reaching out to those in the informal sector, and obviously at this point do not have in place any finalized contractual arrangements (**See Appendix A: Tables/Charts, Chapter VI, Tables 2-3 ("Social Pension Profile: Sub-Saharan Africa," and "Sub-Saharan African Countries With Statutory Social/Civic Pensions").**

The Rationale for Age as the Primary Criteria: Social/Civic Pension

In accordance with the aforementioned definition of a social pension, chronological age as defined by each country, should be the only qualifying factor for determining eligibility. Eligibility for a social pension based on need (determined by a means-test), or pre-old age workplace contributions, should not be included as factors in eligibility determinations for the growing older population. An analysis of the data submitted by country governments, only five countries currently use age as the only qualifying criteria in considering a social pension for older persons; four countries in addition to age utilizes a means or pension test for determining eligibility. Globally, the goal is to guarantee that all older persons have at least basic income security in their retirement years. It is obvious that the vast majority of countries, based on data from the ISSA Annual Country profiles, have not reached that goal. Several countries, based on the definition of social pension have reached the goal. There are other countries making very good progress toward the goal, whereas others are progressing at a much slower pace.

In accordance with the United Nations 1948 Universal Declaration of Human Rights, as well as international labor standards, older persons at retirement age should be guaranteed income security. The major problem, especially in countries such as those in Sub-Saharan Africa where the informal sector represents the majority of the work force, "…pensions are accessible only to a minority, and many older persons can rely only on family support (ILO: World Social Protection Report, ibid, p. 73). But, family support systems and/or the extended family kinship system has been significantly weakened due to a variety of reasons including, modernization, urbanization, famine, political turmoil, and wars. Furthermore, there has not been an ongoing commitment globally for the inclusion of the dominant informal sectors in Sub-Saharan Africa as part of the formal sector's tripartite labor collective bargaining structure.

With declining family support systems, the lack of a collective bargaining structure for the dominant informal sector "…the majority of the world's older women and men have no income security, have no right to retire and have to continue working as long as they can – often badly paid and in precarious conditions (ILO: Social Protection Report, ibid, p. 73 **(See Appendix B: Concepts, Definitions and Special Notes).**

FUTURE EXPECTATIONS: THE NEXT GENERATION IN SUB-SAHARAN AFRICA

A review of data addressing those workers currently in the labor force participating in a tripartite labor contributory system provides an indication regarding who will have access to a pension in the future. Data does not reflect the potential non-contributory pension schemes related to the informal sector. Globally, it is estimated that approximately one-third of the current working age population is contributing to some type of contributory pension scheme. With special interest here for Sub-Saharan Africa, the range of coverage goes from 5.8% to 66,7% of the working age population in Western Europe. It is estimated that approximately 39.9 % of the global labor force are presently making a contribution to an insurance scheme, and can expect to receive a contributory pension when he/she retires from active employment. Whereas, in Sub-Saharan Africa only 8.2% of the current labor force are contributing to an insurance scheme that will provide a contributory pension at the time of retirement. For comparative purposes, the contributory insurance participation in Asia and the Pacific is 33%, approximately four times as Sub-Saharan Africa, the Middle East 36.7, Latin America and the Caribbean 37.6, Northern Africa 47.8, Western Europe/North America 90 and 98% and Central Eastern Europe 69.6 (ILO: World Social Protection Report, ibid, p. 84). Globally, not just in Sub-Saharan Africa, the world is not prepared for the "Silver Tsunami."

So, after more than three quarters of a Century of Declarations, Resolutions, and action oriented policy activities, including the First World Assembly on Aging, Sub-Saharan Africa have not benefited from any significant policy changes inter-intra Region in regards to ensuring that the older retiring population will have at least basic income security. And, as aforementioned there is not evidence to illustrate that the next generation in Sub-Saharan will experience a different fate than the current one.

Coverage Projections for the Next Generation

Considering the aforementioned analysis and discussion the current state of social pension coverage for the old age population in Sub-Saharan Africa is shameful. A very significant question becomes, what about the next generation of older people? It is obvious from the reports that although some countries are making progress, others are lagging behind.

According to data sources (ILO: World Protection Floor 2014/15, Section 4.4.1, pp. 83-84), the picture is not much brighter for the next generation. The ILO uses what is referred to as a contributor ratio that "… gives an indication of the proportion of the population – or the labor force – which will have access to contributory pensions in the future." The contributor ratio does not accurately "… reflect access to non-contributory pensions, it still gives an important signal regarding future levels of coverage, taking into account that benefit levels in contributory pension schemes tend to be higher than those from non-contributory pension schemes (ILO, pp. 83). According to the contributor ratio, globally, only about 1/3, or 29.7% of the current working population is making a contribution to some form of a pension scheme for the future. Well, what about the current population in Sub-Saharan Africa? For Sub-Saharan Africa the coverage is about 5.8 percent.

The International Labor Organization (ILO, pp. 83-84) provides more precise data for future projections in adding the concept "economically active." The reference is to the population that is not only active in the labor force, but is contributing to a pension scheme. Contractually, this population of labor force participants is expected, as a matter of right, will receive a pension at the time of retirement. Globally, the percentage for this population (economically active) is 39.9%; but, as a result of "… the high proportion of informal employment in sub-Saharan Africa, only 8.2 per cent of the labor force contributes to a social pension insurance scheme and earns rights to a contributory pension" (ILO, ibid, p.84).

The most recent report from the International Labor Organization (ILO) illustrates that very little progress, globally from a social protection/social pension perspective since 2014-2015 (World Social Protection Report, 2017-2019, ILO, Switzerland, 29/11/2017).

The latest report, 2017/2019, indicates that only about 29% of the global population has access to comprehensive social security; just a small percentage increase of 27% reported in 2014/2015. Globally, only about 45% of the global population is currently covered by at least one social benefit. Some 55%, approximately 4 Billion are still unprotected. The Report points out that approximately 68% of persons beyond retirement age receive an old age pension or social security. When considering the "…expenditure on pensions and other benefits for older people accounting for 69% of GDP on average with large regional variations, the report underlines that benefit levels are often low and not enough to push older people out of poverty. This trend is often fueled by austerity measures" (ILO World Protection Report 2017/2019, ibid, 2017).

THE 2015 MILLENNIUM DEVELOPMENT GOALS/THE 2020 SUSTAINABLE DEVELOPMENT GOALS

The Inclusion/Exclusion of Social Statutory Social Pensions

During recent years a couple of very important global plans of actions, The 2015 Millennium Development Goals and The 2020 Sustainable Development Goals, have been conceptualized and implemented under the auspices of the United Nations. But, explicit attention or inclusion of goals, measurable objectives and evaluative tools to address the social pension problem, or lack of income security globally of the older populations, were omitted in both documents. These action plans have included explicit and implicit goals and/or target groups, with measurable objectives focused on improving the quality of life for all citizens; yet, no explicit goals and objectives, including timetable for addressing the social pension issue has been included in either document. As aforementioned more than half of older persons globally are without a social pension; and as frequently mentioned, more than 80%, specifically 82.5 of older persons in Sub-Saharan Africa do not have a social pension or income security following retirement. In addition to the issue of the lack of a social pension or income security not being appropriately addressed, the problems related to basic needs for medical, social and health care, including long-term care for a growing older population, are not explicitly addressed as well. The aforementioned facts should set off an alarm or alerts of a basic need for a growing older population, especially regarding a lack of income security in old age.

The year 2015 was the deadline for the completion and reporting of the results from the United Nations Millennium Development Goals (MDG). As discussed in Chapter III the results from the 2015 MDG indicated some progress in Sub-Saharan Africa, especially the increase in primary school enrollments that should result in raising the level of education, but the 2015 Report also revealed a need for more work and actions in some of the other eight areas. It should be noted that none of the nine MDG Goals included a specific one focusing on social pension improvements. Also in 2015 the United Nations shared with the world what was referred to as the Sustained Development Goals (seventeen), including goals and action plans, with a completion deadline set for Calendar Year, 2020. Once again it should be noted that there were no explicit goal(s), measurable objectives, and action plans or timetable included in the 2015 MDGs with a focus on social pensions or social protection for the old-age population. Also, there is no explicit language, goals, objectives, and action plan included in the United Nations Sustainable Development Goals for 2020 with a focus on the older population, especially social pensions.

When considering the fact that only 45% of the global population is currently covered by one social benefit and only 29% of the global population has access to comprehensive social security, why not consider social pension a top priority within the MDG2015 Goals? Furthermore, more than eighty percent, specifically 82.5% of older persons in Sub-Saharan Africa currently do not have a social pension, it would have been quite proactive, relevant and timely to include such a subject matter within the Millennium Development Goals 2015, and the Sustained Development Goals 2020 as part of the United Nations agenda. An explicit goal including measurable objectives, and an implementation plan and evaluation, would have brought to the attention of member countries the plight of older persons globally and a global call for action. Also, as they have done historically, organizations such as the International Labor Organization (ILO), World Bank, and Help Age International could have provided the technical assistance needed to member countries in the conceptualization, design, and implementation of such a goal, measurable objectives, methods for accomplishing the task and timetable. Declarations that have emerged from the various assemblies, forums and conventions in recent decades clearly state that older persons should have the right to basic income security, access to social services and healthcare at the time of retirement. Furthermore, the Declarations have brought to the attention of member countries the rights of older persons, as based on the United Nations Declaration of Human Rights. Human Rights and social justice for older persons especially in the area of social protection have been a global consensus now for decades. Yet, in Sub-Saharan Africa less than twenty percent of the older population has a social pension, also now being referred to by some organizations such as Help Age International as a civic pension.

SUMMARY AND CONCLUSION

According to data from ILO, only 16.9 % of older persons living in Sub-Saharan Africa receive an old age pension, 37% in North Africa, 47% in Asia and Pacific, 56% in Latin America and the Caribbean, and 90% in North America and Europe. Inequalities regarding social protection for the older populations are very difficult to comprehend in a global world where there is so much wealth.

Currently eleven countries in Sub-Saharan Africa are listed as having a statutory guaranteed social pension, categories one and two. Five of the eleven use age as the only eligibility criteria; the remaining six uses some form of a means or pension test in addition to age. The countries listed in category three seem to be making progress toward the goal of a statutory social pension. The remaining countries in categories four and five have a tremendous amount of work to be done in future years of introducing in their countries a statutory social pension. Research illustrates that a social pension, including low-income countries is affordable, achievable and sustainable.

Therefore, in conclusion, the current state of social protection for older citizens in Sub-Saharan Africa is extremely limited; and, social protection into the next generation does not look so well for the majority of countries. It will take some miraculous policy efforts, globally, as well as from the African states to ensure that the current and next populations of older people will have at least basic income security. But, to live in dignity will require more than just a basic income, but access to health care and social services, including long-term care.

As indicated such a commitment to a quality life will need significant cooperation and support from the global community, especially from the colonial occupiers whose countries benefitted greatly from the resources, including forced labor, during the years of occupation by the European Powers. The occupation era contributed significantly to the underdevelopment of Africa (Meredith, Martin and Rodney). The theme question is would it be asking too much for selective countries to contribute a small percentage of their GDP towards ensuring social protection for the older population in Africa?

Although some significant changes have occurred regarding coverage for the older population globally, with the exception of African countries such as Cape Verde, Kenya, Lesotho, Liberia, Mauritius, Mozambique, Namibia, Swaziland, Botswana, Seychelles and South Africa, progress has been extremely slow. Also, on a more positive note, currently some twelve to fifteen countries with existing social insurance schemes but without a statutory mandate for older persons, have invited workers from the informal sectors to enroll in their tripartite collective bargaining systems. It is also very positive to note that Zanzibar, although not quite clear regarding its sovereignty or semi autonomous status with Tanzania has recently introduced a universal social pension scheme for its older population.

As previously noted, the percentage of the older African population that is part of a labor contractual pension scheme (contributory) is extremely low. Also, the number of social pensions (non-contributory cash transfers paid regularly to older people) among the countries is extremely small. Less than 20% of countries in sub-Saharan Africa currently have some form of a non-contributory social pension.

There is a global campaign currently in progress spearheaded by organizations such as ILO, Help Age International, calling for the implementation of a social pension, as a matter of human right for all older citizens.

End of Chapter VI

CHAPTER VII

Social Pensions for the Growing Older Population in Sub-Saharan Africa: Affordable, Achievable and Sustainable The Time For Action Is Now!!!

INTRODUCTION

It is somewhat obvious based on the explicit narrative of Chapter VI that the need for a statutory social pension and/or basic income security for the growing older populations globally, especially in Sub-Saharan Africa, have to be a top priority now! Not only is immediate attention and action needed among countries within the continent of Africa, also low and some middle income countries globally. The call goes out to International Organizations, including The United Nations, The International Labor Organization, The International Social Security Association, Help Age International and the World Bank to address the issue of a lack of income security for the growing older population, the "Silver Tsunami." Without a doubt, there is an urgent and immediate need now for a social pension for the old age population in Sub-Saharan Africa. As aforementioned repeatedly throughout the narrative of Chapter VI, approximately 82.5% of the current older population in Sub-Saharan Africa and 51% globally does not have access to a social pension or basic income security following retirement from the workplace. Furthermore, unless there are proactive policy initiatives on the part of the problem countries, such as those in Sub-Saharan Africa soon, the future generations of older persons will be confronted with the same reality of not having basic income security following retirement. The challenges are great and will require a proactive response from political and activists' leadership, not only from the continents/countries, but also from the global community as well.

The past Global Assemblies and Conventions, including the First World Assembly on Aging in 1982 resulting in numerous Declarations and Policy Statements, have been timely and relevant for international organizations and their member countries in responding to the "silver tsunami." Despite all of the Global Assemblies and Conventions that produced timely and relevant Declarations and Policy Statements, older persons globally, especially in Sub-Saharan Africa, continue not to have basic income security in in later years. As aforementioned not only does the problem exist in Sub-Saharan Africa but on other continents/countries as well. Globally, approximately fifty-one percent of older persons do not have a social pension or income security following retirement. The problem, especially for Sub-Saharan Africa is not just a lack of basic income security, but there are also indications of insufficient or lack of access to health and social services, including proper nutrition and long-term care for a growing older population. Furthermore, as life expectancy increases among the older population accompanied by chronic illnesses such as Dementia and Alzheimer's the need for specialized personnel and services, including long-term medical/health and social care will increase. The need for long-term care becomes more and more challenging, especially the rising cost of caring for the older population as well as increasing demands on medical, health and social systems. It should be noted that the aforementioned challenges have to include the family kinship system largely responsible for a major part of day-to-day caregiving for the growing older population. Chronic illnesses or conditions such as Dementia will continue to require around the clock services and/or caring and a great percentage of the caring will come from family members, especially women. The time is now for some proactive decision-making and/or concrete actions not only on behalf of the older population in Sub-Saharan Africa, but globally.

Once again it is regrettable that an explicit goal focused on a social pension for all was not part of the United Nations 2015 Millennium Development Goals (MDG). The inclusion would not have just drawn attention to the plight of the growing older populations and their lack of income security, it could have raised global consciousness concerning other issues such as lack of access to medical, health and social services. The recognition and awareness of the problems/issues would have encouraged countries to become more proactive in planning for the "Silver Tsunami," the growing older population. Furthermore, an explicit goal, including implementation strategies, for a social pension for all was also excluded from the 2020 United Nations Sustainable Development Goals that was introduced in 2015.

Approximately a decade ago in a policy discussion paper regarding the subject of extending social security for all, the manuscript author (Bailey, Clive, "Extending Social Security in Africa, ESS Paper No. 20, ILO: 2004, p. 20) addressed the challenges to be confronted and overcome for the idea to become a reality. Bailey pointed out that, "...the nature of the problem is such that the extension of social security to the excluded of Sub-Saharan Africa is going to take a long time..."(Bailey, Clive, ibid, 2004). Now, the question from the approximately 82.5% of the uncovered older citizens in Sub-Saharan Africa, and the 51% globally is, how long? How long do they have to wait? The author recommended at the time "...a special effort should be made to gather support for the launching of the Campaign in Africa" (Bailey, ibid, 2004, p. 20). The Minimum Development Goals (MDG) or the Sustainable Development Goals (SDG) would have been a great opportunity for the world to become proactive in responding to the growing older population and their special needs.

Now, it is one decade later after Bailey's recommendation, and there has been no significant percentage change in the percentage of uncovered citizens in Sub-Saharan Africa or globally.

In an effort to increase global awareness of the problem and the lack of social justice for older persons, advocates and activists on behalf of the older populations globally, are beginning not only to mobilize, but are becoming more proactive. The global "Aging Demand Campaign" under the leadership of Help Age International, the International NGO, and other activists, including Bishop Desmond Tutu, Nobel Peace Laureate recipient from South Africa, has been calling attention or awareness to the problem in recent years. The Campaign is calling on The United Nations to convene as soon as possible a Special Session to address the need for a social pension globally, as well other issues facing a growing older population or the "Silver Tsunami." The Aging Demand Campaign has concluded that the time is now to ensure that every older person have income security, access to healthcare (including long-term care), social services, housing, safety from abuse and neglect, and the opportunity to participate with dignity in societal decision-making affecting their lives. Now is also the time to globally move beyond a culture of ageism that affect negatively the older population globally; also the time is now to recognize that the "Silver Tsunami" brings to the policy making tables, years of struggle, experiences, knowledge and skills that could help to create a "World For All Ages," embodied in human rights and social justice.

HUMAN RIGHTS AND SOCIAL JUSTICE: THE GLOBAL FOUNDATION FOR SOCIAL PROTECTION

A social or civic pension is a regular guaranteed non-contributory income paid to older persons in retirement based on citizenship and/or residency rather than any previous contributions within a tripartite organized labor system. A country's decision to enact a statutory social/citizen's pension should be the results of a country's legislated process (Vydmanov, Charles Knox, "Social Protection Floors and Pension Citizens: The Role of a 'citizen's pension," Help Age International, Briefing Paper No. 9, 2012). Age as determined by each country, based on the country's unique aging demographics, and other social and health factors, should be the only eligibility criteria for a social pension.

John Rawls Theory of Social Justice/The UN: Declaration of Human Rights

Approximately one decade prior to the First General Assembly on Aging in Vienna in 1982, John Rawls published what eventually became the foundation for some of the most intellectual discussions and/or debates on the subject matter of social justice. Rawls emphasized or advanced the notion of fairness and social justice for all citizens in a modern society. Prior to the publication of the Theory of Justice, the most dominant theme of the time centered around the Utilitarian Principle of "the greatest good for the greatest number," or the majority of those in society over the minority. But, Rawls was all about justice and fairness for all in society not just based on one's social, economic, birthright, military "might" or dominance, or political status in society, but citizenship" (Rawls, John, Theory and Principles of Justice, London,

Oxford University Press, 1971). Rawls theory of justice and fairness "… revolves around the adaptation of two basic principles of justice which would in turn, guarantee a just and morally acceptable society. The first and second principles of justice and fairness advanced the notion that …each person in society is to have an equal right to the most extensive basic liberty compatible with the similar liberty for others…they are to be of the greatest benefit to the least advantaged members of society" (Rawls, ibid. pages, 3-7 and 60-65).

Now, here we are in the midst of the "Silver Tsunami" witnessing a dramatic global demographic growth in the older population. Not only is this population growing older as a result of medical/health science, technology and improvements in social/economic status, their enhanced health status allows for more independence in day to day activities. But, in our current global society, social justice for the older population is not equal across countries, or regions when it comes to basic income security, access to health and social care, and living their older years in dignity and respect. As aforementioned throughout this manuscript, only 16.9% of the older population in Sub-Saharan Africa, 51% globally has access to a social pension following retirement. According to Rawls theory and principles each older person, including the least advantaged member of society, at the time of retirement should have an equal right to a social or civic pension and social protection compatible with others in society.

"The United Nations: Declaration of Human Rights 1948"

The current global advocacy for a social/citizen pension is not only in accordance with Rawls theory of justice and fairness in society, but the United Nations Universal Declaration of Human Rights adopted in 1948. Article 22 of the Declaration states "Everyone, as a member of society, has the right to social security." The adoption of the Declaration of Human rights clearly recognizes that social security is a basic human right. Also, The UN International Covenant on Economic, Social and Cultural Rights, 1966, Articles 9 and 11, says "The States' Parties to the present Covenant recognize the right of everyone to social security, including social insurance, and "Article 11 recognizing that everyone should have the right to an adequate standard of living, that includes food, shelter, and clothing (ISSA: Strategy for the Extension of Social Security Coverage, ISSA Bureau, Geneva June 2010)/(United Nations: ICESCR, Chapter IV Human Rights, General Assembly Resolution 2000A (XXI), December, 1966).

The International Labor Organization (ILO) Mandate in the Preamble to its Constitution, 1919, the goal is the improvement of conditions related to labor "…through the prevention of unemployment…protection of the worker against sickness, disease, and injury arising out of his employment, the protection of children, young persons and women, provision for old –age and injury. The Declaration of Philadelphia, 1944, the goal "…to pursue the extension of social security measures to provide a basic income to all in need of such protection and comprehensive medical care." Additional ILO Mandates: The ILO 2001, "Reaffirmed social security as a basic human right; launched in 2003 a global campaign with the goal of extending social security; ILO Mandate on Social Justice for all, 2008; ILO's Minimum Standards Convention 102, 1952; ILO Convention 202, Introduction of the two dimensional models for ensuring social security for all, 2012. Let's not forget the World Assemblies on Aging, and their Declarations related to social justice and human rights, beginning with the First World Assembly in 1982.

There seems to be a growing global consensus among advocates for a social justice and human rights approach in the implementation of policies for ensuring a quality of life for older citizens. Those rights should include income security, access to healthcare and social services, a safe and secure environment, decent housing, social participation in decision-making, and a life with dignity and respect (Ginneken, Wouter van, "Civil Society and Social Protection Floor," Journal of International Social Security, Vo. 66, Issue 3-4, July/December, 2013, pages 6986). The global consensus is that a Social pension should be an integral part of a country's governing statutes, or legal mandate, that is non-contributory, and based on age citizenship/residency (as the only eligibility requirements), with an adequate income (Help Age International: Pension Watch Briefing no. 9). There is sufficient evidence to support the notion that a social pension for older citizens could have a major impact on poverty, unemployment, social inequalities as well as economic growth and transformation.

A global recognition of the rights of a growing older population was clearly highlighted in Declarations adopted during the First World Assembly on Ageing in Vienna in 1982. The Assembly in recognition that globally there was a growing older population that should be guaranteed a living environment that will "...allow them to enjoy in mind and in body, fully and freely, their advancing years in peace, health and security..." (World Assembly on Ageing, PREAMBLE, Vienna, July 26 – August 6, 1982). Global States/Delegates at this Assembly reaffirmed "... their belief that the fundamental and inalienable rights enshrined in the Universal Declaration of Human Rights apply fully and undiminished to the aging...that quality of life is no less important than longevity, and that the ageing should therefore, as far as possible, be enabled to enjoy in their own families and communities a life of fulfillment, health, security and contentment, and appreciated as an integral part of society (World Assembly on Ageing, Preamble, ibid, 1982).

On the matter of social justice and human rights 450 older persons representing 22 countries recently expressed that older people globally did not have the autonomy needed for independent decision-making affecting their day-to-day lives. According to the same group the same was true for having some choice or choosing types of care, such as long-term care and support services. Furthermore they expressed that they did not have sufficient knowledge necessary for decision making related to access to palliative care. Palliative care is extremely critical for the growing older population. It is interesting to note following the aforementioned narrative on the subject of Social Justice and Human Rights, based on the Help Age Report 2018, that there is no explicit declaration, policy or standard on behalf of the growing older population related to autonomy and independence, long-term care, including palliative care, currently within the international human rights law **(See Chapter I, page 25).** In regards to palliative care, as life expectancy increases, especially related to chronic illnesses such as Dementia and Alzheimer's, palliative care becomes a very critical need for patients. Palliative care requires very specialized attention and care for those with serious illnesses as aforementioned. The primary focus on the part of specialized medical personnel including family caregivers is providing immediate relief from ongoing symptoms and stress.

THE NEED FOR A SOCIAL PENSION IN SUB-SAHARAN AFRICA IS NOW!!!

Globally, while the vast majority of high-income level countries have social security/pension protection for their citizens such as universal coverage, most countries in Sub-Saharan Africa currently have less than 10% of the working sector with similar social protection coverage. In other words following retirement from the workplace in future years workers and their families will not have basic income security as well as other retirement benefits related medical, health and social services. Once again as indicated in Chapter VI, only 16.9% of the population in Sub-Saharan Africa currently have a social pension; in other words, approximately eighty-two (82%) percent are uncovered or without basic income security in old age. It has been estimated that (80%) percent (342 million) of older people living in developing countries do not have basic or adequate income support, i.e., a social pension (UN: DESA, Policy Brief No. 3, September 2007). The projections are that by the year 2050 the number 342 million of people living in developing countries, without income security will increase to 1.2 billion. This latter projection, 1.2 billion will become a reality if pension coverage "...does not keep pace with demographic trends (UN: DESA, ibid, 2007, p 1). The number in Sub-Saharan Africa will significantly increase as well. As aforementioned unless there are some urgent policy changes regarding social pensions immediately, future generations in Sub-Saharan Africa will be confronted with similar experiences, such as a lack of income security, as those who are currently occupying the category referred to as old age.

It is well documented that globally people are not only living longer, they are enjoying improved or enhanced health in later life. But, despite tremendous progress millions in the older population, especially in Sub-Saharan Africa, will face old age in a poverty environment without a social pension, or basic income security. In low and middle income countries only about one out of every four older persons receive a pension; but in Sub-Saharan Africa only eleven countries currently guarantee a statutory social pension for their old age citizens who worked in the informal sectors or were self-employed. Globally, as aforementioned, it is estimated that only about half of the world's population will have access to a social pension in old age (Help Age International: Global Age Watch Index 2014, Insight Report).

The consensus is that social pensions can and will reduce poverty among the older population; without proactive policy action a significant number of older persons, globally will live out their remaining years in poverty. In reference to retirement a significant number of the growing older population have chosen to continue working, not only in order to maintain at least a minimum level standard of living for themselves but their children and grandchildren as well. Also, for a significant number of the older persons the problem of living in poverty has been exacerbated because many now have additional child caring responsibilities as grandparents; the additional child caring responsibilities are the results of factors such as the HIV/AIDS/Ebola pandemics as well as political and military conflicts (UN: DESA, ibid, 2007, p 1).

The major contributing factor to this reality, lack of income security in old age, has to do with the exclusion of the informal and/or the self-employed from the formal sectors, or the traditional tripartite system of collective bargaining. The concept exclusion may not be appropriate in some instances, considering the fact that some workers within the informal sectors for various reasons have voluntarily chosen not to participate. On a very positive note based on the country survey analysis in Chapter VI, a growing number of countries with traditional tripartite system are now reaching out to workers in the informal sector with an invitation to participate. The aforementioned represents a very positive sign for future generations.

The problem is, not just for the employers/employees including public/private sectors, to solve, but international organizations, national governments including non-governmental as well. All parties will need to come together to look at the causative factors keeping the two labor sectors apart, and taking the initiatives to come up with a long-range plan resulting in a positive outcome. The evidence illustrates that a social pension for older persons contributes to economic development, and the reduction in unemployment and poverty. The vast majority of the working population in Africa continues to be in the informal sector (Jostein Hauge, The Guardian, "Global Development," 9/3/2014). Furthermore, according to Hauge, "Eighty (80%) percent of the population in Sub-Saharan Africa eventually ends up working in what is considered vulnerable jobs, or jobs in the informal sector." Sub-Saharan Africa "… has the highest vulnerable employment rates of all developing regions" (Hauge, ibid, p 2).

Income security is one of the most urgent concerns of older people globally. This is especially true for those living in Sub-Saharan Africa where generation after generation of the older population's work history was in the informal labor market. As a result they end up in old age without basic income security or social protection. The lack of basic income security as well as access to healthcare and social services, are the two areas mostly mentioned by older persons in surveys as problems (UN and Help Age International: Ageing in the 21st Century: A Celebration and a Challenge, 2012).

Many older persons without a social pension will spend their later years, not living in dignity, but working in old age. Africa has some of the highest percentages of labor force participation in the old age category, women and men, especially in the agriculture sector, than any other region of the world. An example is Malawi a country where 80% of older men continue to participate in the labor market. Malawi recorded the highest level of female labor participation, 83% in 2010. Globally, labor force participation in 2010 for those 65 plus was 31% in the less developed regions and only 8% in the more developed regions of the world. The projections are that the overall labor force participation in 2020 will be 39% in the African region, compared to 20% in Asia, 32% in Latin America, 19% in North America, and only 7% in Europe (UN: World Population Aging, 2013).

A global commitment to social pensions, including implementation strategies and actions, has to be a primary goal in the 21st Century, beginning now. The Ageing in the 21st Century document highlights that the investments in pensions are the most important ways for ensuring that the older population has economic independence and security. Also, it will have a major impact on the reduction of poverty, especially for school age children. Significant investments in social pensions could have a major impact on the socialization, or growth and development of children; once again, as a result of diseases such as HIV/AIDS, political and military conflicts, more and more children are living with grandparents. A significant number of these grandparents who have taken on the responsibility of rearing grandchildren will not have a social pension. Furthermore, social protection floors that include a non-contributory scheme must be implemented not only for ensuring income security but access to health and social services for older persons as well (UN and Help Age, 2012, p.14).

THE BENEFITS OF SOCIAL/CIVIC PENSIONS

Reductions in Poverty, Unemployment, Socialization of Children/ Youth and Contribute to Sustained Economic Growth

There is a global consensus that social pensions have a major role in the reduction of poverty, unemployment, the socialization of children (growth and development), contributions to economic growth, as well as other income and social inequalities. "Social security systems in many developed market economies reduce poverty and inequality by half or more" (ILO: Policy Briefing Paper 3, Geneva, 2008, p. 1). There is an increasing number of very successful case histories from regions such as Africa, Latin America and the Caribbean, and Asia, of how instituting statutory social pensions and or social transfers, are reducing poverty; furthermore, the evidence is that results are happening at a much quicker pace, than what has happened historically from anticipated outcomes from traditional economic policies, including Foreign Aid Programs (ILO: Social Security Briefings Paper 3, ibid, Geneva, 2008). In reference to the Millennium Development Goals, for reducing poverty in half by 2015, the enactment of a minimum social pension protection scheme could be the difference in reaching or not reaching the objective (ILO: Briefing Paper 3, ibid, 2008). The theme, "Pay Now or Pay Later" is quite relevant when one considers the consequences of no action. By not being proactive, only increases the likelihood of continuing poverty, resulting in the need for an abundance of resources later on in responding to all of the negative consequences brought on by a failure to take appropriate actions. So, the time is now not later!!!

Although poverty, including extreme poverty has significantly declined in most regions of the world, the evidence shows there has been little change among the poor in Sub-Saharan Africa, especially in the rural areas (UN: Food and Agriculture (F&A) 2015 IN BRIEF, "The State of Food and Agriculture Africa 2015 IN BRIEF"). Research continues to document the impact social protection programs have on reducing poverty and food insecurities. "In 2013 social protection helped lift up to 150 million people out of extreme poverty …those living on less than US$1.25 a day. Social protection allows households to increase and diversify their food consumption…positive impacts on child and maternal welfare are enhanced when programs are gender sensitive or targeted at women" (UN: F&A 2015, p. 7).

Research related to a cost benefit study in Tanzania concluded "…a universal old-age pension would cut poverty rates by 9%, with considerable stronger effect – 36 per cent – for older man and women and 24 percent for individuals living in households with elderly family members…A more balanced effect would be achieved by a child benefit for school age children, which would result in a cut in poverty rates by around 30 percent…The combination of these two benefits would achieve a reduction in poverty rates of 35 percent, with even more substantial effects for individuals living in households with children and elderly (a drop of 46 percent), which face the highest poverty rate" (ILO: Briefing Paper 3, Geneva, 2008, p. 15); the aforementioned content was taken from: Gassman, F., and Behrendt, C., 2006, "Cash Benefits in Low-Income Countries: Simulating the Effects on Poverty Reduction for Senegal and Tanzania, Issues in Social Protection, Policy Discussion Paper 15, ILO, Geneva, 2006).

ILO Briefings Paper 3, also stresses that social protection cash transfer schemes can play a major role in fueling economies that can result in reducing unemployment, poverty, and helping to stabilize families. Such initiatives enhances the incomes of local people, raises the demand levels of the local population as well as providing positive linages and increasing domestic markets. Briefing Paper 3 postulates that "The early investments into a basic set of social security benefits may even become zero or negative, because the fiscal costs might be offset by positive economic returns and the enhanced productivity of a better educated, healthier and better nourished workforce" (ILO: Briefing Paper 3, p. 2).

Factors such as modernization, including urbanization and industrialization, wars, political instability, diseases (HIV/AIDS, now Ebola), have and continue to have a major impact on family support systems, functions and survival. In so many instances the older family members, especially the female, have had to assume additional and/or major responsibilities for family survival. So many of the older family members do not have any form of social protection or social pension. The Ageing in the 21st Century Report points out that the investment in social pensions not only helps the older person but the family as a whole, especially the children. A social pension may be the primary source of income during the time of a family's economic struggles.

The older person taking on the primary duties of rearing their grandchildren assumes major responsibilities. The socialization process involving an environment for the overall growth and development of children requires income security, as well as healthy grandparents. The old age component of the life cycle is quite challenging even for those with income securities, but taking on children, youth, and grandparents exacerbates all of issues. For many of the grandparents, without even basic income supports, continuing in the labor force is an only option. Such family structures would greatly benefit from a country's investment in a social pension. The social pension scheme, including a provision for orphan children would have a much greater impact, not only regarding the overall growth and development of the children, but allows for grandparents to live in dignity and respect.

An investment in the concept of a social pension for Africans in their advanced ages is a strategic investment in children. As aforementioned the family structure in Africa is changing and the old age or grandparents, for a variety of reasons are expected to assume a major responsibility in the socialization of children. In its 2014 State of the World Population Report the United Nations articulated the importance and power of the approximately two billion children globally. The theme of the Report focused on the urgency, especially in Africa and Asia, of investing in children. So says the Report "… a demographic dividend can happen when a country's working age population is larger than its elderly and young population who are dependent." The suggestion is that the world's almost two billion young people have the potential of positively changing society, especially economically. The vast majority of the young people who reside in the less developed countries, are confronted with major obstacles, such as adequate access to education, healthcare, and surrounded by an environment of violence; almost twenty-five percent of the population is out of school. The current demographic shift occurring in some 60 developing countries, especially in Africa, is presenting a great opportunity for what the Report states as a demographic dividend if the countries are willing to make significant investments in the growth and development of these children. The goal for a commitment is to ensure that all of the children are provided with the opportunity to reach their full potential (UN: State of the World, 2014).

The United Nations 2014 Report (The Power of 1.8 Billion: Adolescents, Youth and the Transformation of the Future) shares the results of investments made by East Asia in the 1960's when it committed to making a significant investment in its children. According to the Report East Asia witnessed an economic dividend or a 6% increase in its GDP and in some of the countries observed a quadrupling of per capita income. It was the demographic dividend that was the major factor contributing to the one-third rise in income between the years 1965 to 1995; also, the 6% annual growth in per/capita income during the same time period. The per/capita income during the year 1995 more than quadrupled from $2296 to $9777 between 1965 and 1995. Currently, for every non-worker East Asia has 2.4 workers. It is interesting to note that approximately 2 percent of the annual per/capita income growth during the past two decades is the results of the shifting demographics. The conclusion drawn from experiences in East Asia would be similar in Sub-Saharan Africa if the appropriate human capital investments were made (UN: State of World Report 2014: Fact Sheet, "Youth in Asia," UNFPA). In fifteen of the countries, approximately one-third, in Sub-Saharan Africa half of the population is under the age of 18. If the countries were committed to making the appropriate human capital investments, "…the combined demographic dividends could be at least $500 Billion per/year (equal to one-third of the region's current GDP for up to 30 years" (UN: State of World Report (The Power of 1.8 Billion: Adolescents, Youth and the Transformation of the Future) 2014: Fact Sheet, "Youth in Sub-Saharan Africa," UNFPA).

The evidence is overwhelming when discussing the positive impact when investing in children. Looking at Poverty Through the Eyes of Children, an initiative from the World Bank, provides an excellent policy investment analysis of what the potential is when only a small share of a country's budget is invested in children. Not just the children who are being reared by grandparents as a results of factors such as HIV/AIDS, military conflicts, and job and/or unemployment due to labor/job issues, but all children. According to the World Bank report, "Investing as little as 10% of public savings from recent fuel subsidies cuts in Egypt into child cash grants would actually uplift 1.6 million children out of poverty" (Shiferaw, Bekele, (Blog) "Looking at Poverty Through the Eyes of Children," The World Bank, 10/6/2014). There were similar results in Jordan and Ghana. In Jordan it was the electricity subsidy cuts, and in Ghana it was fuel subsidies. A similar example is given from Uganda. Shiferaw, "…a little under 10% of new oil revenues could finance a 3 percentage point increase in education spending as a share of total public spending. The overall benefits to children and Ugandan society, approximately 1-1.4 million children added to the primary school enrollment; between 340-500,000 skill workers would be added to the labor market, as well as a 1% increase in the country's GDP growth rate. As a result of the aforementioned investments in Ghana some 100,000 children would be moved out of extreme poverty" (Shiferaw, ibid, 2014).

Botswana is the only country currently with a universal social protection scheme for children, provision for Orphans (ISSA: Social Security Around the World). There seems to be a growing consensus that a country's, including the global community, investments in social protection for all (the human infrastructure) is just as critical as a country investing in its physical infrastructure (Cichon, M. Extending Social Security to All, ILO, Social Security

Department, 16 Nov., 2010). There is a saying that goes "Pay Now or Later." A report from the World Bank has pointed out that extreme poverty in a country can be a serious risk to its overall security; in other words, extreme poverty can be a very significant barrier to overall economic growth and transformation. Beyond argument, productivity is a characteristic of people who enjoy a minimum level of material security (World Bank: World Development Report, An enhanced investment climate or environment is positive for all citizens - World Bank, A Better Investment Climate for Everyone, 2005, p. 24). One of the most significant conclusions derived from the World Bank 2005 report was that a country without basic social transfer schemes with provisions for foster/orphan (Botswana), access to health care and services, adequate levels of nutrition and social stability, will not be able to unlock the productive potential of its citizens. In paraphrasing the aforementioned, basic income security should be highlighted. This should especially include the older population with the responsibilities of raising grandchildren. For all countries the children are the future, and therefore need all of the necessary resources to ensure that they grow to their maximum potential. Grandparents without social protection/social pension may not be able to ensure that children will have this opportunity.

Income security is considered a very significant beginning step in the direction of economic growth and transformation. This is especially the case involving investments in children. "For poorer communities and households it is accepted that even a small cash benefit provided on a regular and reliable basis can make a big difference…Such direct improvements in income security for benefit recipients are accompanied also by a number of indirect improvements that extend to recipients and members of their households, including improvements in nutritional intake, children's educational attainment, empowerment and well-being" (ISSA: Development and Trends Africa, Strategic Approaches to improve Income Security 2014, p. 19). And, let's not forget that research concludes that it is affordable even among low and middle-income families.

SOCIAL PENSIONS: AFFORDABLE, ACHIEVABLE AND SUSTAINABLE!!!

Is a social pension affordable? Globally, if international organizations, including member states is going to live up to all of the resolutions and declarations with commitments to human rights and social justice over the past several decades, the answer has to be yes! The question often raised when the subject of a social pension comes up is affordability. Is it feasible for a country where the percentage of older persons without social protection coverage can be as high as 80% afford a social or civic pension? Or, can the country(s) afford not to? From a cost benefit perspective can the country(s) and the global community afford not to? Although there is sufficient global evidence to demonstrate that the benefits of investments in a social pension, in developing and developed countries, can outweigh the future costs of not making such an investment, the question of affordability remains.

Is social security affordable has been addressed by global organizations such as the ILO and concluded that affordability is a reality. "We know that the world can afford to make the right to social security a reality not just a dream … less than 2% of global Gross Domestic Product (GDP) would be necessary to provide a basic set of social security benefits to all of the world's poor" (ILO: Social Security Policy Briefing Paper 3, pp. 3-4, 2008). In response to the question of affordability, Help Age International stresses that the cost of such investments can be significantly less than what is most often stated. Citing its own research the organization makes the point "that a universal pension for all people 65 plus at 20% percent of average income would range from 0.4 of GDP in Burkina Faso to 1.8% in China" (Health Age International: Global Age Watch Index, Insight Report, p. 6, 2014). Burkina Faso a low-income country in Sub-Saharan Africa has a per capita income of US$1149; the country has an extremely high dependency ratio 94.1.

The International Labor Organization conducted a cost study involving twelve developing countries in Africa and Asia. Based on data analysis it was estimated that an initial gross annual cost of a basic social protection package would be in the range of about 3.7 % to 10.6 % of the country's GDP; this would be as indicated the gross annual cost for the country. But, when analyzing individual elements of the package the costs would be significantly lower. For example, the annual cost for the universal old age and disability package would be between 0.6 % and 1.5% of GDP for selected countries, including Burkina Faso, Cameroon, Ethiopia, Kenya, Senegal, Tanzania, Bangladesh, India, Nepal, Pakistan, and Vietnam. The ILO projected that "...the costs for 2010 remain at or below 1.0 % of GDP in six of the 12 countries, while Burkina Faso, Ethiopia, Kenya, Nepal, Senegal and Tanzania find themselves between 1.1 and 1.5 per cent of GDP" (ILO Briefing Paper 3, p.6). Although the ILO data supports the notion that a social pension is affordable in the aforementioned six Sub-Saharan countries, only one of the six, Kenya (recently enacted in April 2018) currently has a universal statutory social pension for older people.

A more recent report, (Help Age, 2015 Report) should provide social pension advocates with additional results to be used as part of their organizing strategies and tactics for promoting social pensions globally. The percentage of GDP for nine (9) countries in Sub-Saharan Africa identified as having a social pension are: Botswana - 0.01%, C. Verde - 0.0024%, Lesotho – 0.15%, Mauritius – 0.01%, Namibia – 0.02%, Seychelles – 1.518, South Africa – 0.02%, Swaziland – 0.03% and Liberia – 2.49%. Two other countries in Sub-Saharan Africa with a social pension not listed in the 2015 report are Mozambique and Kenya. Three of the countries, C. Verde, Lesotho, and Swaziland have been classified, according to the World Bank, as Low Middle-Income countries; the country Liberia, according to the World Bank has been classified as Low-Income. The conclusion drawn is that a low-income country such as Liberia with a per/capita income of $970.00 American dollars, has instituted a statutory pension for older persons who had worked in the informal sector. Although not classified as high income three of the countries with social pensions, low middle-income were capable of finding or creating fiscal space within their country's budget for introducing a social/civic pension. Affordability is no longer a rationale for failure to introduce a social pension. (**See Appendix A: Tables/Charts, Chapter VI, Tables 2-3 - "Social Pension Profile: Sub-Saharan Africa," "Sub-Saharan African Countries With Statutory Social/Civic Pensions."**

Part of the problem related to a lack of investments in social pensions, according to ILO, is that some governments, especially in low-income countries, have not viewed social security as one of their primary goals in conceptualizing development strategies. A country(s) investment in social transfers has often been viewed as more of an obstacle related to economic growth (Cichon,

M. Extending Social Security to All, 2010). A similar observation to the aforementioned, is because countries are low-income, poor, there are those who see social transfers and/social security/protection "...as an unaffordable luxury" (Harris, Elliott, Financing Social Protection Floors: Considerations of fiscal Space, ISS Review, Volume 66 1 Number 3-4, p. 112, 2013). But, in some countries political activists, especially during elections, take the position that the country cannot afford a transfer pension, even if the target was the old age population.

The question of affordability was high on the agenda for some political/civic activists, including administrative officials, during the General Election debates in Kenya in 2014. One major subject and debate centered around expanding the cash transfer program for seniors. In its political Manifesto the Jubilee and Cord Alliances was a proposal to expand the current stipend or cash transfer program to seniors if their campaign to be elected was successful. In other words if they took power an objective would be to increase the coverage of the transfer scheme that was at that time being provided for those Kenyan citizens aged 65 plus. At the time of the debate the program, covering some 500,000 seniors, were supported by the World Bank. The Alliances went further in its Manifesto recommending that the program include persons with disabilities, orphaned and all vulnerable children. Organizationally/administratively, the Alliances recommended the creation of a system whereby social protection payments would be administrated by County Governments.

The debate in Kenya seemed to focus around two major issues, affordability and the right of persons to receive a pension without contributing during previous or prior years of employment. The Zimele Asset Investment Manager Mr. Sammy Muvelah addressed the right issue. His position was that one should only the right to receive a cash transfer pension if those persons had made a contribution during their working years. According to Mr. Muvelah, a right implies an obligation. He also addresses the issue of affordability. The National Social Security Fund, according to Mr. Muvelah, has about 3 million persons covered, which is not enough to provide universal cash transfers for old age poverty. The Chief Executive Officer, Institute of Economic Affairs Mr. Kwame Owino, addressed the issue of affordability. He based his argument on the problem of insufficient tax revenues. He addressed, at that time, the ongoing budget deficits, especially not being able to take care of expenses. He concluded that the objective for introducing a universal cash transfer program at that time in Kenya was not possible.

The aforementioned example related to the subject of social protection and/or social pension illustrates some of the possible dynamics in various countries around some of the issues. What happened in Kenya? Well, the President of Kenya called a Special Cabinet Meeting on the 27th of April 2014. On this day the Cabinet's agenda was to approve Budget Estimates for the Financial Year 2014/2015. This was the Agenda focusing on priorities and for the Jubilee Government. The Budget included an increase of cash transfers for older people from 500,000 to 1 million (Help Age International, Global Age Watch: Data and Analysis on Population Ageing, June 5, 2014). (The Official Website of the President, April 27 2014, Press Brief; Business Daily, Cash Transfers to All Unworkable, Say Experts, Posted February 6, 2013). A progressive initiative on the part of Kenya, 500,000 to 1 million, but the very positive initiative did not guarantee at the time of guaranteeing a statutory social pension for all of the older population in Kenya.

According to Harris (ibid, p. 112) "...shocks to employment can have devastating human and social consequences – less consumption of food and thus poorer nutrition; withdrawal of children from school; loss of access to essential services; and the forced sale of assets, all of which lessen the capacity to recover once the shock passes." The previous observations do raise the question of how governments view population ageing? In a United Nation Nations survey of world governments, globally more than half viewed population ageing as a major concern in their countries; governments in "… more developed countries were more than twice as likely, 92% as those in less developed regions, 42%" that viewed population aging as a major concern (UN: DESA, World Population Policies, 2013).

If and to what extent it is a problem of governments viewing social protection and/or social transfers as a barrier/burden in economic development, the World Banks makes the case that "…the economic arguments in favor of making resources available for investments in social security is overwhelming." Furthermore says the World Bank, "…that poverty is a risk to security and lack of security is a hindrance to the investment climate…. Beyond argument, productivity is a characteristic of people who enjoy a minimum level of material security (World Bank: World Development Report, A Better Investment Climate for Everyone, 2005, p. 24). One of the most significant conclusions derived from the World Bank 2005 report was that a country(s) without basic social transfer schemes with provisions for foster/orphan (Botswana), access health care and services, adequate levels of nutrition and social stability, will not be able to unlock the productive potential of its citizens. In paraphrasing the aforementioned, basic income security should be highlighted. This should especially include the older population with the responsibilities of raising grandchildren. For all countries the children are the future, and therefore need all of the necessary resources to ensure that they grow to their maximum potential. Grandparents without social protection/social pension may not be able to ensure that children will have this opportunity.

Kenya Moving Forward in 2018

Although Kenya came up short of a universal pension for all in 2014 the country finally reached the goal in 2018. In June 2018 Kenya launched a statutory social pension for all; now more than a half million older persons, women and men will now receive monthly a social pension, their first ever. "Under the new Government-funded (Inua Jamil: Swahili meaning 'a country that moves forward') 70 and above universal social pension, launched by President Uhuru Kenyatta on Saturday 2 June, all Kenyans over 70 will receive 2,000 shillings, just under US$20, per month" (Derbyshire, Justin, www.helpage.org/blogs/profile-justin-derbyshire-28211, 11 Jun 2018, pages 1-4). The launching of a universal social pension in Kenya does not come as shocking news in Kenya or globally. As aforementioned providing a social pension for the older population has demonstrated that such policies reduces poverty and unemployment. The launching of statutory social pensions for the older population are desperately needed in countries where a significant number of people, men and women are employed in the informal sector and/or self-employed. Also, in response to those who raise the question of cost, "In most low and middle-income countries, the cost of a universal pension for the over 65s would be less than 1.8% of GDP" (Derbyshire, Ibid).

The launching of the statutory universal social pension in Kenya does ensure that all Kenyans beyond the age of 70 years will have at least basic income security during older age. It is important to know that the statutory social pension "...is owned and funded by the government of Kenya, and does not rely on funding from international donors" (Derbyshire, ibid, page 2). The age of 70 as the basic eligibility requirement may raise some questions; for example, life expectancy in Kenya for women is 63.6, men 59.8. Whereas the statutory pension age is 70 the question is what specific provisions are made for those who live beyond their life expectancy age before reaching the age of 70?

CREATIVE AND INNOVATIVE STRATEGIES FOR ESTABLISHING NON-CONTRIBUTORY PROGRAMS

Identifying Fiscal Space Within Countries' Budgets

There is this strong belief among some governments that a social pension, even though it is targeting one of the most vulnerable groups, the older population, is not affordable within a country's budget. This is especially the case when considering long-term support for pension legislation and/or sustainability. A country's economic specialist can make a very strong argument based on budget analysis in supporting his/her case. Even with overwhelming evidence as previously mentioned, some governments remain skeptical or not convinced. The reality is that the addition of a social pension has to be sustainable, enacted into law, and not supported by a temporary or one time budget contribution. Therefore, the search for fiscal space within a country's budget becomes critical in decision-making regarding the adoption of a social pension.

What is considered fiscal space in regards to budget matters? First of all, "In its broadest sense, fiscal space can be defined as the availability of budgetary room that allows a government to provide resources for a desired purpose without any prejudice to the sustainability of a government's financial position" (International Monetary Fund (IMF), Policy Discussion Paper, Heller, P.S., Understanding Fiscal Space, March 2005, p.3). So, when a government says that the introduction of a particular program, such as a social pension is not affordable, there is no fiscal space, no excess "schillings," or "pula available within the budget for the program to become a reality. If there is no current space with the budget the task becomes how does a government create fiscal space. Let's recall that in response to the Jubilee and Cord announcement during the 2014 Election that if elected the leaders would significantly increase the number of social pensions (cash transfers) for the old age uncovered population. The response from the opposition, including the government's Chief Economist was that the plan was not affordable. The Business Daily prior to the election quoted some experts, "Cash Transfers to all unworkable." But, following the election when the Jubilee Alliance took over, it was announced during a Special Cabinet meeting on April 27, 2014 the increase in cash transfers had been increased from 500,000 thousands to one million. It is obvious that some fiscal space had been created to accommodate an additional 500,000 elders. Now, the major task for Kenya is to legislatively create a universal statute that will include all eligible citizens.

According to Bailey, 2004, p.3, if a country could demonstrate that "...the resulting fiscal outlays would boost medium-term growth and perhaps even pay for itself in terms of future fiscal revenue…" could strengthen the advocacy for a cash transfer program. What are some other incentives that may enter the debate? There is evidence that an investment in a social pension can reduce poverty, create jobs (The Kenyan experiment in remote areas); a social pension to the old age population now with the responsibility of caring for the children, now with parents for a variety of reasons, will contribute significantly to the well being of the children. The country's investment in the socialization of the children now, could result in not having to pay for the negative consequences later; some may refer to it prevention, or "pay now or pay later."

Selective Recommendations for Creating Fiscal Space Within Budgets

The IMF Policy Paper by Bailey, 2004, pp. 3-6 offers several recommendations for creating fiscal space. One strategy for creating fiscal space within the country's budget is by additional revenues, new tax revenues, non-tax revenues. Another means is a government decision process, if political feasible to do so, whereas a program of low priority is deleted and/or expenditures reduced from the budget. The first two, adding new taxes or deleting what may be considered by the government to be a low priority program, could develop into some very interesting debates among the constituents as well as the political leaders within the country. The borrowing of resources and/or donor contributions from domestic or external resources is another government option for creating fiscal space. Also, a very interesting suggestion from Bailey was that a government by the powers invested in it request that the central bank just print money as a loan to the government. Finally, fiscal space for a particular program, such as a social pension, could be created from a financial grant from external sources.

The aforementioned recommendations for creating fiscal space are similar to those offered by Harris, Elliott, "Financing Social Protection Floors: Considerations of Fiscal Space," ISSR, Vol. 66, No. 3-4, 2013, pp. 114-136. According to Harris, ibid p. 115, some primary methods for creating fiscal space "…are domestic tax, and non-tax revenues." Another recommendation, very similar to Bailey's, recommends the redirection of expenditures, or redirecting funds away from a low priority program to a program based on a political and/or civic consensus, a high priority area. An example could be a social pension for the old age population. Another approach by Harris would be on enhancing administrative efficiency. It is highly possible that by strengthening the evaluative model of a particular program, reexamining the goals and measurable objectives, the government may realize, according to Harris, similar "…outcomes or results can be achieved using fewer resources, therefore, freeing up resources for other applications," (Harris, ibid, 2013, p.115) for adding a new program. Harris, ibid, 2013, p. 115, not unlike Bailey, recommends that another way of creating revenues could be the printing of money by the government.

In considering any or all of the aforementioned for creating fiscal space the uniqueness of each country has to be closely examined; the country's politics, the current and future economic growth potential (GDP), country's debt, economic governance (The Ibrahim Index of African Governance: Human Development, Sustainable Economic Opportunity, Participation and Human Rights, Safety and Rule of Law). Also, what about a country's membership and participation in international organizations, such as ILO, the United Nations? Not only membership in those organizations, what about the country's commitment to the various declarations with a focus on social justice and human rights?

The point to be made is related to an observation from ILO in a discussion focused on building social protection floors; "…a one-size-fits-all approach is not appropriate, every member State should design and implement its Social Protection Floor guarantees according to national circumstances and priorities defined with the participation of social partners" (ILO: Social Security for All: Building Social Protection Floors and Comprehensive Social Security systems, 2012). Closely related to fiscal space is sustainability. A future challenge, especially regarding the old age population, will be the change in dependency ratios. Therefore, the growth of the aging population will continue to have a significant impact on future budgets in responding to the needs of this population.

Although the subject of affordability remains the central focus for many of the governments, especially in the low and middle-income countries, there is sufficient evidence that fiscal space for a program such as a social pension is a very strong possibility. In Chapter VI a number of examples were provided of countries in Sub-Saharan Africa that had made tremendous progress in creating a social pension for the older population in their respective countries. In addition to Sub-Saharan Africa, globally there are examples of other countries, such as Brazil and Bolivia, reporting success stories in regards to social pension systems for their older populations.

SOCIAL PENSIONS ARE ACHIEVABLE, NOT JUST HIGH INCOME COUNTRIES BUT LOW-TO MIDDLE INCOME COUNTRIES IN SUB-SAHARAN AFRICA, LATIN AMERICA/CARIBBEAN

There is much to be learned from the successful experiences of some of the low and middle-income countries globally, especially those in Sub-Saharan Africa, about creating fiscal space within budgets for social programs. Not only creating the fiscal space but also taking the next steps in extending social protection to vulnerable members of society. There are excellent global examples from countries, including Sub-Saharan Africa, such as Bolivia, Botswana, Brazil, Costa Rico, Liberia, Lesotho, Namibia, Thailand, and South Africa demonstrating that a social pension can become a reality (ILO: Fabio, Duran-Valverde, Pacheco, J.F., "Fiscal Space and Extension of Social Protection: Lessons Learnt from Developing Countries," 2012). Liberia with a p/capita income of $970, one of the lowest in Africa, has a statutory social pension for those formerly employed in the informal sectors or self-employed. These countries utilized a variety of creative/innovative techniques in their efforts to find fiscal space within their budgets. The case histories from the aforementioned countries reinforce the previous conclusion that low and middle-income countries can find the space considering limited budgets for the purpose of extending social protection to vulnerable populations. The countries have also concluded that the investments they make in regards to human development will play a significant role when it comes to reducing poverty, unemployment economic and social development. It reinforces the theory that there is a strong and positive correlation between the introduction of social pensions and social economic growth and development within a country (ILO: Fabio et al, ibid, 2012).

There is also another very significant trend occurring globally among low-income countries, including some of those in Sub-Saharan Africa. Countries, such as Namibia, have begun to transition away from ad hoc types of interventions as a response to social protection concerns. Instead of offering solutions such as fuel subsidies, temporary cash programs, more and more countries "…in Africa are moving from ad hoc social safety net interventions to more integrated and efficient social protection programs" (ISSA, Development and Trends 2014, Africa: Strategic approaches to improve Social Security, p 7). Another trend emerging is that countries are beginning to transition away from a dependency on external funding and are identifying financial sources or fiscal space within their budgets for social expenditures (ISSA, Development and Trends ibid, 2014).

In regards to separating myths from facts, historically there was a position among many that in order to enact appropriate social protection programs a country would first need to achieve a particular level of economic growth. The acceptance of this position would normally see countries waiting for long periods of time before the readiness button was pushed. But, lessons learned from other countries, especially those in Sub-Saharan Africa, demonstrate that developing countries and/or low and middle income, can identify fiscal space within their budgets for social protection programs such as social pensions for the older population. Liberia with a p/capita income around $970 has a statutory social pension, although a means test is used, for the older population who do not qualify within the traditional tripartite system. On the other hand Equatorial Guinea with a p/capita income of $32,269 does not have a social pension (ISSA, Development and Trends, ibid, 2014/ISSA Annual Survey 2015). The next step for Liberia is to eliminate the means or pension test and use age as the only criteria for eligibility. Furthermore, "…the social security system need not be, in the first instance, comprehensive in its coverage and risks" (ISSA, ibid, 2014, p 18). Once there is the foundation for such a program a country has something to build on, or take an incremental approach to improving on the policy when certain social, economical and political conditions allow. The Social Security policy in the United States has been enhanced, incrementally, over the years with positive amendments for improving the quality of life for the retired population and their families.

Globally, there is a growing recognition that social pensions, as well as other programs for social protection, are major investments in human capital. The results of investments in human capital correlate with sustainable economical growth and development. Also such investments have been known to respond positively to economic and social shocks. The growing recognition on the part of public and private decision-makers, including community activists that social pension programs produce positive results, have contributed significantly to increasing support for such social programs (ISSA, Development and Trends, ibid, 2014).

In regards to global social activism, social protection coverage campaigns, especially for social pensions, have continued to gain momentum during the past decade. One of the most active campaigns has been under the leadership of Help Age International, "Age Demand Campaign" (See Chapter II). In addition to Help Age, "The past decade has witnessed increasingly strong and sustained political will in support of social protection coverage extension in Africa, demonstrated by the adoption of a number of regional and pan-African agreements, including the 2004 Pretoria Declaration on Economic, Social and Cultural Rights in Africa, the 2008 African Union's Social Policy Framework for Africa, and the 2010 Yaounde Tripartite Declaration on the Implementation of the Social Protection Floor" (ISSA Development & Trends ibid, p 3, 2014).

Based on all of the available evidence, the question of affordability and/or the lack of fiscal space should no longer be justification for countries not to include among their statutes a social pension for all older persons at the time of retirement. Research has also demonstrated, as aforementioned that an old age pension contributes to the reduction in poverty, unemployment, the overall growth and development of children, as well as contributing to sustained economic growth and development. Economically, "Africa is rising" with one of the fastest growing economies in the world. One economist has boldly stated the following, "This is Africa's Moment," Robertson, (2012, p. 244). At this historical moment Africa maybe considered the world's best geographical region for economic investments and opportunities (Robertson, ibid, 2014). The economic success story in Africa is critical considering the global consensus of a significant correlation between an investment in social pensions and economic growth. Therefore, why should 80% of older persons in Sub-Saharan Africa not have access to an adequate income, and hopefully in the very near future, access to health and social services, including long-term care as well.

SELECTIVE MISSED OPPORTUNITIES HISTORICALLY TO COMMIT AND IMPLEMENT SOCIAL PENSIONS FOR THE OLDER POPULATIONS IN AFRICA

This is an ideal time for adopting social protection programs, such as a social pension in Sub-Saharan Africa as well as globally. The Continent of Africa has demonstrated in recent decades, not only very positive economic growth and transformation but there is a new spirit, especially among the young of moving beyond the past and getting things done. This could be the time to seize the opportunity for allowing social justice and human rights to reign. It is hoped that Sub-Saharan Africa with support of the United Nations, the International Labor Organization, and other global organizations committed to social justice will not miss this great opportunity to provide social protection for one of its most vulnerable population groups, the "Silver Tsunami." There have been opportunities in the past but the circumstances and/or commitment to do so was not there, especially during the historical period preceding or planning for the day or Freedom or Independence, or immediately following Independence. History has confirmed that the foreign powers were not interested in sharing their knowledge and expertise with the native populations in the development of tripartite labor systems that would ensure the workers and their families of social protection. The former colonizers' priority continued to be focused on their own economic interest back home, especially in Europe.

Pre-Post Independence – After more than three-quarters of a Century involving European domination and/or colonization, the post-World War II era witnessed the cry for freedom and Independence as the top priority on the African Continent. During the era of colonization forced labor operationalized by the colonizers to ensure that their economic needs, especially back home in Europe, were met at the expense of the available native labor force. Not only was forced labor critical for the European powers the building and/or construction of transportation systems became even more critical for the purpose of exporting the very valuable natural resources, ivory, rubber back home to Europe (Gondola, Ch. Didier, <u>The History of the Congo,</u> "Timeline of Historical Events," London: Greenwood Press, 2002, p. xxiii). Also, it was during this era of forced labor that the Missionaries as well as diplomats shared with the global community some of the horrors that took place during the reign of King Leopold II, including mutilations, floggings, repression, as well as slave trading (Gondola, ibid, 2002).

There is no significant evidence to suggest that the European masters had any interest in the workers, especially social protection, beyond meeting their own needs, including the economic transformation that was happening globally as part of the industrial revolution taking place in the Western world. Collective bargaining regarding working conditions, social protection for workers and their families were not priority items. Although a collective bargaining system did exist during the era of colonization native workers were excluded from participation. Following Independence a small percentage of native workers employed in the newly independent governments and/or other civil service positions, became part of a tripartite system of labor. As would eventually happen until this day, the vast majority of the labor or work force in Africa became part of what became known as the informal sector, referred to in Kenya as Jua Kali. There is little or no evidence that the Western powers, especially Germany and the United States made any innovative attempts to incorporate some form of collective bargaining system within the informal system of labor. Germany, a major contributor during the Belgium Conference of 1884-85 ("Scramble for Africa"), was the first country to establish a system of social security under the leadership of Chancellor Bismarck. Other Western powers followed, including the United States who established a system in 1935 approximately two decades prior to Ghana's Independence around 1957. In other words, the Western powers possessed the knowledge base and awareness of the need for social protection programs.

Following Independence a great opportunity existed for the global public and private sectors, including the political units, as well as the former colonizing countries, to develop a plan focused on economic growth and development in the former colonies. A plan that would have included economic investments, not just foreign aid, but economic investments in a continent rich in raw materials, minerals, including diamonds, and oil reserves. The era of Post-Independence could have been a great time for economic growth and transformation in Africa. Africa's "economic rising," or Africa's "Economic Renaissance" would not have had to wait decades later for what Rostow refers to in Chapter V as "take off". If commitments and actions had been taken earlier there would not be 82% of older persons without income security and social protection at this stage in the 21st Century. A major question remains why not a Marshall Plan for Africa similar to what occurred in Europe at the conclusion of WW II? Such an initiative could have been the foundation for a formalized workforce, including future social protection measures for workers and their families.

Following Independence, first Ghana in 1957, the agenda for the continent became one of nation building. In other words, transitioning from a very period of colonization, including the purposefully separation of families, tribes, forced labor, the seizure and exploitation of land and natural resources, to and era of self rule and/or governance. Some academicians or theorists would describe the aforementioned as a move from a traditional to a modernized and industrial society. To conceptualize and implement or carry out such an ambitious process would require tremendous resources, including technical resources (Njoku, R. C., <u>The History of Somalia</u>, Oxford, England: Greenwood Press, pages 101-107, 2013; Lipset, S. M., <u>Political Man: The Social Basis of Politics</u>, London: Heinemann Press, pages 1-54, 1964).

The major question following Independence may have been where will the abundant resources needed for such long-term and future transition come from? As aforementioned there is no evidence that the colonizers committed to such undertaking or the sharing of resources. Also as aforementioned there was no commitment to the development of a labor system for workers and their families. But, thanks to the International Labor Organization (ILO) who became advocates for ensuring that African civil servants, who replaced the expatriates following Independence, had some social protection under a tripartite or collective bargaining system.

A major oversight was, "…unfortunately, colonial rule failed to establish a solid economic foundation under which the governing elite…could craft an enduring national unity…(Njoku, ibid, 2013, p. 102). As a result of a failure to commit to the development of an economic infrastructure on the part of former colonizers and their allies, the newly independent African countries, "…were left in wore shape than it had ever been because colonial rule introduced new institutions, new ideologies new practices of capitalism – new patterns of consumption (Njoku, ibid, 2013). All of these new trends and practices that were introduced during some seventy-five years of colonization were like alien in comparison to the traditional practices and/or cultural traditions of the continent (Njoku, ibid, 2013, p. 102)

The lack of a conceptual plan, including a lack of commitment to resources on the part of the former colonizing countries and their Western allies "…explains why the transition into an independent statehood that started on a peaceful note soon exploded into violent conflict (Njoku, ibid, 2013, p. 102). In view of the conflicts, including wars and coups, a common reaction became, Africa's new leadership is not capable of governing. One can not ignore the latter in the historical struggles of African countries, politically and economically, but, let's not ignore the role or lack of responsibilities of the European and Western powers who came up short in their commitments; the question remains why not Marshall Plan for Africa? Once again social theorists (Chapter V), project that every society or country will follow a historical and irreversible process of a transition from a traditional to a modern and industrialized society over time. The assumption of the modernization theorists is "…that with greater access to education, improved communication, and the shifting of people from the slumbering traditional moral sector, ethnic consciousness will give way to national consciousness (Njoku, ibid, 2013, pages 101-102; Lipset, ibid, 1964, pages, 1-54). The aforementioned process has been more difficult for some African countries to achieve and the question is why? One response has to be what the countries possessed at the starting block? Did they have the sufficient resources and leadership to conceptualize and implement a plan following a quarter-century of colonization? Most importantly considering that the continent's resources, including forced labor had helped to develop the economic empires of Europe, did they have global support for a Western style Marshall Plan that had been introduced in Europe for its recovery following WWII? Maybe the answer to the latter question was discussed in Chapter V, the President of France response to the question why no Marshall Plan for Africa? According to President Macron, Africa unlike the European countries has civilization issues such as women having too many children.

The International Labor Organization (ILO): The Minimum Standards Convention 1952 – In response to an era of rapid economic growth and industrialization following World War II, the ILO 1952 Convention concluded that this was the appropriate time to move quickly in adopting the contributory insurance scheme globally. The major question at the time during the Convention was "…how to significantly extend coverage and help workers to graduate out of non-regulated work into formal regulated employment" (Hagemejer, Krzsztof and McKinnon, Roddy, "The role of national floors in extending social security to all," The International Social Security Review, Volume 66, Number 3-4, July-December 2013, p. 5). A major challenge was how to include within the Minimum Standards the new and emerging countries of the world, such as those in Sub-Saharan Africa; countries that were already decades behind the level of economic growth as the economically powerful Western countries. The Convention concluded that, considering the social, economic, and political realities that would confront the newly developing countries, they would not be prepared to introduce a tripartite labor system anytime soon following independence. Therefore, in an effort to be as inclusive as realities would allow, several proposals were made to include the developing countries such as those in Sub-Saharan Africa. Specifically, the proposals included a revised timeline whereas the developing countries would be able to phase in the various pillars of coverage in accordance with their stage of economic transformation. The Convention by this time had accepted the theory of modernization (Chapter V) in projecting the progress of countries over time. Finally, it was concluded that Modernization, especially the anticipated economic transformation as expressed by theorists, such as Rostow would eventually resolve the issues surrounding future social protection issues in Sub-Saharan Africa. During the Convention there was a degree of optimism and/or expectation that, 'a supposition that was grounded on the experience of industrialized economies – that such graduation would happen automatically in the course of development and would lead to increased population coverage under contributory social security programs' (Hagemejer and McKinnon, ibid, 2013, pp. 5-6). The optimism of the time that the newly developing and independent countries would follow a similar path soon began to fade. More than a half-century later, the vast majority of the labor force in Sub-Saharan Africa remains in the informal sector. It has been more than six decades since the 1952 Minimum Standards Convention, and yet only 16.9% of older people in Sub-Saharan Africa have a social pension. **It is time for global action, including national governments as well as civil society organizations to demand actions on behalf the "silver tsunami."**

In the musical culture known as "Hip Hop" the artist known as Drake expresses the realities that would confront the newly emerging countries, "Starting from the bottom now I am here." Yes, the former colonized countries have started from the bottom, but for the most part not quite here at this point in time. The African Poet, Okri further expounds on the realities of the Continent as it attempts to become a player on the global economic stage. "Africa stepped onto a world stage with its hands tied, the contract of nations negotiated against it favor. It was joining a game in which all of the contestants had been in training for centuries, had set the rules of the game, and had all of the best facilities and the bias of the ages; and it was joining this game with broken arms and legs" (Ben Okri, "The Spirit of Africa.")

As the world is aware, including those decision-makers attending the 1952 Convention, for a variety of reasons, the projections did not materialize as expected. It appears that the global community, especially the former colonizers or Western powers avoided taking a pro-active role in foreign direct investments in Africa's economic growth and transformation. The Western world has had a long history, as illustrated in Conventions, of labor organizing strategies and tactics, including the development of tripartite collective bargaining systems. The International Labor Organization has demonstrated historically, including the 1930 forced Labor Convention its commitment for the social welfare and social protection for workers and their families; the ILO has not find a similar commitment from global governments and their leaders for ensuring social protection for workers and families. Once again why was there not a Marshall Plan for Africa? The results have been a continent dominated by an informal labor system without guarantees of systems for social protection beyond retirement.

Structural Adjustment Programs (SAP) – Western powers, especially the United States and Great Britain, following the collapse of Russia's communist economic system, decided that Capitalism should be the model for economic growth globally, especially in the developing world. So political leaders such as Ronald Regan of the United States, Margaret Thatcher, of Great Britain, were instrumental in the development of two major institutions, The World Bank, and The International Monetary Fund. As developing countries in Sub-Saharan Africa, as well other parts of the world were struggling to survive ongoing economic woes that had stagnated economic growth following independence, the concept structural adjustment was introduced in Africa and other parts of the world. In their efforts, based on their analysis of what was troubling Africa economically, these Western powers in the early 1980's introduced what they considered as solutions to the problems. The primary or major goals were to significantly curtail or decrease the level of government interventions in the economies of the developing countries, reducing the countries deficits, and helping the countries in opening their economies to global markets.

The results of the Western powers conceptualization of the problems, no evidence of input from the developing countries, were strategies focused on what became known as Structural Adjustment Programs (SAP); the Western powers primary strategy of helping the developing countries were based on loans and not foreign direct investments. To qualify for a loan, initially and continuing loans; once again there was no evidence of involvement of countries targeted to benefit. Countries had to agree to the rules that had been set forth by the aforementioned institutions, The World Bank and the International Monetary Fund. Countries who did not comply with the policies would have their loans terminated and/or rejected for future loans; the interest on loans had to be made on a timely basis or loans would be terminated. The structural adjustment policies and programs had been conceptualized for the purpose of providing incentives for generating income, and reducing and/or paying off debts; also creating an environment for promoting economic growth and transformation (Toyin, Falola and Oyenini, Bukola A., "Africa in Focus: Nigeria, Latin America in Focus Series," ADC-CIO, California, 2015).

The SAP policies and programs had a tremendous impact on the formal as well as the informal economy sectors in developing countries. The SAP played a major role in the development of the informal sector. But, there is no evidence to suggest that the SAP decision-making ever approached the subject of social protection in the work place, or encouraged levels of cooperation with the formal sector. "The implementation of SAP invariably led to situations whereby governmental institutions, multinationals corporations, and privately owned firms outsourced labor through a myriad of small scale informal operations" (Toyin, et al, ibid, p. 127). It appears that the practice of job outsourcing, and the loss of jobs, helped to create and/or expand the private informal sector in Nigeria. Approximately 6 out of 10, workers were employed in the informal sector. "The SAP failed to deliver on…promises, and among other things, it weaned an unprecedented high informal sector operation instead" (Toyin, et al, ibid, 2015, p. 127). One of the major goals of the SAP was the privatization of public enterprises, the promotion and advocating for free market fundamentals, and bring about significant reductions in government expenditures, especially as they involved matters related to social welfare and social protection (Toyin et al, ibid, 2015).

Globally, there is a consensus among many that the structural adjustment programs were more detrimental, and/or resulted in, not only increased poverty but a lack of progress ensuring social protection for workers and their families. Western leaders and countries with a great deal of monetary clout creating the World Bank and the International Monetary Fund, seemingly were more interested in imposing an economic concept or system on developing countries at a time when they were more vulnerable. There seemed not to be any consideration of using these global institutions, World Bank and The International Monetary Fund, in providing technical assistance, and foreign direct investments, rather than loans for enhancing economic transformation in the developing world. In the process these global powers possibly could have used their influence to bring together the informal and formal sectors of labor, resulting in a tripartite collective bargaining system that would have greatly reduced the current number of older persons without social protection in their later lives.

Millennium Development Goals: The Exclusion of Social Protection for Older Persons – One would think that after several global assemblies on aging, follow up forums, conventions, as well as declarations on human rights, and social justice for older people, one specific MDG would be the reduction in the number of older people without a social pension. Considering the current percentage of those with s social pension in Sub-Saharan Africa at 16.5%, a 50% increase would have been a nice challenge by 2015. The exclusion of a specific goal as part of the MDGs passed up on a global opportunity to focus on the plight of older person without income security, and access to social and health care. Yes, there is global advocacy currently under-way, including the Age Demand Campaign spearheaded by Help-Age International, but being part of the MDGs would have brought more attention to the problem. Most governments, especially in Sub-Saharan Africa during the past decade have searched for innovative ways for reducing poverty, expanding access to education, health and social services. It would have been appropriate, because of the severity of the problem, to include a measurable objective followed by selective methods for reducing the number of older persons without income security within the Millennium Development Goals.

Sustainable Development Goals 2020: The Exclusion of Social Protection for Older Persons – History keeps repeating itself. The same conclusion reference the United Nations Sustainable Development Goals can be repeated. There were no specific goals for reducing the number of older persons globally without a social pension following retirement.

AFRICA'S RENAISSANCE/AN EMERGING "NEW SPIRIT" FOR GETTING THINGS DONE: IMPLICATIONS FOR SOCIAL PROTECTION/ PENSIONS FOR THE GROWING OLDER POPULATION

The tremendous need for social protection/social pension is very well established for the older population in Sub-Saharan Africa. There is also the evidence that providing a social pension to the older population can have significant benefits, the children, the older people, as well as contributing to economic growth. Research supports the conclusion that it is affordable. Declarations from international policy-making bodies have been presented that justify the need. It is now time for a movement in full collaboration with the Aging Demand Campaign for the enactment of a social pension for the growing older population in all countries.

The "Silver Tsunami," or the growing older population in Sub-Saharan Africa will present many challenges. One major challenge is ensuring that each older person at the time of retirement will be able to live in dignity with income security, adequate housing, and access to health and social services. When one considers that less than 20% of the older population now has a social pension at retirement, the task may seem insurmountable. But there are a new generation of scholars, educators, activists, journalist, that are part of a "new spirit," that have been emerging now for some time on the continent. There appears to be a new spirit for getting things done, rather than a preoccupation with the past. The poetic narrative below coming from Ben Okri expresses the "new spirit." For Okri, Africa "… is perfectly poised for a new destination. The time is now to take the first step in our renaissance…" For Okri "the moment is now".

The current movement in Africa, "Africa Rising" incorporates within the "new spirit," or current proactive behavior that is all about putting the past behind and moving forward. There is a message for all people globally who continue to hang on to all of the historical myths about the continent of Africa, Tarzan does not live there anymore; for a growing number of people globally, Africa is the new frontier (Beckett, Justin and Sudarkasa, E., Investing in Africa, Wiley Publishers, 2002).

As aforementioned a new movement on the African Continent begin in 2016, African Rising for Justice, Peace and Dignity. This new movement was the results of ongoing dialogues among various social movements, non-governmental organizations, social justice activists and intellectuals, including artists, athletes and cultural activists from all across the Continent. The current vision of the movement continues to be focused on enhanced democracy, equality and the eradication of social injustices confronted daily by people across the Continent. In efforts to become more effective in reaching its goals African Rising for Justice, Peace and Dignity has launched a very significant program Activists In Residence (AIR) Second Edition. This program is being launched in partnership with the Training Center for Development Cooperation (TCDC). The primary purpose of AIR is "strengthening the infrastructure of societal transformation by providing a time and space to recharge, re-energize and recuperate leaders, human rights defenders, activists and artists. AIR will provide activists an opportunity to reflect upon their different contextual challenges in the pursuit of justice, peace and dignity in creating the Africa we want. Program (2nd Edition) will be held in Arusha, Tanzania between November 8-30 2018 bringing together 10 activists from 10 different African Continents to build their mental, physical, digital and strategic resilience" (Africans Rising's Edition of the Activist in Residence Program (AIR), engagement@africans-rising.org, pages 1-3, 2018).

"The Spirit of Africa's People Will Transform the Continent" (Ben Okri, African Poetic Leader of the African Renaissance)

"Our nations were shaped by outside forces and faced instability from their creation. But from art to business I can see the resilience and creativity that will help us overcome the challenges...For most of the 20th Century Africa made an epic journey: from its original way, through the trauma of colonialism and into the flawed daylight of independence. It made a journey in 50 years that it took other continents centuries – and, in some nations, thousands of years – to accomplish. We all know that the terms of African Independence were flawed at birth; Africa stepped on to the world stage with its hands tied, the contract of nations negotiated against it favor. It was joining a game in which all the contestants had been in training for centuries, had set the rules of the game, and had all of the best facilities and the bias of the ages; and it was joining this game with broken arms and legs, confidence shattered, spirit shattered... We have been tearing ourselves apart while the world gathered the treasurers of the Earth. The first step in our renaissance has to be putting our house in order. This is a moment in which Africa's road is famished and perfectly poised for a new destination" Excerpt from a lecture by Ben Okri presented to the Centre for African Renaissance Studies, Pretoria, South Africa – Guardian and Observer (Guardian News and Media) Monday 9/7/2015 – 4:45:38 AM.

Ben Okri and African Journalists such as Charlayne Hunter Gault (USA, working as a reporter in South Africa, do represent a new spirit and a way of thinking about Africa. In the new spirit of Africa, especially among the young, there is more of a positive attitude about the continent despite all of the historical injustices. Unlike the Special Edition of The Economist Journal approximately fifteen years ago with its headline, "The Hopeless Continent" (The Economist, Special Edition, "The Hopeless Continent," London, May 13-19, 2000, Journalist such as Hunter-Gault speaks about "the new wind blowing across the Continent...the promise of an African renaissance..." Hunter Gault, Charlayne, New News Out of Africa: Uncovering Africa's Renaissance, New York: Oxford University Press, 2006, p. 107).

It is interesting to note that approximately fifteen years later the Economist published an updated Special Edition, Africa Rising, with reference to Africa's rising economy, The Economist, Special Edition, "Africa Rising," London, December 5, 2011). Africa is no longer viewed as the "The Hopeless Continent." In Africa there is a new spirit and buoyancy capturing or pervading the Continent. A writer for the New York Times recently writing about a city in Cleveland, Ohio USA that last won a major sports Championship (baseball, 1948) approximately sixty-eight years ago. In 2016, the Basketball team won the National Basketball Association Championship, the first in more than a half-century ago that the City had accomplished such a feat. The Championship brought new buoyancy to the city "...that has spilled out, largely undiminished, into some of the less scenic corners of the city" (Hyduk, John, A Year That Can never Be Taken From Cleveland," New York Times, Sunday, 1/1/2017, p. 4). The writer concluded that in Cleveland, Ohio hope can no longer be stopped nor can hope be contained. In other words soon there will be Championships in the other major sports such as football and baseball.

So, why the optimism regarding a social pension for older person much sooner than later? It is that the "new spirit" and the "African renaissance" along with an era of economic growth, and a new way of thinking that will result in policies to protect needs of a growing older population, the "Silver Tsunami." Yes, there will be policies and/or statutes that will ensure that the older population in Sub-Saharan Africa will be able to live their remaining years, not only in dignity, also as full participants in the new renaissance. Yes, there is a new spirit that cannot be stopped nor be contained.

No, it is not considered a very positive note that only eleven countries out of 47 in Sub-Saharan Africa with a statutory social pension for their older populations, on the other hand in an unprecedented positive initiative approximately fifteen countries are now reaching out to the informal and/or informal sectors. The results will eventually be a reduction of older people without social protection, more specifically a social pension among future generations.

SUMMARY/CONCLUSION

For the past three decades, global Conventions, including the World Assemblies, as well as global civic organizations, have reaffirmed the basic human rights of a growing older population. The ILO Convention on Social Protection Floors Recommendation 202 stated that the social protection floors should include four basic social security guarantees. One guarantee called for "... basic income security... for older persons," as well as "... basic income security ... for persons in active age who are unable to earn sufficient income, in particular cases of sickness, unemployment, maternity and disability..." (ILO: Recommendation 202, Geneva, 101st Session, 2012, p.3).

It should be clear from the aforementioned definition and principles that the older population, including the active age group, has the rights to social protection, including basic income security. The problems of extending social protection to the self-employed, and/or those who have labored throughout their lives in the informal sectors of the labor market continue to be a major challenge, especially countries in Sub-Saharan Africa. Although this issue has been around for decades, especially in the developing world, none of the conventions have been able to put forward a conceptual framework and specific strategies toward a solution. The fact that the problem has been around for years and no solution(s) is a major reason why the subject of a social pension is been advocated for extending social protection for the current and future older populations. The advocates for a social or civic pension are addressing the urgent need for a population who has been excluded, for whatever the reasons, from a tripartite labor market system of social protection.

It is difficult to understand how global international organizations, such as the ILO, the ISSA, the United Nations, who have a history of pension reform going back for decades, did not successfully challenge the omission of a social pension as a human right for the population of seniors without coverage, as part of the Millennium Development Goals for 2015, and the 2020 Sustainable Development Goals.

CHAPTER VIII

ECONOMIC GROWTH, THE "YOUTH BULGE" GENERATION AND THE "RISING AFRICAN SPIRIT": IMPLICATIONS FOR SOCIAL POLICIES, PROGRAMS AND ENHANCED QUALITY OF LIFE FOR ALL

INTRODUCTION

The economic status of a country plays a major role in determining its capacity and readiness for enhancing the overall quality of life for all citizens. This applies not only in regards to an old age social pension, although it requires high priority, but also the implementation of social policies and programs addressing the needs of citizens across all age groups. Sustained economic growth and development provide opportunities for children and youth to pursue a quality education that allows for maximum growth in a developing cybernetic society. A country's readiness and commitment to implement new social programs, such as a social pension is not just a matter of affordability but sustainability as well (Heller, Peter, "Understanding Fiscal Space," International Monetary Fund (IMF), 2003 page 3). Sustainability has to do with the "...capacity of a government...to finance its desired expenditure programs, to service any debt obligations (including those that may arise if the created fiscal space arise from government borrowing) and to ensure its solvency" (Heller, ibid, 2003 p 4). So, the challenge becomes more than just determining affordability and finding fiscal space within the budget, but will the countries have the on-going resources from current and future revenues to sustain those program(s) (Heller, ibid, 2003)?

The evidence from global research sources has concluded that a correlation does exist between economic growth and the introduction of statutory social programs such as a social pension. Therefore, it becomes imperative that political, civic leaders, and non-governmental organizations, comprehend the importance of the correlation and/or relationship between the two factors. If social protection programs in Sub-Saharan Africa are going to "...contribute actively to positive social and economic outcomes, social protection policy goals cannot be pursued in isolation; they must be promoted alongside a broad range of coherently applied policy actions…" (ISSA, Africa: Strategic Approaches to Improve Social Security, Development and Trends 2014, pages 26-27). A country's economic growth and transformation becomes critical and essential when there is a commitment for ensuring the overall quality of life, income security, safety, and access to education, health and social services, not only for a growing older population, but enhancing the quality of life for citizens across all age groups.

Although, there seem to be sufficient evidence of sustained economic growth in Africa some economists and scholars have expressed caution in speaking of an economic renaissance. Cautious optimism is understandable when one considers some of the uncontrollable global trends; one example of an external uncontrollable economic trend that could impact Sub-Saharan Africa and other developing countries, has been recent downturns in the economy of China. Despite the downturns China is still considered to have the second best economy globally after the United States. China has become an economic partner on continents such as Sub-Saharan Africa as well as in the Latin American countries. China has made some tremendous investments in Latin America, especially involving infrastructure development projects. The downturns in China's economic growth patterns can have an impact on a country's commodity prices as well as an impact on overall economic growth and transformation. An example of one internal economic threat to sustained economic growth in Sub-Saharan Africa is related to a lack of a strong productive electrical infrastructure. Although there is a great deal of optimism regarding sustained economic growth, the aforementioned examples of potential deterrents, electrical power issues, and commodity prices, could have an impact or become a deterrent to economic growth. Foreign Direct Investments (FDI) in infrastructure developments such as in electric power systems and transportation is one reason African leadership is currently focusing less on foreign aid and more on FDI. China, not just in Latin America, has become a major contributor to FDI in Sub-Saharan Africa. Despite the potential threats or deterrents to continuing economic growth and transformation, there is a growing new spirit, especially among the growing youth population in Sub-Saharan Africa, of confronting the economic, social and political challenges and moving forward.

Chapter, VII highlighted several very important conclusions to be considered as the continent moves forward towards the future: First, there is an urgent and critical need for a social or civic pension in Sub-Saharan Africa in preparing for the "Silver Tsunami." The growing older population will have need of, not just social pensions, also other forms of social protection such as access to health, medical and social services, including long-term care. Secondly, research demonstrates that a statutory social or civic pension is affordable, achievable and sustainable. The success of a number of Sub-Saharan African countries, including Liberia listed by the World Bank as a Low Income country with a p/capita income of only $970 have reinforced that perspective; yes Liberia has a statutory social pension. Thirdly, it is extremely important and research strongly illustrates that there are very significant benefits a country can derive from a social pension, including the reduction in poverty, unemployment and support for the preparation and/or socialization of children, especially educational achievements. Considering the importance of an increasing role grandparents are playing in the socialization of children a social pension becomes an imperative. The aforementioned benefits, not only include a reduction in poverty and unemployment, they also contribute significantly to economic growth and development.

AFRICA'S ECONOMIC RENAISSANCE: CURRENT AND FUTURE PROJECTIONS

The current picture of economic growth occurring throughout Sub-Saharan Africa should be a time for optimism and celebration. For some global experts, especially economists, Africa's economy is in a renaissance phase and that should be a major incentive for the region to move forward, not just the enactment of a social pension, but social polices and programs for enhancing the quality of life of all age groups. The consensus of a significant number of Economists is that Africa's economy was in the midst of an unprecedented growth (Robertson, Charles, et al, The Fastest Billion: The Story Behind Africa's Economic Revolution: The Story Behind Africa's Economic Revolution, UK: Renaissance Capital Securities, 2012). The book highlighted a growing global consensus that "From the vantage point of many in the West, Africa remains a continent of woes, a continent stalked by conflict among various groups, corrupt dictatorships, religious strife, war and famine. Investors, economists, fund managers, and academics are now challenging the narratives that have portrayed Africa as a continent of woes. The world is now being informed that there is a "new spirit" in Africa. According to Beckett, "Tarzan does not live here anymore" (Beckett and Sudarkasa, ibid, 2000, p.3); in other words the new spirit in Africa is saying it's time to move on. Some investment economists are now viewing Africa as the final frontier (Beckett, ibid, 2000). Africa now has more of the world's fastest growing economies than any other continent (Robertson, ibid, 2012 p. 1). Following years of economic and social development struggles, Sub-Saharan Africa is making significant strides in an attempt to play an important role in the global economic community.

As aforementioned by Robertson, Africa has some of the world's fastest growing economies and a good example is Ethiopia. Ethiopia within the last dozen years has achieved double-digit growth; globally, it has now become the fourth fastest growing economy. If the country can maintain its current pace of economic growth by the year 2025 it will transition from the category low-income to middle income status. Ethiopia currently is the fastest growing non-oil producing country in the world. What can other countries learn from Ethiopia's success? Ethiopia primary decision for success has been focused on investments in public infrastructure in the area of energy, transport, communications, and the social sectors. Ethiopia has recognized that what drives economic growth are infrastructure investments (World Bank Blog, African Can End Poverty, "Ethiopia's Great Miracle: What will it take to sustain it?" Blog Submitted by Lars Christian Moller, 12/11/2015). There is evidence that what is being referred to as the "African Economic Renaissance" had not by 2013 begin to stagnate but continued its upward spiral, 5% over the past decade. This was happening when "...most of the developed world was still recovering from the global economic crisis" (The World Bank: The African Competitiveness Report 2013 "Assessing Africa's Competitiveness," World Economic Forum, 2013, pages 3-18).

It is interesting to note that even in the midst of the global financial crisis most of the Sub-Saharan countries were reporting significant economic growth over the past decade. The GDP growth rate was projected to be around 4.9%, according to economists, during the year 2013; the rate in 2012 was 4.2%. The projection for the year 2014 was 5.2%. The projections for the region should reach 5.5% by 2015 according to the World Bank (World Bank – Africa: Working for a World Free of Poverty, Vol. 8, October 7 2013; Vol. 9 April 7 2014). According to the most recent World Bank Report, 2016, the projection of 5.2% in 2014 only reached 4.6% not

5.2; and the projection of 5.5% by 2015 only reached 3.4% **(See Appendix A: Tables/Charts, Chapter VIII, Tables 1-4).**

Past, Current and Future Economic Projections

First of all, the decline in economic growth from 4.6% in 2014 to 3.4% in 2015, represented the "...weakest performance in Sub-Saharan Africa since 2009" (World Bank, ibid, 2016, p. 153). The factors contributing to a significant slowing of the economy during this time period, externally were lower commodity prices, a significant slowdown involving major trading partners, and borrowing conditions became tighter. There were also internal factors to be considered, such as political instability, various conflicts, and infrastructure issues related to shortages of electricity or power sources (World Bank, ibid, 2016).

A slow down in the African economy beginning around 2014 to some experts and naysayers were that Africa had its "day in the sun" or "Renaissance." Globally, all countries will experience economic growth slowdowns but also upswings over a period of years. Africa has demonstrated in recent decades that it is not only ready but prepared to become part of the global economy; not unlike other countries Africa will continue to experience "upswings" and "downswings" in its economy. The United Kingdom and other European countries have been experiencing downturns or economic growth stagnation in recent years **(See Appendix A: Tables/Charts, Chapter VIII, Table 1).**

Factors contributing to the economic slowdown had its most significant impact on countries, such as Nigeria, the oil exporters. Nigeria who has the Region's largest economy as well as the largest exporter of oil, witnessed a slowdown in economic growth from 6.3% in 2014 to 3.3% in 2015. There was, although slight, some positive movement among the countries in the business of exporting minerals and metals, such as Mauritania, South Africa and Zambia. The South Africa economy, for example, did expand by 1.3% in 2015 in comparison with 1.5% in 2014 (World Bank, ibid, 2016).

The impact of the Ebola crisis had a negative impact on some of the countries during the time frame 2014-2015; as the crisis slowed down or decreased in impact, economic activities in Liberia somewhat rebounded. But other countries, such as Guinea, Sierra Leone, the economies of these countries remained rather weak. Economic activities decreased significantly in countries such as Burundi and South Sudan primarily as a result of political instability. It is interesting to note from the World Bank Report that during the aforementioned time period countries such as Cote d'Ivoire, Rwanda, and Tanzania, economically "...remained rather robust partly due to lower exposure from the commodity slowdown, and fallouts from infrastructure investments" (World Bank, ibid, p.153). Two of the countries, Rwanda and Tanzania are classified as Low-Income countries, and the Cote d'Ivoire is classified as Low-Middle Income (World Bank, Country Income Analysis, 2016). It should be noted that the broad variations, economically, culturally, degree of political stability, and a country's history of responding to economic, social and health shocks, across a Region such as Sub-Saharan Africa, affect the populations differently.

In taking a look at the future, one projection and a very important one is that commodity prices will stabilize but continue or remain low through the 2017 year. A continuing major deterrent to economic development has to do with the issue of electrical power; the projections are that this problem will continue. These continuing issues have prognosticators backing away from earlier projections and indicating a moderate recovery in 2016. But, projections are that economic growth is expected to climb to 4.2% by the end of 2016, and to 4.7% in 2017-2018, back to what it was in 2014, 4.6%. "These projections assume that commodity prices will stabilize, and electricity constraints ease. These are, however, considered variations within the region" (World Bank, 2016, p.156).

Africa's Economic Rising

Despite some slowdowns, especially between the time period 2012 to 2015, Africa is beginning to rise again economically. During the year 2016 Africa's GDP was 2.1% following a disappointing decline from 2012 to 2015. Economists are projecting that by the year 2021, just five years away the GDP will reach 4.5%. Two Regions Asia, Pacific and Central America recorded higher growth in 2016 than Africa, 5.2% and 3.9% respectively. The very positive projection is that Africa will become the second fastest region 4.4% GDP growth rate once again in 2019. Asia and the Pacific are the only two regions that will record a higher GDP growth rate 5.4% than Africa. African countries have become some of the best performers in regards to economic growth globally; between 2004 an 2014, despite the slowdowns ten African countries were ranked within the fastest growing economies globally. The two areas considered so critical to economic growth and transformation are services and industrial output. Between the years 2006-2014 of the top twenty countries having the highest growth in services eight were located in Africa; during the same period 2006-2014 nine of the twenty countries with the highest industrial output were in Africa. Ethiopia who ranks four among the fastest growing economies, is ranked 1st among the twenty fastest growing economies related to services. In reference to industrial output Sierra Leone is ranked 2nd among the twenty countries, as aforementioned nine of those twenty are in Africa (Ibrahim Foundation 2017 Forum Report: Africa at a Turning Point, "Back on the Growth Path African Population and Real GDP Growth Rate, Africa," Mo Ibrahim 2017 Forum, p 10-11) **(See Appendix A: Tables/Charts, Chapter VIII, Tables 1-4).**

SELECTIVE FACTORS CONTRIBUTING TO ECONOMIC GROWTH AND TRANSFORMATION IN SUB-SAHARAN AFRICA

Improved Inter-Intra Continent/Country Economic Partnerships

Factors responsible for Sub-Saharan Africa's sustained economic growth in recent decades are related to several significant factors: First, there seems to be a very strong consensus related to investments, public and private as well as intra-inter economic activities taking place within and beyond the continent. Secondly, another factor is related to the increasing growth in household consumption. Thirdly, according to the World Bank, "The rise in commodity prices, and the surge of foreign capital spurred by accommodative monetary policies in high-income economies, is key to the region's sustained growth since the mid-1990's" (World Bank, vol. 9, 4/7/2014).

The diversification of trading partners by Sub-Saharan countries seemingly has had a major impact on economic growth. Trading in expanded markets such as the "BRIC" (Brazil, Russia, China, India, more recently South Africa became a member) countries during the past decade has contributed to economic growth. During the past decade the growth of exports to the BRIC countries increased by approximately 24%; exports to the BRIC countries in 2000 was 9%, but a decade later had reached 34%. Another factor that has played a very important role during a period of strong economic growth is that in the Sub-Saharan countries, government officials seem to have provided more initiatives for investment spending. One of the reasons given for the increase in investment spending, according to the World Bank Annual Doing Business Report, is that the governments in the Sub-Saharan countries have expended a great deal of human energy creating an environment that will "make life better for investors." The World Bank Report of 2013-2014 reported that the countries in Sub-Saharan Africa did more to improve the regulations or regulatory reform, needed for business operations than any other region.

Improved Infrastructure Developments, Energy and Railroads Development

Countries such as Ethiopia, Ghana, Namibia, Niger, Nigeria, South Africa, Tanzania, and Zambia have been focusing investments toward basic infrastructure, including power generation, roads and port facilities (World Bank: vol. 8, 10/7/2013). These are critical areas for investments for enhancing the region's level of competitiveness on a global scale. It should be noted that by the year 2050 three Sub-Saharan countries, Ethiopia and Nigeria, aforementioned in the previous paragraph, and the Democratic Republic of the Congo, would be among the ten countries in the world with the largest populations. With the exit of Russia, Europe does not have a country listed within the top ten (Bloomberg Business: Steve Matthews, "These 10 Countries Will Have the World's Biggest Populations By 2050," August 18, 2013).

Historically, commodities in African countries have been a key factor in exports but there is evidence that a significant change is taking place. Economic growth in the region is beginning to come from places other than basic commodities. "Manufacturing output… is expanding as quickly as the rest of the economy. Growth is even faster in services, which expanded at an average rate of 2.6% p/person across Africa between 1966 and 2011" (The Economist: "The Twilight of the Research Curse," 1/10/2015). Not only manufacturing and services but tourism as well. Between 2000 and 2012, visitors to the country doubled, and receipts tripled. Some countries in Sub-Saharan are revising their GDP estimations in order to provide a more accurate accounting of this all important non-resource sectors. The areas of telecommunications, transportation, as well as finance, are expected to play a future role in economic growth (The Economist, 2015, ibid).

Another major change in factors related to economic transformation is Foreign Direct Investments. African officials for sometime now have been emphasizing the need to dramatically shift from AID programs to Foreign Direct Investments. In recent years the region has seen a significant increase in Foreign Direct Investments as a percentage of GDP; FDI increased from 5% in 2012 to 10% in 2013 (The Economist, 2015, ibid). A change is also occurring in regards to the destination of FDI investments. Historically, the greatest percentage of the FDI investments was channeled towards the resource-rich African countries. The current trend sees the economic-poor countries receiving a share of the FDI investments as well. Although the resource rich countries continue to receive more FDI investments in absolute terms, but when measured as a share of the GDP, the economic-poor countries actually receive more in investments. It is of interest that foreign investors from Africa seem quite interested in non-commodity industries, such as financial services, approximately one-third of their investments (The Economist, 2015, Ibid).

In recent years, Nigeria has been Africa's largest economy and its economic growth has been around 5%. But, its continuing growth during that time has not only come from oil but other sectors as well. Oil has for the most part accounted for about 95% of all exports, but a change in this trend is beginning to emerge. Since there has been what some economists consider a period of oil stagnation, exports have come other sectors, including mobile phones, construction, and banking. Surprisingly, the service sector now represents about 60% of the GDP. Similar trends are occurring in other Sub-Saharan countries such as Angola and Botswana. Angola, the second largest oil producer saw it growth rate reach 5.1%in 2013. But this growth was not primarily due to oil exports but from manufacturing and construction; the fishing industry expanded by 10% and agriculture by 9%. Currently approximately one-third of government revenues are from the non-oil sector of the economy. A decade ago "0" revenues came from the non-oil sector. Botswana, known for it productive diamond fields following Independence, has seen the mining sector, diamonds, gold and copper fall from 46% in 2006 to 35% in 2011 (The Economist, 2015, ibid).

The growing evidence is that Sub-Saharan Africa is no longer totally dependent on International AID packages but now more and more expectations are from inter/intra Direct Investments. In recent years or the last decade, the world has and continues to observe significant growth in Foreign Direct Investments. The commodities boom partly resulting from significant developmental sales in the Asian region, as well as the "...massive expansion of moving international trade activities off shore..." are factors contributing to the successful economic growth in the region. It has been recognized that the expansion and/or increase of Foreign Direct Investment in the region will not just provide expanded job opportunities but the region should anticipate "...new opportunities through deeper global trade integration" (World Bank: Punam Chuhan-Pole, African Pulse, Vol. 9, 4/7/2014, USA: Washington D.C.).

For Sub-Saharan Africa, the natural resources and service sectors are critical when it comes to new opportunities in global trading. "The resources and service sectors are Sub-Saharan Africa's best performers. The share of the Resource Sector rose from 9% during 1995-99 to 12.5% during 2007-2011, while that of the service sector grew from 40% to 47%... During 1995-2012 the region's total exports increased from $68 Billion to over $400 Billion. Most of this increase came from natural resources' exports. Example, petroleum, minerals, and metal exports ballooned from $38 Billion to $300 Billion during the period (World Bank: Chuhan-Pole, 2014, ibid).

Another very significant trend, aforementioned, occurring in Sub-Saharan Africa is an increase in intra-regional market activities. There is a growing emphasis on internal markets. "The value of formal intra African trade has increased almost five-fold in absolute terms between 2001 and 2012; though its relative share has remained constant at around 12% and sits below other regions" (African Development Report, Africa's Development Bank Group, Mthuli Ncube, Chief Economist, Cote d'Ivoire, 2014; "Regional Integration for Inclusive Growth," pages 1-5). Although Sub-Saharan Africa's share of the external markets remain below that of other Regions, the 2014 Development Report maintains that "Regional integration is …a relevant pillar for Africa's development…no new policies are needed but implementation of those formulated in the past" (African Development Report 2014, ibid, pages 9-15).

The agriculture sector is a specific example of intra-regional collaboration. "…Intra-African greenfield Foreign Direct Investment projects as a percentage of greenfield inflows into Africa almost tripled between 2003-2013, from 7% in 2003 to over 21% in 2013. This trend is driven by a continuous rise in South African Foreign Direct Investment in the continent, and supported by a dramatic increase …from Kenya and Nigeria since 2008…firms in these countries accounted for nearly 60% of project overflows into Africa between 2003-2013" (African Development Report 2014, ibid, pages 27-45). Tanzania is another example of changes related to intra-regional collaboration. For example, Tanzania's geographical distribution of exports, during the last decade to the European Union decreased, but intra-regional trade to other Sub-Saharan African countries, specifically South Africa and East Africa expanded (World Bank: Africa's Pulse, vol. 9, 4/7/2014).

The 2014 African Development Forum that convened in October 2014 in Marrakech Morocco addressed the State of Economic Growth and Transformation in Africa. One major Theme on the agenda focused on how internal resources in African countries' can be better mobilized to diversify their financial sources; furthermore, how new strategic partnerships can be established to promote economic growth and transformation. In a major address, Mr. Carlos Lopes, Executive Secretary, United Nations Economic Commission for Africa, challenged the delegates in regards to economic development issues. He noted in his remarks that Africa in the past and present had become too occupied "…trying to get handouts or support from other governments, and too little effort in terms of what you can collect your selves and how you can improve your systems. According to Mr. Lopes, in regards to economic growth, capital flow into Africa in 2013 was higher than the flow of Aid. This particular observation partly supports his observation that more focus in Africa should be on capital investments than on donor aid. To further support his original point reference capital and aid, Capital flowing into Africa in 2013 reached 60 billion, Commercial liquidity that was not used was approximately 80 billion, Central Bank Reserves approximately 600 billion, and Sovereign Funds were worth approximately 18 billion. Furthermore, since 1995 Africa's aggregated GDP has doubled from 700 billion to 1.4 trillion in 2013 (United Nations, Economic Commission for Africa, African Development Forum, Theme: Innovative Financing For Africa's Transformation, 14-16 October 2014).

Another participant at the Africa Forum, Mr. Abdalla Hamdok, Africa Development Forum 2014, Deputy Executive Secretary, Economic Commission for Africa, expressed the need for innovative financing, including sustainable development financing. There seemed to have been a strong consensus during the Forum that development financing was a crucial need and challenge for the region. Included in the package of ideas for a new approach included innovative forms of international relationships, contracts that will ensure mutual accountability within the traditional donor-recipient relationship. Another strong recommendation coming out of the Forum related to some oversight in ensuring that the promises set forth in the UN Millennium Development Goals, especially the 0.7% development assistance target is carried out. Other Themes emerging from the 2014 Forum were a consensus that in order to enhance Africa's economic transformation there was a need for a stronger partnership between the public and private sector; a need for the region to generate more resources from within its own economic sectors; the tracking of Africa's lost or stolen billions; and to support Mr. Lopes narrative, the region was in need of a new AID paradigm.

One Theme of major importance emanating from the 2014 Forum that will no doubt be applauded by the "Age Demand Campaign," was a conclusion that "Private equity and the growth of pension funds provide a massive opportunity to finance investment." The Campaign under the leadership of Help Age International and other global advocates, including Bishop Desmond Tutu, moral leader of South Africa and Noble Peace Laureate, has been calling for the United Nations to address social issues, especially pensions, of older people. Only 16.9% of retirees in Sub-Saharan Africa will have basic income security on reaching retirement age.

The 2014 Forum addressed the role of China as an investment partner in Africa. It appears that China has become Africa's number one Foreign Direct Investment partner (FDI); China's trading currently reaches $210 billion 2013, from $166 billion in 2011, $198 billion in 2012. China's contributions towards economic transformation have been in the areas of trade as well as infrastructure development. Currently China is involved in major projects or multi-million development projects in road construction, railways, ports and airports. These are familiar projects that Western countries have ceased providing fund packages for. China's Foreign Direct Investment in China was $3.5 in 2013 that carried a year-on-year growth rate of 20.3 %. It is projected that China's cumulative direct investment is expected to reach $100 billion by the year 2020. Chinese Premier Li Keqiang in an address before the African Union, Addis Ababa in 2013 announced that China would be increasing loans to African countries by $10 that would bring the current total to $30 billion. He also announced that China would increase the Africa-China Development Fund from $2 billion to $5 billion (Olingo, 11/29/14, page 1).

A "New Spirit" and Growing Optimism in Africa: Implications for Social Protection For All

For social pension advocates there is reason to be optimistic in regards to Sub-Saharan Africa. The Region as aforementioned during the past several decades has been experiencing unprecedented sustained economic growth. Also, accompanying the economic growth phenomenon in Sub-Saharan Africa is a new positive spirit and a growing level of confidence among a growing and highly educated youth movement who has embraced the cybernetic world. One of the new spiritual leaders is described as the poetic leader of the New African Renaissance Era, Ben Okri. For Okri the time is now for the continent to take the initial steps in what is being described as the African Renaissance. For Okri and others, the focus is on getting things done now rather than concentrating on the past. In recent years, college students as well as labor, religious and civic groups have been actively involved in protest in challenging political and government leaders to get rid of corruption as well as other illicit business practices. They now realize that such practices are a major deterrent to economic growth and enhancing the quality of life across all age groups, including the growing older population, the "Silver Tsunami."

Ben Okri is one of a growing number of young Africans who are demanding social, political and economic changes on the continent; they do not want to be just observers with occasional input, but on-going active participation in the decision-making process. As aforementioned, one example is the new "Africa Rising" movement recently focused on justice, peace and dignity launched across the continent on the 25th of May 2017. The movement is comprised of current social movements, non-governmental organizations, artists, intellectuals and cultural artists. The date May 25th symbolizes the day of African Liberation, the founding of the Organization of African Unity that occurred on the aforementioned date in 1963; the mission of the Union at the time was to free the continent and its people from foreign domination. According to the current organizers, the original goal remains the same, but a very important statement has been added: "…determination to liberate ourselves from all exploitation and ensure a better life for all Africans (Naidoo, Kumi (Launch Director) "Africa Rising," africans-rising.org, May 23, 2017.

As aforementioned, The "African Rising" movement was launched on May 25 2017 in all of the African countries and the movement continues to gain momentum not only on the continent it has spread throughout the diaspora. Reports are that African Liberation Day on the historical May 25th date was very successful in 2018. According to the organizers Liberation Day 2018 were successful due to the mobilization of thousands of social activists from various countries; on the aforementioned date approximately seventy activities were carried out in fifty-two countries, forty-seven in Africa. Some of the aforementioned activities included: Youth in Gambia focused on cleaning the pollution residues on the beaches; political prisoners took part in the mobilization from their prison cells; youth in Burkina Faso mobilized to discuss their and the country's future; participants in Cote d'Ivoire came together to discuss human trafficking and the physical and mental abuse being suffered by migrants from Africa in the Middle East (dgtl.africans-rising.org/May 28, 2018, 7:45 PM).

A major or a key goal for the "African Rising" launch "…is to ensure that Africans Rising inspires millions of African people to demand from the government good governance as they work collectively towards common goals of peace, social inclusion and shared prosperity. **We want to let our leaders know that we have had enough of this unjust system and we want to make clear our intention to work together, to build a new Africa" (www. africans-rising/25may/#what25).**

What is so remarkable about the "African Rising" movement is the increasing number of new millenniums; the youth and/or young people of Africa have impressed such leaders as Archbishop Desmond Tutu, Nobel Peace Prize Laureate of South Africa. The Archbishop had this to say in a conversation with a scholarly writer several years ago, 'I wish you could meet some of the young people I've been meeting. They take your breath away. Man! You sit there with your mouth agape, listening to these you people. They really can make the country hum! They do not see themselves as handicapped. They see all the opportunities, all the things they can become. The sky is the limit now! I get the sense we are a scintillating success waiting to happen! It's like, it's like we've become Americans! (Perry, Alex, <u>The Rift: A New Africa Breaks Free</u>, New York: Little, Brown and Company, 2015, p. 391)'

The "Youth Bulge Generation"

Currently there are several phrases that captures Africa's "Renaissance," in regards to economic growth and transformation: "Africa Rising," "It is Africa's Time," "The Fastest Billion, The Story Behind Africa's Economic Revolution," and "Africa's New Spirit." The global consensus is that Africa is one of the fastest growing economies in the world. A major question is can the continent that was described some two decades by a leading global publication, The Economist, as "Africa doomed," be able to continue with a positive level of sustainability? The aforementioned publication ten years later as the world was witnessing a significant period of growth, headlined its publication with the title "Africa Rising." Although there are numerous factors, such as continuous infrastructure development, intra-inter investments, administrative efficiency, and reduction in all forms of corruption, taking advantage of the "youth bulge" generation phenomenon can contribute as well to economic growth and transformation.

Global population growth as a result of declining fertility, mortality, medicine/public health education and practices, improved living standards, could have significant implications for economic growth and transformation, especially regarding changes in the age structure. "Declines in child mortality, followed by decline in fertility produce a 'bulge' generation and a period when a country has a large number of working age individuals and a smaller number of dependents" (Canning, David, Raja, Sangeeta, and Yazbeck, Abdo, "Africa's Demographic Transition Dividend or Disaster?" World Bank: Africa Development Forum, 2015, p. 1). This "youth bulge" working age generation will give a significant boost to a country's economy if there are sufficient job opportunities for them to take advantage of (Canning, et al, 2015). Demographic Scholars with an interest in demographic trends and economic activities are using the concept Demographic Dividend; the concept "...describes the interplay between changes in a population's age structure due to the demographic transition and rapid economic growth" (Canning, et al, 2015, p. 1).

From the perspective of an economist commenting on the subject of demographics as a Growth Factor, "When countries get richer, child mortality rates fall and life expectancy increases significantly. Over the course of a couple of generations, people respond to this by greatly reducing the number of children they have. But during those initial two generations, there is a population explosion. The result is higher demand in the economy but increased labor that help keep wages down" (Robertson, Charles, The Fastest Billion, The Story Behind Africa's Economic Revolution, London: Renaissance Capital, 2012, pages 126-127). Another very significant factor to consider is related to families during the bulge generation having a smaller number of children; the results with a smaller number of children per/family, those families and their governments will be able to invest more into health and education that will enhance the overall development of children (Canning, et al, ibid).

The population explosion or the "youth bulge" generation that takes place usually involves the young workers. Although all of the aforementioned can result in higher demands within the economy, the increased labor supply is a factor contributing to keeping wages down. China is presented as an example of a country with very low inflation in recent years. The contributing factor is related to the very high available supply of young workers. Now, a factor calling for wage increases in the range of about 10-25% is that there is a significant decline in the available supply of young workers (Robertson, ibid, p. 127). "The West is well past this point of decline. The number of 15-24 year olds is expected to stagnate between 2010 and 2020 in North America, to decline by 7%in Western Europe. Eastern Europe is expected to see a dramatic fall 33% fall in the absolute number of 15-24 year olds…China will see its 15-24 year old population shrink by 47 million" (Robertson, ibid, p.128).

Multinational corporations have been forewarned in regards to the significant increase over the next several decades in the age group 15-24, as well as the age group 15-30. Sub-Saharan Africa "…has become a magnet for expansion minded multinational corporations and numerous small and midsize foreign owned businesses"(Beckett, J. and Sudarkasa, E. M., Investing in Africa: An Insider's Guide to the Ultimate Emerging Market, NY: John Wiley & Sons, 2000, p. 94). A key factor in the "Africa Rising" slogan is the anticipation of a growing consumer market, especially in the age group 15-30, the "…the potential for future growth in consumer demand is the fact that in most African countries 45% of the population is at or below the age of 15, while another 26% is between the ages of 15 and 30" (Beckett, et al, ibid, p. 94).

It would seem that countries that are willing to conceptualize, and plan appropriately could take advantage of the "youth bulge generation," in response to this phenomenon. It would mean a strong commitment investment in the youth or young population, including education, as well as overall social wellbeing. Improvements in quality of life or social wellbeing should include social/health policies to insure that they grow to their maximum potential. Currently a significant number of children are living with grandparents without a social pension. An investment in social pensions for parents and grandparents raising children and grandchildren could reduce the number of children living in poverty, and a reduction in unemployment. Due to a number of factors, parents inflicted with diseases and illnesses, political conflicts, wars and parental unemployment issues have resulted in an untold number of orphan children. An investment in those children now could have a significant impact on a country's economic growth in the future.

Africa and China: A Growing Partnership

China's growing Foreign Direct Investment in Africa has raised questions and concerns regarding the relationship. On the one hand there are those who strongly feel that China's goal is to exploit countries such as Kenya. But there are others who feel that China in the long run benefits a country like Kenya. The latter points to China's significant contributions to the current and ongoing infrastructure development in Kenya; an example given is "…the standard gauge railing or the Port at Lamu Island that offers affordable and diverse products to consumers" ((Sanghi, Apurva and Johnson, Dylan, "Three Myths About China and Kenya," The World Bank: Working for a World Free of Poverty, Submitted May 20, 2016).

The World Bank in 2016, in response to some of the concerns addressed several myths regarding the relationship between China and Kenya, a major partner. The first or myth number one claimed that China was "...deliberately flooding the market with cheap products and destroying Kenya's economy." The focus of myth one addressed the bilateral trade difference between the two countries. It was pointed out that not only does Kenya have a trade deficit with China but also Germany a country that is surviving quite well economically. The reality is Kenya is not a great exporter to any country at this point in time. Also, there has been a significant decline in Kenya's "export to GDP ratio...between 2005 and 2012, far from the norm for other high growth economies. Consumers now have greater variety of choice" (Sanghi and Johnson, ibid, 2016).

The second myth to be addressed was that China in all of its development projects, building and construction, imported the workforce from China. Research studies indicates that "Chinese companies hire Kenyans for 78% full time/95% part time roles...93% of companies report hiring Kenyan employees. Chinese companies have created nearly 2,000 direct jobs, 5.3% of the total jobs created through Foreign Direct Investments" (Sanghi and Johnson, ibid, 2016). Currently, China ranks number 5 globally in Foreign Direct Investments, whereas India ranks number 1(Sanghi and Johnson, ibid, 2016). The third myth focused on the role of China or its major interest in the exploitation of natural resources in Africa. Once again, research seems to point out China's interest extends beyond just natural resources. China's interest seems to engage in all major economic sectors. For example, in "2014 the communication sector received 150 million dollars in investment from China, and automotive manufacturing 68 million" (Sanghi and Johnson, ibid, 2016).

Considering all of the investment initiatives currently operational in Africa there is interest and obviously concern regarding the current slowdown in China's economy and what impact will it have on African countries. The current crisis occurring in China's economy could affect not only Sub-Saharan Africa and countries globally as well. Brazil "...is already faltering as weaker Chinese imports of minerals and soybeans have jolted all of Latin America. The uncertainty over China could limit the maneuvering room for officials to address the sluggish Brazilian economy at a time when resentment is festering over proposed austerity measures" (Bradsher K, International New York Times, 8/26/2015, p. 1). Brazilian leadership, especially its President is currently under a great deal of criticism for allowing the country's economy to become so dependent on China. China became Brazil's number one trading partner; the United States dropped to the number two spot six years ago. A great deal of the concern among the citizenry of Brazil relates to the fact that the country's exports decreased 23.6%, $24.7 billion "...in the first seven months of the year from the same period in 2014" (Bradsher, ibid, p. 4). China who has the second largest economy globally, accounts for approximately 13% of the world's GDP.

Russia is another country becoming very concerned regarding the current realities of China's economy. There was very significant financial news during 2014 when Russia and China announced the $400 billion natural gas deal. China's investment was expected to finance a 2,500 - mile pipeline for the purpose of transporting fuel from Siberia. During the happy occasion President Putin of Russia announced that in the near future Russia would be selling more gas to China than Germany; Germany, obviously is currently Russia number one customer. The aftershock considering what is currently happening in China's economy "...the prices that

China is willing to pay for the gas are dropping so low that it may no longer be worthwhile to build a pipeline" (Bradsher, ibid, p. 5).

With recent concerns globally regarding China's economy, countries such as Brazil are being confronted with and having "…to respond to a new reality as a once sure bet becomes uncertain" (Bradsher, ibid, p. 1) China tremendous economic growth in recent years somewhat dominated and reshaped the global economy. Its economy became the driving force dictating "…corporate strategies, financial markets and geopolitical decisions. China seemed to have a one-way trajectory, momentum that would provide a steady source of profit and capital" (Bradsher, ibid, p.2). But, the week of August 24, 2015 will for a long period of time when all of the fears about China's resulted in what is being referred to as a global market rout, including a significant devaluation of the country's currency.

China is in Partnership with five other countries establishing a new bank, The New Development Bank in Africa to support economic growth and transformation initiatives. BRICS (Brazil, Russia, India, China, South Africa) bold new effort was the establishment in July 2014, a new development Bank in Africa. The goal is to offer another alternative to the already established multilateral development financing institutions. Full operation, lending money, was expected to begin in 2016. The new Bank will serve, according to Ikome and Comins, an alternative to the World Bank, but will also provide a mechanism for applying pressure on the global advanced economies to make good on all of their promises/commitments to the developing world.

China, the principle member of the new Bank is already a major economic force globally during the past decade, and other members of BRICS have expressed that they have the capacity to make significant contributions to the new initial. BRICS has demonstrated tremendous growth during the past ten years. It currently has approximately a 25% world economic output. BRICS currently has some 120 billion committed in combined investments in various strategic sectors, such as natural resource extraction, manufacturing, and services and information technology. The new Bank's initial lending pool is expected to facilitate additional capital inflows into Africa. A major theme of the new Bank is Beyond Financial and Economic Gains; it has hopes of solidifying strategic links as well as enhancing relationships in Africa.

Brazil, a major partner within the BRICS structure has been experiencing major economic issues in recent years. Brazil is Latin America's largest economy but its current economic problems seem somewhat overwhelming, and almost out of control. The Minister of Finance appointed by the President just one year ago and given the task of stabilizing the country's finances recently resigned out of frustration. Recently the second of the three major credit rating organizations lowered the country's debt to junk status. The Brazilian economy has been projected to decline by 2.5-3 % during 2016; the fiscal has increased from 2% of the GDP in 2010 to 10% at the end of the year 2015. To make matters worse in Brazil there is a major bribery or corruption scandal involving the state controlled oil-company now on the agenda for the country to resolve with. In the midst of all of the economic woes Rio de Janeiro is preparing to host South America's first Olympic games in August 2016 (Brazil's fall, "Disaster looms for Latin America's biggest economy," The Economist, January 2, 2016).

Should Sub-Saharan African countries be concerned about Brazil's economic problems at this time? Not just Brazil, what about China and Russia, partners in BRICS? One may use Brazil has an example of potential problems for Sub-Saharan African countries. Brazil's economic problems challenging the country at the end of 2015 and now being brought forward to 2016 can be related to its strong trading partnership with China; it is China's number one trading partner. Brazil considered globally as a frontrunner or major leader among emerging economies is also a major partner within BRICS that include South Africa. A current and future goal of Sub-Saharan countries is diversification and/or trading in expanded markets. Sub-Saharan African countries market expansion, including the BRICS countries, has had a major impact on economic growth and transformation in recent years. Therefore, a continuation of the current economic problems in Brazil, Russia, and especially China could become a deterrent to economic growth.

Global concerns regarding a slowdown in China's economy probably will continue. The concern is obvious considering the fact that China has the second largest economy in the world. A significant slowdown would probably raise some level of concern globally considering that China accounts for such a high percentage of the worlds GDP, approximately 13% several years ago. On the other hand developing and/or low-middle income countries have become quite dependent on China's economy. Brazil, second largest economy in Latin America, is an example of a country for a period of time had become quite dependent on China's economy when its economy suffered a significant decline during the period 2014-16. In 2016 Brazil credit rating was lowered to junk status.

For a significant period of time prior to the year 2015 China somewhat shaped the global economy. But around this time period China's economy began to suffer some setbacks such as a devaluation of the country's currency; there were concerns globally, especially those countries such as Brazil that had become quite dependent on China and its economy. Now, it is the year 2017 and once again some concerns regarding China's economy. The story line is that China's economy is once again has slowed, more than anticipated, in two major sectors, manufacturing and services. Not unlike other economies, including the United States, United Kingdom, one can expect China's economy to have slowdowns as well as upswings. China has contributed significantly, especially in Foreign Direct Investments in Africa, more so than any other global economic giant, including the United States. China will no doubt continue to have a significant impact on growth and development in Africa.

POTENTIAL INTERNAL THREATS TO ECONOMIC GROWTH IN SUB-SAHARAN AFRICA

Management and/or Business Practices/Regulatory Reforms

Despite the optimism surrounding Africa's Renaissance there are some factors the continent has to be on guard against; these are historical factors that could, if countries are not constantly on alert become a threat to sustained economic growth. Good sound management practices, including regulatory reforms, are crucial as the continent continues its forward thrust of sustained economic growth and transformation. In recent years the World Bank has as one of its goals has monitored changes or lack of in business management practices. In such a business climate it becomes very difficult to carry out sound business practices. But, according to the World Bank Africa in recent years has been closing the gap in comparison with other countries as they go about introducing significant reforms. In reference to business friendly economies globally, five of the top ten most improved countries are in Sub-Saharan Africa; at the top of the list, number one, of business friendly economies is Singapore (World Bank: Doing Business 2015 Rankings, 12th Edition). According to the World Bank Report 2015, it is becoming easier to do business in Sub-Saharan Africa. In 2005 it took approximately 235 days to transfer property in the lowest rank countries but only 42 days in the top ranked countries. The gap is closing, whereas in 2014, it was 90 days for the low rank countries compared to 40 for the high rank countries, a difference of 193 days. According to Doing Business 2015, the gap has narrowed to 62 days.

The World Bank reports that Sub-Saharan Africa accounted for the largest number of regulatory reforms for enhancing the opportunities for implementing positive business practices. Senegal, on the West Coast of Africa, implemented reforms in 6 of the 10 areas monitored by Doing Business. An example resulting from regulatory reform is the length of time it took to implement the necessary procedures for importing goods overseas. In 2005 it took Senegal 27 days; now it takes only 14 days. One critical measurement had to do with the "...the ease of doing business in 189 economies based on 11 business-related regulations, including business start up, getting credit, getting electricity, and trading across borders." The data gathering does not include corruption. (World Bank: Ramalho, Rita, Doing Business 2015: Going Beyond Efficiency, World Bank Group Flagship Report (12th Edition), pages 3-14). Ramalho, R. ibid (2015) of the World Bank, "No one, looking ahead would start a business if its very hard to close one...Failure is a part of life, so you want to have a legal system that knows how to deal with failure."

The World Bank highlights some significant and positive regulatory reforms currently underway in Africa. The changes could have a major impact relating to economic development, increased capital investments, an expanded infrastructure, as well as an expanded labor market system. One can only hope that the changes will contribute to growth in the more technological oriented manufacturing sector whereas Africa will become more globally competitively. The latter could contribute significantly to providing social protection for all, but especially the old age population. The recurring theme is that currently 75-80 % of those 60 plus do not have social protection, such as income security, access to health care and services. This is why positive signs in economic transformation are so crucial (The World Bank, ibid 12th Edition, "Doing Business: "Going Beyond Efficiency," 2015).

According to international organizations such as the World Bank, Sub-Saharan Africa in the past has been noted for having some of the most complex business and management practices. But, all that is changing in the era of "Africa Rising." Now, Sub-Saharan Africa stands out when it comes to regulatory reforms and creating an environment for implementing positive business and management practices. The ISSA views "Excellence in Administration" as a tool for the development of quality social protection/social security programs for the welfare of all citizens, including the old age population. Therefore, the development and implementation of solid business and management practices are crucial (ISSA: Africa Strategic Approaches to Improve Social Security, Development and Trends, 2014).

"The ISSA defines excellence in social security administration in relation to the achievement of good governance, high performance and improved service quality" (ISSA: Africa Strategic Approaches to Improve Social Security, Development and Trends, 2014, p. 9). Furthermore, according to the ISSA, "Excellence" should not be seen as a constraint for completing a particular task, but should be viewed as a guiding mind-set. Also, it should be viewed and "… understood as an administrative 'end' in the management of resources, and also as a 'means' to engender citizen-centered delivery and to achieve societal-level policy goals" (ISSA, 2014, ibid, p. 10).

With a goal of achieving "Excellence" in administration, a number of countries in Sub-Saharan Africa have taken the initiative to incorporate educational, training and practice modals into the work place; an example comes from Swaziland. Swaziland is one of the very few countries in Sub-Saharan Africa that has adopted a universal social pension for the older population, age being the sole eligibility requirement. A very critical business practice instituted was a strategic planning model with the goals and objectives of identifying what weaknesses existed within the management structure. Although not clearly stated in the reporting research the strategic planning process probably provided the opportunity to identify strengths, opportunities and threats as well as method of analysis used in strategic planning known as "SWOT" Analysis (ISSA, 2014, ibid, p. 12).

The National Security Fund in Uganda has established "…the Strategic Management Framework…providing a roadmap to clarify the vision and mission of the Fund, offers an example of the need to develop a robust administrative framework as a condition for improving the social security of the population. This should be the starting point for all organizations to effectively and efficiently manage resources and meet citizen's expectations" (ISSA, 2014, ibid, p. 12). It could be pointed out that the first phase of the strategic planning process used in Swaziland provides a similar opportunity for clarifying the mission of an organization as well.

Being referred to as "Setting the Rates Right," Cameroon's National Social Insurance Fund, introduced this program model to illustrate "…how giving specific attention to establishing the prices of services has led to a measurable decrease in the costs of many of those services, and consequently the release of funds for other strategic activities" (ISSA, 2014, ibid, p. 12). In addition to the aforementioned other programs for improving management and business practices. The National Insurance Fund in Mauritius has introduced a project focusing on organizational transparency known as the "The Disclosure of Information Model." This management program model has focused on the very serious subject of transparency and the results have been a significant boost in the public image of the organization. The country of Tanzania and its National Health Insurance Fund established the Annual "Clients Day." This model provides the opportunity for the Fund to bring together face-to-face local and regional leaders for constructive dialogue with significant stakeholders.

A business and management "culture of excellence" is considered essential in the implementation of performance objectives within a country's administrative units. Although this particular area has presented challenges for some countries in Sub-Saharan Africa, just like there is an "economic rising," research is showing a significant improvement in business and management practices. The Ibrahim Index of African Governance, 2014 points out that globally, five of the top ten most improved countries are in Sub-Saharan Africa. The aforementioned Section on Business and Management Practices, provide examples of countries that have been very successful in improving or enhancing a "culture of excellence." These countries provide specific models and how used to improve practices within their units of services.

The aforementioned initiatives being developed and implemented by the various countries in Sub-Saharan Africa is a demonstration that the countries are committed to sound management practices. They are positive indicators of contributions now being made toward economic transformation that will have a very significant impact on social protection and social security in the future. The overall improvements and progress in management and business practices, including regulatory reforms will continue to boost "Africa Rising."

The "Elephant in the Room:" Corruption

The most recent Corruption Perception Index reports that globally more than two-thirds, 66%, of the 176 countries under study are below the midpoint scale (50); the scale goes from 0, (very clean) to 100 (highly corrupt). According to Transparency International the results of the 2016 survey illustrates the strong relationship between the concepts corruption and inequality. "In some countries, "…collusion between businesses and politicians siphons off billions of dollars in revenue from national economies, benefitting the few at the expense of the many. This kind of systemic grand corruption violates human rights, prevents sustainable development and fuels social exclusion…Higher ranked countries tend to have higher degrees of press freedom…access to information about public expenditure, stronger standards of integrity for public officials, and independent judicial systems (Transparency International, "Corruption Perceptions Index 2016," Surveys, 25 January 2017) **See Appendix A: Tables/ Charts, Chapter VI, Table 10).**

It has been suggested that the elections that took place throughout Africa in 2016 provided for Africa and the world a glimpse of the impact corruption and other financial illicit activities had on the electoral process. Most importantly, the election results confirm the strong correlation between corruption, other financial illicit operations in countries and social inequalities. Two countries, Cape Verde and Sao and Principe with elections held 2016, political observer teams identified both countries as achieving exemplary status during their electoral processes. President Jorge Carlos Fonseca won re-election in Cape Verde without any electoral turmoil. In Sao and Principe, the elections held in July 2016, a complete change in government was accomplished very peacefully minus turmoil. It is the change in governments that normally presents the greatest challenge for countries during the electoral process (Transparency International, "Correction Perceptions Index 2016," ibid, 2017).

The electoral process in other African countries illustrated the negative impact corruption can have on the electoral process. As a result of serious corruption activities in Ghana, citizens of this historic country (first to achieve Independence in 1957), articulated their frustrations and anger throughout the electoral process. As a result of the citizens' disappointments and frustrations with the government's role in corruption activities they responded in the voting booths; the results, for the first time in Ghana's historic past an incumbent President lost the election.

At the end of the electoral process in Gambia the incumbent President, Yahya Jammeh, who had been in power for more than 20 years, refused to accept the final count from the voters and announced he would not step down as President. It was only after dialogues or interactions with the leadership of nearby countries, such as Senegal and donor giving countries, he agreed to step down and went into exile in Equatorial Guinea (Transparency International, "Correction Perceptions Index 2016," ibid, 2017). Prior to his departure into exile he withdrew Euro 11.4 million from various Banks in Gambia. Gambia currently has a public debt totaling more than 100% of its annual GDP; the youth unemployment rate in the country is approximately 40% (Ruth MacLean, African Correspondent, "EU pledges Euro 225 million rescue package for the Gambia as new democracy dawns," The Guardian, 10/2/2017: 09/02 EST).

Shortly after former President Yahya Jammeh went into exile in Equatorial Guinea, updated information related to his corruption and other financial illicit activities while in office begin to emerge; the earlier reports of his looting and stealing from the country was significantly higher than first reported. His methods for obtaining the cash or money were carried out by using members of the Republic Guard who took his Executive Directives and used them for making cash withdrawals from various state entities. He left the country in approximately $1b in debt; fifty million dollars were taken from entities such as the country ports, social security and the National Telecoms Company. The cost of his private jet was $4.5 m (Euro 3.6m) withdrawn from the State Pension Fund. A very sad conclusion, especially since the focus of this Manuscript is on social pension reform, pensioners are now being refused their pension, or they are now receiving less (as low as $5.00) than normal (Guardian: MacLean, Ruth/Dakar and Saikou, Jammeh/Banjul, "New Claims Over Scale of ex-Gambian Leader's Theft from State Coffers" 2/23/2017: 07:16 EST).

Somalia, not surprising considering its history over the past two decades, ranks last 176 of all the countries under study on the "Corruption Perception Index 2016." The country had to postpone the Presidential electoral process three times in 2016; the process was hopefully to be resolved in 2017. The electoral process in Somalia has been marked by malpractice and corruption for years. The country has not had a centralized functioning government since 1991. It was in 1991 when warlords took charge and practically tore the country apart at a time when a serious famine broke out. For approximately two decades without a functioning government, the country has received billions of dollars in aide from foreign countries, including the United States. The turmoil and the fighting have continued including the Capital City of Mogadishu where in January 2017, Shabab fighters set off two large bombs; the results from the bombing included the deaths of dozens of peacekeepers from Kenya (Jeffrey Gettleman, New York Times, African News Events, "Fueled by Bribes, Somalia's Election Seem as a Milestone of Corruption," February 7, 2017).

The plan has been to complete the electoral process by electing a President in 2017; countries having supported Somalia with foreign aid in recent decades, including the United States, have been instrumental in ensuring that an electoral democratic process would become a reality. In reference to provisions for foreign aid to Somalia the United States during the past decade has allocated or given to the country 1.5 billion dollars in humanitarian aid; an additional 240 million dollars was given by the United States that would assist Somalia in its political and economical recovery. Considering the support from countries other than the United States related to economical and political recovery, it is obvious why a democratic and peaceful electoral process would be critical in 2017 following three failed attempts in 2016. The United States was committed to 196 million dollars in overall funding in 2017. In the midst of proceeding with the electoral process in 2017, there was concern, based on report that surfaced, "Growing evidence of systematic purchase of votes risks undermining Wednesday's long awaited poll, which has been described as a 'way station' to political stability and full democracy' (Jason Burke, African Correspondent, The Guardian "Its Pretty Brave, Mogadishu on Lockdown as General MPs Elect President, 8/2/2017, p 1, 07:02 EST). Yes, the process did get underway as PMs begin casting their ballots on February 8, 2017; the voting took place "…in a high security compound at an airport in the Somalia Capital Mogadishu to elect a President for the unstable East African State (Burke, ibid, 2017). The electoral process was finally completed 8/2/2017. The newly elected President is Mohamed Abdullah Mohamed, age 55, former Prime Minister, and a US-Somali National. The United States and several European states were largely responsible for financing the elections (Jason Burke, African Correspondent, The Guardian, "Somalis greet new dawn as US dual national wins President," 8/2/17, p 1, 13:25, 2017 EST).

Although Rwanda did not go through the Presidential electoral process recently is an example of a country and it President with a commitment of fighting corruption. Rwanda the 3rd least corrupt country in Sub Saharan Africa, recently fired 200 police officers on charges of corruption; two-hundred (200) civilians were arrested for giving money or bribes to police officers. The President of Rwanda has been praised during his tenure for fighting corruption; the country has been depending on foreign aid for a significant part of its budget. The African Union reports that each year some 50 billion dollars are lost to corruption and other financial crimes across Africa. (News 24: Breaking News, Associated Press, February 2, 2017, 23:2; Transparency International, Daily Reports, February 7, 2017).

But, in South Africa the drama around corruption and other financial illicit activities continue to take the spotlight. In January 2017, a South African Court ruled that President Jacob Zuma could be charged over corruption matters that occurred prior to his election as President in 2009. The more than 800 corruption charges had been dropped weeks before he was elected President of South Africa in 2009. The 800 charges included, racketeering, fraud and money laundering that involved a multi-billion dollar arms Bill. During his current tenure in office since 2009 the President has been confronted with a number corruption scandals; during the same period he has been criticized frequently about South Africa's very poor economic growth rate, and a record high unemployment rates (Transparency International, Daily Reports, June 24, 2016). Approximately two weeks following the decision by South Africa's High Court that the charges against the President dropped before 2009 could be reinstated, brawls and chaos broke out in the South African Parliament; the major issue underlying the chaos related to corruption. Opposition leaders of Parliament shouted out that the President was a 'scoundrel and "rotten to the core' because of his corruption activities while in office. The opposition leaders were forced to leave the Chambers by guards (Associated Press, Johannesburg, February 9, 2017, 14:29 EST).

Zimbabwe has had its share of scrutiny regarding corruption in recent years. The Herald, Zimbabwe's largest newspaper ran the following headline on October 27, 2015, "Sculptor Fights Corruption." The headline was also part of Transparency International Daily Blog. Melody Fombe, the Sculptor, expressed that the country's fight against corruption has to be a collective movement involving all of the citizens of Zimbabwe. Corruption to Mr. Fombe is the worst enemy of economic growth, and the overall development of the country. As a sculptor he has chosen to use his artistic skills, stone carvings, in bringing awareness about corruption in Zimbabwe. After observing corruption practices running rampant in various governmental entities, Mr. Fombe decided to focus his stone carving on the subject of corruption. His most notable carving crafted from sphinx stone was given the title "corruption." The carving depicts a man with a gold tooth holding a bag of money. His interpretation of the figure is a "money monger" who is "greedy." He wanted to use the carving, corruption, to rally and encourage people to fight against corruption. His wish is that one-day Zimbabwe will be free from corruption and everybody will be happy. Corruption, the stone carving, was entered into an International Art Exhibition at the Arts Centre on October 27, 2015 in Zimbabwe (Marwizi, Tawanda, Arts Correspondent, The Herald Newspaper, Zimbabwe, October 27, 2015); Transparency International, Daily Corruption News, "Sculptor Fights Corruption," October 27, 2015.

To highlight current corruption practices two Zimbabwe Revenue Authority officials, Revenue Officer and a Revenue Supervisor appeared in Court before the Magistrate in Harare in October 2015. They are being charged with solicitation for a $70,000 bribe for the purpose of slashing a $900,000 stamp duty. The two officials have been charged with criminal abuse of their duties as public officials. The Magistrate granted bail of $300.00 each, ordered to appear in Court on 11/16/2015 (Fungai Lupande, Court Reporter, Zimbabwe Herald, "2 Zimra Officials up for $70,000 Bribery, 11/2/2015; Transparency International, Daily Corruption News, 11/2/2015.

Zimbabwe was not the only country in Sub-Saharan Africa during the year 2015 focusing on corruption. In South Africa religious leaders (known as the Western Cape Forum), labor unions, non-governmental organizations, university/college academics, and civil servants planned a demonstration and March to the Parliament Offices. The purpose of the demonstration, estimated to be approximately 300 registered organizations (20,000 people expected), was to take a position against corruption. The consensus of those participating was that South has not taken corruption seriously. The participants were asking that society as a whole refrain from corruption; a specific demand, end corrupt business practices as well as tax evasion. A major concern was that too many citizens were living in poverty while corruption was running rampant Kekang, Masa, Transparency International, Daily Corruption News, "Religious Leaders to Join Anti-Corruption Marches," September 23, 2015.

Nigeria under the leadership of newly elected President Muhammadu Buhari, seemingly has committed to stopping corruption in the oil industry. His new policy is "Nigeria will buy and sell oil products directly, cut out middlemen in bid to curb corruption" (Michelle Faul, Associated Press, 11/3/15; Article quoted in Transparency International: Daily Corruption News, 11/4/15). The President's plan is bring a halt to the corruption epidemic in the oil industry in Nigeria, Sub-Saharan Africa's largest producer. The obvious goal of the President is to eliminate all illicit practices of middlemen in business exchanges in the oil industry. The outgoing or previous President Goodluck Jonathan had been warned by the Central Bank Government during his tenure, and chose to ignore, that approximately $20 billion dollars during a three year period was missing (Faul, AP, 2015, ibid, Transparency International, 2015).

As aforementioned, Nigeria is the largest producer of oil in Africa, approximately 2 million barrels of crude oil daily. The population of Nigeria consumes approximately 2.4 million

(9 million liters) daily. It is interesting to note that most of the oil consumed is imported; the major reason is that the local refiners are considered inefficient for the task (Faul, AP, ibid; Transparency International, ibid). One could conclude that Nigeria, Africa's largest oil producer for many years, has some serious problems related to the industry's infrastructure.

In a related matter, oil not gas, the World Bank has pledged Sh54 billion, $600 million to fund an oil pipeline that will link upstream operations of Kenya, Uganda and South Sudan. This funding is made possible by the International Finance Corporation (IFC) and is part of loan Sh160 billion for projects in the Horn of Africa. The IFC is the private sector lending arm of the World Bank. The entire pipeline project is estimated to cost $5 billion; the funds are also intended to support various renewal energy projects, including wind energy as well as access to markets (World Bank: Leaders commit Billions in Major New Development Initiative for the Horn of Africa, October 27, 2014, Press Release).

Sub-Saharan Africa is becoming a major source of global wealth, but it has to find ways to maximize the potential benefits coming from all of its natural resources, including domestic markets and equally important export markets. The consensus is that Africa's current growth could be significantly higher if investments were staying, not leaving the Continent illicitly. "As illicit financial flows are hidden from African tax authorities, they undermine Africa's fiscal policy space, deny the continent additional tax revenues, which could be used to fund government programs and enhance productivity, which in turn would increase the tax base to raise more revenue and fund development requirements" (Hamdok, ibid, Africa Development Forum 2014).

Although the World Bank did not use the concept/variable corruption among the measures for doing business, it is like the "Elephant in the room;" to what extent is there a correlation between good business practices/governance and capital investments? Let's look at a current case history in Tanzania. Although this is not a specific case of corruption the average observer will view it as having the potential for it to happen. A headline in a recent edition of Financial Times "Tanzania natural gas investment threatened by arrest of officials." The narrative states that the arrest of the officials threatens to complicate and delay billions of dollars of investment into the sector. The foreign companies who have already reached agreements with the government to exploit the reserves are: Exxon Mobil (US), Statoil (Norway), and BG Group and Ophir (UK). The arrests occurred when the two officials refused to comply with demands from lawmakers to release details of 26 contracts, known in the industry as production sharing agreements. The arrests will delay the publishing of key legislation for the gas industry as well as plans to introduce a new constitution ahead of elections in 2015 when the current President is scheduled to step down. The aforementioned energy groups have not made final investment decisions and production now may be many years away, or at lease a decade. Opposition lawmakers are refusing to drop their demands for transparency within the industry. Mr. Zitto Kabwe, Head of the Parliamentary Committee overseeing the matter, and opposition lawmaker, expressed that transparency would help to determine if the government would be getting its share of potential revenues, determine if contracts differ between agreements, and if any bribes had been paid in securing the contracts?

The opposition has intensified following the leaking of a contract showing new terms with two of the foreign companies. The leaked contract revealed that ExxonMobil (US) and

Statoil (Norway) would pay Tanzania no more than 50% from a natural gas field in the Indian Ocean. There is also some concern in the country that those representing Tanzania during the negotiations will be taken advantage of by the more experienced international gas magnets. Civil society are now pressing for open contracts in the industry (transparency, accountability), as well as demanding more public discussions regarding how the revenues will be invested in the country. People are reminded that Uganda has been involved over a number of years attempting to develop a deal with foreign groups in developing its vast oilfields, including a pipeline through Kenya to the Indian Ocean.

Corruption has been and continues to be a global concern and activists from around the world are becoming more assertive in their demands for action. They are organizing with the goal of presenting their concerns before the G20 Leadership Conference that will take place in 2014 in Brisbane, Australia. The global activist group includes the Nobel Peace Laureates Archbishop Desmond Tutu (South African Social Rights Activist, Retired Anglican Bishop), and Tawakkul Karman (Youngest woman to receive the prize, and the second Muslim woman). The group is calling on the G20 Leaders to make corruption a top priority in their discussions of multi-national organizations/companies; the Leaders should adopt and action oriented plan to pressure multi-national corporations to publish financial (transparency) information in each operating country, including profits and taxes paid. Also, they are calling on the G20 Leaders to implement a complete action oriented plan to stop and prevent the billions of corrupt money currently flowing around the world.

There is more and more global recognition, especially among global organizations, that corruption is a major barrier in social and economic development, including the enactment of social programs that would ensure the quality of life for all. The finding of fiscal space within country's budget would be less complicated if the problem of corruption was significantly curtailed. According to the Financial Times "Hugh offshore gas finds promise to lift the East African Nation into the ranks of middle-income countries by 2030 and free it from dependency on foreign aid. But, there has been a governmental agreement to keep the terms of the production sharing agreement secret, and this obviously will raise suspicion. There was no mention regarding transparency.

The problem of corruption or the illicit management of public funds as aforementioned has become a major concern not only of citizens but governmental and/or political officials as well. It is interesting to note that the African Union Summit convened its 30th Session on the 22nd day of January 2018 in Addis Ababa, Ethiopia. The theme was, "Winning the fight against Corruption: A Sustainable Path to Africa's Transformation," African News, The Morning Call, "Africa's Fight Against Corruption," reported in Transparency International, Daily Corruption News, 22 January 2018. A consensus during the Summit expressed by Nigerian President Muhammad Buhari seems to have been that, "Corruption is indeed one of the greatest evils of our time… Corruption rewards those who do not play by the rules…I cannot overemphasize the value of strong institutions. A judiciary which stands firm against arbitrariness and injustice by the executive is a vital pillar in the anti-corruption fight, Buhari added" (DW.Com, "African Union, Trade, Security and Anti-Corruption Top AU Agenda," 29.01 2018, pages 1-2).

The agenda for the Summit also included Trade and Security on the Continent. In regards to trade the delegation was promoting a single African air transport market. The leadership behind the launching of a Single African Transport Market was the President for the year 2018 Paul Kagame who had committed to reforming the African Union. There seemingly was "… an agreement between 23 out of 55 countries to lower the cost and ease of inner-African travel. The move will also likely see a boost for countries like South Africa, Rwanda, Kenya and Ethiopia who have the biggest commercial airlines and have been pushing for the agreement for the past few years" (DW.Com, Ibid, pages 1-2).

Workforce Separation: Informal and Formal Sectors

The most disrespected, unappreciated and less protective within the global workforce are those described as informal workers or the self-employed. Globally, the vast majority of the older population, globally without a social pension is those who worked in the informal sector or as self-employed. The organization, Women in Informal Employment: Globalizing and Organizing (WIEGO) provides its definition of this growing workforce, including implications for this significant labor sector. The organizational theme of WIEGO is "Empowering Informal Workers, Securing Informal Livelihoods." According to WIEGO, "The informal economy is comprised of economic activities, enterprises and workers that do not receive social protection through work or legal protection through the state…often stigmatized as 'illegal,' 'underground,' 'black' or 'grey,' the generalization is unfair…The vast majority of informal workers are trying to earn an honest living against great odds (WIEGO, wiego.org, 2017). The informal sector and/or the self-employed have increased significantly in recent decades, "emerging in unexpected places and in new guises. Today, half to three-quarters of non-agricultural workers in developing countries earn their living informally (WIEGO, ibid, 2017). What this means is that the vast majority of workers will not have basic social protection, including income security following retirement.

The International Labor Organization (ILO) the historical advocate group on behalf of workers express similar observations regarding the plight of the informal and/or self- employed workforce. The ILO refers to the aforementioned sector under the category vulnerable employment; the vulnerable employed as defined by ILO as unpaid work when carrying out family duties and/or responsibilities. The vulnerable employed normally receives low wages for their work and the working hours are usually long and can be under very difficult working conditions. According to the ILO workers have no rights to grievance procedures or legal process in protecting the rights of workers, including social protection. The jobs are considered vulnerable and part of the informal labor sector; as part of the informal sector workers and their families do not have the benefits of paid sick days, no representation by trade unions, and most importantly retirement benefits such as a social pension (ILO, "Key Indicators of the Labor Market," 9th Edition, Geneva ILO 2015/Lee, Marlene, Christianson, Hanna and Bietsch, Kristin, "Global Employment and the Sustainable Development Goals," Population Reference Bureau, Vol. 71, #2, Washington, DC, 2017).

The aforementioned workers as indicated by WIEGO and the ILO are those, globally without social protection, especially social pension in retirement. One major barrier to overcome for ensuring that the older population will have access to basic income security, health, medical care and social services, is the current lack of collaborative labor ties between the informal and formal sectors. The working together of these two sectors could significantly increase the chances of reducing the number of persons without a social pension at the time of retirement. Keeping in mind that currently less than 20%, 16.5 % more specifically, of older persons in Sub-Saharan Africa do not have a social pension at the time of retirement. In regards to the overall labor force in Sub-Saharan Africa the informal sector of labor continues to dominate as it has done historically following Independence. But, there is one very positive note, based on an analysis of Country profiles in Chapter V, is that approximately fifteen countries in Sub-Saharan Africa with contributory tripartite labor systems have introduced provisions that eventually would allow the informal or self-employed to voluntarily participate in the formal sector's system of collective bargaining

One major factor that has to be addressed in any discussions and/or debates regarding barriers to social pensions is the fact that the informal labor sector remains dominant or continues to comprise a significant percentage of the labor force in Sub-Saharan Africa. The informal economy not only can be a deterrent or barrier to pension reform, but also slows the process allowing for sustained economic growth. Knowledge of the informal and formal labor sectors historically indicates that the two sectors have a very limited history of collaboration or partnerships regarding matters of social protection for workers and their families. Therefore, the evidence strongly indicates that the vast majority of older persons without a social pension were part of the informal sector's labor force.

The employment of workers in the formal sectors has historically been the primary factor in ensuring that the older population will have an adequate or basic income following retirement. Formal sector employment has also provided social protection for workers and their families during job tenure providing medical and health benefits, financial support resulting from temporary and/or permanent disability, and of course as aforementioned, social pensions following retirement. But, for a significant number of the world's population that is engaged in the informal sector, social protection or a social pension following retirement is not guaranteed (Harris, Elliott, "Financing Social Protection Floors: Considerations of Fiscal Space," in International Social Review, Vol. 66 1 Number 3-4, July-December 2013). The fact is most countries where the informal sector represents the majority of workers are considered low-income or poor. It is in those countries, for the most part that "…social protection has long been thought of as an unaffordable luxury" (Harris, 2013, ibid, p 112). Not only would a social pension be considered an unaffordable luxury in some low-income countries, but there are other social and economic issues to be considered, "…shocks to employment can have devastating human and social consequences – less consumption of food and thus, poorer nutrition; withdrawal of children from school; loss of access to essential services; and the forced sales of assets, all of which lessen the capacity to recover once the shock passes" (Harris, 2014, ibid). Once again regarding the subject of affordability, research findings and/or case histories addressed in Chapters VI and VII demonstrate that social programs such as pensions are affordable and achievable.

The origins or beginning of global recognition of the informal economy in Africa dates back almost six decades beginning around the early 1950's. There have been several historical milestones relating to the origins of the concept informal sector (King, Kenneth, "Jua Kali: Change and Development in an Informal Economy 1970-95," Eastern African Studies, Great

Britain, Long House Publishers, 1996). The first milestone occurred beginning in the early 1950's and involved the East African Royal Commission (EARC) 1953-55. The composition of the East African Royal Commission consisted of individuals or experts from Britain and Africa, experts on conditions in East Africa. The Commission addressed a number of issues on the African conditions, including those related to the acquisition and sale of land. During its research in Kenya the Commission observed what was described as a cluster of settlements. These settlements were observed beyond the main boundaries of the existing towns. The Commission concluded that the settlements should "...not be viewed as a eyesore but key centers of African trade" (King, ibid, p. 4; NOTE: QUOTATION is from King, whose quote was from (EARC Report, 1955, p. 208). The concept "...informal sector was first publicly applied to these kinds of clusters..."(King, ibid, p. 4).

The discovery of the informal sectors for carrying out trade activities were very significant in reference to the origins of the concept, but the Commission as well addressed other issues related to commerce and land acquisition. It addressed some of the regulatory practices, including restrictions related to the acquisition of credit and licensure, as well as land purchases and sale, for the purpose of micro-enterprise development. "The Commission also argued for the individualizing of land tenure, and initiative that was rapidly put into place in parts of Kenya, and which would soon have a powerful influence on the development of cash crops and on farm incomes more generally. In a rather forward-looking comment, the Commission affirmed its belief that African enterprise development was inseparable from urban land reform" (King, ibid, p. 4). The Commission research, analysis, and advocacy, no doubt laid a foundation for the future development of informal as well as former enterprises.

Another important timeline in the development of the informal sector economy took place around 1966. It was at this time, just three years post-independence, that a major conference or meeting was convened in Kenya. The proceedings of this Conference have been published as "Education, Employment and Rural Development" (Sheffield, J. R. (ed.), East African Publishing House, Kenya, Nairobi 1967). The primary incentive for such a meeting/conference at the time was an increasing awareness, and obviously major concern of the significant numbers of "...primary school leavers...and what was conceived of as the stark arithmetic of unemployment that faced the dramatically numbers of young people"(King, ibid, p.5). It can be assumed that a significant number of the potentially unemployed youth, as well as other age groupings would find employment in the growing informal sector of Kenya, to include the rural and urban informal sector. Why not? By this time in Kenya the informal sector had a strong foothold, and would have some opportunities for the unemployed, including the school leavers.

A third phase to consider in any discussion regarding the origin and history of the informal sector are the contributions of the International Labor Organization (ILO). Although the findings and analysis from the ILO became available in 1971, the field research work had begun approximately five years earlier. The ILO research included the study of 90 micro businesses and 850 micro enterprises scattered throughout the country. A major focus of the research and analysis of these micro enterprises was an attempt "...to understand the 100 years of continuities and discontinuities between pre-colonial trading patterns and the emergence of African business in the post-Independence period" (King, ibid, p. 5). One significant discovery from the project was "...a distinctive trading culture and a business ethic amongst the Kikuyu in parts of Central

Province...their acknowledgement of this enterprise culture amongst the Kikuyu might well prove to have been a significant milestone in trying to explain the differential involvement of Kenya's various communities in both formal and informal sectors" (King, ibid, pp. 5-6).

A significant event during this particular timeline was the arrival in Kenya of The Comprehensive Employment Strategy Mission at the invitation/request of the ILO in 1971. It was the Strategy Mission under the auspices of the ILO who began "...dramatizing the concept of the informal sector... It is intriguing that this concept was disseminated as a result of the Kenya Mission and published in 1972 in the report Employment, Incomes and Equality: A Strategy for increasing Productive Employment in Kenya (ILO, 1972" (King, ibid, pp. 6-7).

In regards to the origin of the concept informal sector, did it originate during the research of the Strategy Mission with the ILO in Kenya around 1971, or the research carried out by researcher Keith Hart involving his work in Northern Ghana with the Frafra migrants? It has been suggested that the "...first paper using the term informal sector had been read in a Conference on Urban Employment in Africa in Sussex in September 1971" (King, ibid, p. 7). Keith Hart, based on his research in Ghana, read the aforementioned paper at the Sussex Conference.

A final question regarding the origin and history of the concept is why was Kenya the geographical area where the concept globally became best known? Why not Ghana or Nigeria? One response is related to the ILO's Employment Mission in Kenya who focused it research and analysis around policy priorities. "What favored its application in Kenya was that petty enterprise and services had quite rapidly, since Independence, attached themselves to Nairobi and other towns that had been colonial and racially segregated conditions. These African beginnings of micro-enterprise were therefore suddenly becoming quite visible" (King, ibid, p. 7). Other reasons given in response to the question were (1) all the research, analysis and the production of manuscripts that had emerged from the University of Nairobi, especially it Department of Developmental Studies; (2) also, scholars had been using similar concepts, such as 'intermediate sector,' and (3) it was in Kenya that a history involving what was referred to as non-formal education emerged, or education and training that was taking place separately from the traditional formal or the official system of education, and had been included in employment policy considerations (King, ibid, pp. 7-8).

So, a conclusion can be drawn that the concept informal sector, or now being referred to as "jua Kali," meaning "under the hot sun" has been used to describe a country's economy dating back to 1971/1972. One can also conclude that the International Labor Organization in Kenya played a major role in the origins and history of the concept (Orwa, Bani, 2007). During this early history a large percentage of the Kenyan population expressed "...jua Kali to be the most important economic sector in Kenya, the one in which they all work" (Orwa, ibid, p. 1).

Another name given to the informal economy is "shadow economy" (World Bank: Working for a World Free of Poverty, "Informal = Illegal? Think Again", Blog submitted by Truman Packard (9/10/2012). More explicitly, the informal economy has also been defined as "...the sum of production of goods and services that are, in essence, legal under prevailing laws, like construction, driving cabs, and selling things...but are partially or totally concealed to avoid payment of taxes and social security contributions, or to escape regulations" (World Bank, ibid, p.1).

The informal sector in developing countries, in reference to non-agriculture labor or employment, ranges between 1/4 and 4/5; but most significantly contribution to a country's Gross Domestic Product (GDP) ranges between 25% and 40% of annual output (World Bank, "Workers in the Informal Economy"). More specifically, one source estimated that the informal sector makes up approximately 72% of the total labor force in developing countries, and contributes approximately 18% to a country's GDP (Bani Orwa, "Jua Kali association in Kenya: A Force for Development and Reform," Center for International Private Enterprise (Affiliate of the US Chamber of Congress): Reform Case Study, No. 0701, Washington, DC, 1/25/2007. More current data, 2013 estimates the share of non-agricultural workforce globally in the informal employment sector is 75% within the top five countries: Uganda 94%, Madagascar 90%, India 85%, Pakistan 75%, and Nicaragua 75% (Lee, Christianson, Bietsch, PRB, ibid).

There is a consensus that the process embodied into labor's tripartite collective bargaining mechanism is a major reason that globally so many older persons at the time of retirement will not have basic income security and access to health and social service. Furthermore, workers and their families have had access to health and/or medical services, and protection against job loss due to injuries in the workplace. In moving forward with the goal of removing barriers to social pensions that ensure social protection for older persons, several questions/issues have to be addresses. One question, do workers and/or their business enterprise in the informal sector have the opportunity to participate in the formal sector? How aggressive has the formal sector as well as the appropriate governmental entities reached out to the formal sector? Do workers not see any values or benefits of becoming part of the formal sector? In other words are there more negatives than positives from the workers' perspective? Does the formal system see too many disadvantages of aggressively pursuing the entrepreneurs and/or workers in the informal sector? Another major issue is what impact does such a dominant labor sector of informal workers have regarding a country's GDP, or tax supported revenues needed for providing services for the people, and/or economic growth and development?

First of all, are the informal workers reluctant to engage with the formal sector, or become part of mandatory pension schemes? There is a feeling among some workers that if they became part of such a mandatory system "…their pensions will not increase commensurately with their contributions" (World Bank, "Averting the Old Age Crisis," Issue Brief 7 Evasion, 1994, p. 319). It was also suggested that workers were more concerned about their present consumption needs than social protection or future pension needs. The most difficult factor for comprehending was that workers "…expected to die relatively early" (World Bank, Issue Brief 7 p. 319).

But, the major reason provided or shared by the World Bank, Issue Brief 7 was related to payroll taxes and regulations. Taxes and regulations not only seem to be a problem for the workers, but the business as well. The Issue Brief 7 on reasons why the informal sector workers actually evade or avoid participation in the formal sector are concerns related to taxes. The addition of social security taxes added to existing taxes, and regulatory mechanisms provide incentives for workers to escape or use the informal sector as some safe haven. An example of the issues related to social security payroll taxes is cited from Venezuela where the payroll taxes represent approximately 1/3 of what it cost for becoming part of the formal sector. Business owners are very sensitive in reference to taxes and regulatory practices. "In Brazil, escape to the informal sector and other forms of evasion increased as payroll tax rate rose during the economic down turn of the 1980's" (World Bank: Issue Paper 7, ibid, p. 319). The other forms of evasion can include on the part of entrepreneurs not reporting the full amount of a company's earnings, working hours of employees, not properly complying with rules and regulations, or not following the required schedule for payment contributions (World Bank, ibid).

It is interesting to note that from a small sample of formal sector employers who have provided an opportunity for the self-employed and/or workers in the informal sector, to voluntarily participate in their formal sectors, the defined contribution to the scheme from the self-employed is significant higher than the regular employees **(See Appendix A: Tables/ Charts, Chapter VI, Table 5).**

When a large segment of the labor force is not participating in the traditional tripartite system of collective bargaining, regardless of reasons what are the consequences? One consequence can result in many older persons, the current state of affairs in Sub-Saharan Africa, not having the minimal income security and/or social protection in old age. But from a country's perspective, the lack of full participation of the very large informal sector in the formal sector, "...entails a loss in budget revenues by reducing taxes and social security contributions paid and therefore the availability of funds to improve infrastructure and other public goods and services. It invariably leads to a high tax burden on registered labor" (World Bank: "Workers in the Informal Economy"). There are additional government concerns such as not having the appropriate revenues for providing the necessary social or entitlement programs (healthcare/social services, education, children allowances, and social pensions. Also, the lack of participation can result in much needed economic transformation activity (World Bank, ibid).

Although the issue and major concern is focused on social protection another emerging concern has to be related to future economic growth and transformation. A major priority, it seems in countries in Sub-Saharan Africa, is to continue the recent levels of sustained economic growth as well as become a major competitor globally. The current slogans emerging out of Africa, "Africa Rising," "Africa's Economic Renaissance," "The New Spirit," "The New Frontier," is more than just slogans but represent the economic realities that have been occurring during recent decades. There seems to be awareness that infrastructure development, expanding markets, continuing improvements in regulatory reforms, as well as management practices are key factors reference sustained economic growth. But, what draws attention to the dominant informal sector/economy, is need for the development of a highly skilled productive workforce. A highly skilled workforce with an emphasis on productivity is what will be needed to become a competitive force in a global world. But, the current informal sector which dominate the workforce, working within its organizational labor structure and culture, becomes more of a deterrent to the development of a highly skilled workforce to meet future needs in a cybernetic society. In reality the informal sector/economy can be characterized as a sector of low wages and low productivity in a highly competitive world.

The issues related to the needs of a skilled workforce is critical as the continent pass through a demographic transition with the anticipation of a growing and/or increasing number of youth, especially in the 15-24, 15-30 age groups **(SEE CHAPTER I – Section related to Demographic Transition/Dividend).** Also, the need for investments in the socialization of this young population in health, and especially education, to become the highly skilled workers that will drive or oversee and contribute to sustained economic growth in the future. By investing in the youth the Continent will become a demographic dividend and not a demographic disaster.

Multinationals are extremely excited about what is being referred to globally as the "youth bulge," the generation explosion within the youth population. They are looking at not only the potential of a highly skilled workforce, if proper investments are made, and potentially a very large consumer market. A major positive for Sub-Saharan Africa, considering fertility rates, is that it has potentially the largest number of 15-30 year olds than any other Region (See Chapter I section on fertility and mortality). With a skilled workforce this represents a demographic dividend regarding economic growth and development. But, this potential age group will need to become part of the formal economy with all of the rights and obligations for the results to be a demographic dividend.

Considering the aforementioned factors related to the significance of the informal/formal sectors in regards to social protection to move forward with the goal of increasing the percentage of social pensions, problems and issues within both sectors will have to be addressed. This discussion has to include not just the two labor sectors involved, but government/public and private entities. Also, and most importantly international organization, including the International Labor Organization, the World Bank, as well as the global non-governmental organization, such as Help Age International.

One Sub-Saharan country has become proactive in an attempt improve on the situation separating the informal sector from a pension system. Kenya during the year 2011 introduced a new "jua Kali" (informal sector) "Mbao Pension Scheme." The pension scheme was launched by the Kenyan National "jua Kali" Cooperative Society Limited. This is Kenya's attempt to include the very large number of informal sector workers in some form of a contributory/define benefits scheme that would provide some social protection, pension, following retirement. According to the Kenyan Retirement Authority of the more than 10 million labor force participants only approximately 15% are part of a retirement scheme. This means that more than 70% of those without not in a retirement scheme are part of the informal sector. The majority of the 70% are likely to end up following retirement in poverty. One factor that raises an alarm is that Kenya is currently seeing a significant, not from the informal to the formal sector, but from the formal to the informal sector during the recent decade; labor economists expect that this current trend will continue.

Kenya has set a target of some 8.5 million workers, especially those employed in small and median sized enterprises. Some experts are expressing a level of pessimism relating to the difficulties reaching the informal workers considering the complex structure of the informal sector. The new scheme is requesting that the informal sector workers contribute at least KES 20 p/day to qualify for a pension. The amount of return at the time of retirement will be based on the overall performance of the Fund. Kenya taking advantage of current communication technology will make their contributions by way of a money transfer system; participants will be able to receive updates regarding their account with the use of the cell phone. The Kenyan National jua kali Cooperative Society has hopes that as the new scheme becomes successful it will serve as a model for other countries with a dominant informal sector labor force (ISSA: Country Profiles, Section on Reforms by Kenya, Last input from Kenya, 2014

The ISSA has recommended that the extension of social protection coverage can be accomplished by doing exactly what is happening in Kenya, targeting the informal labor network that "... more than 70% of the African labor force is engaged in the informal economy and rural activities...the last national survey of the informal economy in Senegal showed 2.2 million workers in the informal (non-agricultural) economy in 2012 (82 percent of whom are entrepreneurs). Formal contributory social security schemes, which do not cover independent workers, have around 25,000 employers affiliated. The implementation of a scheme adapted to the needs of the informal (non-agricultural) economy, combined with other policies, can dramatically increase levels of social security coverage. As a measure of its potential to extend coverage, the affiliation of only 1 percent of this very large group of excluded informal workers in Senegal would double the national social security coverage rate" (ISSA: Africa Strategic Approaches to Improve Social Security, Development and Trends, 2014, page 7). (**Note: As recently as April 2018 Kenya became the 11th Sub-Saharan African Country to enact a statutory universal social pension plan) (See Appendix A, Tables and Charts, Chapter VI, Tables 2 -3).**

It has been strongly suggested that for social programs, such as a social pension, it is crucial that all parties/units of public and private systems work together or form strategic alliances to achieve the overall goals of social protection. The dominant informal labor sector in Sub-Saharan Africa is an excellent example of the need for stakeholders, especially the formal sector to work together. The informal sector remains on the outside resulting in the fact that retirees will not have a social pension on leaving the work force. "If informal labor markets remain the norm, then approaches that do not recognize this will not only mean that coverage targets are not met, but that social security systems' positive social and economic impacts are not realized more fully... In practice, this means the danger of an increasingly marginalized and vulnerable labor force working in precarious conditions without basic social protection..." (ISSA: Africa Strategic Approaches to Improve Social Security, Executive Summary, ibid, 2014, page v).

It seems obvious that the percent of current retirees or former employees without a social pension are related to there being employed in the informal sector. Furthermore, without some innovative policies immediately or in the near future, future older populations will not have basic income security; not only will a lack of policies impact negatively on the quality of life of older people, it can also be a significant deterrent to sustained economic growth and development. It seems urgent that countries identify and put in place innovative policies for the purpose of the two employee sectors, formal and informal, working together for the benefit of the current and future older populations.

One challenge from the International Social Security Association (ISSA) begins with the development of integrated systems in the various countries. In order "...to build comprehensive and coherent social security systems that take full advantage of the diversity of possible social protection mechanisms found in Africa will require greater political support and public trust and, perhaps most importantly, the design, financing and delivery of benefits which take into account a rapidly changing economic, social, demographic and environmental context. Also, to be taken into account are the contributory capacities and needs of workers in rural and informal economies and the respective disincentives/incentives associated with mandatory and voluntary coverage" (ISSA Developments and Trends: Africa, Strategic approaches to improve social security, Executive Summary, 2014). The ISSA, based on a number of success stories from Sub-Saharan Africa and Latin American countries, have observed some very positive indicators that have significantly increased political support as well as public trust in moving forward. The political support has come as a result of the growing research that the development of social pensions can be major contributions to economic development (ISSA, ibid, Executive Summary).

Globally, countries, although at different paces, are going through a demographic transition. Africa's Demographic Transition: Dividend or Disaster? The theme is the focus of the Africa Development Forum 2015. The global demographic transition, especially regarding changes in age structures, as well as dependency ratios, is critical in regards to economic growth and transformation. It seems especially critical in discussions related to the education and training of a future highly skilled productive workforce to compete in a global economy.

Failure to Take Advantage of Africa's Demographic Dividend: The "Youth Bulge" Generation

A major factor that could become quite a deterrent to economic growth would be a failure on the part of the continent to take advantage of what is being referred to as the Demographic Dividend. All countries in Sub-Saharan Africa have a major strength that other continents/countries for the most part do not have at this timeline in history. The evidence indicates that Africa is the only Region globally that will experience a significant population growth, the 15-24 age group during the next several decades (Chapter II, p. 29). The most significant growth of this specific age group will occur in Sub-Saharan Africa; during the current decade this particular cohort of young people will rise by 15%, 20% to 2030, 13% to 2040 and still 10% by the year 2050. Globally, Nigeria by the year 2050 will become the fourth most populous country in the world; by the year 2050 Africa will have seven of the 20 largest countries in the world (Robertson, ibid, p. 128). Currently, approximately 45% of the population is at or below the age of 15 and another 20% of the population is between 15-30 (Beckett, ibid, p. 94).

Africa with no global equals is currently the youngest continent. The population age group 15-24 in 2015 represented one/fifth (1/5th) of Africa's 1.2 billion people; by the year 2050 half of the population on the continent of Africa will represent the age group below 25 years of age. By the end of the 21st Century almost half, 47% to be more specific, of the world's youth will be African. Now, what is happening in Africa in regards to population growth is being described as the "youth bulge" generation or a generation population explosion that is taking place globally within the age groups 15 to 24. Globally, this demographic trend, generation explosion among the youth on a continent is being considered a demographic dividend; such significant changes in a population's age structure, could have a significant contribution to make regarding future economic growth and development. Hopefully, the "youth bulge" will contribute more than a population of future consumers but become part of the movement, "Africa Rising," not just economically, also actively participating in overall societal decision-making. The "youth bulge" "… constitutes a source of both labor inputs and human capital in production, improving total factor productivity in a region of the world where capital formation is limited (Ibrahim Forum Report 2017, Mo Ibrahim Foundation, 2017, p. 14; United Nations: DESA).

The "youth bulge" generation can contribute to what is described as a country or continent's demographic dividend. "A demographic dividend can occur during a window of opportunity created by reductions in child mortality and a demographic shift to fewer dependent people relative to working-age individuals...The full realization of the sexual and reproductive rights health and rights (SRHR) of adolescents and youth (ages 10-24) can facilitate gains in their health, well-being, and educational attainment. Long-term investments in the health of adolescents and youth, including their sexual and reproductive health, can help accelerate economic growth when combined with the appropriate investments in education and economic planning" (Gay, Elizabeth (Senior Policy Analyst/Author) et.al, Population Reference Bureau (PRB): In Collaboration with the African Union Commission (AUC) Department of Human Resource Science and Technology, "The Demographic Dividend in Africa Relies on Investments in Reproductive Health and Rights of Adolescents and Youth," Policy Brief, February 2017, p. 2).

In recognition of the importance of the "youth bulge" and the "demographic dividend," the African Union during its 2016 Assembly, "...established the theme for 2017 as "Harnessing the Demographic Dividend Through Investments in Youth...AU heads of states and governments recognize a country-level demographic dividend as central to the continent's economic transformation in the context of AU Agenda 2063-the AU global strategy for economic transformation within the next 50 years (Gay, PRB, February 2017, ibid). In its Agenda 2063 Framework Document: The Africa We Want, the African Union stated specifically, "Africa's young people are the primary vehicle for realizing the demographic dividend and the principle engine for fostering development at all levels. By 2063, Africa's children and youth will be fully engaged as the talent pipeline, principal innovators, and indeed the sustainers of Africa's advantages from transformation...Youth overt unemployment will have been eliminated and they would have full access to educational training opportunities, health services, recreational and cultural activities, as well as to financial means to allow each youth to fully realize their full potential. The youth will be incubators of new knowledge driven business start-ups and will contribute significantly to the economy" (Gay, PRB, February 2017, ibid, p. 4).

In reference to sexual and reproductive health and rights the question is did all the Presidents vote on and/or in consensus with the 2063 Agenda? Recently the President of Tanzania, John Magufuli, declared publicly that he was endorsing a 1960 law that allows the state school systems to expel young girls who become pregnant (Ratcliffe, Rebecca, The Guardian: Global Education, Women's Rights and Gender Equality, (UK), "After getting pregnant, you are done: no more school for Tanzania's mums-to-be," Friday June 30 2017). During the past decade approximately 55,000 young girls have been expelled from Tanzanian's state schools. It is reported that approximately 21% of girls 15-19 have given birth. The Women's campaign has publicly stated that the "...high numbers are result of rape, sexual violence and coercion" (Ratcliffe, The Guardian, June 2017, ibid). Although the African Union has declared a goal focusing on sexual behavior and reproductive health and rights in its 2063 agenda, there maybe need to ensure that all countries are on board.

The "youth bulge" also "...constitutes a reliable source of demand for a country's economy through their consumption activity. Simply lowering the youth unemployment rate to that of adults would lead to a 10-20% increase in Africa's GDP. Is fundamental for the development of a new class of African entrepreneurs (Ibrahim Forum Report 2017, ibid). The "youth bulge" considering the aforementioned factors, is obvious why it is being counted on as a demographic dividend. "...Africa has the opportunity to reap a "demographic dividend." As the total dependency ratio is projected to decrease steadily until 2085 (55.7% compared to 82.6% in 2005), there will be a larger workforce supporting fewer children and elderly people. The lower dependency burden will free up resources for development...the consequences of not taking full advantage of the youth's potential are wide-ranging, including significant economic losses, armed conflict, brain drain, as well as political and social unrest and instability (Ibrahim Forum Report 2017, ibid, 2017).

The question for countries, especially policy makers on all levels is are the political leaders, civic leaders, including non-governmental organization committed to providing all of the resources needed in preparing the current and future "bulge" generations as leaders to move the Continent forward? One of the major threats, and most critical, to economic growth and development will be a lack of commitment and resources for educating and preparing this population for greatness. The continent's current leadership has to take note of the new developing spirit, especially among the young of moving forward and getting things done. The leadership needs to listen to youth such as Ben Okri, the poetic leader of the African Renaissance, calling on leaders to take action now **(Chapter VIII, page 9).**

The African Forum concluded that the future of Africa depends to a great extent on the capacity of countries' leaders to respond positively to the needs and expectations of the growing youth population. The Forum challenged the leaders to utilize their capacity for harnessing the energy and expectations of the youth. During the year 2015 approximately 30 million of young people in Africa were unemployed. Although considered one of the fastest growing economies globally, the Forum concluded that Africa had not created enough jobs in responding to the demands and needs of youth (Ibrahim Forum 2017, ibid). One source has estimated that Sub-Saharan Africa will have to generate approximately "...one million jobs (new jobs) per/month to keep employment rates stable and will need to generate almost two million new jobs per/month by 2030... The labor force has been defined as those individuals beginning at 15 years and older within the population...is economically active, employed or unemployed (Lee, Christianson, Bietsch, ibid, 2017, pages 2-7).

The African Forum addressed several threats existing within the youth population; "too many young Africans feel devoid of economic prospects and robbed of any say on the future of their own Continent...Voter turnout is declining and skepticism about elected representatives is growing, especially among the young...Disenchantment with democracy and lack of economic opportunities form a 'toxic brew' bound to strengthen the appeal of migration and violent extremism (Ibrahim Forum 2017 Full Report, "Africa at a Tipping Point," April 7-9 2017, pages 10-86, Marrakech, Morocco). In reference to the subject of migration, approximately one-third of the young population classified as the tertiary (specialist) educated in Kenya, Uganda, Liberia, Mozambique and Ghana have left their countries. Also, in regards to the aforementioned 'toxic brew' leading to violence terrorist attacks have increased in Africa more than 1,000% (Ibrahim Forum 2017 Full Report, ibid).

Recently, as aforementioned there has been a new developing movement, Africans Rising for Justice, Peace and Dignity. In 2016 approximately 275 individuals, especially youth leaders, representing various civil societies, the trade union movement, women, men, persons with disabilities, political leaders, and faith based groups from across Africa and the Diaspora gathered in Tanzania. The results of the gathering were the creation of the Kilimanjaro Declaration that included the following statement regarding youth: "African youth are a critical foundation of building the success in our Continent and must play a central role in building African Rising." Furthermore, the Declaration calls for the movement to "…build an African wide solidarity and unity of purpose of the peoples of Africa to build the future we want: A Right to Peace, Social inclusion and Shared prosperity" (Ibrahim Forum, 2017 ibid).

It has to concern the continent's leadership when witnessing the departure or the migration of many young people each year, some risking their lives to do so, to Western and European countries seeking an enhanced quality of life. Many of upset because of the lack of opportunities for growth and development, excluded from the opportunity to become prepared and actively participate in their country's political process. Also, more and more they recognize the negative impact illicit financial practices, especially corruption can have on economic growth. Young people, especially in South Africa have begun to take to the streets in protest in reference to corruption practices. The Kilimanjaro Movement and Declaration is an attempt, especially the youth for the Continent to take note and proceed with corrective actions to create a society of "justice, peace and dignity. A major step will be a greater investment in youth, especially education and preparation for living in an information and/or cybernetic society. The launching for the movement took place on 25 May 2017 (Africans Rising for Justice, Peace and Dignity, media@Africans-rising.org.

If countries in Sub-Saharan Africa following conceptualization, design and implementation of appropriate social policies, especially those investing in youth, the results could be a demographic dividend for all concerned. All countries in Sub-Saharan Africa will be in a position to "reap the benefits." By taking actions immediately everybody benefits, especially the youth and future generations from the bulge explosion and/or the demographic dividend related to economic growth and transformation. "Policy choices and actions can transform the population of a nation into a healthy, educated, empowered labor force that can contribute to real and sustained growth and lifts people out of poverty" (Canning, et al, 2015, p.1). No progressive actions on the part of leadership in regards to significant investments in youth will become a major threat to economic growth and development.

On a very positive note the African Union has spoken. At an Assembly Meeting of the Union in June 2016 the theme was "Harnessing the Demographic Dividend Through Investments in Youth." The leadership, Heads of State, during the Assembly recognized that a demographic dividend for the countries was central to Africa's economic transformation within the context of its agenda 2063; the global strategy for the African Union strategy for economic transformation within the following 50 years. The Union concluded that, "Long-term investments in the health of adolescents and youth, including their sexual an reproductive health, can accelerate economic growth when combines with the appropriate investments in education and economic planning (Population Reference Bureau, Policy Brief 2017 "Harnessing the Demographic Dividend Through Investments in Youth," Washington, D.C., 2017).

In regards to the African Union commitment and strategy to long-term investments in youth, an International Foundation Leader has been speaking out on the subject. The Philanthropist is Bill Gates, Founder of Microsoft, until recently considered the richest person globally, now ranks second, recently expressed in an interview, "…stability in Africa makes a huge difference to the entire world, and that investing in the health and education of its young people is vital… By the end of this Century there will be four billion more people on earth and three billion of these extra souls will be born in Africa" (Toynbee, Polly, "The African Youth Boom: What's Worrying Bill Gates," The Guardian (USA Edition): Now Generation Global Development: Young People, Poverty, Africa, Interviews, 18 September 2018). It should be noted as revealed in the aforementioned interview with Polly Toynbee that "…half of the Bill and Melinda Gates Foundation spending goes to Africa" (Toynbee, ibid, 2018).

NON-CONTRIBUTORY SOCIAL PENSIONS: LESSONS LEARNED FROM SUCCESSFUL COUNTRIES

There is global research and sufficient evidence to illustrate that a non-contributory social or civic pension is affordable regardless of a country's income status. There is evidence demonstrating that if countries are strongly committed regardless of global income classification, they can create fiscal space and extend social protection to vulnerable populations such as the "Silver Tsunami." Examples from some committed countries, including Bolivia, Botswana, Brazil, C. Verde, Costa Rica, Kenya, Lesotho, Liberia, Mozambique, Namibia, Seychelles, Swaziland, Thailand, and South Africa have demonstrated that fiscal space can be identified for the purpose of extending social protection. It should be noted that nine of the aforementioned countries are from Sub-Saharan Africa. During the past decade these countries have accomplished their goal of extending social protection for the older population, especially those who were self employed and/or worked in the dominant informal sectors. Botswana, has not only extended social protection to its older population, but has included a universal social protection program for vulnerable children, especially orphans (Fabio, Duran-Valverde and Pacheco, Jose Franciso, "Fiscal Space and the Extension of Social Protection: Lessons Learned From Developing Countries," ESS Paper No. 33, ILO: Social Security Department, Geneva, 2012).

Countries without a social pension have considered several possible approaches or methods in an effort to provide some form of social protection, especially income security, for their older populations. The first consideration has been the process of extending their existence system of social insurance coverage to the uncovered population; secondly, the development of a mutual or micro system of coverage, lastly, the introduction of a non- contributory social assistance model for the older population. According to research the first two options were '…difficult to apply to high risk groups…and that social assistance schemes have more promise for rural populations than do other two possibilities' (Shen, Ce and Williamson, John B., "Does a Universal Non-Contributory Pension Scheme Make Sense for Rural China?" Journal of International Social Welfare, Vol. 22, No. 2, October 2006, pages 146-149).

Chapter VI, The Current State of Social Pensions in Sub-Saharan Africa, addresses the fact that a number of countries globally, including Sub-Saharan Africa, have introduced statutory non-contributory pension systems for the older population. Five of those countries (Botswana, Lesotho, Namibia, Mauritius and Seychelles) use age as the only eligibility criteria, others use a combination of age and the "means test" or "pension test" for determining eligibility. Also, as indicated in Chapter V, Brazil began with the use of a "means test" in addition to age, but later it was discarded as part of the process for determining eligibility. A couple of reasons were given for the change, administratively inefficiencies and a significant number of potential eligible citizens were overlooked during the eligibility screening process.

Under the auspices of the International Labor Organization, Social Security Department, and its "Global Campaign on Social Security and Coverage for all," a study was conceptualized, designed and implemented in eight countries that had successfully extended social protection programs (Duran-Valverde and Pacheco, ibid). The primary lessons from the aforementioned successful country experiences that other countries may want to consider are: the strategies/options utilized by the countries in extending social protection, especially how budget or fiscal space was created for financing. One very important lesson for other countries is the reality that a number of components have to be considered, especially in the creation of fiscal space, such as economic growth and transformation, what the countries consider to be their micro/macro economic priorities, and strong political/government support (Duran-Valverde and Pacheco, ibid).

It is very interesting to note some of the diversity of the countries under study by the ILO, geographically, population, economic growth/transformation, and human development. Three of the eight countries were in Latin America (Bolivia, Brazil, Costa Rica), one in Asia (Thailand), and four countries located in Sub-Saharan Africa (Botswana, Lesotho, Namibia, South Africa). Botswana, Costa Rica, and Lesotho, Namibia had populations ranging between 2 to 5 million; Bolivia approximately10 million; Brazil, South Africa, and Thailand over 50 million. Another area where diversity of the eight is noticeable is in the size of the economy, "… Brazil ranks among the top economies in the world, and is the biggest economy in the group followed by Thailand and South Africa…In terms of GDP per capita, the four top countries are Botswana, Brazil, Costa Rica, and South Africa (All with GDP per capita above US$10,000 in PPP terms; at the bottom of the group…poor countries like Lesotho, US$1,613 and Bolivia US$4,426… the sample contain a group of economies at very different stages of development and institutional maturity and with very different political models…With respect to GDP growth, one can identify three groups of countries. A first group, to which Botswana, Costa Rica and Namibia belong, presented an average annual growth rate above 4 percent between 1995-2009. A second group comprises Bolivia, Lesotho, South Africa and Thailand, with average growth rates in the range of 3.0 to 3.9 percent. Brazil lagged behind the other countries with an average GDP growth rate of 2,9 percent, partially attributable to low rates during the 1990s crisis" (Duran-Valverde and Pacheco, ibid, p. 7).

The countries under study are at various levels of economic growth and transformation, including human development. One measurable indicator that illustrates differences among the countries is the Human Development Index (HDI). The primary focus of the HDI is on people, their growth and development, especially their capacities, and not just economics. It looks at the average achievement of people in several areas or dimensions, including, Education, Standard of Living, and Health. The HDI does not focus specifically on poverty, social/economic inequalities, and human security (UN Development Reports). The Education Dimension looks at the mean years of schooling for adults aged 25 years and the projected years of schooling for children of school entering age; HDI assesses the Gross National Income p/capita. The HDI looks at a range of income from a minimum of $100 (PPP) to a maximum of $75,000 (PPP). The World Bank formula states that GDP per/capita is based on purchasing power parity. The PPP GDP is converted to international dollars using purchasing power parity. The Health Dimension looks at life expectancy at birth using a minimum value of 20 years and a maximum of 85 years (UN Development Reports). The overall value points that include the three aforementioned dimensions provide somewhat of a summary profile of the average achievement of an individual in significant dimensions of human development: a long and healthy life, level of knowledge, and having a decent standard of living (UNPD: Human Development Reports, "Human Development Index," 2009). **See Appendix B: Concepts, Definitions and Special Notes**).

The HDI value, of the three dimensions, for the eight countries that was under study ranges from 0.514 (Lowest) to 0.854 (Highest) (Duran-Valverde and Pacheco, ibid, 2014, p. 7).

Lesotho	0.514
South Africa	0.683
Namibia	0.686
Botswana	0.694
Bolivia	0.729
Thailand	0.783
Brazil	0.813
Costa Rica	0.854

It has also been noted that the countries under study have a history of commitment to social welfare programs that enhance the quality of life across age groups. All eight of the countries had programs focused on health and nutrition, education, and social protection (old-age pension); also other social welfare benefits including maternal and child health, and disability. Three of the eight countries reported to have conditional cash transfer programs. Five of the countries described their cash transfer programs as unconditional (Duran-Valverde and Pacheco, ibid, 2014, p. 13). Programs normally described as conditional cash transfer programs involves some form of a "means test" in determining eligibility for service. An example of an unconditional cash transfer program is the old age pension, including orphan care in Botswana. This particular program does not require a "means test," and eligibility is based on the country's definition of old age in determining eligibility for services.

According to the authors, there are two very significant lessons that can be learned from the countries' successful experiences. First of all, "…the creation of sustained fiscal space for social protection is feasible and there are multiple options for expanding this fiscal space…policy makers are not restricted to one or two options only; on the contrary, there is a considerable range of options to explore. The necessary tools are at hand and even the poorest countries considered in this study achieved extra ordinary results" (Fabio and Pacheco, ibid, p. 5). As aforementioned the country of Liberia, low-income with a per/capita income of $970.00, has instituted a social pension for those who had been employed in the informal sector or self-employed.

The matrix illustrating the range of strategies available that were used by the countries in the study included ten: (1) Mineral-based taxation or the use of similar taxes, (2) An increase in general taxation, (3) An increase in Social contributions, (4) Budget surplus, (5) A reduction in non-priority spending, such as a decline in military expenditures, (6) A reduction in the national debt, (7) Official development assistance, (8) The sale of government or state assets, (9) Gains from efforts in efficiency, and (10) Amendment to the Constitution (Fabio and Pacheco, ibid, Table 4, p. 15).

The second major lesson to be taken from the successful country experiences also demonstrated that there is no single recipe, or "cookie cutter" approach for raising the level of social protection financing. Although these countries have several points in common, the decisions adopted by government depend on the social, political, economic and cultural environment of each nation. In other words, the best strategy has a strongly idiosyncratic component" (Fabio and Pacheco, ibid, pages 16-21).

It becomes obvious that there was no "cookie cutter" model or approach that countries used in achieving their goals of social protection; each country made use of a wide range of strategies to create fiscal space. Once again, although the countries under study have some common factors, they differ in significant ways, or each is at somewhat of a different phase of economic growth and transformation. In other words under close analysis one could find some similar attributes within the social, political, economical and cultural settings, one would also discover some significant differences, especially in regards to social/economic growth. But, the key focus here is that despite the existing differences each country has achieved the goal of social protection (Fabio and Pacheco, ibid).

Additional or other recent experiences in Latin America also offer blueprints to be considered by countries seeking to expand program coverage to their respective older populations. A review of these experiences reinforces the observation that there is no uniform or "cookie cutter" approach or model. Beginning around the year 2000 the subject of social protection for the older population fueled by intense debates among stakeholders in the political and academic arena created a proactive environment for action (Rofman, Rafael, Apella, Ignacio, and Vezza, Evelyn, "Expanding Economic Protection to the Elderly in Latin America," International Social Security Review, Vol. 68, 1/2015). A major goal of the initiative was to expand or extend coverage of social protection within the informal labor sector. Some fourteen countries within the "...region introduced inclusive reforms – involving non-contributory schemes – which sought to expand coverage for the elderly" (Rofman, et al, ibid, p. 2, 2015). Evidence shows that non-contributory schemes related to social protection, including the elderly, were not a new initiative, but had been in existence for years. But, it was between the years 2000-2013 that the proactive intensity magnified.

Several factors were presented by the researchers that contributed to the proactive movement, "...including the exhaustion of the contributory model for extending statutory coverage developed in the second half of the twentieth century, an improvement in the fiscal situation in most countries in the region, and social pressure demanding better adapted social protection policies, with an emphasis on addressing the needs of vulnerable populations"

(Rofman, et al, ibid). Results of the more recent initiatives have made it possible for a larger group from the elderly population, who in the past had no protection, to become part of the social protection system, especially a statutory social pension scheme (Rofman, et al, ibid).

There are a couple of strategies that may be very helpful for those countries with the goal of extending or expanding social protection to the older population. Within the Latin America experience, "Inclusion strategies have been based on two alternative models: the expansion of traditional contributory pension schemes; and the development of poverty reduction programs focused on the elderly. The two models show differences regarding the legal and institutional means used, the adequacy of benefits, the fiscal and economic sustainability of the new programs, and their impact on and interaction with other areas of public policy. This diversity provides a fertile environment for the analysis and evaluation of policies regarding coverage" (Rofman, et al, Ibid). It should be emphasized that the success of program extensions in Latin America had a great deal to do with and/or partnerships with other public policies. In other words some countries recognize that there is a relationship between a social pension policy and policies related to economic growth and transformation. This may be a very important area for other countries with similar ambitions to consider.

The initiatives that were introduced and implemented in Latin America during the critical time period between 2000-2013 demonstrated "...a clear paradigm shift in social protection models in Latin America, from systems based strongly on the contributory model to others that are mixed, combining non-contributory components to a degree never previously recorded in the history of such programs" (Rofman, et al, Ibid, p. 21). Once again as aforementioned in the previous paragraph much of the success in Latin America could be attributed to "... their sustainability under both fiscal and economic policy...created under particularly good macroeconomic and fiscal conditions, given the international economic context of the first decade of this century" (Rofman et al, ibid p 21).

THE ULTIMATE GOAL IS A SOCIAL PENSION FOR ALL: FACTORS TO CONSIDER IN MOVING FORWARD

Affordability and Fiscal Space in Budgets, Technical Assistance

Global research has demonstrated that a social/citizen pension for the non-tripartite labor sector for the current and future populations of older persons is affordable. It is strongly recommended that countries in the process of enacting a social pension review the success stories whereas social protection programs, such as a social pension have been adopted; the key factor here is that not only review the middle to upper income countries, but the successful low-income countries as well. Also, during the pre or initial stages during the process countries should be aware of and make use of the technical assistance available from global organizations such as the International Social Security Association (ISSA), The International Labor Organization (ILO), The World Bank, as well as Help Age International, the global non-governmental organization. In reference to the ISSA the following are highly recommended: ISSA Guidelines for Social Security Administration, the ISSA Barometer, and the ISSA Academy, and The ILO's Social Protection Floors Recommendations 202, dated 2012.

Country Diversity

International organizations based on global experiences, recognize that there is no one model fits all approach "cookie cutter" pension system for all countries. For each country, keeping in mind the goal of a social pension for all, a variety of methods and/or approaches should be considered. Countries are very diverse, politically, socially, culturally, and economically. The political readiness and/or support can be very critical; demographic and various economic shocks, as well a country's history of responding to social shocks will vary. The challenges of country diversity in most instances will call into play an exploration or critical analysis of innovative methods/approaches during the conceptualization and planning process.

Non-Contributory Cash Transfers: Experiences from Successful Countries

The book or manuscript's primary focus has been to address the plight of older persons in Sub-Saharan Africa without a social pension. They represent the large percentage of former workers without a history of participation in a tripartite (worker, employer, public) collective bargaining system. There are significant lessons, including innovative approaches, to be learned from low and middle-income countries, Botswana, Lesotho, Namibia, and Swaziland, from their experiences. The non-contributory cash transfer programs that are financed primarily from tax revenues in the aforementioned countries are more common in countries where the informal labor sector remains a large part of the labor market, 70%. Within a multi-pillar approach the non-contributory cash transfer program represents the first level of the ladder. The future goal for a country could be that as the numbers of workers within the informal sector are added to formal sector the beginning pillar will no longer be needed. In Sub-Saharan Africa there are eleven countries to learn from, two representing low-income countries, that have instituted statutory non-contributory social pensions for the older population.

In addition to the countries listed above, countries should seriously consider the experiences in Latin America. First, the approach used in combining the traditional contributory models with those that were mixed, and the blending of the non-contributory models; in other words, take a serious look at the inclusion strategies utilized. Secondly, the major focus on interactions with other areas of macroeconomic public policies, to ensure sustainability of new programs, especially social pensions for the elderly population (Rofman, et al, ibid).

The Administrative Use of a Means/Pension Tests for Eligibility Determination

In order to determine a person's eligibility for a particular service or program some countries will utilize a method known as a means or pension test (See Chapter V). Some countries when establishing a social pension for older persons will utilize such a test. It is recommended that a country may want to research the countries employing such a method for determining eligibility for an older person's to receive a social pension or transfer program. One recommendation is that if such a test is used, "…it should be harmonized (and possibly administered jointly) with other social assistance programs—although eligibility criteria should take into account the low capacity of the old to work productively and benefit levels might vary by age, according to estimated consumption needs" (James, Estelle, et al, A World Bank Policy Research Report, Averting the Old Age Crisis: Policies to Protect the Old and Promote Growth, New York: Oxford University Press, 1994, p 239). Some countries following the adoption of the means test (Chapter V, the Brazilian experience) later eliminated it from the process of determining eligibility. Brazil discovered that the overall administrative costs far outweighed its usefulness, and also discovered that the process was omitting persons that should have been included. It should be noted that countries in Sub-Saharan Africa, Botswana, Lesotho, Namibia and Swaziland with very successful outcomes, only use age in determining eligibility.

Several negative factors were excited by (Shen and Williamson, ibid, pages 147-148) in their research related to the use of the "means test:" According to the Authors, 'Means-tested pension schemes limit benefits to those who fall below a specified income (or assets) limit. Means tests tend to discourage working and savings by increasing the effective marginal tax rate; simultaneously, they encourage working in the informal sector, and reduce the tax base and size of the formal sector of the economy…').

Collaboration with All Stakeholders

Research has demonstrated a strong correlation between social protection programs, including social pensions, and economic growth and transformation. In other words, the two concepts reinforce each other. As aforementioned, a social pension can reduce poverty, unemployment, and contribute to economic growth. The conceptualization, design, and development of social protection policies should not be done in isolation and consideration given serious collaboration with other stakeholders. Social protection policies need to be promoted and developed alongside a wide range of other policy activities, especially those related to economic growth and transformation.

Chronic Illness/Disability and the Aging Process

The central focus of this book has been the subject, the lack of a social pension or more specifically, income insecurities in old age. Once again, approximately 80% of older persons in Sub-Saharan Africa are without a basic or adequate income for retirement. If it has been such an historical struggle to ensure a basic income one can imagine the struggle for access to health care and social service coverage. But, the reality is that countries will have to devote more attention to a growing older population with health and social service needs. Chapters I, and V have addressed the health and social service needs, especially those related to chronic illnesses such as Dementia and Alzheimer's. This will become a major challenge for all of the stakeholders, especially health systems, government policy makers, and health and social service activists. Also, there are very important learning experiences, Chapter V, from countries, such as the United Kingdom and the United States from the challenges they have faced in meeting the long-term care needs of a growing older population.

SUMMARY/CONCLUSION

The evidence from global research sources has concluded that a correlation does exist between economic growth and social protection programs, including social pensions. Therefore, it becomes imperative that political and civic leaders, governmental and non-governmental organizations, comprehend the relationship between economic growth and social protection policies. If social protection programs are going to benefit from and contribute to economic growth, a country's comprehensive social policy goals cannot be pursued in isolation. They must be promoted alongside a broad range of coherently applied policy actions, including macroeconomics, labor, social, health and education (ISSA, "Africa: Strategic Approaches to Improve Social Security, Development and Trends," 2014, pages 26-27). The future success of social pensions in Sub-Saharan Africa for the older population will depend on the Region's economic growth and transformation.

Sub-Saharan Africa has demonstrated over the past couple of decades that the Region is ready to takes its place in the global economic arena. Regardless of what the naysayers may say, economically Africa is positioning itself, not only to benefit also contribute to the global economies. Although there has been a slowdown in growth since 2014, Africa is like other global regions, countries experiencing slowdowns in growth; see aforementioned Table (World Bank country projections 1961 – 2015). Research evidence illustrates the sustained economic experiences in recent decades for Sub-Saharan Africa.

Some of the economic successes experienced by countries in Sub-Saharan Africa can be attributed to factors such as a diversification of trading partners, or trading in more expanded markets; successes have also come from more public and private investments, inter-intra regional. Globally, countries have seen, research confirms, enhanced business/administrative practices, and very good progress in regulatory reforms. There is also a major shift away from Aid Programs and more toward Foreign Direct Investments.

Although tremendous strides have been made for enhanced economic growth, there exist some major potential threats to future successes. The countries will need to continue to improve in the areas of management and business practices, especially in the areas of regulatory reforms. Countries for the most part, aforementioned, have demonstrated a commitment and willingness to continue making advancements in this area. Two of the major potential threats continue to be corruption and the lack of a partnership or collaboration between the informal and formal labor sectors. Recent examples in countries such as The Gambia, Somali demonstrate the impact corruption can have during the electoral process. Corruption is not just a matter of the electoral process but the financial and illicit practices have invaded the day-to-day lives of citizens. Secondly, there is a desperate need for the two labor sectors, formal and informal to become collaborative partners in increasing the number of older persons with a pension following retirement from 16.9% to 100%. The lack of affordability for a social pension can no longer be the reason for a lack of social pensions. Approximately fifteen countries in Sub-Saharan Africa now have statutory pension systems, some of the countries have been classified by the World Bank as low-income, for the older population; they represent the retirees who spent their work history as self-employed or worked in the informal sector.

Once again, there is a "new spirit" in Africa, especially among the youth bulge generation and considering the recent successes in sustained economic growth there are reasons to be optimistic. The goal is social protection/pension for all; countries such as Botswana, Lesotho, Liberia and Swaziland have demonstrated that it is possible with a small amount of a country's GDP. Botswana, not only has a social pension for the older population who worked in the informal sector or self-employed, but have included provisions for children and/or orphans. Keep in mind many children have been left with grandparents due to a variety of reasons, military/political conflicts and parental health issues. A large number of these children are living with grandparents without a social pension.

CONCLUSION

The book began with a major focus on the dynamic global demographic population explosion that had begun in the early 1800's. The dynamics of this unprecedented demographic phenomenon were highlighted by an increasing global population growth across all age groups especially the growing older population. As aforementioned the world had reached the population mark of one billion around 1800 and since that time the growth has continued not only at a rapid pace over the years but requiring significantly less time to reach designated timelines; for example between one billion to two or six billion. This demographic growth phenomenon, sometimes referred to as a demographic shock or explosion, has and will continue to affect or have an impact on all continents, countries and regions, especially their critical societal systems. Those systems as aforementioned throughout the previous chapters include: the family, political, economic, occupational, medical, health and social welfare.

One major question as the world observed these demographic dynamics taking place was what were the causative factors contributing to this growth phenomenon? The responses over the years, based on research findings and other scholarly pursuits were that the major factors contributing to this demographic phenomenon included medical discoveries, innovations in medical, health and public education. Public health education, especially historically has played a very significant role. Also, there were other factors to consider as well such as the evolution in agricultural technology, production and distribution, infrastructure development beginning with the industrial revolution that included rail transportation. Yes, with the coming of the Industrial era there were the developments of various infrastructure systems including the construction of roads, transportation and electric power systems.

The growing older population, "Silver Tsunami," has received special attention because of the impact this growing population group, referred to by some as 60 plus or the beginning of the ageing process in the Western or developed world. A reminder is that beginning age group for the aging process will vary according to a continent's or country's culture, traditions, social and economic factors; in other words, the beginning of the aging process in the developing world could begin around age 55 to 58 years. The major importance of the growing older population is the major significance it will have on all societal systems, especially the family, medical, health and social. In regards to this particular population group globally a very critical question arises, to what extent does population-aging matters in the 21st Century? Chapter II thoroughly addresses the question. The question was not to downplay other age groups, but to respond to projections globally of the impact the growing older population, especially the chronic illnesses accompanying the demographic growth phenomenon, could possibly have on all of the aforementioned critical and/or essential societal systems.

As international organizations, countries, political leaders, social activists began to recognize the demographic growth occurring and the potential impact on key societal systems, somewhat of a belated alarm went off. The United Nations, for example organized the First General Assembly on Aging in 1982 with an overall goal(s) of providing an opportunity for member countries to gather, share information regarding the demographic phenomenon taking place and make preparation for the "Silver Tsunami," the growing older population. Since 1982 there have been a number of Assemblies, Forums, Conferences resulting in policy and program declarations with a focus on making preparations to ensure that the older population live in dignity with sufficient income security in their later lives. Despite all the assemblies, pledges and declarations since 1982, the aforementioned have had little impact on ensuring social protection for the growing older population; an example is Sub-Saharan Africa where 82.5 % of retirees do not have a social pension. Globally, those lacking social protection such as social pensions or basic income are 51% or more than half the older population globally. In other words the problem is global.

The consensus is that globally all countries, some more so than others, will feel the impact of a growing older population. Continents and/or countries, listed as low to middle income, especially Sub-Saharan Africa will be extremely challenged. The critical question is how well are the countries, not only in Sub-Saharan Africa, but other low to middle income countries globally, prepared for a growing older population? Sub-Saharan Africa has a history of caring for its vulnerable members, especially the elderly and children. The caring system commonly referred to as the extended family system has been weakened following years of colonization, including forced labor, the taking of critical land resources as well as the forced separation of tribes/people from their family's historical caring for each other. The major challenge for Sub-Saharan Africa as well other low to middle income countries will be to become innovative in finding ways for responding to their growing older population. Adding to the aforementioned challenge(s) a number of the aforementioned countries will be confronted with modernization, industrialization and urbanization. It will be difficult for historical traditions and customs, especially the extended family system, to perform as in the past in caring for family members including the growing older population.

As aforementioned all of the Assemblies, forums and conferences beginning around 1982, including adopted declarations, have had little impact on the older population regarding income security as well as access to medical, social and health systems including long-term care. The State of social protection/social pensions has changed very little in recent years. The United Nations introduced in recent years Minimum Development Goals and Sustainable Development Goals designed with specific measurable objectives for improving the quality of life of people globally. Goals and objectives, including specific methods for reducing the number of older persons globally without social pensions or basic income security were not included.

The time is now, not just for the countries in Sub-Saharan Africa, but globally in honor of social justice and human rights. Action is needed to ensure that the older population of retirees be ensured of social protection, especially a social pension. As aforementioned, only half, approximately fifty-one percent of the current population of older persons globally have a social pension. Research tells us that a social pension, regardless of p/capita income is not just affordable and achievable also sustainable. Global research has also demonstrated that even low-income countries, including some in Sub-Saharan Africa with very low per/capita incomes have come up with innovative ways to provide a social pension for a population who worked for years as self employed or in the informal sectors. Liberia is one example of a country with a p/capita income of about $970 dollars who has come up with an innovative way of providing a social pension for those who worked in the informal sectors or self employed. Although not listed under the specific category of low-income other countries in Sub-Saharan Africa have come up with innovative ways of providing a social pension for the older population and in some instances a special provision for children. The aforementioned countries include: Botswana, Kenya, Namibia, C. Verde and Swaziland; not only have countries in Sub-Saharan Africa discovered ways for providing a social pension for those who were not part of a tripartite collective bargaining system, similar progress comes from countries in Latin America/Caribbean.

Finally there is hope for the future in Sub-Saharan Africa for providing not only social protection for a growing older population but policies and programs for ensuring enhanced quality of life across all age groups. The optimism is related to the following: (1) The Continent has been experiencing economic growth and according to economists has one of the fastest growing economies globally. (2) There has been an increase in foreign direct investment, infrastructure development, especially inter-regional activities. (3) There is a "new spirit" in Africa especially among the growing youth population. The growing commitment of the youth is getting things done. The current youth movement, "Africa Rising" is gaining momentum observed by the theme conferences across Africa during the past several years. The "new spirit" among the youth, includes the phrase, "Tarzan" does not live in Africa anymore. Social protection for all, including a growing older population is coming to the Continent.

It should be pointed out that there is a global movement underway for the purpose of ensuring that that all of the growing older population, the "Silver Tsunami" has basic income security, and access to other systems of care including social welfare, medical and health that include long-term care. Most importantly, there is also movement to do away with all forms of ageism and/or stereotypes that prevent the growing older population from living in their later lives with dignity and respect. This global movement, as aforementioned has been under the leadership of Help Age International, a global non-governmental organization with a goal of enhancing the quality of life for the growing older population. In recent years, with assistance from international activists including Bishop Desmond Tutu Noble Prize Laureate from South Africa has been petitioning the United Nations to have a Special Session focused on the problems and issues being confronted daily by the growing older population. A very happy note is that the United Nations is currently working with activists from around the world in addressing the aforementioned concerns.

APPENDIX A

TABLES/CHARTS

CHAPTER I
Global Population Growth: A Historical Perspective 8000 B.C. to 2100

Table 1
Global Population The 1 Billion Mark (1800/1804:
Population Percentages By Major Regions

REGION		% OF POP 1800				
Asia		65				
Africa		10.9				
Europe		20.8				
N. America		0.7				
Oceania		0.2				
Latin America/Caribbean		2.5				
Although Historians use	1800 for the	One (1) B				
Mark, some have preferred the date 1804						

Table 2
Global Population By Major Regions: 2015, 2030, 2050, 2100

MAJOR AREAS/REGIONS		POPULATION (MIL)			
		2015	2030	2050	2100
World		7,349	8,501	9,725	11,213
Africa		1,186	1,679	2,478	4,387
Asia		4,393	4,923	5,267	4,889
Europe		738	734	707	646
Latin Amer. & Caribbean		634	721	784	721
North America		358	396	433	500
Oceania		39	47	57	71
Ref: United Nations: DESA, Population Division, World Population Prospects: The 2015 Revisions, Key Findings and Advanced Tables, page1					

Table 3
Percentage of the World Population By Major Regions

Regions		2015	2030	2050	2100	
World		100	100	100	100	
Africa		16	20	25	39	
Asia		60	58	54	44	
Europe		10	9	7	6	
LA/Caribbean		9	8	8	6	
N. America		5	5	4	4	

Oceania		1	1	1	1	
Dev. Countries		17	15	13	11	
Developing Countries		70	69	67	60	
Least Developed		13	16	20	28	
	UN: DESA, Pop. Division, World Pop. Prospects 2015					

Table 4
Percentage of World Population Distribution by Regions 1800(4) - 2050

HISTORICAL MILESTONES IN WORLD POPULATION:
1804 – 2050 WORLD POPULATION: 1804 - 2050

POPULATION (B)	YEAR REACHED	NUMBER OF YEARS TO INCREASE BY ONE BILLION				
1	1804					
2	1927	123				
3	1960	33				
4	1974	14				
5	1987	13				
6	1999	12				
	PROJECTIONS	FOLLOWING 2000				
7	2012	13				

8	2026	13				
9	2043	17				
9.3	2050					
UN: Pop. Div., World Pop. Prospects: The 2000 Rev., Vil. III, 2001						

Table 5
Life Expectancy At Birth, Dev. Groups, Major Regions: 2005-2010; 2045-2050; 2095-2100

MAJOR AREA		2005-2010	2045-2050	2095-2100			
World		68.7	75.9	81.8			
More Dev. Regions		76.9	82.8	88.9			
Less Dev. Regions		67.0	74.8	80.8			
Least Dev. Countries		58.4	70.4	77.6			
Other less Dev. Countries		68.8	76.0	82.2			
Africa		55.6	68.9	77.1			
Asia		70.3	76.9	83.0			
Europe		75.3	81.3	87.9			
Latin America/Caribbean		73.4	81.8	87.9			
Northern America		78.4	83.7	89.0			
Oceania		76.8	81.7	86.6			
SOURCE: UN: DESA, Pop. Div., World Pop. Prospects, 2012 Revision							

Table 6
Life Expectancy At Birth (Years) By Gender Globally and Development Groups

Major Areas		2005-2010	2045-2050	2095-2100		
		Male Female	Male Female	Male Female		
World		66.5 71.0	73.7 78.2	79.9 83.7		
More Dev. Regions		73.4 80.4	79.9 85.7	86.5 91.4		
Less Dev. Regions		65.2 68.8	72.7 76.8	79.1 82.7		
Least Dev. Countries		57.3 59.5	68.5 72.3	75.6 79.7		
SOURCE: UN, DESA, Pop. Division, World Pop. Prospects, 2012 Revision						

Table 7
Global Life Expectancy at Age 60 By Developmental Regions

REGIONS		2010-2015	2010-2025	2045-2050		
WORLD		20	21	22		
MORE DEV.		23	24	26		
LESS DEV.		19	20	21		
LEAST DEV.		17	18	20		

Table 8
Life Expectancy at Age 80 By Developmental Regions

| | 2010 - 2015 | 2020 - 2025 | 2045 2050 | | |
	80 + # of Years	80 + # of Years	80 + # of Years		
DEV. REGIONS					
World	8	8	9		
More Developed	9	10	11		
Less Developed	7	7	8		
Least Developed	6	7	8		

Table 9
The Dynamics of Population Aging in the modern World:
Percent 65 Plus By Regions

MAJOR REGION/COUNTRY	1950		2000		2050	
World	5.2		6.9		19.3	
Africa	3.2		3.3		6.9	
L America & Caribbean	3.7		5.4		16.9	
China	4.5		6.9		22.7	
India	3.3		5.0		14.8	
Japan	4.9		17.2		36.4	
Europe	8.2		14.7		29.2	
Italy	8.3		18.1		35.9	
Germany	9.7		16.4		31	
Sweden	10.3		17.4		30.4	

USA		8.3		12.3		21.1		
Ref: MAJOR SOURCE / UN 2001 - Leonid A. Gavrilou & Patrick Heuveline, "Aging of Pop.," IN: Paul Demeny & Geoffrey McNicoll (Eds), The Ency. of Population, NY: MacMillian, 2003								

Table 10
Global Population 65 Plus By Gender: 2015-2030-2050

YEAR	TOT. POP BOTH SEXES	MALE	FEMALE	POP 65 PLUS BOTH SEXES	MALE	FEMALE	% AGE 65 PLUS BOTH SEXES	MALE	FEMALE	
2015	7,253.3	3,652.0	3,601.3	617.1	274.9	342.2	8.5	7.5	9.5	
2030	8,315.8	4,176.7	4,139.1	998.7	445.2	553.4	12.0	10.7	13.4	
2050	9,376.4	4,681.7	4,694.7	1,565.8	698.5	867.3	16.7	14.9	18.5	
	An Aging World	2015; Issued 3/20/16, Dept. Commerce - Census Bureau	Wan He, Daniel Goodkind, Paul Kowal Authors							

Table 11
Globally The Most Populous Countries: 2016 - 2050

COUNTRY 2016	POPULATION (M)		COUNTRY 2050	POPULATION (M)		
China	1,378		India	1,708		
India	1,329		China	1,344		
United States	324		United States	398		
Indonesia	259		Nigeria	398		
Brazil	206		Indonesia	360		
Pakistan	203		Pakistan	344		
Nigeria	187		Brazil	226		
Bangladesh	163		Congo Dem. Rep.	214		
Russia	144		Bangladesh	202		
Mexico	129		Egypt	169		
UN: PRB, 2016 World Pop. Data Sheet, PRB, Wash., DC, 2016						

Table 12
Globally Highest and Lowest Fertility Rates 2016

HIGHEST			LOWEST			
Niger	7.6		So. Korea	1.2		
So. Sudan	6.7		Romania	1.2		
Congo Dem. Rep.	6.5		Singapore	1.2		
Chad	6.4		Taiwan	1.2		
Somalia	6.4		Bosnia Herzego.	1.3		

Burundi	6.1		Greece	1.3	
Angola	6.0		Moldova	1.3	
Mali	6.0		Poland	1.3	
Mozambique	5.9		Portugal	1.3	
Uganda	5.8		Spain	1.3	
UN: PRB 2016 Pop. Data Sheet, Wash., DC, 2016					

Table 13
Projected Global Population Decline 2006-2030

COUNTRY		PERCENT DECLINE (MIL)				
Russia		-18.0				
Japan		-11.1				
Ukraine		-7.1				
South Africa		-5.8				
Germany		-2.9				
Italy		-2.8				
Poland		-2.0				
Romania		-1.5				
Bulgaria		-1.4				
Spain		-1.4				
		REF: Why Pop. Aging Matters, Trend 5:Aging and Pop. Decline, Publications No. 07-6134, National Institute on Aging, Washington, D.C., USA				

Table 14
Population Growth Sub-Saharan Africa 2010 – 2050 - % 60 Plus

COUNTRY	TOTAL POP 2010	% 60+	TOTAL POP 2050	% 60+		
Angola	749,199	4%	3,564,096	8%		
Benin	461,649	5%	2,307,410	10%		
Botswana	117,057	6%	373,027	13%		
Burkina Faso	535,519	3%	3,060.730	7%		
Burundi	376,857	4%	1,960,831	13%		
Cameroon	1,084,229	5%	4,077,071	11%		
Cape Verde	27,665	5%	162,927	23%		
Central Af. Repub	263,517	6%	827,775	11%		
Chad	510,000	4%	2,073,561	7%		
Comoros	32,242	5%	185,067	15%		
Congo	214,150	6%	856,590	12%		
Congo Dem Rep	2,857,759	4%	11,965,177	8%		
Cote d'Ivoire	1,308,319	6%	5,202,786	12%		
Djibouti	47,773	5%	208,766	14%		
Guinea	533,063	5%	2,545,641	11%		
Guinea Bissau	89,914	5%	300,270	8%		
Guinea Equatorial	29,606	4%	136,807	9%		
Eritrea	214,188	4%	1,242,502	11%		
Ethiopia	4,297,304	5%	18,245,248	10%		
Gabon	96,742	6%	390,993	16%		
Gambia	86,120	5%	355,548	9%		
Ghana	1,400.144	6%	5,875,110	13%		
Kenya	2,089,634	4%	8,623,102	10%		
Lesotho	133,128	7%	254,141	10%		
Liberia	200,071	5%	958,730	11%		
Madagascar	932,275	5%	4,856,324	11%		
Malawi	762,748	5%	2,908,793	8%		
Mali	502,770	4%	2,183,580	8%		
Mauritana	148,963	4%	747,844	12%		

Mauritius	150,602	12%	456,321	30%		
Morocco	2,610,934	8%	11,178,411	25%		
Mozambique	1,190,767	5%	3,779,388	8%		
Namibia	124,865	6%	482,225	13%		
Niger	554,145	3%	2,959,242	5%		
Nigeria	8,158,284	5%	29,981,880	10%		
Rwanda	393,757	4%	2,280,040	10%		
Sao Tome Princip	8,691	5%	42,689	14%		
Senegal	504,753	4%	2,548,160	10%		
Seychelles	10,274	0				
Sierre Leone	202,677	3%	866,176	7%		
South Africa	3,694,968	7%	9,286,054	16%		
Sudan	2,480,261	6%	10,636,279	14%		
Swaziland	63,638	5%	148,555	8%		
Tanzania	2,189,234	5%	9,196,160	8%		
Togo	372,536	5%	1,818,111	14%		
Uganda	1,397,349	4%	6,376,474	7%		
Zambia	632,235	5%	1,979,770	7%		
Zimbabwe	731,869	6%	2,819,762	13%		

Table 15
Sub-Saharan Africa: Dependency and Support Ratios/Social Pension
2015 - 2030

Regions		Dependency Ratio	Support Ratio	Social Pension		
		2015 2030	2015 2030	Yes No		
East Africa						
Burundi		133.6 130.0	17.3 13.6	No		
Comoros		115.1 99.5	16.6 13.2	No		
Djibouti		88.3 75.6	12.7 9.5	No		

Eritrea		124.4 98.2		16.9 16.9		No	
Ethiopia		131.2 94.4		12.4 12.7		No	
Kenya		122.3 102.7		16.1 13.4		Yes	
Madagascar		125.7 109.0		15.6 12.9		No	
Malawi		147.9 120.8		11.7 14.4		No	
Mauritius		57.7 62.1		6.6 3.6		Yes	
Mayotte		126.4 95.8		11.8 9.4		No	
Mozambique		147.8 127.5		12.1 12.5		Yes	
Reunion		71.2 79.3		5.7 3.0		No	
Rwanda		119.4 91.6		16.3 12.0		No	
Seychelles		59.2 71.4		9.1 4.4		Yes	
Somalia		154.3 137.3		13.9 14.8		No	
South Sudan		130.0 110.0		12.5 13.2		No	
Uganda		161.0 130.9		15.4 18.4		No	
Tanzania		142.5 127.3		12.9 12.8		No	
Zambia		147.9 126.4		13.9 16.6		No	
Zimbabwe		123.5 100.2		15.1 16.3		No	
Middle Africa							
Angola		154.4 136.4		17.0 15.8		No	
Cameroon		129.8 108.1		13.6 14.1		No	
C. Africa Rep.		116.6 95.8		12.0 12.3		No	
Chad		158.4 134.3		15.8 16.8		No	
Congo		129.2 116.3		11.9 11.5		No	
Dem. R. Congo		147.3 128.4		13.6 13.9		No	
Equal. Guinea		108.6 106.0		16.6 8.8		No	
Gabon		110.3 92.8		9.3 9.9		No	
Sao Tome Prin.		129.0 105.2		14.2 13.3		No	
Sou. Africa							
Botswana		82.9 72.8		15.2 11.1		Yes	
Lesotho		108.0 92.0		11.6 13.5		Yes	
Namibia		104.2 91.4		13.9 11.3		Yes	
South Africa		78.4 70.2		11.1 8.3		Yes	

Swaziland		110.0 95.5	13.3 12.4	Yes		
Western Africa						
Benin		126.4 105.4	15.3 14.2	No		
Burkina Faso		142.9 120.6	17.2 17.0	No		
C. Verde		80.7 66.2	12.1 8.7	Yes		
Cote d'Ivoire		130.2 115.3	14.4 14.6	No		
Gambia		148.8 129.2	17.7 16.3	No		
Ghana		109.7 96.3	14.0 12.7	No		
Guinea		128.8 111.4	14.3 13.3	No		
Guinea Bissau		119.4 104.3	14.4 13.4	No		
Liberia		126.8 106.0	14.6 13.9	Yes		
Mali		153.9 133.8	15.6 17.4	No		
Mauritania		115.9 100.7	14.4 12.2	No		
Niger		172.3 171.4	14.2 13.3	No		
Nigeria		132.9 119.5	15.7 15.7	No		
Senegal		133.4 117.6	14.6 14.3	No		
Sierra Leone		126.5 101.0	16.5 17.2	No		
Togo		124.1 105.7	16.1 15.2	No		
	Definitions:	Total Age Dependency Ratio/ Potential Support Ratio – **See Appendix B**				
	Ref. UN: DESA, 2015 World Pop. Aging	Report, 2015 Revision, "World Social Protection Report"				

Table 16
Total Dependency Ratio and Potential Support Ratio
By Regions and/or Countries: 2015 - 2030

Region and/or Country		Dep. Ratio	Support (PSR) Ratio			
		2015 2030	2015 2030			
The World		73.5 75.7	7.0 4.9			
More Developed Regions		65.1 80.1	3.4 2.4			
Less Developed Regions		75.4 75.0	9.0 5.9			
Least Developed Countries		118.5 100.4	12.8 11.5			
Other Less Developed Countries		69.2 70.1	8.6 5.4			
Less Dev. Regions, Excluding China		85.6 78.9	10.0 7.2			
High Income Countries		64.8 78.0	3.7 2.6			
Middle Income Countries		70.8 71.0	8.7 5.6			
Upper Middle Income Countries		56.8 64.6	7.4 4.2			
Lower Middle Income Countries		84.2 75.9	10.4 7.6			
Low Income Countries		131.1 110.5	12,7 12.5			
Sub-Saharan Africa		131.3 113.9	14.0 13.6			
Africa		121.0 108.2	12.9 11.7			
North Africa		85.6 83.8	10.3 7.3			
Asia		66.5 67.2	8.0 5.1			
Europe		62.3 78.0	3.5 2.4			
Latin America/the Caribbean		72.8 67.9	7.6 5.0			
Northern America		66.5 81.3	4.0 2.6			
Canada		61.3 80.7	3.8 2.4			
United States		67.2 81.4	4.0 2.7			
	REF. UN: DESA	World Pop. Aging, 2015 Rev.				

288

CHAPTER II
Why Population Aging Matters in the 21st Century
Tables/Charts

Table 1:
Potential Support Ratios By Geographical Regions

Region	Potential Support Ratio (PSR)
Africa	13
Asia	8.0
Latin America/Caribbean	7.6
Oceania	4.8
Europe/North America	4
Japan	2.1

SOURCE: UN: DESA Pop. Div.
Ref. 2015; SPR defined by
Number of people age 20-64
Divided by the number of people
Age 65 plus

CHAPTER III
**The World Responds to the Dramatic Demographic Explosion
Especially the "Silver Tsunami"**

Tables/Charts

No Tables/Charts

CHAPTER IV
Social Protection in Traditional African Societies:
Transcending All Age Groups

Tables/Charts

No Tables/Charts

CHAPTER V
Pre-Post Independence Africa:
The Challenges of Modernization, Industrialization and Urbanization

Table 1
Percent of Non-Agricultural Informal Employment By Region and Gender

COUNTRY		WOMEN	MEN			
Sub-Saharan Africa		74%	66%			
Middle East N. Africa		35%	45%			
Latin America Caribbean		54%	51%			
South Asia		83%	82%			
East/South East Asia		64%	65%			
Urban China		36%	33%			
Vanek, Joanne, et.al						
WIEGO Working Paper 2						
Cambridge, MA, 4/2014						
"Statistics on the Informal Economy: Definitions, Regulations, Estimates and Challenges"						

Table 2
Global Growth in Working Age Population (Millions)
By Regions and Development: 2000 - 2030

Region	Year 2000	2015	2030	% Change 2000 to 2015	% Projection Change 2015 to 2030	
World	3,860	4,825	5,496	25	13.9	
Asia	2,370	2,988	3,306	26.1	10.6	
Europe	452	446	405	-1.3	-9.2	
Latin America	305	395	452	29.5	14.4	
North America	197	217	220	10.2	1.4	
Sub Saharan Africa	338	519	803	53.6	54.7	
China	888	1,031	983	16.1	-4.7	
India	641	860	1,034	34.2	20.2	
More Developed	802	825	784	2.9	-5.0	
Less Developed	2,170	2,969	3,729	36.8	25.6	
Ref: Pop Division, World Pop Prospects: The 2015 Revisions, 2015						

CHAPTER VI
The State of Social Protection/Social Pensions in Sub-Saharan Africa

Table 1
Global Social Pension Coverage By Geographical Regions

Region	Percent (%) Coverage				
Sub-Saharan Africa	16.9				
Middle East	29.5				
North Africa	36.7				
Asia/Pacific	47.0				
Latin America/Caribbean	56.0				
North America/Europe	90.0				
Source: ILO: World Social Protection Report 2014/15, Section 4.4.1, pp. 83-84, 2015					

Table 2
Social Pension Profile: Sub-Saharan Africa

Country	Population	% 65 Plus	Stat. Soc. Pen.	Program Type	Current State or Progress	Income (WB)	Dep. Ratio
Algeria	39.5	4.6	No	Soc. Insurance	4 ****	U M	48.5
Angola	22.1	2.4	No	Soc. Insurance	3 ***	U M	98.7

292

Benin	10.6	2.9	No	Soc. Insurance	5 *****	Low Income	83.0
Botswana	2.3	3.7	Yes	Universal	1 *	U M	55.3
Burkina Faso	17.42	2.4	No	Soc. Insurance	3 ***	Low Income	91.3
Burundi	10.5	2.4	No	Soc. Insurance	5 *****	Low Income	89.2
C. Verde	0.5	5.2	Yes	S. Ins/Soc. Asst.	2*	Low Middle	51.7
Cameroon	22.8	3.2	No	Soc. Insurance	5 *****	Low Middle	85.1
C. Afr. Republic	4.7	3.8	No	Soc. Insurance	4 ****	Low Income	76.5
Chad	13.2	2.4	No	Soc. Insurance	5 *****	Low Income	102.2
Comoros	NO DATA BASE						
Congo	4.6	3.4	No	Soc. Insurance	3 ***	Low Middle	85
Congo Dem. R	NO DATA BASE						
Cote d'Ivoire	20.8	3.2	No	Soc. Insurance	5 *****	Low Middle	79.7
Djibouti	0.9	4.1	No	Soc. Insurance	5 *****	Low Middle	60.5
Egypt (NA)	83.4	5.9	No	Soc. Insurance	5 *****	Low Middle	58.3
Eritrea	NO DATA BASE						
Ethiopia	96.5	3.5	No	Soc. Insurance	3 ***	Low Income	83.5
Gabon	1.7	5.1	No	Soc. Insurance	4 ****	Upper Middle	77.0
Gambia	1.9	2.4	No	Soc. Ins. Provident	4 ****	Low Income	93.0
Ghana	26.4	3.5	No	Soc. Ins./M. Occupation	3 ***	Low Middle	71.6
Guinea	12.0	3.1	No	Soc. Insurance	5 *****	Low Income	82.4

Guinea/Bissau	NO DATA BASE						
Guinea/Eq.	0.8	2.8	No	Soc. Insurance	5 *****	Low Middle	70.8
Kenya	48.5	2.9	Yes	S. Ins/Soc. Asst.	2*	Low Middle	81.0
Lesotho	2.2	4.2	Yes	Universal	1 *	Low Middle	67.1
Liberia	4.4	3.0	Yes	S. Ins/Soc. Asst.	2 *	Low Income	83.9
Libya (NA)	6.3	4.9	No	Soc. Insurance	3 ***	Upper Middle	52.2
Madagascar	23.6	2.8	No	Soc. Insurance	5 *****	Low Income	81.4
Malawi	16.8	3.2	No	Mandatory Ind. Act	5 *****	Low Income	93.3
Mali	15.8	2.7	No	Soc. Insurance	3 ***	Low Income	100.9
Mauritania	4.0	3.2	No	Soc. Insurance	5 *****	Low Middle	75.7
Mauritius	1.3	9.1	Yes	Univ. Soc. Ins	1 *	Upper Middle	39.8
Morocco	33.5	5.0	No	Soc. Insurance	5 *****	Low Middle	49.1
Mozambique	28.8	3.4	Yes	S. Ins/Soc. Asst.	2*8	Low Income	94.2
Namibia	2.3	3.6	Yes	S. Ins/Soc. Asst.	1 *	Upper Middle	67.1
Niger	18.5	2.6	No	Soc. Insurance	5 *****	Low Income	111.6
Nigeria	178.5	2.7	No	Mandatory Ind. Act	5 *****	Low Middle	89.2
Reunion	NO DATA BASE						
Rwanda	12.1	2.4	No	Soc. Insurance	3 ***	Low Income	80.2
Sao Tome P.	0.2	3.3	No	Soc. Insurance	3 ***	Low Middle	81.3
Senegal	14.5	2.9	No	Soc. Insurance	5 *****	Low Income	86.5
Seychelles	0.1	7.8	Yes	Universal	1 *	High Income	42.8

Sierra Leone	6.2	2.7	No	Soc. Insurance	3 ***	Low Income	78.3
Somalia	NO DATA BASE						
South Africa	54	5.6	Yes	S. Ins/Soc. Asst.	2 *	Upper Middle	53.9
Sudan (NA)	38.8	3.3	No	Soc. Insurance		Low Middle	79
South Sudan	NO DATA BASE						
Swaziland	1.3	3.5	Yes	Soc. Asst./ Prov.	2 *	Low Middle	69.7
Tanzania	50.8	3.3	No	Soc. Insurance	3 ***	Low Income	92.4
Togo	7.0	2.8	No	Soc. Insurance	3 ***	Low Income	80.1
Tunisia	11.0	7.3	No	Soc. Insurance	4 ****	Low Middle	43.9
Uganda	38.8	2.4	No	Provident Fund	4 ****	Low Income	
Zambia	15.0	2.6	No	Soc. Insurance	3 ***	Low Middle	96.4
Zimbabwe	16.2	3.0	No	Soc. Insurance	5 *****	Low Income	80.2

Table 3
Sub-Saharan African Countries With Statutory
Social/Civic Pensions

COUNTRY	TOT. POPULATION	% 65 PLUS	DEP. RATIO	LIFE EXP/ BIRTH	STAT. SOC. PEN.	GDP/P CAPITA	W BANK INC. GP.
				M W	M W	US $	
Botswana	2.3	3.7	55.3	66.2 66.9	65 65	16,735	UM
Cape Verde	0.54	4.5	51.2	71.6 75.2	65 60	6,553	LM
Kenya	48.5	2.9	80.3	60.3 64.1	60 60	3,156	LM
Lesotho	2.2	4.2	67.1	49.9 50.0	70 70	3,029	LM

Liberia	4.6	3.0	81.9	60.2 62.2	60 60	813	LOW INCOME
Mauritius	1.3	10.0	40.6	71.1 77.8	60 60	21,088	UM
Mozambique	28.8	3.4	94.2	54.0 56.8	60 55	1,217	LOW INCOME
Namibia	2.5	3.6	67.1	62.5 67.5	60 60	10,585	UM
Seychelles	0.095	7.1	44.2	68.4 78.3	63 63	28,391	HIGH INCOME
South Africa	55.9	5.1	51.6	55.5 59.5	60 60	13,225	UM
Swaziland	1.3	3.7	69.2	49.6 48.1	50 50	8,343	LM
	SOURCE: SOCIAL	SECURITY					
	PROGRAMS THROUGH OUT THE WORLD, ISSA, 2017						

Table 4
Population Growth/Percent 60 Plus Sub-Saharan Africa: 2010-2050

COUNTRY	TOTAL POP 2010	% 60+	TOTAL POP 2050	% 60+		
Angola	749,199	4%	3,564,096	8%		
Benin	461,649	5%	2,307,410	10%		
Botswana	117,057	6%	373,027	13%		
Burkina Faso	535,519	3%	3,060.730	7%		
Burundi	376,857	4%	1,960,831	13%		
Cameroon	1,084,229	5%	4,077,071	11%		
Cape Verde	27,665	5%	162,927	23%		
Central African Republic	263,517	6%	827,775	11%		
Chad	510,000	4%	2,073,561	7%		
Comoros	32,242	5%	185,067	15%		

Congo	214,150	6%	856,590	12%		
Congo Dem Rep	2,857,759	4%	11,965,177	8%		
Cote d'Ivoire	1,308,319	6%	5,202,786	12%		
Djibouti	47,773	5%	208,766	14%		
Guinea	533,063	5%	2,545,641	11%		
Guinea Bissau	89,914	5%	300,270	8%		
Guinea Equatorial	29,606	4%	136,807	9%		
Eritrea	214,188	4%	1,242,502	11%		
Ethiopia	4,297,304	5%	18,245,248	10%		
Gabon	96,742	6%	390,993	16%		
Gambia	86,120	5%	355,548	9%		
Ghana	1,400.144	6%	5,875,110	13%		
Kenya	2,089,634	4%	8,623,102	10%		
Lesotho	133,128	7%	254,141	10%		
Liberia	200,071	5%	958,730	11%		
Madagascar	932,275	5%	4,856,324	11%		
Malawi	762,748	5%	2,908,793	8%		
Mali	502,770	4%	2,183,580	8%		
Mauritius	148,963	4%	747,844	12%		
Mauritius	150,602	12%	456,321	30%		
Morocco	2,610,934	8%	11,178,411	25%		
Mozambique	1,190,767	5%	3,779,388	8%		
Namibia	124,865	6%	482,225	13%		
Niger	554,145	3%	2,959,242	5%		
Nigeria	8,158,284	5%	29,981,880	10%		
Rwanda	393,757	4%	2,280,040	10%		
Sao Tome Princip	8,691	5%	42,689	14%		
Senegal	504,753	4%	2,548,160	10%		
Seychelles	10,274	0				
Sierra Leone	202,677	3%	866,176	7%		
South Africa	3,694,968	7%	9,286,054	16%		
Sudan	2,480,261	6%	10,636,279	14%		
Swaziland	63,638	5%	148,555	8%		
Tanzania	2,189,234	5%	9,196,160	8%		
Togo	372,536	5%	1,818,111	14%		

Uganda	1,397,349	4%	6,376,474	7%		
Zambia	632,235	5%	1,979,770	7%		
Zimbabwe	731,869	6%	2,819,762	13%		

Table 5
Informal Sector and Self-Employed Workers Voluntary Participation:
Tripartite Contributory Schemes

COUNTRY	INSURED CONTRIBUTIONS	SELF EMPLOYED CONTRIBUTIONS				
Angola	3%	11%				
Burkina Faso	5.5%	11%				
Congo	4%	12%				
Ethiopia	7%	18%				
Ghana	5.5%	11%				
Liberia	3%	5%				
Mali	3.6%	9%				
Rwanda	3%	6%				
Sao Tome Principe	6%	14%				
Sierra Leone	5%	15%				
Sudan	8%	25%				
Togo	4%	16.5%				
Zambia	5%	10%				
	NOTE: Some countries with contributory schemes provided an opportunity for the self-employed to become part of the scheme.		NOTE #2: The Self employed voluntarily agreed to contribute a defined payment, % of salary, in order to qualify for defined programs and payments.			

Table 6
Human Development Index 2015: Sub-Saharan Africa

COUNTRY	HDI RANK	HDI VALUE	GNI P/CAPITA	GNI MINUS HDI	HDI RANK 2014
	VERY HIGH HD	SSA: NONE			
	HIGH HD				
Seychelles	63	0.782	23,886	-15	63
Mauritius	64	0.781	17,948	1	64
	MEDIUM HD				
Botswana	108	0.698	14,663	-33	107
Gabon	109	0.697	19,044	-46	109
South Africa	119	0.666	12,087	-30	119
Cape Verde	122	0.648	6,049	3	122
Namibia	125	0.640	9,770	-18	126
Congo	135	0.592	5,503	-7	135
Equal. Guinea	135	0.592	21,517	-79	137
Ghana	139	0.579	3,839	5	140
Zambia	139	0.579	3,464	7	139
Sao Tome/ Principe	142	0.574	3,070	12	142
Kenya	146	0.555	2,881	10	147
	LOW HD				
Swaziland	148	0.541	7,522	-33	149
Angola	150	0.533	6,291	-27	150
Tanzania	151	0.531	2,467	10	152
Nigeria	152	0.527	5,443	-23	151
Cameroon	153	0.518	2,894	2	154
Zimbabwe	154	0.516	1,588	20	158
Mauritania	157	0.513	3,527	-12	155

Madagascar	158	0.512	1,320	25	157
Rwanda	159	0.498	1,617	14	162
Comoros	160	0.497	1,335	22	160
Lesotho	160	0.497	3,319	-12	161
Senegal	162	0.494	2,250	3	163
Uganda	163	0.493	1,670	8	165
Sudan (Now NA)	165	0.490	3,846	-22	165
Togo	166	0.487	1,262	18	167
Benin	167	0.485	1,979	1	168
Malawi	170	0.476	1,073	16	170
Cote d'ivoire	171	0.474	3,163	-20	172
Djibouti	172	0.473	3,216	-22	171
Gambia	173	0.452	1,541	3	173
Ethiopia	174	0.448	1,523	5	174
Mali	175	0.442	2,218	-9	175
Congo Dem. Rep.	176	0.435	680	15	178
Liberia	177	0.427	683	13	177
Guinea-Bissau	178	0.424	1,369	3	179
Eritrea	179	0.420	1,490	1	181
Sierra Leone	179	0.420	1,529	-1	176
Mozambique	181	0.418	1,098	4	182
So. Sudan (SSA)	181	0.418	1,882	-12	179
Guinea	183	0.414	1,058	4	182
Burundi	184	0.404	691	5	184
Burkina Faso	185	0.402	1,537	-8	185
Chad	186	0.396	1,991	-19	186
Niger	187	0.353	889	1	187
C. Afr. Republic	188	0.352	587	4	188
	HD GROUPS				
	VERY HIGH HD	0.892			

	HIGH HD	0.746			
	MEDIUM HD	0.631			
	LOW HD	0.497			
	DEV. COUNTRIES				
	ARAB STATES	0.687			
	E. ASIA/PACIFIC	0.720			
	EUROPE/C. ASIA	0.756			
	LATIN AMER/CAR.	0.751			
	SOUTH ASIA	0.621			
	SUB-SAH. AFRICA	0.523			
	LEAST DEV. COU.	0.508			
	NOTE: NORWAY RANK, 1, VALUE 949; C. AF. REP.	RANK 188, VALUE 0.352	FOR CONCEPTS & DEFINITIONS, I.E.	HDI, GNI, SEE APPENDIX B	

Table 10
Ibrahim Index of African Governance (IIAG) 2017

COUNTRY	II SCORE	RANK	% CHANGE FROM 2011		
Angola	40.8	43	+0.2		
Benin	58.8	15	_0.2		
Botswana	74.2	3	_1.8		
Burkina Faso	52.2	22	+0.3		
Burundi	45.8	38	+1.2		
C. Verde	74	2	_1.9		
Cameroon	45.9	37	_1.3		
Cent. Afr. Rep.	24.9	52	_8.4		

Chad	32.8	49	+0.5			
Comoros	48.5	32	+0.9			
Congo	42.8	42	+0.6			
Congo Dem. Re	33.9	48	+0.1			
Cote d'Ivoire	48.3	35	+8.5			
Djibouti	45.9	36	+0.5			
Equal. Guinea	35.5	46	_0.7			
Eritrea	29.9	50	_0.4			
Ethiopia	48.6	31	+3.4			
Gabon	52.2	23	+1.2			
Gambia	50.5	27	_1.7			
Guinea	43.7	40	_0.1			
Guinea Bissau	35.7	45	_3.2			
Kenya	58.8	14	+4.3			
Lesotho	61.1	10	+2.2			
Liberia	50.7	26	+0.9			
Madagascar	49.1	29	+2.8			
Malawi	56.7	17	_0.2			
Mali	48.7	30	_8.1			
Mauritania	43.0	41	+0.1			
Mauritius	79.9	1	_0.7			
Mozambique	52.3	21	_2.2			
Namibia	70.4	5	+2.0			
Niger	48.4	33	_0.6			
Nigeria	44.9	39	+0.9			
Rwanda	60.7	11	+2.9			
Sao Tome P.	59.1	13	+0.7			
Senegal	62.4	9	+4.5			
Seychelles	70.3	6	_0.8			
Sierra Leone	51.0	25	+0.7			
South Africa	73.0	4	+0.9			
Somali	8.5	54	+1.2			
South Sudan	19.9	53	_9.6			
Sudan	28.3	51	+0.4			

Swaziland	49.6	28	+0.7			
Tanzania	56.7	18	_1.0			
Togo	48.4	34	+4.0			
Uganda	54.6	19	_1.3			
Zambia	59.5	12	+0.5			
Zimbabwe	40.4	44	+4.6			
	Definitions and Concept:	See Appendix B				
	NOTE: 1 The IIAG score includes 4 components, (1) Safety and Rules of Law: accountability, personal safety, national security;	(2) Participation and Human Rights: rights, gender; (3) Sustainable Economic Growth; public management, business environment, infrastructure, rural sector;	(4) Human Development: social welfare, education, and health	NOTE: 3 Average score each component: Safety Rule of Law 51.8 (H 82.7 Mauritius - L 5.5 Somalia), Economy 42.6 (H 77.5 Mauritius - L 4.1 Somalia), Human Rights 50.1 (H 50.1 C Verde - L 10.4 Somalia), Human Development 55.1 (H 85.7 Mauritius - L 14 Somalia).		
	NOTE: 2 The average IIAG overall score for all countries 4 components 49.9. Highest score 79.9 Mauritius/ Lowest 8.5 Somalia.					

Table 11
Corruption Perception Index (CPI) 2017

COUNTRY	RANK 2016	SCORE 2016	SCORE 2015	SCORE 12		
Botswana	35	60	63	65		
Cape Verde	38	59	55	60		
Mauritius	50	54	52	57		
Rwanda	50	54	54	53		
Namibia	53	53	48	48		
Sao Tome Principe	62	46	42	42		
Senegal	64	45	44	36		
South Africa	64	45	44	43		
Ghana	70	43	47	45		
Burkina Faso	72	42	38	38		
Lesotho	83	39	44	45		
Zambia	87	38	38	37		
Liberia	90	37	37	41		
Benin	95	36	37	36		
Gabon	101	35	34	35		
Niger	101	35	34	33		
Cote d'Ivoire	108	34	32	29		
Ethiopia	108	34	33	33		
Mali	116	32	35	34		
Tanzania	116	32	30	35		
Togo	116	32	32	30		
Malawi	120	31	31	37		
Djibouti	123	30	34	36		
Sierra Leone	123	30	29	31		
Nigeria	136	28	26	27		
Guinea	142	27	25	24		
Mozambique	142	27	31	31		
Cameroon	145	26	27	26		
Gambia	145	26	28	34		

Kenya	145	26	25	27		
Madagascar	145	26	28	32		
Uganda	151	25	25	29		
Comoros	153	24	26	28		
Zimbabwe	154	22	21	20		
Dem. Rep. Congo	156	21	22	21		
Burundi	159	20	21	19		
Cen. Afr. Republic	159	20	24	26		
Chad	159	20	22	19		
Rep. of Congo	159	20	23	26		
Angola	164	18	15	22		
Eritrea	164	18	18	25		
Guinea-Bissau	168	16	17	25		
South Sudan	175	11	15	N/A		
Somalia	176	10	8	8		
Definitions/Concepts: – Corruption Perception Index:	See Appendix B					

CHAPTER VII
Social Pensions in Sub-Saharan Africa: Affordable, Achievable and Sustainable

Tables/Charts

No Tables/Charts

CHAPTER VIII
Economic Growth, the "Youth Bulge" Generation and the "Rising African Spirit:"
Implications for Social Policies, Programs and Enhanced Quality of Life for All

Table 1
World Bank GDP Growth: 1961 - 2015

			1961	2015			
Country			1961	2015			
Belgium			5.0	1.5			
Finland			7.6	0.2			
Israel			11.2	2.5			
France			5.5	1.3			
Japan			12.0	1.2			
Sweden			5.7	4.1			
UK			2.6	2.6			
USA			2.3	3.0			
World			4.3	2.6			
Sub-Saharan Africa			1.5	3.0			
	Source: World Bank "GDP Growth Annual, 2016"						

Table 2
World's Fastest Growing Economies 2004-2014: "Africa Rising"

WORLD RANK	COUNTRY	ANNUAL GDP GROWTH %				
4th	Ethiopia	10.8				
7th	Angola	9.9				

13th	Rwanda	7.8				
13th	Sierra Leone	7.8				
17th	Zambia	7.6				
19th	Nigeria	7.4				
20th	Ghana	7.3				
20th	Mozambique	7.3				
23rd	Uganda	6.8				
25th	Liberia	6.9				
	Av. Annual % Real Terms					
	Ibrahim Foundation	2017 Forum Report	Data Source:	The Economist		
	Of the 25 fastest growing economies					
	Globally, 2004-2014	Ten were Africans				

Table 3
World's Fastest Growing Economies/Growth in Services 2006-2014:
"Africa Rising"

WORLD	COUNTRY	ANNUAL GDP GROWTH %				
1ST	Ethiopia	13.5				
9TH	Nigeria	9.5				
11TH	Zambia	9.4				
13TH	Rwanda	9.3				
14TH	Zimbabwe	9.1				
15TH	DRC	8.4				
16TH	Mozambique	8.3				
17TH	Ghana	8.0				

	Ibrahim Foundation	2017 Forum Report		Data Source: The Economist		
	Of the 20 countries in the highest growth in services 2006-2014 Eight of the 20 are Countries in African.					

Table 4
World's Fastest Growing Economies/Industrial Output 2006-2014: "Africa Rising"

WORLD	COUNTRY	ANNUAL GDP GROWTH %				
2ND	Sierra Leone	23.6				
3RD	Liberia	19.9				
4TH	Ethiopia	14.4				
7TH	Ghana	11.0				
10TH	Niger	10.1				
11TH	Rwanda	9.3				
13TH	Tanzania	8.2				
16TH	Zambia	7.5				
17TH	Burkina Faso	7.4				
	Ibrahim Foundation	2017 Forum Report		Data Source: Economist		
	Of the 20 countries in the highest growth, industrial output Nine are in African Countries					

APPENDIX B

DRAMATIC GLOBAL POPULATION GROWTH EMBRACES THE GROWING OLDER POPULATION, THE "SILVER TSUNAMI,"

CONCEPTS, DEFINITIONS AND SPECIAL NOTES RELATED TO SOCIAL PROTECTION/SOCIAL PENSIONS

INTRODUCTION

Globally, in referring to some of the basic needs of citizens across all age groups, gender, and work status, a number of concepts are commonly referred to. The following concepts as defined by experts in the area of human and occupational welfare are an attempt at clarifications when used by governments, employers, employees, civic leaders and/or citizens.

In addition to the aforementioned, Appendix B Section 2 also provides specific definitions for the numerical classifications used to describe progress already accomplished towards a statutory social pension; not only the accomplishments made towards that goal, but a numerical concept to illustrate how far countries have progressed or not progressed toward a statutory social pension for the older population globally. In other words, the primary focus is on those within the workforce that were not part of a traditional tripartite collective bargaining system, therefore not eligible for a social pension at the time of retirement.

Appendix B: Section 1

<u>Ageism</u> – The concept ageism should be discussed with the same level of concern, as racism, and sexism. Globally, The First World Assembly on Ageing in 1982 with the delegates reaffirming "... their belief that the fundamental and alienable rights enshrined in the Universal Declaration of Human Rights apply fully and undiminished to the aging...that quality of life is no less important than longevity and that ageing therefore, as far as possible, be enabled to enjoy in their own families and communities a life of fulfillment, health, security and contentment, and

appreciated as an integral part of society" (World Assembly on Ageing, PREAMBLE, ibid). "Ageism is the stereotyping of and discrimination against individuals or groups based on their age. Ageism can take many forms, including prejudicial attitudes, discriminatory practices, or institutional policies and practices that perpetuate stereotypical beliefs (World Health Report on Ageing and Health, WHO 2015, NLM Classification: WT 104, Geneva).

Social or Citizen Pension — A common or consensual definition of a Social/Citizen pension is, "A non-contributory cash transfer paid regularly to older citizens (age as defined by the country) by government." Unlike contributory pensions, social or citizen pensions do not require any previous contributions from recipients" (Help Age International, Pension Watch, Pensions Glossary) (ILO: Social Protection Floors Recommendations, No. 202, 2012; Knox-Vydmanov: Help Age International, 2013, pp. 1-5). A social or civic pension is the result of a legislative or parliamentary action by government, which becomes a statue or law within a particular country. Therefore, a social pension could fall under the category of social assistance. A social pension is now being referred to by many global activists, such as Help Age International, for the rights and social justice on behalf of older people as a "Citizen pension." A "Citizen pension," according to Help Age International, "...is a guaranteed minimum income in old age based on citizenship/ residency rather than previous formal contributions... It must be legislated, adequate and regular" (Help Age International: Pension Watch, Pension Glossary, page 1). Globally, social pension activists, including Bishop Tutu of South Africa, are the key players supporting the call on the United Nations to schedule a special session to address concerns, such as the disparities related to social pensions and other issues affecting a growing older population.

Social Security – The concept social security is used in Western countries such as the United States to describe a contributory social insurance scheme. Considered one of the most significant social policy initiatives in the United States, was The Social Security Act of 1935; adopted more than six decades following the first global Social Security Act enacted in Germany under the leadership of Chancellor Bismarck. The concept "...refers to programs established by statute that insure individuals against interruption or loss of earning power and for certain special expenditures arising from marriage, birth or death. This definition also includes allowances to families for the support of children (SSPTW: Africa, 2013). An example, in the US children can continue to collect their social security allowances until age 21.

Social Protection – One of the most universal concepts used is Social Protection. The concept involves a variety of initiatives or policies "...that provide cash or in-kind transfers to the poor, protect the vulnerable against risks and enhance the social status and rights of the marginalized... all with the overall goal of reducing poverty and economic and social vulnerability (UN: Food and Agriculture Organization (FAO)," The State of Food and Agriculture, 2015, p. 4). The concept Social Protection involves several broad areas of assistance. First, is the category of social assistance; social assistance is "publicly provided conditional or unconditional cash or in-kind transfers or public work programs" (UN: FAO, ibid, p.4). The second category of social protection is commonly referred to as contributory programs, usually part of a tripartite labor employer/employee/public collective bargaining arrangement within the formal labor sector. These contributory programs are designed to "...provide cover for designated contingencies affecting household welfare and income (UN: FAO, ibid, p. 4). Lastly is the category of labor market programs. "Labor market programs provide unemployment benefits, build skills and enhance workers' productivity and employability" (UN: FAO, ibid, p. 4; Help Age International, ibid).

Although the concept Social Protection has been somewhat clarified, there are other concepts that are more commonly used but falls within the general area of Social Protection. The concept Social pension is one of those concepts.

<u>Social Assistance</u> – Social Assistance are cash transfer programs that provide cash assistance to eligible individuals or households. The program may include a children allowance, a social pension; need based transfers as well as conditional cash transfers. Conditional cash transfers are cash provided to families based on need. Conditional means that the recipients are required to make some human investment commitment such as keeping the kids in school, and/or making sure that appointments with health providers are carried out (Help Age International, ibid).

<u>Social Insurance</u> – Unlike the Social or Citizen Pension, a Contributory Pension is paid to a person according to a defined rate of contributions and benefits, or pro rata to a person with a history or record of incomplete contributions. The defined contributions and/or benefits are normally agreed upon within the framework of a tripartite or collective bargaining agreement. The Contributory pension scheme, including defined contributory payments and benefits are related to the worker or retiree's salary or other agreed upon values that have been predetermined in advance (Help Age International, ibid).

<u>The Provident Fund</u> – This particular scheme is a form of savings that may be mandatory or voluntary and are considered as a defined contribution scheme. The Fund will pay out the contributions made by the worker and interest accumulated as a lump sum at the time of retirement or under other circumstances that were predetermined. Also, as predetermined the retiree may receive part of the payment in cash or as an annuity. The Provident Fund normally will have predetermined arrangements that contributions are equally made by the employee and the employer (Help Age, ibid).

<u>Targeting</u> – The primary purpose of targeting by a government is a conviction that the program or resources will be directed toward those consumers that are most in need (Help Age, ibid).

<u>Replacement Rate</u> – A very significant factor in reference to retirement; the purpose of the retirement rate is that it analyzes or measures the amount of income following retirement as a percentage of income prior to retirement (Help Age, ibid). Income replacement following retirement is a matter of concern for many pensioners. A major problem seems to be that pension systems do not have a reliable generic model, or comparable model to use as a framework. "One possible solution is to compare the average level of pensions received to the average level of earnings in the economy, as a national snapshot at a given point in time of the relative income situation of the employed population (World Protection Report 2014/15, ibid, p. 90). Data is available, from OECD countries for such purposes, but it is quite complicated to carry out, '… impossible to replicate on a wider scale for countries outside these groups, mainly due to lack of comparable earnings statistics as well as the limited availability of the household survey data that would enable such comparisons' (World Protection Report, ibid).

Although the subject of replacement rate has little relevancy for the current social assistance pension population, it does raise questions and considerations for the appropriate model to use in deciding on the amount that a social pension for a country that is adequate for income security. What are the factors that should be included for determining, for each country, the amount needed by an older person on a social assistance pension to live in dignity?

<u>Pension Testing</u> – The use or purpose of such a method is for the government to exclude applicants that are already receiving a pension (Help Age, ibid).

<u>Means Test</u> – The Means Test is a targeting method utilized by countries, more specifically programs, that are based on income that collects information related to household income and/or wealth and verifies all of the information collected against independent sources. A "proxy means tests generate a score for applicant's households based on observable characteristics of the household, such as the location and quality of household, the education and, possibly, the occupations of adult members. Eligibility is determined by comparing the household's score against a predetermined cutoff point (Help Age International, Pension Watch, Glossary, page 3). Although means testing is currently used by a number of countries in Sub-Saharan Africa, the method as indicated in the narrative, some governments are beginning to reject the method for determining eligibility for programs, especially the social pension. Research from the government of Mauritius, one of a very small number of countries in Sub-Saharan Africa with a universal non-contributory social pension, indicated that the use of the test could omit about 20% of older persons. Furthermore, the administrative cost for implementing such a program does not justify the cost savings. In other words, the savings do not justify the added administrative cost (Help Age International, ibid).

<u>Informal Economy</u> – All units, activities, and workers in informal employment and out-put from them (UN: HABITAT III Issue Papers on the Informal Sector, p 2, New York, 5/31/2015).

<u>Informal Sector</u> – Comprised of informal production units or informal sector enterprises, as defined below: The informal sector includes informal agricultural production units but does not include households as employers of domestic workers (HABITAT, ibid).

<u>Informal Employment</u> – Employment that leaves individuals in employment relationships without labor and social protection through their work, or without entitlement benefits, whether or not the economic units they operate or work for are formal enterprises, informal enterprises or households (HABITAT, ibid).

<u>Total Dependency Ratio</u> – Persons aged 0-19 and aged 65 or over per 100 persons aged 20-64.

<u>Potential Support Ratio</u> – Persons aged 20-64 per person aged 65 or over.

Appendix B: Section 2

<u>Current State or Progress of Statutory Social Pensions: Sub-Saharan Africa</u>

The Column Social Pension Progress provides indicators, numbering one (1) through five (5) illustrating the current state or progress of the African countries:

1. The numerical number 1(A Grade) indicates that the particular country has met the basic requirement of establishing a social pension for older persons who during their working years were primarily employed, self-employed or worked in the informal sectors. It indicates that only the factor age as established by the country, is the only requirement for determining eligibility. For the country there is no additional criteria/ requirement. The factor age has been established in the Statutory Laws of the country as the only requirement for a social pension. The global consensus is that age only should be the goal of each country for ensuring that all older persons will have a social pension, especially basic income security in later life.

2. The number 2 (B Grade) is an indication that a country has chosen to use an additional factor for determining eligibility. A "Means Test" based on a person's need is commonly used by countries in determining eligibility for a social pension. Research has demonstrated that the Means Test is not only administratively inefficient, but significant numbers of persons are lost during the process. Finally, number 2 indicates that a country has additional work to do in reaching the goal of having age only as the basic criteria.

3. The number 3 (C Grade) represents countries that have not established any form of a statutory pension system for those who had been employed primarily within the informal sector or were self-employed. The positive aspect in this category is that the aforementioned countries have initiated contacts with the self-employed/informal sector employees for the purpose of voluntarily including those workers as part of the country's tripartite system. The interactions have included a discussion around establishing defined contributions and benefit packages. This process helps to ensure that the next generation of older persons will have social protection in later life. It should be noted that the fact the scheme is voluntarily is no guarantee that all informal sector employees will participate. But, it represents a step forward in the process.

4. The basic difference between number 3 (C Grade) and 4 (D Grade) is that level 4 countries or those classified as 4 do not at this point provide specifics regarding the inclusion of the informal sector workers; for example contractual factors such as monthly or annual contributions and benefits. In other words there may be relationship building process but no specifics at this point in time.

5. The number 5 (F Grade) indicates that the countries have failed so far to institute two very important elements that eventually could ensure that all older persons will be provided a social pension: (a) the lack of statutory law establishing a social pension for older persons, and (b) have not reached out to the self-employed or the informal sector for the purpose of working together towards the goal of a social pension. Furthermore, these are the countries in their response in the Coverage sector of the annual survey from the ISSA that the Self-Employed or the informal sectors were excluded.

Appendix B: Section 3

<u>Concepts and Definitions Related to Quality of Life, Human Development, Country Governance including Corruption and/or Illicit Business Practices</u>

The major theme of the current or 2016 Report focuses on "Human Development for everyone." The Report emphasizes that the goals for todays as well as future generations should be, "Good health, access to knowledge, human rights, human security, decent standards of living, nondiscrimination, dignity, self determination...Human development is about enlarging freedoms so that all human beings can pursue choices they value...Human development focuses on the richness of human lives rather than on the richness of economics" (Human Development Report 2016, United Nations Development Programs (UNDP), "Human Development for Everyone," New York, NY, page 1).

"The Report conveys five basic messages: Universalism is key to human development for every one is attainable; Various groups of people still suffer from basic deprivations and face substantial barriers to overcoming them; Human development for everyone calls for refocusing some analytical issues and assessment perspectives; Policy options exist and, if implemented, would contribute to achieving human development for everyone; A reformed global governance, with fairer multilateralism, would help attain human development for everyone" (UNDP, ibid).

OECD Countries: Who are the countries and what is their Mission?

Thirty-six countries comprise the OECD network: Australia, Austria, Belgium, Canada, Chile, Czech Republic, Denmark, Estonia, Finland, France, Germany, Greece, Hungary, Iceland, Ireland, Israel, Italy, Japan, Korea, Latvia, Lithuania, Luxembourg, Mexico, Netherlands, New Zealand, Norway, Poland, Portugal, Slovak Republic, Slovenia, Spain, Sweden, Switzerland, Turkey, United Kingdom, United States.

The Mission Statement (Better Policies for Better Lives OECD: Organization for Economic Co-Operation and Development. The Organization dates back almost a half-century, 1960 when 18 countries came together to develop a global organization with a commitment to economic development. Although they represent globally the most advanced countries, especially economically, the organization also works with emerging countries, such as Mexico, Chile and Turkey; also works with emerging economies such as China, India, Brazil, including countries in Africa, Asia, Latin America and Caribbean (OECD.org)

Selective Key Definitions and Concepts Related to Human Development (inequalities), Corruption, Governance and Business Practices:

Human Development Index (HDI):

"A composite index measuring average achievement in three basic dimensions of human development – <u>a long and healthy life, knowledge and a decent standard of living.</u>"

Gross National Income (GNI) per capita:

"Aggregate income of an economy generated by its production and its ownership of factors of production, less the incomes paid for the use of factors of production own by the rest of the world converted to international dollars using PPP rates, divided by midyear population."

GNI per capita rank minus HDI rank:

"Difference in ranking by GNI per capita and by HDI value. A negative value means that the country is better ranked by GNI than by HDI value."
"Ranking by HDI value for 2014, which was calculated using the same most recently revised data available in 2016 that were used to calculate HDI values for 2015."

Corruption Perception Index 2017:

"A country or territory's score indicates the perceived level of public sector corruption on a scale of 0 (highly corrupt) to 100 (very clean). A country's rank indicates its position relative

314

to the other countries in the index. This years index includes 168 countries and territories... Sixty-eight per cent of countries worldwide have a serious corruption problem. Half of the G20 are among them. Not one single country, anywhere in the world is corruption free."

<u>Ibrahim Index of African Governance IIAG</u>

<u>Note</u> the Four Major Components: Safety and Rules of Law, Human Rights Participation, Economic Growth and Human Development

NOTE: 1 The IIAG score includes 4 components, (1) Safety and Rules of Law: accountability, personal safety, national security;	(2) Participation and Human Rights: rights, gender; (3) Sustainable Economic Growth; public management, business environment, infrastructure, rural sector;	(4) Human Development: social welfare, education, and health	NOTE: 3 Average score each component: Safety Rule of Law 51.8 (H 82.7 Mauritius - L 5.5 Somalia), Economy 42.6 (H 77.5 Mauritius - L 4.1 Somalia), Human Rights 50.1 (H 50.1 C Verde - L 10.4 Somalia), Human Development 55.1 (H 85.7 Mauritius - L 14 Somalia).
NOTE: 2 The average IIAG overall score for all countries 4 components 49.9. Highest score 79.9 Mauritius/ Lowest 8.5 Somalia.			

<u>Traditional English Translation of "Mother to Son," by Langston Hughes</u>

Well, son I am going to tell you:
Life for me has not been a crystal stair.
It has had tacks in it, and splinters, and boards torn up, and places with no carpet on the floor, just plain bare son.
But all the time I have been climbing on, reaching landings, and sometimes going in the dark where there is no light.
So, boy, don't you turn back.
Don't you sit down on the steps because you find it to be kind of rough!!!
Don't you fall down now!!! Because as you see I am still going, climbing honey. Yes, I am still climbing, and life for me has not been a crystal stair.

<u>Traditional English Translation:</u> McKinney, Edward A.

ACKNOWLEDGEMENTS

The successful completion of a book or manuscript is a very long journey that requires overcoming major obstacles and challenges along the way. There were times during the journey when I had to turn to others, especially writers for inspiration. One of those writers from the past that I turned to for inspiration was the great poetic scholar and writer Langston Hughes. Looking down from the Heavens Langston would remind me of how difficult life could be during various journeys in life but one should not quit just keep on climbing and climbing until you reach the goal. Langston Hughes literary masterpiece "Mother to Son" became quite an inspiration during the current journey as it had been during other journeys throughout my life.

First of all, Langston's aforementioned poem was written in what is described as "Black Dialect." Out of great respect for Langston and my elementary school teachers from years ago who first introduced me to Langston and other Black writers such as Phyllis Wheatley, I will not use the English translation at this point but will share with readers the poem as it was originally written in "Black Dialect." By the way, Phyllis Wheatley who became an outstanding American writer was born in Senegal came to America at the age of seven as a young slave with her family. Phyllis Wheatley was the name of my racially segregated elementary school in Macon (Bibb County) Georgia.

Langston Hughes poetic inspirational masterpiece "Mother to Son" speaks: "Well, son, I'll tell you: Life for me ain't been no crystal stair. It's had tacks in it, And splinters, And boards torn up, And places with no carpet on the floor – Bare. But all the time I'se been a-climbin' on, And reachin' landin's And turnin corners, And sometimes goin' in the dark Where there ain't been no light. So, boy, don't you turn back. Don't you set down on the steps 'Cause you finds it's kinder hard. Don't you fall now – For I'se still goin', honey. I'se still climbin', And Life for me ain't been no crystal stair." (**Note:** Langston Hughes, American Poet was born February 1, 1901 in Joplin, Mo; he died on May 22 1967. **(For a traditional English Translation, no dialect of "Mother to Son," See Appendix B: Concepts, Definitions and Special Notes).**

When Langston was not enough to keep the journey moving smoothly, I could also reach back and thank about my Sunday Schools' lessons (biblical scriptures) and the Richard Allen Endeavor Leagues of Churches such as Fountain Temple African Methodist Episcopal (AME) Church and Grants Chapel AME Church, Macon, Georgia. The aforementioned institutions introduced to me as a youth biblical verses that focused on having Faith for achieving goals. The primary verses were found in the 11th Chapter of Hebrew. The verses were highlighted to be used when confronting and managing challenges. Currently there is the "Up North" AME Church, Historic St. John in Cleveland, Ohio where the biblical verses continue help keep the journeys going smoothly.

In addition to inspirational figures such as Langston Hughes, the completion of such a research and writing task, book or manuscript, is not possible without a very supportive environment, including for the most part immediate family, colleagues, educational institutions and social organizations. It all began with the family, my wife Louise and two sons, Bill, Craig and extended family members Melton, Dora, Fred and Bruce. No, let's not forget extended family members, especially the in-laws, colleagues and friends who also played a very significant role(s). Also, most importantly let's not forget my *Fictive Kin* Mrs. Alice, Murray, Rose, Julia, Emma, Ethel, Mr. Benny and Dennis, the older members of the little village like community where I grew up in Georgia ("It takes a village to raise a child') who from the first day I can remember repeatedly impressed on me that regardless of the environment and the social problems surrounding me I could grow up to be anything I wanted to be.

The book, for the most part a scholarly look globally at one of the most critical issues in the modern era, the growing older population, or the "Silver Tsunami," and the lack of social protection for the unprecedented growing older population. The idea for the book came about as a result of being exposed to the continent of Africa. Africa, more specifically Sub-Saharan Africa, is where my ancestors were taken away more than four centuries ago. As a social work/public health scholar I have had the opportunity, special thanks to the United States International J. William Fulbright Senior Scholar Program, to travel and work at several distinguished universities, University of Botswana (Southern Africa), and Nairobi and Kenyatta Universities (East Africa). The aforementioned universities allowed me the opportunity to expand my academic interest beyond the boundaries of the United States becoming a global scholar in the area of public/social policy, more specifically Aging Policy.

I am extremely grateful/thankful of several opportunities that emerged during my academic years in the aforementioned countries and universities. Most importantly was the increased interest on the part of students' reference curriculum matters, including research and the social caring practices related to the growing older population, not just Africa but globally. It is well known that historically Africa utilizing extended family customs/traditions has made sure that the older population, including children were well taken care of. The continent including its political leaders, academics as well as social activists, are now recognizing that historical traditions and customs are changing; these changes include the extended family system. The changes are occurring as a result of modernization, industrialization and urbanization. Let's not forget the negative impact of colonization on the continent for more than three quarters of a century. Countries in Sub-Saharan Africa are recognizing that changes, political and social will have to be made that ensures that the growing older population will have income and other social supports during their later lives. Educational institutions will be challenged to provide educational content for the purpose of developing policies and programs in response to the growing older population, or the "Silver Tsunami." Speaking of problems related to the older population, currently 82.5% of the older population in Sub-Saharan Africa does not have a social pension or income security during retirement. I am so thankful to the students who became part of the academic exercises, especially my Aging Seminars including the policy and practice simulations. Most importantly for me were those students who had chosen other areas of specialty study were now beginning to select aging as a major research area; several students eventually came to the USA for graduate study, including master and doctoral education. It was those aforementioned students that I am so thankful. They did not just expand their interest but gave me the inspiration and the incentives to continue in expanding my policy interest globally with an increased focus on aging.

In addition to institutions and organizations such as the Fulbright Association and educational institutions, I am extremely thankful to the global organization Help Age International. Help Age is a Non-governmental (NGO) global activist organization with a major focus on aging. The opportunity to participate and work with this organization was a major highlight of my tenure in Africa. Help Age provided me with a great opportunity in 1998-99 to participate in the International Year for Older Persons in Nairobi, Kenya. Most importantly was a special invitation to participate as the guest speaker during the organization's Regional Conference on Aging; theme of the Conference, "A Society for All Ages." Yes, I was the featured speaker, a replacement for The First Lady of South Africa at the time Mrs. Graca Mandela (President Mandela and Mrs. Graca Mandela was married in 1998), who for business reasons could not participate during the Conference. I feel greatly indebted to Help Age International for helping me to grow in my scholarship and activism related to ageing globally. Currently, Help Age is providing the global leadership with activists such as Bishop Desmond Tutu, Nobel Prize Laureate, South Africa, to convince the United Nations to have a Special Session on Global aging issues, especially the lack of social protection/social pensions for the growing older population. Finally thanks to the staff of the Michael Schwartz Library Cleveland State University for physical space, assistance and support during my journey. Finally, Author House Publishing of Indianapolis, Indiana for providing me the academic support needed for completing the journey.

Edward A. McKinney, PhD
Professor Emeritus
College of Liberal Arts and Social Sciences
School of Social work
Cleveland State University
Cleveland, Ohio 44118

ABOUT THE AUTHOR

EDWARD ARTHUR MCKINNEY, PH.D.

Dr. McKinney is the recipient of the Bachelor degree (BA) in Sociology Morehouse College (1962) Atlanta, Georgia and Master of Social Work degree (MSW) Atlanta University (1964), Atlanta, Georgia; Master in Public Health Education (MPH) (1967), University of Pittsburgh and a Doctorate in Social work (Ph.D.) (1970), University of Pittsburgh, Pittsburgh, PA.

Dr. McKinney has held faculty positions at the following Universities in the United States: Department of Social Work, State University of New York/SUNY, Brockport, NY, The School of Applied Social Sciences (MSASS) Case Western Reserve University, Cleveland Ohio and The School of Social Work, Cleveland State University, Cleveland, Ohio.

He has been the recipient of several outstanding international scholarly awards including faculty appointments on the continent of Africa, specifically Sub-Saharan Africa. The aforementioned appointments include The J. William Fulbright Senior Scholar Award, The University of Botswana 1988-1989. He was also a recipient of a second J. William Fulbright Senior Scholar Award, Joint Appointment at Nairobi and Kenyatta Universities, Kenya, East Africa 1998-1999. Also, Dr. McKinney received a Special Academic Invitation as a Visiting Professor/Scholar in Residence, School of Social work University of Botswana, 2007-2008. He also received a Special Invitation in 2004 to participate in a Street Children Project in Addis Ababa, Ethiopia. The global project involved working with non-governmental organizations (NGO's) from Ethiopia and the USA; the project was focused on assisting youth and/or young adults in Ethiopia, especially females in preparing for future careers.

Dr. McKinney has also been the recipient of a number of national, regional and local Awards in the United States, examples are: Distinguished University Faculty Award, Cleveland State University 2001-2003, The Black Faculty and Staff Organization Distinguished Faculty Award 2001, The Ohio School Social Work Association: Friends of School Social Work Award for Dedication to the Advancement of School Social Work 2011. The Cuyahoga County Commissioners' Award: In Recognition of Time, Dedication and Commitment to the Elderly Population of Cuyahoga County Serving as Chair of the Advisory Council 2006. The Cuyahoga County, Division of Senior and Adult Services: The Anna V. Brown Award Recognizing Continued Dedication and Support to the African American Senior Community 2013 and The PVA Circle of Homes Award: In Recognition of Leadership as Board Member and Outstanding Commitment to Individuals with Developmental Disabilities 1995.

He has held memberships in the following scholarly organizations: The Delta Omega National Honor Society in Public Health and The Golden Key National Honor Society in Sociology. As aforementioned, Dr. McKinney has served on a number of national, regional and local professional boards and committees: National Council on Social Work Education (CSWE) Academic Accreditation Committee, The National Board of the American Association of Public Health (During service time was selected National Public Health Social Worker of the Year), The Special Health Committee, U.S. Congressional Black Caucus, Washington, D.C. (appointed by Congressperson Louis Stokes Ohio D-OH 14), currently Board Member Western Reserve Area Agency on Aging, Chairperson Education and Research Committee, The Greater Cleveland Council on Older Persons (Program Committee) and The Greater Cleveland Interdenominational Clergy Alliance as Special Program Consultant including project proposal writing.

In 1981 Dr. McKinney and Clergy students from the Ministerial Education/Training Project, sponsored by Case Western Reserve University School of Applied Social Sciences, received a Special Invitation from the Television Program: CBS Sunday Morning News Hosted by Charles Kuralt. The purpose of the appearance on CBS by Dr. McKinney, Academic Program Coordinator was to share with the nation how indigenous leadership, Clergy in Cleveland was being trained and prepared to work with social activists, professionals and political leaders in the community. The purpose of the groups working together was to do away with all of the social evils such as poverty, unemployment, poor housing conditions and a lack of access to essential programs and services, including health and social services preventing citizens from across all age groups from enhancing their overall quality of life.

Dr. McKinney has also served on several National Scholarly Editorial Boards: The Journal of Health and Social Policy, The Journal of Applied Social Sciences and The Journal of Health and Social work. Also, he has published numerous articles including a number of professional conference presentations relating to his professional and academic work beginning around 1975 to the present. Selective examples of relevant publications and presentations includes: Book, The Black Aged: Understanding Diversity and Human Service Needs, California: Sage Publishing, California, 1990, Presentation: "The Impact of Modernization on the Extended Family System in Africa, Who Will Care For the Elderly and Children?" The presentation was part of the 33rd International Congress, Schools of Social Work Santiago, Chile August 2006, Article: "Global Population Growth, Aging Policy Implications for Sub-Saharan Africa," National Association of Social Work (NASW) Specialty Practice Sections, Fall/Winter Publication 2015.

Edward A. McKinney, BA, MSW, MPH, PHD
Professor Emeritus/School of Social work
College of Liberal Arts and Social Sciences
Cleveland State University
Cleveland, Ohio 44118

Printed in the United States
By Bookmasters